Best-Loved
Favorite
Brand Name
R E C I P E S™

Publications International, Ltd.

Favorite Brand Name Recipes at www.fbnr.com

Pictured on the front cover *(clockwise from top left):* Manicotti Marinara *(page 106),* Holiday Double Chocolate Cookies *(page 344),* Roasted Turkey Breast with Cherry & Apple Rice Stuffing *(page 214)* and Fluffy Lemon Berry Pie *(page 348).*
Pictured on the back cover *(clockwise from top):* Chicken Tuscany *(page 128),* Thai-Style Beef & Rice *(page 192),* Strawberry Cheesecake Pie *(page 368)* and Italian Beef Burrito *(page 124).*

ISBN-13: 978-1-4127-2471-5
ISBN-10: 1-4127-2471-6

Manufactured in China.

8 7 6 5 4 3 2 1

Microwave Cooking: Microwave ovens vary in wattage. Use the cooking times as guidelines and check for doneness before adding more time.

Preparation/Cooking Times: Preparation times are based on the approximate amount of time required to assemble the recipe before cooking, baking, chilling or serving. These times include preparation steps such as measuring, chopping and mixing. The fact that some preparations and cooking can be done simultaneously is taken into account. Preparation of optional ingredients and serving suggestions is not included.

CONTENTS

Greet the Day   4

Soups & Stews   46

Dining In   94

The Old Country   144

Everything Veggie   198

On Holiday   214

Bread Baking   246

Make a Cake   308

Cookies & Pies   338

Acknowledgments   376

Index   377

Greet the Day

Get your day started off right with breakfast recipes that will fill you up and please your palate. From omelettes to pigs in a blanket, the choice is yours.

Cheesy Potato Pancakes

1½ quarts prepared instant mashed
    potatoes, cooked dry and cooled
1½ cups (6 ounces) shredded Wisconsin
    Colby or Muenster cheese
4 eggs, lightly beaten
1½ cups all-purpose flour, divided
¾ cup chopped fresh parsley
⅓ cup chopped fresh chives
1½ teaspoons dried thyme, rosemary or
    sage leaves
2 eggs, lightly beaten

1. In large bowl, combine potatoes, cheese, 4 beaten eggs, ¾ cup flour and herbs; mix well. Cover and refrigerate at least 4 hours before molding and preparing.

2. To prepare, form 18 (3-inch) patties. Dip in 2 beaten eggs and dredge in remaining ¾ cup flour. Cook each patty in nonstick skillet over medium heat 3 minutes per side or until crisp, golden brown and heated through.

3. Serve warm with eggs or omelets, or serve with sour cream and sliced pan-fried apples or applesauce. *Makes 4 to 6 servings*

Variation: Substitute Wisconsin Cheddar or Smoked Cheddar for Colby or Muenster.

Favorite recipe from **Wisconsin Milk Marketing Board**

Crêpes

1 cup all-purpose flour
1 cup fat-free (skim) milk
½ cup EGG BEATERS® Healthy Real Egg
    Product
1 tablespoon FLEISCHMANN'S®
    Original Margarine, melted

In medium bowl, blend flour, milk, Egg Beaters® and margarine; let stand 30 minutes.

Heat lightly greased 8-inch nonstick skillet or crêpe pan over medium-high heat. Pour in scant ¼ cup batter, tilting pan to cover bottom. Cook 1 to 2 minutes; turn crêpe over and cook 30 seconds to 1 minute more. Place on waxed paper. Stir batter and repeat process to make a total of 10 crêpes.

Makes 10 servings

Cheesy Potato Pancakes

Potato Breakfast Custard

3 large Colorado russet variety potatoes, peeled and thinly sliced
Salt and black pepper
8 ounces low-fat bulk sausage, cooked and crumbled*
⅓ cup roasted red pepper, thinly sliced, or 1 jar (2 ounces) sliced pimientos, drained
3 eggs
1 cup low-fat milk
3 tablespoons chopped chives or green onion tops
¾ teaspoon dried thyme or oregano leaves, crushed
Salsa and sour cream (optional)

Substitute 6 ounces finely diced lean ham or 6 ounces crumbled, cooked turkey bacon for sausage, if desired.

Preheat oven to 375°F. Butter 8- or 9-inch square baking dish or other small casserole. Arrange ½ of potatoes in baking dish. Season to taste with salt and black pepper. Cover with ½ of sausage. Arrange remaining potatoes over sausage; season to taste with salt and black pepper. Top with remaining sausage and red peppers. Beat eggs, milk, chives and thyme until blended. Pour over potatoes. Cover baking dish with foil and bake 45 to 50 minutes or until potatoes are tender. Uncover and bake 5 to 10 minutes longer. Serve with salsa and sour cream, if desired.

Makes 4 to 5 servings

Favorite recipe from **Colorado Potato Administrative Committee**

Cocoa Nut Bundles

1 can (8 ounces) refrigerated quick crescent dinner rolls
2 tablespoons butter or margarine, softened
1 tablespoon granulated sugar
2 teaspoons HERSHEY'S Cocoa
¼ cup chopped nuts
Powdered sugar

1. Heat oven to 375°F. On ungreased cookie sheet, unroll dough and separate to form 8 triangles.

2. Combine butter, granulated sugar and cocoa in small bowl. Add nuts; mix thoroughly. Divide chocolate mixture evenly among the triangles, placing on wide end of triangle. Take dough on either side of mixture and pull up and over mixture, tucking ends under. Continue rolling dough toward the opposite point.

3. Bake 9 to 10 minutes or until golden brown. Sprinkle with powdered sugar; serve warm. *Makes 8 rolls*

Huevos Con Arroz

1 package (6.8 ounces) RICE-A-RONI® Spanish Rice
2 cups chopped tomatoes
4 eggs
½ cup (2 ounces) shredded Cheddar cheese or Monterey Jack cheese
2 tablespoons chopped cilantro or parsley
¼ cup salsa or picante sauce (optional)

1. Prepare Rice-A-Roni® Mix as package directs, substituting fresh tomatoes for 1 can (14½ ounces) tomatoes. Bring to a boil over high heat. Cover; reduce heat. Simmer 20 minutes.

2. Make 4 round indentations in rice with back of large spoon. Break 1 egg into each indentation. Cover; cook over low heat 5 to 7 minutes or until eggs are cooked to desired doneness.

3. Sprinkle with cheese and cilantro. Serve topped with salsa, if desired.

Makes 4 servings

Potato Breakfast Custard

Stuffed French Toast with Fresh Berry Topping

2 cups mixed fresh berries (strawberries, raspberries, blueberries and/or blackberries)
2 tablespoons granulated sugar
⅔ cup lowfat ricotta cheese
¼ cup strawberry preserves
3 large eggs
⅔ cup NESTLÉ® CARNATION® Evaporated Fat Free Milk
2 tablespoons packed brown sugar
2 teaspoons vanilla extract
12 slices (about ¾ inch thick) French bread
    Vegetable oil, butter or margarine
    Powdered sugar (optional)
    Maple syrup, heated (optional)

COMBINE berries and granulated sugar in small bowl. Combine ricotta cheese and strawberry preserves in small bowl; mix well. Combine eggs, evaporated milk, brown sugar and vanilla extract in pie plate or shallow bowl; mix well.

SPREAD ricotta-preserve mixture evenly over *6 slices* of bread. Top with *remaining* slices of bread to form sandwiches.

HEAT small amount of vegetable oil in large nonstick skillet or griddle over medium heat. Dip sandwiches in egg mixture, coating both sides. Cook on each side for about 2 minutes or until golden brown.

SPRINKLE with powdered sugar; top with berries. Serve with maple syrup.

Makes 6 servings

Apple Brunch Strata

½ pound sausage, casing removed
4 cups cubed French bread
2 cups diced peeled Michigan Apples
¼ cup sliced green onions
⅓ cup sliced black olives
1½ cups (6 ounces) shredded sharp Cheddar cheese
2 cups reduced-fat milk
8 eggs
2 teaspoons spicy brown mustard
½ teaspoon salt
¼ teaspoon black pepper
    Paprika

1. Brown sausage in skillet over medium-high heat. Drain on paper towels; set aside.

2. Spray 13×9×2-inch baking dish with nonstick cooking spray. Layer half of bread cubes in bottom of dish. Crumble sausage over bread. Top with Michigan Apples, green onions, olives and cheese. Place remaining bread on top.

3. Mix milk, eggs, mustard, salt and pepper in medium bowl; pour over bread. Cover with foil and refrigerate 4 hours or overnight.

4. Preheat oven to 350°F. Bake, covered, 45 minutes. Remove foil and bake 15 minutes or until center is set. Let stand 15 minutes before serving. Sprinkle with paprika, if desired.

Makes 8 servings

Tip: Suggested Michigan Apple varieties to use include Empire, Gala, Golden Delicious, Ida Red, Jonagold, Jonathan, McIntosh and Rome.

Variation: Substitute 1 can (20 ounces) sliced Michigan Apples, drained and chopped, for fresh Apples.

Favorite recipe from **Michigan Apple Committee**

Stuffed French Toast with Fresh Berry Topping

Buttermilk Doughnuts

Doughnuts
3½ cups unsifted all-purpose flour, divided
¾ cup sugar
2 teaspoons baking powder
1 teaspoon baking soda
1 teaspoon ground cinnamon
¾ teaspoon salt
½ teaspoon ground nutmeg
¾ cup buttermilk
¼ Butter Flavor CRISCO® Stick or ¼ cup Butter Flavor CRISCO® all-vegetable shortening
2 eggs
1 teaspoon vanilla
CRISCO® Oil* for frying

Glaze
1 cup confectioners' sugar
2 tablespoons hot water

Use your favorite Crisco Oil product.

1. For doughnuts, combine 2 cups flour with sugar, baking powder, baking soda, cinnamon, salt, nutmeg, buttermilk, shortening, eggs and vanilla in large mixing bowl. Beat at low speed of electric mixer until blended. Beat at medium speed 2 minutes. Stir in remaining flour. Chill several hours or overnight.

2. Divide dough in half. Sprinkle lightly with flour. Roll each half to slightly less than ½-inch thickness on well-floured board. Cut with floured 2¾- to 3-inch doughnut cutter. Reserve doughnut holes.

3. Heat 2 inches oil to 375°F in deep-fat fryer or deep saucepan. Fry a few doughnuts at a time in hot oil, 1 minute on each side, or until golden brown. Fry doughnut holes 1 to 1½ minutes total time. Drain on paper towels. Serve plain, dip tops in glaze, or cool and shake in plastic bag of confectioners' sugar.

4. For glaze, combine confectioners' sugar and water in small bowl; stir until smooth. Dip tops of doughnuts in glaze. Invert on wire racks until glaze is set.

Makes 1½ to 2 dozen doughnuts and doughnut holes

Omelet Italiano

3 medium mushrooms, sliced
½ teaspoon dried oregano
4 teaspoons butter
1 can (14½ ounces) DEL MONTE® Stewed Tomatoes - Italian Recipe
4 eggs, beaten
½ cup shredded mozzarella cheese
⅓ cup diced pepperoni or ham
2 green onions, sliced

1. Cook mushrooms and oregano in large saucepan in 1 teaspoon butter. Add tomatoes. Cook, uncovered, over medium-high heat 10 minutes or until thickened; set aside.

2. Heat remaining 3 teaspoons butter in large skillet over medium-high heat. Beat together eggs and ¼ cup water; season with salt and pepper, if desired. Pour into skillet. Once eggs begin to set, run spatula around edge of pan, lifting to allow uncooked eggs to flow underneath.

3. When eggs are set, sprinkle left side with cheese, pepperoni and green onions. Fold right half over filling. When cheese melts, remove to serving platter. Pour mushroom-tomato sauce over omelet. *Makes 2 servings*

Prep & Cook Time: 15 minutes

Cherry Danish

2½ to 3 cups all-purpose flour, divided
1 package (¼ ounce) quick-rising yeast
¼ teaspoon salt
¾ cup milk
¼ cup sugar
   Butter or margarine
1 egg
4 ounces almond paste
2 tablespoons light corn syrup
1½ cups pitted and chopped Northwest
      fresh sweet cherries
2 tablespoons sugar
½ teaspoon ground cinnamon

In large bowl, combine 1 cup flour, yeast and salt. In small saucepan, heat milk, sugar and ¼ cup butter to 125° to 130°F. Add warm milk mixture to flour mixture; beat until smooth. Add egg; blend well. Add remaining flour to make soft dough. Knead until smooth and satiny. Cover; let rest 10 minutes.

Roll dough on lightly floured surface to 18×11-inch rectangle; spread with 2 tablespoons softened butter. In small bowl, combine almond paste and corn syrup; spread over butter layer. Combine cherries, sugar and cinnamon; spoon over almond paste. Roll up jelly-roll fashion, starting at long edge. Cut into 16 rolls.

Place on greased baking sheet; cover and let rise about 45 minutes or until doubled in bulk. Bake in 375°F oven 15 to 20 minutes or until golden.   *Makes 16 rolls*

Tip: Glaze and garnish with sliced almonds if desired.

Freezing Tip: Cherry Danish can be frozen in a plastic food storage bag or wrapped in foil. Thaw, wrapped, at room temperature at least 1 hour. Place danish on baking sheet, loosely cover and bake in 325°F oven about 15 minutes or until thoroughly heated.

*Favorite recipe from **Northwest Cherry Growers***

Ham and Rice Pie

1 bag SUCCESS® Rice
   Vegetable cooking spray
1 cup (4 ounces) shredded low-fat
   Cheddar cheese
8 ounces egg substitute, divided
2 tablespoons reduced-calorie margarine
1 cup sliced fresh mushrooms
½ cup chopped green onions
½ cup chopped red bell pepper
½ teaspoon salt
¼ teaspoon dried tarragon leaves,
   crushed
¼ teaspoon black pepper
6 ounces turkey ham, cut into strips
1 cup broccoli flowerets, cooked
½ cup fat-free sour cream
¼ cup flour

Prepare rice according to package directions.

Preheat oven to 350°F. Spray 10-inch pie plate with cooking spray; set aside.

Place hot rice in medium bowl. Add cheese; stir until melted. Stir in ½ of the egg substitute. With back of spoon, spread rice mixture onto bottom and up side of prepared pie plate to form shell.

Melt margarine in large saucepan over medium heat. Add mushrooms, green onions, red pepper, salt, tarragon and black pepper. Cook, stirring occasionally, until vegetables are crisp-tender. Remove from heat. Stir in turkey ham and broccoli. In small bowl, beat remaining egg substitute, sour cream and flour until blended. Add to ham mixture; mix well. Pour into rice shell. Bake just until center is set, about 30 minutes. Let stand 5 minutes before cutting into wedges to serve.

Makes 8 servings

Mini Vegetable Quiches

2 cups cut-up vegetables (bell peppers, broccoli, zucchini and/or carrots)
2 tablespoons chopped green onions
2 tablespoons FLEISCHMANN'S® Original Margarine
4 (8-inch) flour tortillas, each cut into 8 triangles
1 cup EGG BEATERS® Healthy Real Egg Product
1 cup fat-free (skim) milk
½ teaspoon dried basil leaves

In medium nonstick skillet, over medium-high heat, sauté vegetables and green onions in margarine until tender.

Arrange 4 tortilla pieces in each of 8 (6-ounce) greased custard cups or ramekins, placing points of tortilla pieces at center of bottom of each cup and pressing lightly to form shape of cup. Divide vegetable mixture evenly among cups. In small bowl, combine Egg Beaters®, milk and basil. Pour evenly over vegetable mixture. Place cups on baking sheet. Bake at 375°F for 20 to 25 minutes or until puffed and knife inserted into centers comes out clean. Let stand 5 minutes. *Makes 8 servings*

Bayou Yam Muffins

1 cup flour
1 cup yellow cornmeal
¼ cup sugar
1 tablespoon baking powder
1¼ teaspoons ground cinnamon
½ teaspoon salt
2 eggs
1 cup mashed yams or sweet potatoes
½ cup very strong cold coffee
¼ cup butter or margarine, melted
½ teaspoon TABASCO® brand Pepper Sauce

Preheat oven to 425°F. Grease 12 (3×1½-inch) muffin cups. Combine flour, cornmeal, sugar, baking powder, cinnamon and salt in large bowl. Beat eggs in medium bowl; stir in yams, coffee, butter and TABASCO® Sauce. Make a well in center of dry ingredients; add yam mixture and stir just to combine. Spoon batter into prepared muffin cups. Bake 20 to 25 minutes or until cake tester inserted into center of muffin comes out clean. Cool 5 minutes on wire rack. Remove from pans. Serve warm or at room temperature.
Makes 12 muffins

Microwave Directions: Prepare muffin batter as directed above. Spoon approximately ⅓ cup batter into each of 6 paper baking cup-lined 6-ounce custard cups. Cook uncovered on HIGH (100% power) 4 to 5½ minutes or until cake tester inserted into center of muffin comes out clean; turn and rearrange cups once during cooking. Remove muffins with small spatula. Cool 5 minutes on wire rack. Remove from pans. Repeat procedure with remaining batter. Serve warm or at room temperature.

Honey Grapefruit Delight

2 pink or red grapefruit
4 tablespoons honey, divided
1 cup plain nonfat yogurt
¼ teaspoon grated grapefruit peel
¼ teaspoon almond extract
3 tablespoons toasted sliced almonds

Peel and slice grapefruit into ½-inch-thick rounds, reserving peel. Gently toss grapefruit rounds and 2 tablespoons honey; refrigerate until ready to serve. Combine yogurt, remaining 2 tablespoons honey, grapefruit peel and almond extract in small bowl; mix well. Spoon grapefruit into individual dishes. Top with yogurt sauce; sprinkle with almonds.
Makes 2 servings

*Favorite recipe from **National Honey Board***

Mini Vegetable Quiches

Quick Cinnamon Sticky Buns

1 cup packed light brown sugar, divided
10 tablespoons butter, softened and
    divided
1 package (16-ounce) hot roll mix
2 tablespoons granulated sugar
1 cup hot water (120° to 130°F)
1 egg
1⅔ cups (10-ounce package) HERSHEY'S
    Cinnamon Chips

1. Lightly grease two 9-inch round baking pans. Combine ½ cup brown sugar and 4 tablespoons softened butter in small bowl with pastry blender; sprinkle mixture evenly onto bottom of prepared pans. Set aside.

2. Combine contents of hot roll mix package, including yeast packet, and granulated sugar in large bowl. Using spoon, stir in water, 2 tablespoons butter and egg until dough pulls away from side of bowl. Turn dough onto lightly floured surface. With lightly floured hands, shape into ball. Knead 5 minutes or until smooth, using additional flour if necessary.

3. To shape: Using lightly floured rolling pin, roll into 15×12-inch rectangle. Spread with remaining 4 tablespoons butter. Sprinkle with remaining ½ cup brown sugar and cinnamon chips, pressing lightly into dough. Starting with 12-inch side, roll tightly as for jelly-roll; seal edges.

4. Cut into 1-inch-wide slices with floured knife. Arrange 6 slices, cut sides down, in each prepared pan. Cover with towel; let rise in warm place until doubled, about 30 minutes.

5. Heat oven to 350°F. Uncover rolls. Bake 25 to 30 minutes or until golden brown. Cool 2 minutes in pan; with knife, loosen around edge of pan. Invert onto serving plates. Serve warm or at room temperature.

Makes 12 cinnamon buns

Tomato and Salmon Quiche

1 tablespoon olive or vegetable oil
1½ cups chopped fresh mushrooms
½ cup chopped shallots
1 can (14.5 ounces) CONTADINA®
    Recipe Ready Diced Tomatoes,
    drained
½ teaspoon salt
¼ teaspoon ground white pepper
2 cans (7½ ounces each) pink salmon,
    drained
3 tablespoons thinly sliced green onion
2 tablespoons grated Parmesan cheese
3 eggs
¾ cup heavy whipping cream
1 unbaked 9-inch pie shell

1. Heat oil in medium skillet. Add mushrooms and shallots; sauté for 2 minutes. Stir in tomatoes, salt and pepper. Cook for 2 minutes or until most of liquid is evaporated. Remove from heat.

2. Remove skin and bones from salmon, if desired; discard. Stir salmon, green onion and Parmesan cheese into mushroom mixture.

3. Beat eggs lightly in medium bowl; stir in cream.

4. Bake pie shell in preheated 400°F oven for 5 minutes. Spoon salmon filling into hot pie shell; pour egg mixture over filling.

5. Bake at 350°F for 25 minutes or until center is set. Let stand for 5 minutes before cutting to serve. *Makes 6 servings*

Prep Time: 10 minutes
Cook Time: 35 minutes
Stand Time: 5 minutes

Quick Cinnamon Sticky Buns

Potato Straw Cake with Ham & Gruyère

4 medium Colorado russet variety potatoes
1 tablespoon water
2 teaspoons lemon juice
2 teaspoons Dijon mustard
1 cup (4 ounces) thinly sliced ham, cut into strips
¾ cup (3 ounces) shredded Gruyère cheese
½ teaspoon dried tarragon, crushed *or* ¼ teaspoon ground nutmeg
3 to 4 green onions, thinly sliced, white parts separated from dark green tops
3 teaspoons oil, divided
Salt and black pepper

Peel and grate potatoes. Place in bowl with water to cover; let stand at room temperature about ½ hour while preparing other ingredients. Blend 1 tablespoon water, lemon juice and mustard in bowl. Stir in ham, cheese, tarragon and white parts of onions. Reserve green onion tops. Drain potatoes; wrap in several thicknesses of paper towels or clean dish towel and squeeze to wring out much of liquid.

Heat 1½ teaspoons oil in heavy 8- or 10-inch nonstick skillet over high heat. Add half the potatoes, pressing into skillet with back of spoon. Season to taste with salt and pepper. Spread evenly with ham mixture. Cover with remaining potatoes. Season to taste with salt and pepper. Reduce heat to medium-low. Cover and cook 20 to 30 minutes or until potatoes are crisp and golden brown on bottom. Uncover and place rimless baking sheet over skillet. Invert skillet onto baking sheet to release potato cake. Add remaining 1½ teaspoons oil to skillet. Slide cake into skillet, uncooked side down. Cook, uncovered, over medium-low heat 10 to 15 minutes.

Increase heat to medium-high and cook until brown and crisp, shaking pan several times to prevent sticking. Slide potato cake onto serving plate. Garnish with reserved green onion tops. Cut into wedges.

Makes 5 to 6 servings

Favorite recipe from **Colorado Potato Administrative Committee**

Raspberry Crumb Coffee Cake

Coffee Cake
1 (18.25-ounce) package deluxe white cake mix
1 cup all-purpose flour
1 package (¼ ounce) active dry yeast
⅔ cup warm water
2 eggs
1½ cups (18-ounce jar) SMUCKER'S® Red Raspberry Preserves
¼ cup sugar
1 teaspoon cinnamon
6 tablespoons butter or margarine

Topping
1 cup powdered sugar
1 tablespoon corn syrup
1 to 3 tablespoons milk

Grease 13×9-inch pan. Reserve 2½ cups dry cake mix. Combine remaining cake mix, flour, yeast, water and eggs. Mix by hand 100 strokes. Spread batter into greased pan. Spoon preserves evenly over batter.

Combine reserved cake mix, sugar and cinnamon; cut in butter with fork until fine particles form. Sprinkle over preserves.

Bake at 375°F for 30 to 35 minutes or until golden brown.

Combine all topping ingredients, adding enough milk for desired drizzling consistency. Drizzle over warm or cooled coffee cake.

Makes 12 to 16 servings

Biscuits 'n Gravy

Biscuits
> PAM® No-Stick Cooking Spray
> 2 cups self-rising flour
> 2 teaspoons sugar
> 1½ teaspoons baking powder
> ¾ cup buttermilk
> ¼ cup WESSON® Vegetable Oil

Gravy
> 1 pound bulk pork sausage
> ¼ cup all-purpose flour
> 2 cups milk
> ¼ teaspoon salt
> ¼ teaspoon pepper

Biscuits

Preheat oven to 450°F. Lightly spray a baking sheet with PAM® Cooking Spray. In a large bowl, combine flour, sugar and baking powder; blend well. In a small bowl, whisk together buttermilk and Wesson® Oil; add to dry ingredients and mix until dough is moist but not sticky. On a lightly floured surface, knead dough lightly 4 or 5 times. Roll dough to a ¾-inch thickness; cut with a 4-inch biscuit cutter. Knead any scraps together and repeat cutting method. Place biscuits on baking sheet and bake 10 to 15 minutes or until lightly browned. Keep warm.

Gravy

Meanwhile, in a large skillet, cook and crumble sausage until brown. Reserve ¼ cup of drippings in skillet; drain sausage well. Set aside. Add flour to drippings in skillet; stir until smooth. Cook over medium heat for 2 to 3 minutes or until dark brown, stirring constantly. Gradually add milk, stirring constantly until smooth and thickened. (Use more milk, if necessary, to achieve desired consistency.) Stir in salt, pepper and sausage; heat through. Serve over hot split biscuits.

Makes 6 servings (2 biscuits each)

Chilean Puff Pastry Fruit Band

> 1 sheet frozen puff pastry, thawed
> 1 egg yolk mixed with 1 teaspoon water
> 3 ounces soft white goat cheese, crumbled, or cream cheese, softened
> 3 tablespoons powdered sugar
> 2 tablespoons whipping cream or dairy sour cream
> 1 tablespoon orange liqueur *or* ½ teaspoon grated orange zest
> 1 ripe Chilean kiwifruit
> ½ cup Chilean blueberries
> ½ cup Chilean raspberries
> ½ cup apricot jam, warmed and strained

On lightly floured surface, roll pastry sheet to form 12×10-inch rectangle. Using sharp knife and ruler, cut rectangle to measure 11×6 inches; place on baking sheet. Make sure all 4 sides are cut smooth.

Cut 2 (11×1-inch) strips from remaining pastry. Brush long edges of large pastry piece with 1-inch-wide band of egg yolk mixture. Press strips lightly on top. With fork tines, thoroughly poke holes in center to prevent pastry from "puffing" as it bakes. Chill for 30 minutes.

Preheat oven to 400°F. Bake pastry 15 minutes until golden. (Check frequently; if center rises, deflate with a knife tip.) Remove from baking sheet and let cool on wire rack.

Beat cheese, powdered sugar, cream and orange liqueur until smooth. Place pastry base on foil-wrapped chopping board. Spread cheese mixture over pastry. Peel and slice kiwifruit into ¼-inch-thick rounds. Arrange overlapping kiwifruit slices, blueberries and raspberries in bands or stripes over cheese filling. Brush fruit with apricot jam. Refrigerate 1 to 2 hours. Using serrated knife, trim each short side to make neat edges; transfer tart to serving platter. *Makes 4 to 6 servings*

*Favorite recipe from **Chilean Fresh Fruit Association***

Hash Brown Casserole

3 cartons (4 ounces *each*) cholesterol-
   free egg product or 6 large eggs,
   well beaten
1 can (12 fluid ounces) NESTLÉ®
   CARNATION® Evaporated Milk
1 teaspoon salt
½ teaspoon ground black pepper
1 package (30 ounces) frozen shredded
   hash brown potatoes
2 cups (8 ounces) shredded cheddar
   cheese
1 medium onion, chopped
1 small green bell pepper, chopped
1 cup diced ham (optional)

PREHEAT oven to 350°F. Grease 13×9-inch baking dish.

COMBINE egg product, evaporated milk, salt and black pepper in large bowl. Add potatoes, cheese, onion, bell pepper and ham; mix well. Pour mixture into prepared baking dish.

BAKE for 60 to 65 minutes or until set.

Makes 12 servings

Note: For a lower fat version of this recipe, use cholesterol-free egg product, substitute NESTLÉ® CARNATION® Evaporated Fat Free Milk for Evaporated Milk and 10 slices turkey bacon, cooked and chopped, for the diced ham. Proceed as above.

Rice Bran Buttermilk Pancakes

1 cup rice flour or all-purpose flour
¾ cup rice bran
1 tablespoon sugar
1 teaspoon baking powder
½ teaspoon baking soda
1¼ cups low-fat buttermilk
3 egg whites, beaten
   Vegetable cooking spray
   Fresh fruit, reduced-calorie syrup or
     reduced-calorie margarine (optional)

Sift together flour, bran, sugar, baking powder and baking soda into large bowl. Combine buttermilk and egg whites in small bowl; add to flour mixture. Stir until smooth. Pour ¼ cup batter onto hot griddle coated with cooking spray. Cook over medium heat until bubbles form on top and underside is lightly browned. Turn to brown other side. Serve with fresh fruit, syrup or margarine.

Makes about 10 (4-inch) pancakes

Variation: For Cinnamon Pancakes, add 1 teaspoon ground cinnamon to dry ingredients.

Favorite recipe from **USA Rice Federation**

Potato-Ham Scallop

2 cups cubed HILLSHIRE FARM® Ham
6 potatoes, peeled and thinly sliced
¼ cup chopped onion
⅓ cup all-purpose flour
   Salt and black pepper to taste
2 cups milk
3 tablespoons bread crumbs
1 tablespoon butter or margarine, melted

Preheat oven to 350°F.

Place ½ of Ham in medium casserole. Cover with ½ of potatoes and ½ of onion. Sift ½ of flour over onions; sprinkle with salt and pepper. Repeat layers with remaining ham, potatoes, onion, flour, salt and pepper. Pour milk over casserole. Bake, covered, 1¼ hours. Combine bread crumbs and butter in small bowl; sprinkle over top of casserole. Bake, uncovered, 15 minutes or until topping is golden brown.

Makes 6 servings

Hash Brown Casserole

Apple Yogurt Muffins

12 REYNOLDS® Baking Cups

Topping
    2 tablespoons flour
    2 tablespoons sugar
    1 tablespoon butter or margarine,
        softened
    ½ teaspoon ground cinnamon

Muffins
    2 cups flour
    ½ cup sugar
    1 tablespoon baking powder
    ½ teaspoon salt
    ¼ teaspoon ground cinnamon
    1 carton (8 ounces) low-fat vanilla
        yogurt
    1 egg
    ¼ cup vegetable oil
    2 tablespoons low fat milk
    ¾ cup peeled and chopped apples
    ⅓ cup raisins
        REYNOLDS® Color Plastic Wrap

PREHEAT oven to 400°F. Place Reynolds Baking Cups in a muffin pan; set aside.

For Topping
COMBINE topping ingredients until crumbly; set aside.

For Muffins
COMBINE flour, sugar, baking powder, salt and cinnamon in large bowl. Beat together yogurt, egg, oil and milk in small bowl. Add to flour mixture; stir just until dry ingredients are moistened. Gently stir in apples and raisins. Spoon batter into baking cups, filling even with top of baking cups. Sprinkle topping over each muffin.

BAKE 23 to 25 minutes or until golden brown. Cool in pan. Wrap muffins individually in plastic wrap.   *Makes 12 muffins*

Muffin Tip: When preparing low-fat muffin recipes, use Reynolds Foil Bake Cups and spray them with nonstick cooking spray before adding batter. Muffins won't stick, and you haven't added extra fat to the recipe.

Eggs Santa Fe

    2 eggs
    ½ cup GUILTLESS GOURMET® Black
        Bean Dip (Spicy or Mild)
    ¼ cup GUILTLESS GOURMET®
        Southwestern Grill Salsa
    1 ounce (about 20) GUILTLESS
        GOURMET® Unsalted Baked Tortilla
        Chips
    2 tablespoons low fat sour cream
    1 teaspoon chopped fresh cilantro
        Fresh cilantro sprigs (optional)

To poach eggs, bring water to a boil in small skillet over high heat; reduce heat to medium-low and maintain a simmer. Gently break eggs into water, being careful not to break yolks. Cover and simmer 5 minutes or until desired firmness.

Meanwhile, place bean dip in small microwave-safe bowl or small saucepan. Microwave bean dip on HIGH (100% power) 2 to 3 minutes or heat over medium heat until warm. To serve, spread ¼ cup warm bean dip in center of serving plate; top with 1 poached egg and 2 tablespoons salsa. Arrange 10 tortilla chips around egg. Dollop with 1 tablespoon sour cream and sprinkle with ½ teaspoon chopped cilantro. Repeat with remaining ingredients. Garnish with cilantro sprigs, if desired.   *Makes 2 servings*

Apple Yogurt Muffins

Western Omelet

½ cup finely chopped red or green bell pepper
⅓ cup cubed cooked potato
2 slices turkey bacon, diced
¼ teaspoon dried oregano leaves
2 teaspoons FLEISCHMANN'S® Original Margarine, divided
1 cup EGG BEATERS® Healthy Real Egg Product
Fresh oregano sprig, for garnish

In 8-inch nonstick skillet, over medium heat, sauté bell pepper, potato, turkey bacon and dried oregano in 1 teaspoon margarine until tender. Remove from skillet; keep warm.

In same skillet, over medium heat, melt remaining margarine. Pour Egg Beaters® into skillet. Cook, lifting edges to allow uncooked portion to flow underneath. When almost set, spoon vegetable mixture over half of omelet. Fold other half over vegetable mixture; slide onto serving plate. Garnish with fresh oregano.

Makes 2 servings

Variation: For frittata, sauté vegetables, turkey bacon and dried oregano in 2 teaspoons margarine. Pour Egg Beaters® evenly into skillet over vegetable mixture. Cook, without stirring, for 4 to 5 minutes or until cooked on bottom and almost set on top. Carefully turn frittata; cook for 1 to 2 minutes more or until done. Slide onto serving platter; cut into wedges to serve.

Prep Time: 15 minutes
Cook Time: 10 minutes

Cranberry Sausage Quiche

1 (9-inch) frozen deep-dish pie shell
½ pound BOB EVANS® Savory Sage Roll Sausage
¼ cup chopped yellow onion
¾ cup dried cranberries
1½ cups (6 ounces) shredded Monterey Jack cheese
3 eggs, lightly beaten
1½ cups half-and-half
Fresh parsley or sage leaves for garnish

Preheat oven to 400°F. Let frozen pie shell stand at room temperature 10 minutes; do not prick shell. Bake 7 minutes. Remove from oven and set aside. Reduce oven temperature to 375°F. Crumble and cook sausage and onion in large skillet over medium-high heat until sausage is browned. Drain off any drippings. Remove from heat; stir in cranberries. Sprinkle cheese on bottom of pie shell; top evenly with sausage mixture. Combine eggs and half-and-half in medium bowl; whisk until blended but not frothy. Pour egg mixture over sausage mixture in pie shell. Bake 40 to 45 minutes or until knife inserted into center comes out clean. Let stand 10 minutes before serving. Garnish with fresh parsley. Refrigerate leftovers.

Makes 6 servings

Western Omelet

Sunday Morning Upside-Down Rolls

¼ cup warm water (105°F to 115°F)
1 envelope quick-rising yeast
¼ teaspoon sugar
1 cup scalded milk, slightly cooled
½ cup WESSON® Canola Oil
½ cup sugar
3 eggs, beaten
1½ teaspoons salt
4½ cups all-purpose flour
¾ cup (1½ sticks) butter, softened
2 cups packed brown sugar
1 cup maraschino cherries, chopped
1 (16-ounce) jar KNOTT'S BERRY FARM® Light Apricot Pineapple Preserves

Pour water into a large bowl. Sprinkle yeast, then ¼ teaspoon sugar into water; stir well. Let stand 5 to 8 minutes or until mixture is slightly foamy. Meanwhile, in a small bowl, whisk milk, Wesson® Oil, ½ cup sugar, eggs and salt until well blended. Pour milk mixture into yeast mixture; blend well. Gradually add flour to mixture; mix until smooth. Knead dough in bowl (about 5 minutes) until smooth. Add more flour if dough is sticky. Cover with towel and let rise in warm place for 30 minutes or until dough nearly doubles in size. Punch down dough once; cover.

Meanwhile, in small bowl, cream together butter and brown sugar. Spoon (be careful not to pack) 2 teaspoons of creamed sugar mixture into *each* of 24 muffin cups. Sprinkle maraschino cherries over creamed sugar mixture; then add 2 teaspoons Knott's® preserves to *each* muffin cup. Tear small pillows of dough and place on preserves, filling *each* muffin cup to the rim. Cover; let rise about 15 to 20 minutes. Preheat oven to 375°F. Bake for 12 to 15 minutes or until golden brown. Immediately invert rolls onto cookie sheet. *Do not remove rolls from muffin cups.*

Allow a few minutes for preserves to drip down the sides. Lift muffin pans from rolls; cool 5 minutes. Remove muffins to wire rack. Serve warm.   *Makes 2 dozen rolls*

Zucchini Mushroom Frittata

1½ cups EGG BEATERS® Healthy Real Egg Product
½ cup (2 ounces) shredded reduced-fat Swiss cheese
¼ cup fat-free (skim) milk
½ teaspoon garlic powder
¼ teaspoon seasoned pepper
    Nonstick cooking spray
1 medium zucchini, shredded (1 cup)
1 medium tomato, chopped
1 (4-ounce) can sliced mushrooms, drained
    Tomato slices and fresh basil leaves, for garnish

In medium bowl, combine Egg Beaters®, cheese, milk, garlic powder and seasoned pepper; set aside.

Spray 10-inch ovenproof nonstick skillet lightly with nonstick cooking spray. Over medium-high heat, sauté zucchini, tomato and mushrooms in skillet until tender. Pour egg mixture into skillet, stirring well. Cover; cook over low heat for 15 minutes or until cooked on bottom and almost set on top. Remove lid and place skillet under broiler for 2 to 3 minutes or until desired doneness. Slide onto serving platter; cut into wedges to serve. Garnish with tomato slices and basil.

Makes 6 servings

Prep Time: 20 minutes
Cook Time: 20 minutes

Turkey Sausage Potato Pancakes

1 pound turkey breakfast sausage
1 small onion
2 large potatoes, peeled
½ cup cholesterol-free egg substitute
¼ teaspoon black pepper
  Nonstick cooking spray

1. Cook and stir turkey sausage in large nonstick skillet over medium-high heat 6 to 10 minutes or until sausage is no longer pink. Drain; set aside.

2. Place onion in food processor fitted with metal blade. Process, using on/off pulsing action, until onion is chopped. Remove metal blade; fit processor with grating disc. Grate potatoes.

3. Combine sausage, potato mixture, egg substitute and pepper in medium bowl until blended. Shape ½ cup sausage mixture into 5-inch round pancake. Repeat with remaining mixture.

4. Spray large nonstick skillet with cooking spray. Heat over medium heat. Cook pancakes 2 to 3 minutes per side or until brown and potatoes are tender. Serve with applesauce or apple pie filling, if desired.

Makes 4 servings

Favorite recipe from **National Turkey Federation**

Spring Break Blueberry Coffeecake

Topping
  ½ cup flaked coconut
  ¼ cup firmly packed brown sugar
  2 tablespoons butter or margarine, softened
  1 tablespoon all-purpose flour

Coffeecake
  1 package DUNCAN HINES®
    Bakery-Style Wild Maine Blueberry
    Muffin Mix
  1 can (8 ounces) crushed pineapple with
    juice, undrained
  1 egg
  ¼ cup water

1. Preheat oven to 350°F. Grease 9-inch square pan.

2. For topping, combine coconut, brown sugar, butter and flour in small bowl. Mix with fork until well blended. Set aside.

3. Rinse blueberries from Mix with cold water and drain.

4. For cake, place muffin mix in medium bowl. Break up any lumps. Add pineapple with juice, egg and water. Stir until moistened, about 50 strokes. Fold in blueberries. Spread in pan. Sprinkle reserved topping over batter. Bake at 350°F for 30 to 35 minutes or until toothpick inserted into center comes out clean. Serve warm, or cool completely.

Makes 9 servings

Tip: To keep blueberries from discoloring the batter, drain them on paper towels after rinsing.

Blueberry Breakfast Braid

5 to 5⅓ cups all-purpose flour
½ cup sugar
2 envelopes FLEISCHMANN'S®
    RapidRise™ Yeast
1 teaspoon salt
1 tablespoon finely shredded orange peel
½ teaspoon ground cinnamon
1 cup milk
½ cup orange juice
½ cup butter or margarine
2 large eggs
    Blueberry Filling (recipe follows)
1 egg yolk plus 1 tablespoon milk (egg
    mixture)

In large bowl, combine 2 cups flour, sugar, undissolved yeast, salt, orange peel and cinnamon. Heat milk, orange juice and butter until very warm (120° to 130°F). Stir into dry ingredients. Beat 2 minutes at medium speed of electric mixer, scraping bowl occasionally. Add eggs and 1 cup flour; beat 2 minutes at high speed. Stir in enough remaining flour to make a soft dough. Knead on lightly floured surface until smooth and elastic, about 8 to 10 minutes. Cover; let rest 10 minutes.

Divide dough in half; divide each half into 3 equal portions. Roll each to 20×6-inch rectangle. Spread Blueberry Filling evenly. Beginning at long end, roll each up tightly as for jelly-roll. Pinch seams to seal to form ropes. Braid ropes; place on greased baking sheet. Cover; let rise in warm, draft-free place until doubled in size, about 1 hour. Brush with egg mixture.

Bake at 350°F for 30 to 35 minutes or until done. Remove from sheet; cool on wire rack.

Makes one loaf (24 slices)

Blueberry Filling: Combine 1 cup fresh or frozen blueberries, 1 cup sugar and ¼ cup water in medium saucepan; bring to a boil over medium heat. Cook 20 minutes, stirring occasionally, until very thick. Stir in 3 tablespoons cornstarch dissolved in 3 tablespoons water; cook 5 minutes, stirring constantly. Let cool.

Country Fare Breakfast with Wisconsin Fontina

¼ cup butter
2 cups frozen hash brown potatoes
¼ cup finely chopped onion
6 eggs, beaten
2 tablespoons milk
¾ teaspoon salt
⅛ teaspoon pepper
¼ cup chopped fresh parsley, divided
1 cup (4 ounces) shredded Wisconsin
    Fontina cheese, divided
1 cup cubed cooked turkey

Melt butter in 10-inch ovenproof skillet; add potatoes and onion. Cook, covered, over medium heat 15 minutes until tender and lightly browned; stir occasionally. Beat together eggs, milk, salt and pepper; stir in 3 tablespoons parsley and ½ cup cheese. Pour egg mixture over potatoes; sprinkle with turkey. Bake, uncovered, in preheated 350°F oven for 20 minutes or until eggs are set. Sprinkle remaining ½ cup cheese over eggs; return to oven for about 2 minutes until cheese is melted. Remove from oven and garnish with remaining parsley. Cut into wedges and serve with salsa, if desired.

Makes 6 servings

Note: Ham can be substituted for turkey.

Favorite recipe from **Wisconsin Milk Marketing Board**

Blueberry Breakfast Braids

Apple Sauce Cinnamon Rolls

Rolls

>4 cups all-purpose flour, divided
>1 package active dry yeast
>1 cup MOTT'S® Natural Apple Sauce, divided
>½ cup skim milk
>⅓ cup plus 2 tablespoons granulated sugar, divided
>2 tablespoons margarine
>½ teaspoon salt
>1 egg, beaten lightly
>2 teaspoons ground cinnamon

Icing

>1 cup sifted powdered sugar
>1 tablespoon skim milk
>½ teaspoon vanilla extract

1. To prepare Rolls, in large bowl, combine 1½ cups flour and yeast. In small saucepan, combine ¾ cup apple sauce, ½ cup milk, 2 tablespoons granulated sugar, margarine and salt. Cook over medium heat, stirring frequently, until mixture reaches 120° to 130°F and margarine is almost melted (milk will appear curdled). Add to flour mixture along with egg. Beat with electric mixer on low speed 30 seconds, scraping bowl frequently. Beat on high speed 3 minutes. Stir in 2¼ cups flour until soft dough forms.

2. Turn out dough onto lightly floured surface; flatten slightly. Knead 3 to 5 minutes or until smooth and elastic, adding remaining ¼ cup flour, if necessary, to prevent sticking. Shape dough into ball; place in large bowl sprayed with nonstick cooking spray. Turn dough over so top is greased. Cover with towel; let rise in warm place about 1 hour or until doubled in bulk.

3. Spray two 8- or 9-inch round baking pans with nonstick cooking spray.

4. Punch down dough; turn out onto lightly floured surface. Cover with towel; let rest 10 minutes. Roll out dough into 12-inch square. Spread remaining ¼ cup apple sauce over dough to within ½ inch of edges. In small bowl, combine remaining ⅓ cup granulated sugar and cinnamon; sprinkle over apple sauce. Roll up dough jelly-roll style. Moisten edge with water; pinch to seal seam. Cut roll into 12 (1-inch) slices with sharp floured knife. Arrange 6 rolls ½ inch apart in each prepared pan. Cover with towel; let rise in warm place about 30 minutes or until nearly doubled in bulk.

5. Preheat oven to 375°F. Bake 20 to 25 minutes or until lightly browned. Cool on wire rack 5 minutes. Invert each pan onto serving plate.

6. To prepare Icing, in small bowl, combine powdered sugar, 1 tablespoon milk and vanilla until smooth. Drizzle over tops of rolls. Serve warm.
Makes 12 servings

Down-Home Sausage Gravy

>1 package (16 ounces) fresh breakfast sausage
>2 tablespoons finely chopped onion
>6 tablespoons all-purpose flour
>2 cans (12 fluid ounces *each*) NESTLÉ® CARNATION® Evaporated Milk
>1 cup water
>¼ teaspoon salt
>Hot pepper sauce to taste
>Hot biscuits

COMBINE sausage and onion in large skillet. Cook over medium-low heat, stirring occasionally, until sausage is no longer pink. Stir in flour; mix well. Stir in evaporated milk, water, salt and hot pepper sauce. Cook, stirring occasionally, until mixture comes to a boil. Cook for 1 to 2 minutes.

SERVE immediately over biscuits.
Makes 8 to 10 servings

Huevos y Frijoles Frittata

1 (16-ounce) can ROSARITA® Refried
    Beans
1 cup picante sauce, mild
½ cup chopped zucchini
½ cup chopped red bell pepper
1 tablespoon WESSON® Oil
1 (4-ounce) can diced green chilies
¼ teaspoon garlic powder
3 (4-ounce) containers fat-free egg
    substitute *or* 6 eggs
    PAM® No-Stick Cooking Spray
½ cup *each:* no-fat shredded Monterey
    Jack and Cheddar cheeses, blended
¼ cup sliced green onion
    Fat-free sour cream (optional)

1. Preheat oven to 400°F.

2. In medium bowl, combine beans and picante sauce; mix well and set aside.

3. In large nonstick skillet, sauté zucchini and bell pepper in hot oil until crisp-tender. Add chilies and garlic powder; mix well.

4. Add eggs to skillet; cook over medium heat until center is almost set. Turn frittata over; continue to cook 1 minute.

5. Place frittata on cookie sheet sprayed with PAM cooking spray. Spread bean mixture over frittata; top with cheeses and green onion. Bake for 10 minutes. Garnish with sour cream.
Makes 8 (6-ounce) servings

Maple Apple Oatmeal

2 cups apple juice
1½ cups water
⅓ cup AUNT JEMIMA® Syrup
½ teaspoon ground cinnamon
¼ teaspoon salt (optional)
2 cups QUAKER® Oats (quick or old
    fashioned, uncooked)
1 cup chopped fresh unpeeled apple
    (about 1 medium)

In a 3-quart saucepan, bring juice, water, syrup, cinnamon and salt to a boil. Stir in oats and apple. Return to a boil; reduce heat to medium-low. Cook about 1 minute for quick oats (or 5 minutes for old fashioned oats) or until most of liquid is absorbed, stirring occasionally. Let stand until of desired consistency. *Makes 4 servings*

Norwegian Almond Muffins (for bread machines)

Muffins
½ cup water (80°F)
¼ cup milk (80°F)
1 egg (¼ cup), at room temperature
¼ cup cool butter, cut into pieces
¼ cup almond paste
½ teaspoon almond extract
2 cups bread flour
1 teaspoon salt
¼ cup sugar
1 teaspoon ground cardamom
1 package RED STAR® Active Dry Yeast
    or QUICK•RISE™ Yeast

Topping
2 tablespoons cherry preserves
¼ cup slivered almonds
1 tablespoon sugar

Place muffin ingredients into the pan in the order listed (all sizes, all models).

Select the "DOUGH" setting on machine. Dough is a soft batter. Use rubber spatula to help mix ingredients.

After the machine has completed the cycle, spoon batter into 12 well-greased muffin pan cups. Cover; let rise in warm place until almost double in size. Before baking, make an indentation in the top of each muffin; spoon about ½ teaspoon cherry preserves into each muffin. Combine almonds and sugar; sprinkle over muffins. Bake at 350°F for 20 to 25 minutes until golden brown. Cool in pan 3 minutes; remove from pan. Serve warm or cool. *Makes 12 muffins*

Crunchy Ranch-Style Eggs

2 cans (10 ounces each) tomatoes and green chilies, drained
1⅓ cups *French's*® French Fried Onions, divided
2 tablespoons *Frank's*® *RedHot*® Cayenne Pepper Sauce
2 tablespoons *French's*® Worcestershire Sauce
6 eggs
1 cup (4 ounces) shredded Cheddar cheese

Preheat oven to 400°F. Grease 2-quart shallow baking dish. Combine tomatoes, ⅔ *cup* French Fried Onions, **Frank's RedHot** Sauce and Worcestershire in prepared dish. Make 6 indentations in mixture. Break 1 egg into each indentation.

Bake, uncovered, 15 to 20 minutes or until eggs are set. Top with cheese and remaining ⅔ *cup* onions. Bake 1 minute or until onions are golden.   *Makes 6 servings*

Tip: Recipe may be prepared in individual ramekin dishes. Bake until eggs are set.

Prep Time: 5 minutes
Cook Time: 16 minutes

Tuna Cream Cheese Omelets

1 teaspoon butter or margarine
4 to 6 large eggs
    Water
2 ounces cream cheese with chives, cut into ½-inch cubes, divided
2 tablespoons drained and chopped roasted red peppers, divided
1 (3-ounce) pouch of STARKIST® Premium Albacore or Chunk Light Tuna
1 tablespoon light sour cream, divided
    Salt and pepper to taste

In small nonstick skillet, melt butter over medium-high heat. Beat 2 or 3 large eggs with 1 teaspoon water per egg. Stir in half of cream cheese and half of peppers. Pour into hot skillet; cook, using back of spatula to push cooked portion of eggs toward center, letting liquid flow underneath.

When eggs are cooked on bottom and top is nearly dry, sprinkle half the tuna over half the omelet. Fold omelet in half; slide onto plate. Top with half of sour cream; sprinkle with salt and pepper. Repeat for second omelet.
                    Makes 2 omelets

Prep Time: 8 minutes

Apple-Potato Pancakes

1¼ cups unpeeled, finely chopped apples
1 cup peeled, grated potatoes
½ cup MOTT'S® Natural Apple Sauce
½ cup all-purpose flour
2 egg whites
1 teaspoon salt
    Additional MOTT'S® Natural Apple Sauce or apple slices (optional)

1. Preheat oven to 475°F. Spray cookie sheet with nonstick cooking spray.

2. In medium bowl, combine apples, potatoes, ½ cup apple sauce, flour, egg whites and salt.

3. Spray large nonstick skillet with nonstick cooking spray; heat over medium heat until hot. Drop rounded tablespoonfuls of batter 2 inches apart into skillet. Cook 2 to 3 minutes on each side or until lightly browned. Place pancakes on prepared cookie sheet.

4. Bake 10 to 15 minutes or until crisp. Serve with additional apple sauce or apple slices, if desired. Refrigerate leftovers.
                    Makes 12 servings

Crunchy Ranch-Style Eggs

Toll House® Mini Morsel Pancakes

2½ cups all-purpose flour
1 cup (6 ounces) NESTLÉ® TOLL
    HOUSE® Semi-Sweet Chocolate Mini
    Morsels
1 tablespoon baking powder
½ teaspoon salt
1¾ cups milk
2 large eggs
⅓ cup vegetable oil
⅓ cup packed brown sugar
    Powdered sugar
    Fresh sliced strawberries
    Maple syrup

COMBINE flour, morsels, baking powder and salt in large bowl. Combine milk, eggs, vegetable oil and brown sugar in medium bowl; add to flour mixture. Stir just until moistened (batter may be lumpy).

HEAT griddle or skillet over medium heat; brush lightly with vegetable oil. Pour ¼ *cup* of batter onto hot griddle; cook until bubbles begin to burst. Turn; continue to cook for about 1 minute longer or until golden. Repeat with *remaining* batter.

SPRINKLE with powdered sugar; top with strawberries. Serve with maple syrup.

Makes about 18 pancakes

Baked Banana Doughnuts

2 ripe bananas, mashed
2 egg whites
1 tablespoon vegetable oil
1 cup packed brown sugar
1½ cups all-purpose flour
¾ cup whole wheat flour
2 teaspoons baking powder
½ teaspoon baking soda
¼ teaspoon pumpkin pie spice
1 tablespoon granulated sugar
2 tablespoons chopped walnuts
    (optional)

Preheat oven to 425°F. Spray baking sheet with nonstick cooking spray. Beat bananas, egg whites, oil and brown sugar in large bowl or food processor. Add flours, baking powder, baking soda and pumpkin pie spice. Mix until well blended. Let stand for five minutes for dough to rise. Scoop out heaping tablespoonfuls of dough onto prepared baking sheet. Using thin rubber spatula or butter knife, round out doughnut hole in center of dough (if dough sticks to knife or spatula, spray with cooking spray). With spatula, smooth outside edge of dough into round doughnut shape. Repeat until all dough is used. Sprinkle with granulated sugar and walnuts, if desired. Bake 6 to 10 minutes or until tops are golden.

Makes about 22 doughnuts

Variation: Use 8 ounces solid pack pumpkin instead of bananas to make pumpkin doughnuts.

Favorite recipe from **The Sugar Association, Inc.**

Toll House® Mini Morsel Pancakes

Cheddar Broccoli Tart

1½ cups milk
3 eggs
1 package KNORR® Recipe Classics™ Leek Soup, Dip and Recipe Mix
1 package (10 ounces) frozen chopped broccoli, thawed and drained
1½ cups shredded Cheddar, Swiss or Monterey Jack cheese (about 6 ounces)
1 (9-inch) unbaked or frozen deep-dish pie crust*

If using 9-inch deep-dish frozen prepared pie crust, do not thaw. Preheat oven and cookie sheet. Pour filling into pie crust; bake on cookie sheet.

• Preheat oven to 375°F. In large bowl, with fork, beat milk, eggs and recipe mix until blended. Stir in broccoli and cheese; spoon into pie crust.

• Bake 40 minutes or until knife inserted 1 inch from edge comes out clean. Let stand 10 minutes before serving.

Makes 6 servings

Recipe Tip: Cheddar Broccoli Tart is perfect for brunch or lunch. Or serve it with a mixed green salad and soup for a hearty dinner.

Prep Time: 10 minutes
Cook Time: 40 minutes

Tacos de Huevos

10 eggs, beaten
½ cup salsa
¼ cup chopped green onions
½ teaspoon LAWRY'S® Seasoned Salt
2 tablespoons butter or margarine
1 package (10 count) LAWRY'S® Taco Shells
3 medium tomatoes, chopped
Shredded lettuce
1 cup (4 ounces) shredded cheddar cheese

In large bowl, combine eggs, ½ cup salsa, green onions and Seasoned Salt; mix well. In large nonstick skillet, heat butter. Add eggs and scramble over medium heat to desired doneness. Meanwhile, heat Taco Shells in 350°F oven 5 minutes. When eggs are cooked, spoon equal amount into each Taco Shell. Top with tomatoes, lettuce and cheese. Serve immediately. *Makes 10 tacos*

Serving Suggestion: Serve with salsa and fresh fruit.

Hint: Double the recipe for a larger fiesta!

Breakfast Kabobs

2 cups plain yogurt
4 tablespoons honey
1 (12-ounce) package BOB EVANS® Original or Maple Links
1 medium cantaloupe melon, peeled, seeded and cut into 1-inch cubes
1 medium honeydew melon, peeled, seeded and cut into 1-inch cubes
1 small bunch green seedless grapes
1 small bunch red seedless grapes
2 medium red apples, cored and cut into 1-inch cubes
1 pint strawberries, hulled and cut into halves

Combine yogurt and honey in small bowl; refrigerate until ready to serve. Cook sausage in medium skillet over medium heat until browned. Drain on paper towels; cut each link in half. Alternately place sausage and fruit on wooden skewers (about 7). Serve kabobs with yogurt sauce for dipping.

Makes about 7 kabobs

Note: The fruit can be prepared ahead and refrigerated until ready to assemble kabobs with warm sausage. Brush apples with lemon juice or orange juice to prevent discoloration.

Cheddar Broccoli Tart

Creamy Fruit Blintzes

Cheese Filling
- 1 egg yolk
- 2 tablespoons sugar
- 1 (8-ounce) package cream cheese, softened
- 2 cups (12-ounce carton) dry or creamed cottage cheese
- ¼ teaspoon vanilla

Blintzes
- 3 eggs
- 3 tablespoons oil
- 1½ cups milk
- 1 cup all-purpose flour
- ½ teaspoon salt
- ⅓ cup butter or margarine, melted
- 2 tablespoons butter or margarine (unmelted)
- Powdered sugar
- 1 cup sour cream
- 1 cup (12-ounce jar) SMUCKER'S® Strawberry, Cherry or Blueberry Preserves

Combine egg yolk and sugar; beat with electric mixer until thick and yellow. Add cream cheese, cottage cheese and vanilla; mix well. Refrigerate until ready to use.

Combine eggs, oil and milk; beat with electric mixer until well blended. Add flour and salt; continue to beat until batter is smooth and flour is dissolved. Refrigerate, covered, for 30 minutes or until ready to use.

Slowly heat small skillet. To test temperature, drop a little cold water onto surface; water should bead up and bounce. For each blintz, brush pan lightly with melted butter. Measure 3 tablespoons of batter into cup. Pour in all at once, rotating skillet quickly to spread evenly. Cook for 1 minute until golden brown on underside; loosen edge with spatula and remove. Dry on paper towels. Stack, brown side up, with waxed paper between blitzes.

Spread 3 tablespoons of filling onto browned side of each blintz, making a rectangle 4 inches long. Fold two sides in over filling, overlapping edges and covering filling completely. Melt 1 tablespoon butter in large skillet over medium heat. Add half of blintzes, seam-side-down and not touching. Sauté until golden brown, turning once. Keep warm in low oven while cooking second half of blintzes. Serve hot, sprinkled with powdered sugar and topped with sour cream and preserves. *Makes 16 blintzes*

Frittata with Artichokes

- 1 envelope LIPTON® RECIPE SECRETS® Savory Herb with Garlic Soup Mix*
- 8 eggs
- ¾ cup milk
- 1 teaspoon I CAN'T BELIEVE IT'S NOT BUTTER!® Spread
- 1 cup diced and drained canned artichoke hearts (about 4 ounces)

*Also terrific with Lipton® Recipe Secrets® or Golden Onion Soup Mix.

In medium bowl, blend soup mix, eggs and milk; set aside.

In omelet pan or 8-inch skillet, melt I Can't Believe It's Not Butter!® Spread over low heat and cook egg mixture, lifting set edges with spatula and tilting pan to allow uncooked mixture to flow to bottom. When bottom is set, top with artichokes. Reduce heat to low and simmer covered 3 minutes or until eggs are set. *Makes about 4 servings*

Country Skillet Hash

2 tablespoons butter or margarine
4 boneless pork chops (¾ inch thick), diced
¼ teaspoon black pepper
¼ teaspoon cayenne pepper (optional)
1 medium onion, chopped
2 cloves garlic, minced
1 can (14½ ounces) DEL MONTE® Whole New Potatoes, drained and diced
1 can (14½ ounces) DEL MONTE Diced Tomatoes, undrained
1 medium green bell pepper, chopped
½ teaspoon thyme, crushed

1. Melt butter in large skillet over medium heat. Add meat; cook, stirring occasionally, until no longer pink in center. Season with black pepper and cayenne pepper, if desired.

2. Add onion and garlic; cook until tender. Stir in potatoes, tomatoes, green pepper and thyme. Cook 5 minutes, stirring frequently. Season with salt, if desired.

Makes 4 servings

Tip: The hash may be topped with a poached or fried egg.

Prep Time: 10 minutes
Cook Time: 15 minutes

Rise and Shine Sausage Oatmeal Cups

Oatmeal Cups
1 pound BOB EVANS® Original Recipe Roll Sausage
⅔ cup quick or old-fashioned oats
¼ cup milk
1 egg white
1 tablespoon finely chopped onion

Filling
2 teaspoons butter
8 eggs, beaten
½ cup soft cream cheese (plain or herb)
¾ cup chopped seeded tomato, drained
2 tablespoons snipped fresh chives, fresh dill or green onion tops
Salt and black pepper to taste

Preheat oven to 350°F. To prepare oatmeal cups, combine sausage, oats, milk, egg white and onion in medium bowl. Divide mixture evenly among 12 muffin pan cups. Press mixture firmly onto bottoms and up sides to form hollow cups. Bake 12 to 15 minutes or until cooked through. Drain cups on paper towels and keep warm.

To prepare filling, melt butter in large skillet. Add eggs; cook, stirring frequently. When almost done, fold in remaining ingredients; cook until eggs reach desired doneness. Divide mixture evenly among sausage cups; serve hot. Refrigerate leftovers.

Makes 12 sausage cups

Note: Oatmeal cups can be prepared in advance and refrigerated overnight or frozen up to 1 month. Reheat when ready to fill.

Breakfast in a Cup

3 cups cooked rice
1 cup (4 ounces) shredded Cheddar
    cheese, divided
1 can (4 ounces) diced green chilies
1 jar (2 ounces) diced pimientos,
    drained
⅓ cup skim milk
2 eggs, beaten
½ teaspoon ground cumin
½ teaspoon salt
½ teaspoon ground black pepper
    Vegetable cooking spray

Combine rice, ½ cup cheese, chilies, pimientos, milk, eggs, cumin, salt and pepper in large bowl. Evenly divide mixture among 12 muffin cups coated with cooking spray. Sprinkle with remaining ½ cup cheese. Bake at 400°F for 15 minutes or until set.

Makes 12 servings

Tip: Breakfast cups may be stored in the freezer in a freezer bag or tightly sealed container. To reheat frozen breakfast cups, microwave each cup on HIGH 1 minute.

Favorite recipe from **USA Rice Federation**

Smoked Cheese and Muffin Strata

6 BAYS® English Muffins, cubed
8 ounces smoked Gouda cheese, sliced
8 ounces Cheddar cheese, sliced
8 ounces pork or turkey bulk sausage,
    cooked and crumbled
4¾ cups milk
8 eggs
⅓ cup red pepper, diced
⅓ cup green pepper, diced
1 teaspoon salt
    Pinch ground black pepper
    Paprika, to taste

Line bottom of 13×9-inch pan with half of the muffin cubes. Divide cheeses evenly over muffin cubes in pan. Sprinkle on crumbled sausage. Arrange remaining muffin cubes in pan over sausage and cheese layers.

Mix together milk, eggs, peppers, salt and black pepper. Pour over ingredients in pan. Press down on muffin cubes to soak thoroughly. Sprinkle with paprika. Cover with plastic. Refrigerate 8 hours or overnight.

Bake uncovered in 325°F oven for just over 2 hours or until a knife inserted near center comes out clean. Let stand 5 minutes before serving.

Makes 6 servings

Note: Recipe may be halved. Bake in an 8-inch square pan for 1 hour and 15 minutes or until a knife inserted near center comes out clean.

Brunch Sandwiches

4 English muffins, split, lightly toasted
8 thin slices CURE 81® ham
8 teaspoons Dijon mustard
8 large eggs, fried or poached
8 slices SARGENTO® Deli Style Sliced
    Swiss Cheese

1. Top each muffin half with a slice of ham, folding to fit. Spread mustard lightly over ham; top with an egg and one slice cheese.

2. Transfer to foil-lined baking sheet. Broil 4 to 5 inches from heat source until cheese is melted and sandwiches are hot, 2 to 3 minutes.

Makes 4 servings

Prep Time: 5 minutes
Cook Time: 10 minutes

Breakfast in a Cup

Huevos Rancheros in Tortilla Cups

6 taco-size corn tortillas, about 6-inch diameter
Olive oil cooking spray
1 can (14½ ounces) diced tomatoes
1 can (8 ounces) no salt added tomato sauce
1 can (4 ounces) diced mild green chilies
⅓ cup *Frank's® RedHot®* Cayenne Pepper Sauce
½ to 1 teaspoon ground cumin
6 large eggs
1 cup shredded Mexican 4-cheese blend
Garnish: cilantro, black beans (optional)

1. Preheat oven to 425°F. Place tortillas in damp paper towels. Soften in microwave for 30 seconds. Coat both sides of tortillas with cooking spray. Place tortillas in 10-ounce custard cups, pressing in sides. Place a ball of foil in center of each to hold in side of tortilla. Bake 15 minutes until golden. Cool tortilla cups on rack and remove foil.

2. In 12-inch ovenproof skillet, combine tomatoes, tomato sauce, chilies, *Frank's RedHot* Sauce and cumin. Bring to a boil. Simmer for 4 minutes until flavors are blended. Remove from heat. With large spoon, make an indentation in sauce; pour 1 egg into indentation. Repeat with remaining eggs.

3. Bake 7 minutes more or until eggs are almost set. Sprinkle cheese on eggs and bake 1 minute or until melted. To serve, spoon sauce and eggs into tortilla cups. Garnish with cilantro and black beans, if desired.

Makes 6 servings

Prep Time: 10 minutes
Cook Time: 25 minutes

Butterscotch Sticky Buns

3 tablespoons butter or margarine, *divided*
2 packages (8 ounces *each*) refrigerated crescent dinner rolls
1⅔ cups (11-ounce package) NESTLÉ® TOLL HOUSE® Butterscotch Flavored Morsels, *divided*
½ cup chopped pecans
¼ cup granulated sugar
1½ teaspoons lemon juice
1½ teaspoons water
1 teaspoon ground cinnamon

PREHEAT oven to 375°F.

PLACE *1 tablespoon* butter in 13×9-inch baking pan; melt in oven for 2 to 4 minutes or until butter sizzles. Unroll dinner rolls; separate into 16 triangles. Sprinkle triangles with *1⅓ cups* morsels. Starting at shortest side, roll up each triangle; arrange in prepared baking pan.

BAKE for 15 to 20 minutes or until lightly browned.

MICROWAVE *remaining* morsels and *remaining* butter in medium, microwave-safe bowl on MEDIUM-HIGH (70%) power for 30 seconds; stir. Microwave at additional 10- to 20-second intervals, stirring until smooth. Stir in nuts, sugar, lemon juice, water and cinnamon. Pour over hot rolls.

BAKE for 5 minutes or until bubbly. Immediately loosen buns from pan. Cool in pan on wire rack for 10 minutes; serve warm.

Makes 16 buns

Huevos Rancheros in Tortilla Cups

Cinnamon Coffee-Crumb Muffins

    3 cups all-purpose flour
    1 tablespoon baking powder
    1 teaspoon ground cinnamon
    ¼ teaspoon salt
    1¼ cups sugar
    ½ cup (1 stick) SHEDD'S® Spread
        Country Crock Spread-Sticks
    2 eggs
    1 tablespoon instant coffee crystals or
        instant espresso
    1 teaspoon vanilla extract
    1 cup milk
    Crumb Topping (recipe follows)

Preheat oven to 400°F. Grease 12-cup muffin pan or line with paper cupcake liners; set aside.

In large bowl, combine flour, baking powder, cinnamon and salt; set aside.

In large bowl, with electric mixer, beat sugar and SHEDD'S® Spread Country Crock Spread on medium-high speed until light and fluffy, about 5 minutes. Beat in eggs, coffee and vanilla, scraping side occasionally. Alternately beat in flour mixture and milk until blended. Evenly spoon batter into prepared pan; sprinkle with Crumb Topping.

Bake 23 minutes or until toothpick inserted into centers comes out clean. On wire rack, cool 10 minutes; remove from pan and cool completely. *Makes 12 muffins*

Crumb Topping: In small bowl, combine ¼ cup all-purpose flour, 2 tablespoons sugar and ¼ teaspoon ground cinnamon. With pastry blender or 2 knives, cut in 2 tablespoons Shedd's® Spread Country Crock Spread-Sticks until mixture is size of coarse crumbs.

Baked Ham & Cheese Monte Cristo

    6 slices bread, divided
    2 cups (8 ounces) shredded Cheddar
        cheese, divided
    1⅓ cups *French's*® French Fried Onions,
        divided
    1 package (10 ounces) frozen broccoli
        spears, thawed, drained and cut into
        1-inch pieces
    2 cups (10 ounces) cubed cooked ham
    5 eggs
    2 cups milk
    ½ teaspoon ground mustard
    ½ teaspoon seasoned salt
    ¼ teaspoon coarsely ground black pepper

Preheat oven to 325°F. Cut 3 bread slices into cubes; place in greased 12×8-inch baking dish. Top bread with 1 cup cheese, ⅔ cup French Fried Onions, the broccoli and ham. Cut remaining bread slices diagonally into halves. Arrange bread halves down center of casserole, overlapping slightly, crusted points all in one direction. In medium bowl, beat eggs, milk and seasonings; pour evenly over casserole. Bake, uncovered, at 325°F for 1 hour or until center is set. Top with remaining 1 cup cheese and ⅔ cup onions; bake, uncovered, 5 minutes or until onions are golden brown. Let stand 10 minutes before serving. *Makes 6 to 8 servings*

Roman Meal® Waffles

1⅓ cups all-purpose flour
2 tablespoons sugar
1 tablespoon baking powder
½ teaspoon salt
⅔ cup ROMAN MEAL® Original Cereal
1½ cups milk (may be skim milk)
⅓ cup vegetable oil
2 stiffly beaten egg whites

Preheat waffle iron. In medium bowl, combine flour, sugar, baking powder, salt and cereal. Mix together milk and oil; add all at once to dry ingredients. Mix well. Fold in egg whites. Pour batter onto hot waffle iron.

Makes 8 to 10 waffles, 4½ inches each

Scrambled Eggs with Chicken and Sun-Dried Tomatoes

4 eggs
2 tablespoons milk
1 teaspoon dried basil leaves
  Ground black pepper
5 ounces cooked chicken, chopped
¼ cup oil-packed sun-dried tomatoes, drained and cut into thin strips
2 tablespoons chopped green onion
1 tablespoon butter
1 tablespoon grated BELGIOIOSO® Romano Cheese

In medium bowl, beat together eggs, milk, basil and pepper to taste. Stir in chicken, tomatoes and onion. In large skillet, melt butter over medium heat; pour in egg mixture. Cook, without stirring, until mixture begins to set on bottom and around edges. Using large spoon or spatula, lift and fold partially cooked eggs so uncooked portion flows underneath. Continue cooking over medium heat 2 to 3 minutes. Remove from heat. Sprinkle with BelGioioso Romano Cheese and serve immediately. *Makes 3 servings*

Chiles Rellenos Monte Cristos

1 can (4 ounces) whole roasted green chiles
8 large slices sourdough bread
4 slices SARGENTO® Deli Style Sliced Monterey Jack Cheese
4 slices SARGENTO® Deli Style Sliced Colby Cheese
2 eggs
¼ cup milk
1 teaspoon ground cumin
¼ cup butter or margarine
  Powdered sugar, optional
  Thick and chunky salsa, optional

1. Cut open chiles and remove any remaining seeds. Equally divide the chiles over 4 slices of bread. Top each with Monterey Jack and Colby cheeses. Place remaining bread slices on top.

2. In shallow bowl, beat eggs, milk and cumin until blended. Dip each sandwich in the egg mixture, turning carefully to coat until all liquid is absorbed by all sandwiches equally.

3. Melt butter in large skillet over medium heat. Place sandwiches in skillet. Grill (in batches if necessary) 3 to 4 minutes per side, or until browned and cheese has melted. Serve immediately. Serve with powdered sugar sprinkled on top and a spoonful of salsa, if desired. *Makes 4 servings*

Prep Time: 5 minutes
Cook Time: 16 minutes

Ham & Asparagus Brunch Bake

2 boxes UNCLE BEN'S® Long Grain
    & Wild Rice Original Recipe
1 pound asparagus, cut into 1-inch
    pieces (about 2½ cups)
2 cups chopped ham
1 cup chopped yellow or red bell pepper
¼ cup finely chopped red onion
1 cup (4 ounces) shredded Swiss cheese

1. In large saucepan, prepare rice mixes according to package directions, adding asparagus during last 5 minutes of cooking.

2. Meanwhile, preheat oven to 350°F. Grease 11×7½-inch baking dish.

3. Remove rice mixture from heat. Add ham, bell pepper and onion; mix well. Place mixture in prepared baking dish; sprinkle with cheese.

4. Bake 25 to 30 minutes or until mixture is heated through.   *Makes 8 servings*

Variation: Substitute UNCLE BEN'S® Brand Butter & Herb Long Grain & Wild Rice for the Original Recipe Long Grain & Wild Rice.

Tip: This dish can be prepared ahead of time through step 3. Cover with foil and refrigerate several hours or overnight. Bake, covered, in preheated 350°F oven for 15 minutes. Remove foil and continue to bake until heated through, about 10 minutes.

Jam French Toast Triangles

¼ cup preserves, any flavor
6 slices whole wheat bread, divided
6 tablespoons EGG BEATERS® Healthy
    Real Egg Product
¼ cup skim milk
2 tablespoons FLEISCHMANN'S®
    Original Margarine
1 tablespoon sugar
¼ teaspoon ground cinnamon

Evenly divide and spread preserves on 3 bread slices; top with remaining bread slices to make 3 sandwiches, pressing to seal. Cut each sandwich diagonally in half. In shallow bowl, combine Egg Beaters® and skim milk. Dip each sandwich in egg mixture to coat.

In skillet or on griddle, over medium-high heat, brown sandwiches in margarine until golden brown on both sides. Combine sugar and cinnamon; sprinkle over sandwiches. Garnish as desired and serve warm.

Makes 6 pieces

Peach Orchard Muffins

PAM® No-Stick Cooking Spray
1 (16-ounce) can sliced peaches in heavy
    syrup, diced, syrup reserved
⅓ cup WESSON® Vegetable Oil
2 eggs, slightly beaten
1 teaspoon vanilla
2 cups all-purpose flour
⅓ cup sugar
3 teaspoons baking powder
½ teaspoon salt
½ cup KNOTT'S BERRY FARM® Peach
    Preserves
Sugar for topping

Preheat oven to 400°F. Spray 12 muffin cups with PAM® Cooking Spray. In a small bowl, combine syrup, Wesson® Oil, eggs and vanilla; mix well. In a large bowl, mix together flour, sugar, baking powder and salt. Pour egg mixture into flour mixture; stir just until dry ingredients are moistened. Fold in diced peaches. Fill muffin cups to rim. Bake for 15 to 22 minutes or until wooden pick inserted into center comes out clean. Cool 5 minutes. Remove muffins to wire racks. Brush with Knott's® preserves and sprinkle with desired amount of sugar.

Makes 1 dozen muffins

Ham & Asparagus Brunch Bake

Soups & Stews

Cioppino, chili and chowder take the chill out of any day. Plus there's a whole lot more to choose here. So pour yourself a bowlful of something hot.

Golden Gate Wild Rice Cioppino

2 cups chopped onions
1 medium green bell pepper, chopped
4 cloves garlic, minced
2 tablespoons olive oil
1 cup white wine
1 can (28 ounces) whole tomatoes, drained and chopped
1 bottle (8 ounces) clam juice
1 bay leaf
½ teaspoon dried basil leaves
½ teaspoon dried oregano leaves
½ teaspoon dried rosemary
¼ teaspoon red pepper flakes
2 cups cooked California wild rice
6 large *or* 12 small clams, well scrubbed
½ pound uncooked medium shrimp, peeled and deveined
½ pound uncooked scallops, cut into halves crosswise
Chopped parsley

In large stockpot or Dutch oven, sauté onions, bell pepper and garlic in oil until onion is soft. Add wine, tomatoes, clam juice, bay leaf, basil, oregano, rosemary and pepper flakes. Bring to a boil, reduce heat and simmer 30 minutes, stirring often. Add rice and bring to a simmer. Add clams; cook until clams open. Discard any clams that do not open. Add shrimp and scallops; cook until shrimp turn pink, about 2 to 3 minutes; do not overcook. Sprinkle with parsley. *Makes 4 servings*

Favorite recipe from **California Wild Rice Advisory Board**

Golden Gate
Wild Rice Cioppino

Chunky Vegetarian Chili

1 tablespoon vegetable oil
1 medium green bell pepper, chopped
1 medium onion, chopped
3 cloves garlic, minced
2 cans (14½ ounces each) Mexican-style tomatoes, undrained
1 can (15 ounces) kidney beans, rinsed, drained
1 can (15 ounces) pinto beans, rinsed, drained
1 can (11 ounces) whole-kernel corn, drained
2½ cups water
1 cup uncooked rice
2 tablespoons chili powder
1½ teaspoons ground cumin

Heat oil in 3-quart saucepan or Dutch oven over medium-high heat. Add bell pepper, onion and garlic; cook and stir 5 minutes or until tender. Add tomatoes, beans, corn, water, rice, chili powder and cumin; stir well. Bring to boil. Reduce heat; cover. Simmer 30 minutes, stirring occasionally.   *Makes 6 servings*

Favorite recipe from **USA Rice Federation**

Black Bean Bisque with Crab

3 cups low sodium chicken broth, defatted
1 jar (16 ounces) GUILTLESS GOURMET® Black Bean Dip (Spicy or Mild)
1 can (6 ounces) crabmeat, drained
2 tablespoons brandy (optional)
6 tablespoons low fat sour cream
    Chopped fresh chives (optional)

Microwave Directions
Combine broth and bean dip in 2-quart glass measure or microwave-safe casserole. Cover with vented plastic wrap or lid; microwave on HIGH (100% power) 6 minutes or until soup starts to bubble.

Stir in crabmeat and brandy, if desired; microwave on MEDIUM (50% power) 2 minutes or to desired serving temperature. To serve, ladle bisque into 8 individual ramekins or soup bowls, dividing evenly. Swirl 1 tablespoon sour cream into each serving. Garnish with chives, if desired.

Makes 8 servings

Stove Top Directions: Combine broth and bean dip in 2-quart saucepan; bring to a boil over medium heat. Stir in crabmeat and brandy, if desired; cook 2 minutes or to desired serving temperature. Serve as directed.

Dutch Potage

2 medium potatoes, peeled and diced
1 medium onion, chopped
1½ cups thinly sliced carrots
1 quart water
¼ teaspoon black pepper
½ cup prepared HIDDEN VALLEY® The Original Ranch® Dressing
    Salt, to taste

In large saucepan, combine vegetables, water and pepper. Bring to boil; cover and cook over medium heat until vegetables are tender, about 15 minutes. Drain vegetables, reserving liquid. In blender, purée vegetables with 1 cup reserved liquid until smooth. Return purée and remaining liquid to pan; add salad dressing and salt. Cook until heated through. Serve hot. Spoon additional salad dressing into center of each serving.

Makes 4 to 6 servings

Chunky Vegetarian Chili

Cioppino

2 tablespoons olive or vegetable oil
1½ cups chopped onion
1 cup chopped celery
½ cup chopped green bell pepper
1 large clove garlic, minced
1 can (28 ounces) CONTADINA® Recipe
    Ready Crushed Tomatoes
1 can (6 ounces) CONTADINA Tomato
    Paste
1 teaspoon Italian herb seasoning
1 teaspoon salt
½ teaspoon ground black pepper
2 cups water
1 cup dry red wine or chicken broth
3 pounds white fish, shrimp, scallops,
    cooked crab, cooked lobster, clams
    and/or oysters (in any proportion)

1. Heat oil in large saucepan. Add onion, celery, bell pepper and garlic; sauté until vegetables are tender. Add tomatoes, tomato paste, Italian seasoning, salt, black pepper, water and wine.

2. Bring to a boil. Reduce heat to low; simmer, uncovered, for 15 minutes.

3. To prepare fish and seafood: scrub clams and oysters under running water. Place in ½ inch boiling water in separate large saucepan; cover. Bring to a boil. Reduce heat to low; simmer just until shells open, about 3 minutes. Set aside.

4. Cut crab, lobster, fish and scallops into bite-size pieces.

5. Shell and devein shrimp. Add fish to tomato mixture; simmer 5 minutes. Add scallops and shrimp; simmer 5 minutes.

6. Add crab, lobster, reserved clams and oysters; simmer until heated through.

Makes about 14 cups

Prep Time: 30 minutes
Cook Time: 35 minutes

Meatless Italian Minestrone

1 tablespoon CRISCO® Oil*
1⅓ cups chopped celery
½ cup chopped onion
2 to 3 cloves garlic, minced
2 cans (14½ ounces each) no salt added
    tomatoes, undrained and chopped
4 cups chopped cabbage
1⅓ cups chopped carrots
1 can (46 ounces) no salt added tomato
    juice
1 can (19 ounces) white kidney beans
    (cannellini), drained
1 can (15½ ounces) red kidney beans,
    drained
1 can (15 ounces) garbanzo beans,
    drained
¼ cup chopped fresh parsley
1 tablespoon plus 1 teaspoon dried
    oregano leaves
1 tablespoon plus 1 teaspoon dried basil
    leaves
¾ cup (4 ounces) uncooked small elbow
    macaroni, cooked (without salt or
    fat) and well drained
¼ cup grated Parmesan cheese
    Salt and pepper (optional)

Use your favorite Crisco Oil product.

1. Heat oil in large saucepan on medium heat. Add celery, onion and garlic. Cook and stir until crisp-tender. Stir in tomatoes with liquid, cabbage and carrots. Reduce heat to low. Cover. Simmer until vegetables are tender.

2. Stir in tomato juice, beans, parsley, oregano and basil. Simmer until beans are heated. Stir in macaroni just before serving. Serve sprinkled with Parmesan cheese. Season with salt and pepper, if desired.

Makes 16 servings

Albóndigas Soup

1 pound ground beef
¼ cup long-grain rice
1 egg
1 tablespoon chopped fresh cilantro
1 teaspoon LAWRY'S® Seasoned Salt
¼ cup ice water
2 cans (14½ ounces each) chicken broth
1 can (14½ ounces) whole peeled
    tomatoes, undrained and cut up
1 stalk celery, diced
1 large carrot, diced
1 medium potato, diced
¼ cup chopped onion
¼ teaspoon LAWRY'S® Garlic Powder
    with Parsley

In medium bowl, combine ground beef, rice, egg, cilantro, Seasoned Salt and ice water; mix well and form into small meatballs. In large saucepan, combine broth, vegetables and Garlic Powder with Parsley. Bring to a boil over medium-high heat; add meatballs. Reduce heat to low; cover and cook 30 to 40 minutes, stirring occasionally.   *Makes 6 to 8 servings*

Serving Suggestion: Serve with lemon wedges and warm tortillas.

Hint: For a lower salt version, use homemade chicken broth or low-sodium chicken broth.

Fancy Florida Seafood Gumbo

12 ounces Florida oysters, drained
 8 ounces Florida blue crab claw meat
½ cup chopped onion
½ cup chopped Florida celery
1 clove garlic, minced
1 tablespoon butter
1 teaspoon anise seeds
1 teaspoon salt
½ teaspoon sugar
1 teaspoon crushed red pepper
1 (10-ounce) package frozen okra
2 (20-ounce) cans diced tomatoes

Remove remaining shell or cartilage from oysters and crab and set aside. Cook onion, celery and garlic in butter until tender. Add anise, salt, sugar, red pepper, okra and tomatoes. Cover and simmer for 15 minutes. Add oysters and simmer an additional 15 minutes. Add crab and heat thoroughly. Serve over rice.   *Makes 8 to 10 servings*

*Favorite recipe from **Florida Department of Agriculture and Consumer Services Bureau of Seafood and Aquaculture***

Hearty Sausage Stew

¼ cup olive oil
4 carrots, chopped
1 onion, cut into quarters
1 cup chopped celery
2 cloves garlic, finely chopped
1 teaspoon finely chopped fennel
    Salt and black pepper to taste
12 small new potatoes
1 pound mushrooms, cut into halves
2 cans (12 ounces each) diced tomatoes,
    undrained
1 can (8 ounces) tomato sauce
1 tablespoon dried oregano leaves
1 pound HILLSHIRE FARM® Polska
    Kielbasa,* sliced

Or use any variety Hillshire Farm® Smoked Sausage.

Heat oil in heavy skillet over medium-high heat; add carrots, onion, celery, garlic, fennel, salt and pepper. Sauté until vegetables are soft. Add potatoes, mushrooms, tomatoes with liquid, tomato sauce and oregano; cook 20 minutes over low heat. Add Polska Kielbasa; simmer 15 minutes or until heated through.   *Makes 6 servings*

Fisherman's Soup

⅛ teaspoon dried thyme, crushed
½ pound halibut or other firm white fish
2 tablespoons vegetable oil
1 medium onion, chopped
1 clove garlic, crushed
3 tablespoons all-purpose flour
2 cans (14 ounces each) low-salt chicken broth
1 can (15¼ ounces) DEL MONTE® Whole Kernel Golden Sweet Corn, undrained
1 can (14½ ounces) DEL MONTE Whole New Potatoes, drained and chopped

1. Sprinkle thyme over both sides of fish. In large saucepan, cook fish in 1 tablespoon hot oil over medium-high heat until fish flakes easily when tested with a fork. Remove fish from saucepan; set aside.

2. Heat remaining 1 tablespoon oil in same saucepan over medium heat. Add onion and garlic; cook until onion is tender. Stir in flour; cook 1 minute. Stir in broth; cook until thickened, stirring occasionally. Stir in corn and potatoes.

3. Discard skin and bones from fish; cut fish into bite-size pieces.

4. Add fish to soup just before serving; heat through. Stir in chopped parsley or sliced green onions, if desired.

Makes 4 to 6 servings

Prep Time: 5 minutes
Cook Time: 12 minutes

Hearty Minestrone Soup

2 cans (10¾ ounces each) condensed Italian tomato soup
3 cups water
3 cups cooked vegetables, such as zucchini, peas, corn or beans
2 cups cooked ditalini pasta
1⅓ cups *French's*® French Fried Onions

Combine soup and water in large saucepan. Add vegetables and pasta. Bring to a boil. Reduce heat. Cook until heated through, stirring often.

Place French Fried Onions in microwavable dish. Microwave on HIGH 1 minute or until onions are golden.

Ladle soup into individual bowls. Sprinkle with French Fried Onions.

Makes 6 servings

Prep Time: 10 minutes
Cook Time: 5 minutes

Nacho Cheese Soup

1 package (about 5 ounces) dry au gratin potatoes
1 can (about 15 ounces) whole kernel corn, undrained
2 cups water
1 cup salsa
2 cups milk
1½ cups (6 ounces) SARGENTO® Taco Blend Shredded Cheese
1 can (about 2 ounces) sliced ripe olives, drained
Tortilla chips (optional)

In large saucepan, combine potatoes, dry au gratin sauce mix, corn with liquid, water and salsa. Heat to a boil; reduce heat. Cover and simmer 25 minutes or until potatoes are tender, stirring occasionally. Add milk, cheese and olives. Cook until cheese is melted and soup is heated through, stirring occasionally. Garnish with tortilla chips.

Makes 6 servings

Fisherman's Soup

1-2-3 Steak Soup

1 pound boneless beef sirloin steak, cut into 1-inch cubes
1 tablespoon vegetable oil
½ pound sliced mushrooms (about 2½ cups)
2 cups *French's*® French Fried Onions, divided
1 package (16 ounces) frozen vegetables for stew (potatoes, carrots, celery and pearl onions)
2 cans (14½ ounces each) beef broth
1 can (8 ounces) tomato sauce
1 tablespoon *French's*® Worcestershire Sauce
Garnish: chopped parsley (optional)

1. Cook beef in hot oil in large saucepan over medium heat until browned, stirring frequently. Remove beef from pan; set aside.

2. Sauté mushrooms and ⅔ *cup* French Fried Onions in drippings in same pan over medium heat until golden, stirring occasionally. Stir in vegetables, broth, tomato sauce and Worcestershire. Return beef to pan.

3. Heat to a boil over high heat; reduce heat to low. Cover and simmer 20 minutes or until vegetables are tender, stirring occasionally. Spoon soup into serving bowls; top with remaining onions. Garnish with chopped parsley, if desired. *Makes 8 servings*

Prep Time: 5 minutes
Cook Time: 30 minutes

Mexican Chicken Stew

1 tablespoon olive oil
1 pound boneless, skinless chicken breasts, cut into ½-inch cubes
1 can (16 ounces) whole-kernel corn, drained
1 can (15 ounces) red kidney beans, undrained
1 can (15 ounces) black beans, drained and rinsed
1 can (4 ounces) chopped green chilies, undrained
1 cup chicken broth
1½ teaspoons McCORMICK® California Style Garlic Powder
1½ teaspoons McCORMICK® Ground Cumin
1 teaspoon McCORMICK® Oregano Leaves
1 teaspoon McCORMICK® Chili Powder
½ cup sliced scallions
Red bell pepper cut into flower shapes to garnish, if desired

1. Heat oil in large skillet over medium-high heat. Add chicken cubes and cook 5 minutes, stirring often. Remove chicken from skillet and set aside.

2. Add remaining ingredients, except scallions and garnish, to skillet and stir to mix well. Heat to a boil. Reduce heat to medium; cover and cook 10 minutes.

3. Stir in reserved chicken and scallions. Cover and simmer 5 to 10 minutes.

4. Spoon into serving bowl and garnish with red bell pepper flowers. *Makes 6 servings*

1-2-3 Steak Soup

Cheddar Broccoli Soup

1 tablespoon BERTOLLI® Olive Oil
1 rib celery, chopped (about ½ cup)
1 carrot, chopped (about ½ cup)
1 small onion, chopped (about ½ cup)
½ teaspoon dried thyme leaves, crushed
    (optional)
2 cans (13¾ ounces each) chicken broth
1 jar (1 pound) RAGÚ® Cheese
    Creations!® Double Cheddar Sauce
1 box (10 ounces) frozen chopped
    broccoli, thawed and drained

In 3-quart saucepan, heat oil over medium heat and cook celery, carrot, onion and thyme 3 minutes or until vegetables are almost tender. Add chicken broth and bring to a boil over high heat. Reduce heat to medium and simmer, uncovered, 10 minutes.

In food processor or blender, purée vegetable mixture until smooth; return to saucepan. Stir in Ragú Cheese Creations! Sauce and broccoli. Cook 10 minutes or until heated through.

Makes 6 (1-cup) servings

Spinach and Mushroom Soup

1½ cups 1% milk
    3 medium potatoes, peeled and chopped
        (1 cup)
    1 box (10 ounces) BIRDS EYE® frozen
        Chopped Spinach
    1 can (10¾ ounces) cream of mushroom
        soup

• In large saucepan, heat milk and potatoes over medium-low heat 10 minutes.

• Add spinach and soup.

• Cook about 10 minutes or until soup begins to bubble and potatoes are tender, stirring frequently.   *Makes 4 servings*

Prep Time: 5 minutes
Cook Time: 20 minutes

Hearty Beef Stew with Noodles

2 tablespoons BERTOLLI® Olive Oil
1 teaspoon finely chopped garlic
1 pound boneless beef sirloin steak, cut
    into ½-inch cubes
3 cups water
½ cup dry red wine
4 medium new potatoes, quartered
1 large carrot, thinly sliced
1 cup sliced mushrooms
1 cup sliced celery
1 large onion, cut into eighths
1 tablespoon tomato paste
¼ teaspoon dried thyme leaves, crushed
1 bay leaf
1 package LIPTON® Noodles & Sauce—
    Beef Flavor
1 tablespoon finely chopped parsley
    Salt and pepper to taste

In 3-quart saucepan, heat oil over medium heat and cook garlic 30 seconds. Add beef and cook over medium heat, stirring frequently, 2 minutes or until browned. Stir in water, wine, potatoes, carrot, mushrooms, celery, onion, tomato paste, thyme and bay leaf. Bring to a boil, then simmer, stirring occasionally, 30 minutes or until beef is almost tender. Stir in Noodles & Sauce—Beef Flavor and cook 10 minutes or until noodles are tender. Stir in parsley, salt and pepper. Remove bay leaf.

Makes about 4 (2-cup) servings

Cheddar Broccoli Soup

Sausage & Zucchini Soup

1 pound BOB EVANS® Italian Roll
    Sausage
1 medium onion, diced
1 (28-ounce) can stewed tomatoes
2 (14-ounce) cans beef broth
2 medium zucchini, diced or sliced
    (about 2 cups)
2 small carrots, diced
2 stalks celery, diced
4 large mushrooms, sliced
    Grated Parmesan cheese for garnish

Crumble and cook sausage and onion in large saucepan over medium heat until sausage is browned. Drain off any drippings. Add remaining ingredients except cheese; simmer, uncovered, over low heat about 40 minutes or until vegetables are tender. Garnish with cheese. Refrigerate leftovers.

Makes 8 servings

Tuna Minestrone with Parmesan Cheese

2 cans (14½ ounces *each*) chicken broth
    plus water to equal 4 cups
1 can (14½ ounces) ready-cut Italian-
    style tomatoes, undrained
1 can (15¼ ounces) kidney beans,
    drained
¼ cup tomato paste
1 teaspoon Italian herb seasoning
½ teaspoon salt
⅛ teaspoon ground red pepper
½ cup uncooked small shell pasta
2 cups Italian-style frozen vegetables
    (zucchini, carrots, cauliflower,
    Italian green beans, lima beans)
1 (7-ounce) pouch of STARKIST®
    Premium Albacore Tuna
3 cups fresh romaine lettuce, cut
    crosswise into 1-inch strips
    Freshly grated Parmesan cheese

In 4-quart saucepan, combine chicken broth mixture, tomatoes with liquid, kidney beans, tomato paste, herb seasoning, salt and red pepper; bring to a boil over high heat. Add pasta and frozen vegetables; simmer 8 minutes. Remove from heat; add tuna and romaine. Serve with cheese.

Makes 6 to 8 servings

Prep Time: 10 minutes

Chickpea and Shrimp Soup

1 tablespoon olive or vegetable oil
1 cup diced onion
2 cloves garlic, minced
4 cans (10.5 ounces each) beef broth
1 can (14.5 ounces) CONTADINA®
    Recipe Ready Diced Tomatoes with
    Roasted Garlic, undrained
1 can (15 ounces) chickpeas or garbanzo
    beans, drained
1 can (6 ounces) CONTADINA Italian
    Paste with Italian Seasonings
8 ounces small cooked shrimp
2 tablespoons chopped fresh Italian
    parsley *or* 2 teaspoons dried parsley
    flakes, crushed
½ teaspoon salt
¼ teaspoon ground black pepper

1. Heat oil over medium-high heat in large saucepan. Add onion and garlic; sauté for 1 minute.

2. Stir in broth, undrained tomatoes, chickpeas and tomato paste. Bring to boil.

3. Reduce heat to low; simmer, uncovered, 10 minutes. Add shrimp, parsley, salt and pepper; simmer 3 minutes or until heated through. Stir before serving.

Makes 8 to 10 servings

Golden Tomato Soup

4 teaspoons reduced-calorie margarine
1 cup chopped onion
2 cloves garlic, coarsely chopped
½ cup chopped carrot
¼ cup chopped celery
8 medium Florida tomatoes, blanched, peeled, seeded and chopped
6 cups chicken broth
¼ cup uncooked rice
2 tablespoons tomato paste
1 tablespoon Worcestershire sauce
½ teaspoon dried thyme leaves, crushed
¼ to ½ teaspoon ground black pepper
5 drops hot pepper sauce

Melt margarine in large Dutch oven over medium-high heat. Add onion and garlic; cook and stir 1 to 2 minutes or until onion is tender. Add carrot and celery; cook and stir 7 to 9 minutes or until tender, stirring frequently. Stir in tomatoes, broth, rice, tomato paste, Worcestershire sauce, thyme, black pepper and hot pepper sauce. Reduce heat to low; cook about 30 minutes, stirring frequently.

Remove from heat. Let cool about 10 minutes. In food processor or blender, process soup in small batches until smooth. Return soup to Dutch oven; simmer 3 to 5 minutes or until heated through. Garnish as desired.

Makes 8 servings

Favorite recipe from **Florida Tomato Committee**

Vegetable Soup with Delicious Dumplings

Soup

2 tablespoons WESSON® Vegetable Oil
1 cup diced onion
¾ cup sliced celery
7 cups homemade chicken broth *or* 4 (14.5-ounce) cans chicken broth
2 (14.5-ounce) cans HUNT'S® Stewed Tomatoes
½ teaspoon garlic powder
½ teaspoon salt
½ teaspoon fines herbs seasoning
⅛ teaspoon pepper
1 (16-ounce) bag frozen mixed vegetables
1 (15.5-ounce) can HUNT'S® Red Kidney Beans, drained
⅓ cup uncooked long-grain rice

Dumplings

2 cups all-purpose flour
3 tablespoons baking powder
1 teaspoon salt
⅔ cup milk
⅓ cup WESSON® Vegetable Oil
1½ teaspoons chopped fresh parsley

Soup

In a large Dutch oven, heat 2 tablespoons Wesson® Oil. Add onion and celery; sauté until crisp-tender. Stir in *next 6* ingredients, ending with pepper; bring to a boil. Add vegetables, beans and rice. Reduce heat; cover and simmer 15 to 20 minutes or until rice is cooked and vegetables are tender.

Dumplings

Meanwhile, in a medium bowl, combine flour, baking powder and salt; blend well. Add milk, ⅓ cup Wesson® Oil and parsley; mix until batter forms a ball in the bowl. Drop dough by rounded tablespoons into simmering soup. Cook, covered, 10 minutes; remove lid and cook an additional 10 minutes.

Makes 10 servings

Cajun Chili

6 ounces spicy sausage links, sliced
4 boneless, skinless chicken thighs, cut
  into cubes
1 medium onion, chopped
1/8 teaspoon cayenne pepper
1 can (15 ounces) black-eyed peas or
  kidney beans, drained
1 can (14½ ounces) DEL MONTE® Diced
  Tomatoes with Zesty Mild Green
  Chilies
1 medium green bell pepper, chopped

1. Lightly brown sausage in large skillet over medium-high heat. Add chicken, onion and cayenne pepper; cook until browned. Drain.

2. Stir in remaining ingredients. Cook 5 minutes, stirring occasionally.

Makes 4 servings

Prep and Cook Time: 20 minutes

Fruit Soup

5 fresh California nectarines, peeled,
  halved, pitted and diced
1 cup plain low fat yogurt
½ cup low fat milk
1 tablespoon sugar
1 teaspoon almond extract
¼ teaspoon curry powder
½ cup diced strawberries
  Mint leaves (optional)

Reserve ½ cup nectarines. Add remaining nectarines, yogurt, milk, sugar, almond extract and curry to blender; blend until smooth. Stir in reserved nectarines and strawberries. Refrigerate; garnish with mint.

Makes 6 servings

*Favorite recipe from **California Tree Fruit Agreement***

Hearty Tortilla Chip Soup

1 cup chopped onion
¾ cup finely chopped carrots
1 clove garlic, minced
6 ounces GUILTLESS GOURMET®
  Unsalted Baked Tortilla Chips
3 cans (14½ ounces each) low sodium
  chicken broth, defatted
2 cups water
1 cup GUILTLESS GOURMET® Roasted
  Red Pepper Salsa
1 can (6 ounces) low sodium tomato
  paste
1 cup (4 ounces) shredded low fat
  Monterey Jack cheese

Microwave Directions

Combine onion, carrots and garlic in 3-quart microwave-safe casserole. Cover with vented plastic wrap or lid; microwave on HIGH (100% power) 7 minutes or until vegetables are tender. Finely crush half the tortilla chips. Add crushed chips, broth, water, salsa and tomato paste; stir well. Cover; microwave on HIGH 6 minutes or until soup bubbles. Microwave on MEDIUM (50% power) 5 minutes. To serve, divide remaining tortilla chips and half the cheese among 6 individual soup bowls. Ladle soup over cheese and chips, dividing evenly. Sprinkle with remaining cheese. *Makes 8 servings*

Stove Top Directions: Bring 2 tablespoons broth to a boil in 3-quart saucepan over medium-high heat. Add onion, carrots and garlic; cook and stir about 5 minutes until vegetables are tender. Finely crush half the tortilla chips. Add crushed chips, remaining broth, water, salsa and tomato paste; stir well. Cook over medium heat until soup comes to a boil. Reduce heat to low; simmer 5 minutes. Serve as directed.

Cajun Chili

Idaho Potato Gazpacho

2 teaspoons olive oil
2 tablespoons minced garlic
2 medium onions, chopped
4 medium Idaho Potatoes, well scrubbed and diced
1 cup water
10 plum tomatoes, washed, halved crosswise and seeded
1 red or yellow bell pepper, washed, seeded and chopped
1 large cucumber, peeled and seeded
4 cups tomato juice
Salt and black pepper to taste
½ cup chopped fresh dill
Juice of 1 lemon
Dill sprigs for garnish

1. Heat olive oil in large heavy stockpot over high heat. Add garlic and stir about 30 seconds. Add onions and stir 2 minutes, until onions are tender. Reduce heat to medium; add potatoes and water and stir. Cover; cook 8 minutes or until potatoes are tender. Cool.

2. Meanwhile, finely chop tomatoes, peppers and cucumber in food processor, working in small batches. Add vegetables to stockpot with potatoes, stirring to scrape up all browned bits. Add tomato juice, salt and pepper to taste and fresh dill. Stir to combine.

3. Chill soup in refrigerator. Just before serving, add lemon juice and stir. Serve cold, with dill sprigs for garnish, if desired.

Makes 10 (1-cup) servings

Favorite recipe from **Idaho Potato Commission**

Quick Beef Soup

1½ pounds lean ground beef
1 cup chopped onion
2 cloves garlic, finely chopped
1 can (28 ounces) tomatoes, undrained
6 cups water
6 beef bouillon cubes
¼ teaspoon black pepper
1½ cups frozen peas, carrots and corn vegetable blend
½ cup uncooked orzo
French bread (optional)

Cook beef, onion and garlic in large saucepan over medium-high heat until beef is brown, stirring to separate meat; drain fat.

Purée tomatoes with juice in covered blender or food processor. Add tomatoes with juice, water, bouillon cubes and pepper to meat mixture. Bring to a boil; reduce heat to low. Simmer, uncovered, 20 minutes. Add vegetables and orzo. Simmer 15 minutes more. Serve with French bread. *Makes 6 servings*

Favorite recipe from **North Dakota Beef Commission**

Southwestern Soup

1 bag (16 ounces) BIRDS EYE® frozen Corn
2 cans (15 ounces each) chili
1 cup hot water
½ cup chopped green bell pepper

• Combine all ingredients in saucepan.

• Cook over medium heat 10 to 12 minutes.

Makes 4 to 6 servings

Prep Time: 1 to 2 minutes
Cook Time: 10 to 12 minutes

Classic Matzoh Ball Soup

1 whole chicken (about 3½ pounds), cut into serving pieces
7 cups plus 2 tablespoons water, divided
3 carrots, cut into 1-inch pieces
3 ribs celery, cut into 1-inch pieces
1 medium onion, unpeeled, quartered
1 large parsnip, cut into 1-inch pieces (optional)
1 head garlic, separated into cloves, unpeeled
3 sprigs parsley
8 to 10 whole black peppercorns
4 eggs
1 cup matzoh meal
¼ cup parve margarine, melted, cooled
1 tablespoon grated onion
½ teaspoon salt
⅛ teaspoon ground white pepper *or*
    ¼ teaspoon freshly ground black pepper
  Chopped fresh parsley, for garnish

Combine chicken and 7 cups water in Dutch oven. Bring to a boil over medium heat. Remove any foam from surface of water with large metal spoon; discard. Add carrots, celery, unpeeled onion, parsnip, garlic, parsley and whole peppercorns. Cover; simmer 3 hours or until chicken is no longer pink in center. Remove from heat; cool 30 minutes. Strain soup; reserve chicken and broth separately. Discard vegetables. Remove skin and bones from chicken; discard.* Reserve chicken for another use.

Beat eggs in large bowl on medium speed of electric mixer. Add matzoh meal, margarine, remaining 2 tablespoons water, grated onion, salt and ground pepper. Mix at low speed until well blended. Let stand 15 to 30 minutes. With wet hands, form matzoh mixture into 12 (2-inch) balls.

Bring 8 cups water to a boil in Dutch oven. Drop matzoh balls, one at a time, into boiling water. Reduce heat. Cover; simmer 35 to 40 minutes or until matzoh balls are cooked through. Drain well.

Add reserved broth to Dutch oven. Bring to a boil over high heat. Add salt to taste. Reduce heat; cover. Simmer 5 minutes or until matzoh balls are heated through. Garnish with parsley, if desired.   *Makes 6 servings*

*Chicken and broth may be covered and refrigerated up to 3 days or frozen up to 3 months.

Favorite recipe from Hebrew National®

Taco Soup

1 pound BOB EVANS® Original Recipe or Zesty Hot Roll Sausage
1½ tablespoons olive oil
½ small Spanish onion, diced
1 jalapeño pepper, seeded and diced
1½ cups beef broth
1 cup peeled, seeded, diced fresh or canned tomatoes
1 cup vegetable juice
½ tablespoon ground cumin
½ tablespoon chili powder
¼ teaspoon salt
⅓ cup shredded Cheddar cheese
12 tortilla chips, broken into pieces

Crumble and cook sausage in olive oil in Dutch oven until no longer pink but not yet browned. Add onion and pepper; cook until onion is tender. Add remaining ingredients except cheese and chips; bring to a boil over high heat. Reduce heat to low and simmer, uncovered, 15 minutes. Ladle soup into bowls; garnish with cheese and chips. Refrigerate leftovers.   *Makes 6 servings*

Old-Fashioned Beef Stew

1 tablespoon CRISCO® Oil*
1¼ pounds boneless beef round steak, trimmed and cut into 1-inch cubes
2¾ cups water, divided
1 teaspoon Worcestershire sauce
2 bay leaves
1 clove garlic, minced
½ teaspoon paprika
¼ teaspoon black pepper
8 medium carrots, quartered
8 small potatoes, peeled and quartered
4 small onions, quartered
1 package (9 ounces) frozen cut green beans
1 tablespoon cornstarch
Salt (optional)

Use your favorite Crisco Oil product.

1. Heat oil in Dutch oven on medium-high heat. Add beef. Cook and stir until browned. Add 1½ cups water, Worcestershire sauce, bay leaves, garlic, paprika and pepper. Bring to a boil. Reduce heat to low. Cover. Simmer 1 hour 15 minutes, stirring occasionally. Remove and discard bay leaves.

2. Add carrots, potatoes and onions. Cover. Simmer 30 to 45 minutes or until vegetables are almost tender. Add beans. Simmer 5 minutes or until tender. Remove from heat. Add 1 cup water to Dutch oven.

3. Combine remaining ¼ cup water and cornstarch in small bowl. Stir well. Stir into ingredients in Dutch oven. Return to low heat. Cook and stir until thickened. Season with salt, if desired. *Makes 8 servings*

Chicken Ragoût with Chilies, Tortillas and Goat Cheese

1 cup BLUE DIAMOND® Sliced Natural Almonds
6 tablespoons vegetable oil, divided
6 corn tortillas
2 boneless skinless chicken breasts, halved (about 1¼ pounds)
1 cup chicken stock or broth
1 onion, chopped
1 red bell pepper, cut into strips
1 can (7 ounces) whole green chilies, cut crosswise into ¼-inch strips
1½ teaspoons ground cumin
1 cup heavy cream
8 ounces goat cheese
1 tablespoon lime juice
½ to 1 teaspoon salt

Cook and stir almonds in 1 tablespoon oil over medium-high heat in small saucepan until golden; reserve. Heat 4 tablespoons oil; soften tortillas in oil, one at a time, about 30 seconds. Drain on paper towels and cut into ½-inch strips; reserve.

Poach chicken breasts, covered, in barely simmering chicken stock in medium saucepan about 10 minutes or just until tender and chicken is no longer pink in center. Remove chicken from stock; reserve stock. Slice chicken into strips. In large skillet, cook and stir onion and bell pepper in remaining 1 tablespoon oil until onion is translucent. Add chilies and cumin; cook and stir 1 minute. Stir in reserved chicken stock and cream; simmer 2 to 3 minutes. Add chicken. Stir in goat cheese; do not boil. Add lime juice and salt. Fold in reserved tortilla strips and almonds. *Makes 4 servings*

Old-Fashioned Beef Stew

Santa Fe Tomato Chowder

1 tablespoon butter or margarine
2 teaspoons minced garlic
4 ripe tomatoes, chopped
1 can (15 ounces) tomato sauce
1 cup frozen corn kernels
¼ cup chopped fresh cilantro
1 tablespoon *Frank's® RedHot®* Cayenne
    Pepper Sauce
½ teaspoon chili powder
1 ripe avocado, peeled and chopped
1 cup (4 ounces) shredded Monterey
    Jack cheese
1⅓ cups *French's®* French Fried Onions

1. Melt butter in large saucepan; sauté garlic for 1 minute. Add tomatoes and cook 5 minutes. Stir in 1 cup water, tomato sauce, corn, cilantro, **Frank's RedHot Sauce** and chili powder.

2. Bring to a boil over high heat. Reduce heat; simmer 10 minutes. Spoon soup into serving bowls; sprinkle with avocado, cheese and French Fried Onions.

Makes 4 servings

Variation: For added Cheddar flavor, substitute *French's®* new **Cheddar French Fried Onions** for the original flavor.

Prep Time: 10 minutes
Cook Time: 20 minutes

Chicken Vegetable Soup

1 bag SUCCESS® Rice
5 cups chicken broth
1½ cups chopped uncooked chicken
1 cup sliced celery
1 cup sliced carrots
½ cup chopped onion
¼ cup chopped fresh parsley
½ teaspoon pepper
½ teaspoon dried thyme leaves, crushed
1 bay leaf
1 tablespoon lime juice

Prepare rice according to package directions.

Combine broth, chicken, celery, carrots, onion, parsley, pepper, thyme and bay leaf in large saucepan or Dutch oven. Bring to a boil over medium-high heat, stirring once or twice. Reduce heat to low; simmer 10 to 15 minutes or until chicken is no longer pink in center. Remove bay leaf; discard. Stir in rice and lime juice. Garnish, if desired.

Makes 4 servings

Onion Soup with Bel Paese®

1 to 1½ pounds onions, sliced
    Vegetable oil for frying
1 teaspoon all-purpose flour
4 cups beef broth or beef bouillon,
    prepared
¼ teaspoon salt
⅛ teaspoon black pepper
4 slices Italian bread, toasted
4 ounces BEL PAESE® Cheese,* cut into
    4 slices
½ cup CUCINA CLASSICA™ Grated
    Parmesan Cheese (about 1 ounce)

*Remove wax coating and moist, white crust from cheese.

Preheat oven to 350°F. In large saucepan, cook and stir onions in oil until golden. Sprinkle with flour and cook an additional 5 minutes. Add broth, salt and pepper. Reduce heat and simmer for 30 minutes.

In each of 4 small ovenproof crocks, place 1 slice toast. Top with 1 slice Bel Paese® Cheese and 2 tablespoons Cucina Classica™ Grated Parmesan Cheese. Ladle onion soup into crocks. Bake for 10 minutes. Serve hot.

Makes 4 servings

Santa Fe Tomato Chowder

Hearty Potato-Ham Chowder

5 pounds COLORADO potatoes, peeled and cubed (about 15 cups)
3 large onions, finely chopped (about 1 pound)
3 tablespoons instant chicken bouillon granules
2 tablespoons dried marjoram leaves
1 tablespoon dry mustard
1 teaspoon ground black pepper
4 quarts milk, divided
1¼ cups all-purpose flour
1 pound process Swiss cheese, shredded
1½ pounds sodium-reduced ham, diced
½ cup snipped fresh parsley

Steam potatoes and onions in 1 quart water 20 to 30 minutes or until tender. *Do not drain.* Mash slightly. Stir in bouillon granules, marjoram, mustard and pepper. Combine about 1 quart milk with flour; whisk to blend until smooth. Add remaining milk, cheese and milk/flour mixture to potato mixture. Cook and stir over medium high heat until slightly thickened and bubbly. Cook and stir 2 minutes longer. Stir in ham and parsley; return to near boiling. Reduce heat; serve hot.

Makes 24 servings

Favorite recipe from **Colorado Potato Administrative Committee**

Patrick's Irish Lamb Soup

1 tablespoon olive oil
1 medium onion, coarsely chopped
1½ pounds fresh lean American lamb boneless shoulder, cut into ¾-inch cubes
1 bottle (12 ounces) beer *or* ¾ cup water
1 teaspoon seasoned pepper
2 cans (14½ ounces each) beef broth
1 package (0.93 ounce) brown gravy mix
3 cups cubed potatoes
2 cups thinly sliced carrots
2 cups shredded green cabbage
⅓ cup chopped fresh parsley (optional)

In 3-quart saucepan with cover, heat oil. Add onion and sauté until brown, stirring occasionally. Add lamb and sauté, stirring until browned. Stir in beer and pepper. Cover and simmer 30 minutes.

Mix in broth and gravy mix. Add potatoes and carrots; cover and simmer 15 to 20 minutes or until vegetables are tender. Stir in cabbage and cook just until cabbage turns bright green. Garnish with chopped parsley, if desired.

Makes 8 servings

Favorite recipe from **American Lamb Council**

Rosarita Refried Soup

PAM® No-Stick Cooking Spray
1 cup diced onion
1 can (16 ounces) ROSARITA® Traditional No-Fat Refried Beans
6 cups fat free, low sodium chicken broth
1 can (14.5-ounce) HUNT'S® Diced Tomatoes in Juice
4 cups baked tortilla chips
½ cup shredded reduced fat Monterey Jack cheese
¼ cup chopped fresh cilantro

1. Spray a large saucepan with PAM® Cooking Spray. Sauté onion over low heat for 5 minutes.

2. Add Rosarita® Beans, broth and Hunt's® Tomatoes; mix well. Cook until heated through.

3. Place ⅓ cup tortilla chips in *each* bowl. Ladle soup into bowls. Garnish with cheese and cilantro. *Makes 12 (1-cup) servings*

Hearty Potato-Ham Chowder

Tomato French Onion Soup

4 medium onions, chopped
2 tablespoons butter or margarine
1 can (14½ ounces) DEL MONTE® Diced
    Tomatoes
1 can (10½ ounces) condensed beef
    consommé
¼ cup dry sherry
4 French bread slices, toasted
1½ cups (6 ounces) shredded Swiss
    cheese
¼ cup (1 ounce) grated Parmesan cheese

1. Cook onions in butter in large saucepan about 10 minutes. Add undrained tomatoes, 2 cups water, consommé and sherry to saucepan. Bring to boil, skimming off foam.

2. Reduce heat to medium-low; simmer 10 minutes. Place soup in four broilerproof bowls; top with bread and cheeses. Broil until cheeses are melted and golden.

Makes 4 servings

Hint: If broilerproof bowls are not available, place soup in ovenproof bowls and bake at 350°F, 10 minutes.

Prep and Cook Time: 35 minutes

Turkey Chili

1 tablespoon vegetable oil
1 pound ground turkey
1 large onion, chopped
1 large green pepper, chopped
1 can (14 ounces) chunky tomatoes,
    salsa-style
1 can (8 ounces) no-salt-added tomato
    sauce
¾ cup HOLLAND HOUSE® Red Cooking
    Wine
1 package (1¼ ounces) chili seasoning
    mix
1 can (15 ounces) kidney beans, drained
    (optional)

In large saucepan, heat oil. Add turkey, onion and green pepper. Cook until onion is tender. Stir in tomatoes, tomato sauce, Holland House® Red Cooking Wine and chili seasoning mix. Bring to a boil and simmer, partially covered, 10 minutes. Stir in beans and heat through.

Serve, if desired, with rice, shredded cheese and chopped onion.

Makes about 4 servings

Note: Serve this healthy chili with a crisp green salad and cornbread for a delicious meal.

Butch's Black Bean Soup

¼ cup olive oil
1 medium onion, diced
4 cloves garlic, minced
4 cups water
2 chicken-flavored bouillon cubes
1 large can (2 pounds 8 ounces) black
    beans, rinsed and drained
1 can (15 ounces) corn, undrained
1 medium potato, peeled and diced
3 ribs celery, diced
2 carrots, diced
1 cup uncooked rice or orzo
¼ cup fresh cilantro, minced
2 (11-ounce) jars NEWMAN'S OWN®
    Bandito Salsa (medium or hot) *or*
    1 (26-ounce) jar NEWMAN'S OWN®
    Diavolo Spicy Simmer Sauce

Heat oil in large saucepan; cook and stir onion and garlic over high heat until onion is translucent. Add water and bouillon cubes; bring to a boil. Reduce heat to medium; add beans, corn, potato, celery, carrots, rice and cilantro. Stir in Newman's Own® Bandito Salsa and simmer until rice and vegetables are cooked, about 30 minutes.

Makes 8 servings

Tomato French Onion Soup

Summer Minestrone with Pesto

4 tablespoons BERTOLLI® Olive Oil, divided

2 cups diced carrots

3 medium zucchini and/or yellow squash, diced

1 jar (1 pound 10 ounces) RAGÚ® Light Pasta Sauce

2 cans (13¾ ounces each) chicken or vegetable broth

1 can (19 ounces) cannellini or white kidney beans, rinsed and drained

1 cup packed fresh basil leaves

1 large clove garlic, finely chopped

¼ teaspoon salt

In 5-quart saucepan, heat 1 tablespoon oil over medium-high heat and cook carrots and zucchini, stirring occasionally, 8 minutes. Stir in Ragú® Light Pasta Sauce and chicken broth. Bring to a boil over high heat. Reduce heat to low and simmer covered, stirring occasionally, 20 minutes or until vegetables are tender. Stir in beans; heat through.

Meanwhile, for pesto, in blender or food processor, blend basil, garlic, salt and remaining 3 tablespoons oil until basil is finely chopped. To serve, ladle soup into bowls and garnish each with spoonful of pesto. Serve, if desired, with crusty Italian bread.

Makes 8 (1-cup) servings

Prep Time: 20 minutes
Cook Time: 30 minutes

Pizza Soup

2 cans (10¾ ounces each) condensed tomato soup

¾ teaspoon garlic powder

½ teaspoon dried oregano leaves

¾ cup uncooked tiny pasta shells (¼-inch)

1 cup shredded quick-melting mozzarella cheese

1 cup *French's®* French Fried Onions

1. Combine soup, *2 soup cans of water,* garlic powder and oregano in small saucepan. Bring to boiling over medium-high heat.

2. Add pasta. Cook 8 minutes or until pasta is tender.

3. Stir in cheese. Cook until cheese melts. Sprinkle with French Fried Onions.

Makes 4 servings

Prep Time: 5 minutes
Cook Time: 10 minutes

Native American Wild Rice Soup

2 cups water

½ cup wild rice, uncooked, rinsed in cold water and drained

½ cup (1 stick) butter

1½ cups diced onions

8 ounces fresh button mushrooms, sliced

2 teaspoons fresh rosemary, stemmed, minced *or* ¾ teaspoon dried rosemary, crumbled

¾ cup flour

8 cups chicken broth

1 teaspoon salt

½ teaspoon freshly ground black pepper

1 cup whipping cream

2 tablespoons sherry or dry white wine

Place water in medium saucepan. Add wild rice and bring to a boil over medium heat. Reduce heat to low, cover and simmer about 45 minutes. Do not drain; set aside. Melt butter in 5-quart Dutch oven over medium heat. Add onions and mushrooms. Sauté about 3 minutes, until vegetables soften; add rosemary. Add flour gradually to mushroom mixture, cooking and stirring frequently over medium-high heat until mixture boils. Boil 1 minute. Stir in reserved wild rice and any remaining liquid, salt and pepper. Stir in whipping cream and sherry; do not boil. Serve immediately.　*Makes 12 servings*

Favorite recipe from **Wisconsin Milk Marketing Board**

Pimento-Cheese Soup

2 tablespoons butter or margarine
1 medium onion, chopped (about ⅔ cup)
3 jars (4 ounces each) diced pimentos,
    well drained
1 tablespoon all-purpose flour
2½ cups chicken broth
1 cup shredded regular or low-fat sharp
    Cheddar cheese
¼ cup heavy cream
    Salt and pepper, to taste
    Parsley sprigs for garnish (optional)

Melt butter in medium saucepan. Sauté onion over moderately low heat, stirring occasionally, for 10 minutes or until wilted. Add pimentos and cook, stirring occasionally, until onion is very soft but not brown, about 15 minutes. Cool slightly and purée until smooth in blender or food processor fitted with metal blade.

Return mixture to saucepan and whisk in flour. Add broth and bring to a simmer. Stir in cheese and cream until blended. Remove from heat and season to taste with salt and pepper.

Garnish each serving with parsley sprigs, if desired.   *Makes 8 (½-cup) servings*

Note: The base for this soup may be made ahead and refrigerated up to 2 days or frozen. Add cheese, cream and seasonings to base and heat thoroughly prior to serving.

Favorite recipe from **Dromedary Pimientos®**

Catch of the Day Stew

1 can (14½ ounces) reduced-sodium
    chicken broth
1 can (10½ ounces) French onion soup,
    undiluted
1 cup potatoes, peeled and cubed
1 cup baby carrots
½ cup sliced celery
1 pound fish fillets, cut into 1-inch
    pieces
1 cup zucchini, thinly sliced
1 cup mushrooms, sliced
1 can (14½ ounces) diced tomatoes,
    undrained
½ teaspoon *each* dried thyme and
    rosemary, crushed

Combine broth, soup, potatoes, carrots and celery in large Dutch oven; bring to a boil over high heat. Reduce heat to medium; cover and cook 5 minutes. Add remaining ingredients; cook 5 to 10 minutes or until fish flakes easily with fork and vegetables are tender.

Makes 4 to 6 servings

Favorite recipe from **National Fisheries Institute**

Italian Tomato Soup

½ pound lean ground beef
½ cup chopped onion
1 clove garlic, minced
1 can (28 ounces) tomatoes, undrained,
    cut into pieces
1 can (15 ounces) white kidney beans,
    drained, rinsed
¾ cup HEINZ® Tomato Ketchup
½ cup thinly sliced carrots
1 teaspoon dried basil leaves
¼ teaspoon salt

In medium saucepan, brown beef, onion and garlic; drain excess fat. Add tomatoes with juices and remaining ingredients. Cover; simmer 15 minutes.

Makes 4 to 6 servings (about 6 cups)

Bouillabaisse

2 cups water
1 package KNORR® Recipe Classics™
    Vegetable or Spring Vegetable Soup,
    Dip and Recipe Mix
1 bottle or can (8 to 10 ounces) clam
    juice
2 teaspoons tomato paste
½ teaspoon paprika
¼ teaspoon saffron threads (optional)
12 mussels or clams, well scrubbed
1½ pounds mixed seafood (cubed cod,
    snapper, scallops or shrimp)

• In 3-quart saucepan, bring water, recipe mix, clam juice, tomato paste, paprika and saffron to a boil over medium-high heat, stirring occasionally.

• Add mussels and seafood. Bring to a boil over high heat.

• Reduce heat to low and simmer 5 minutes or until shells open and seafood is cooked through and flakes easily when tested with a fork. Discard any unopened shells.

Makes 6 servings

Prep Time: 15 minutes
Cook Time: 10 minutes

Creamy Shell Soup

4 cups water
3 or 4 chicken pieces
1 cup chopped onion
¼ cup chopped celery
¼ cup minced fresh parsley *or*
    1 tablespoon dried parsley flakes
1 bay leaf
1 teaspoon salt
¼ teaspoon white pepper
2 medium potatoes, diced
4 or 5 green onions, chopped
3 chicken bouillon cubes
½ teaspoon seasoned salt
½ teaspoon poultry seasoning
4 cups milk
2 cups medium shell macaroni, cooked
    and drained
¼ cup butter or margarine
¼ cup all-purpose flour

Combine water, chicken, chopped onion, celery, minced parsley, bay leaf, salt and pepper in Dutch oven. Bring to a boil. Reduce heat to low; simmer until chicken is tender. Remove bay leaf; discard. Remove chicken; cool. Skin, debone and cut into small cubes; set aside.

Add potatoes, green onions, bouillon cubes, seasoned salt and poultry seasoning to broth. Simmer 15 minutes. Add milk, macaroni and chicken; return to a simmer.

Melt butter in skillet over medium heat. Add flour, stirring constantly, until mixture begins to brown. Add to soup; blend well. Let soup simmer on very low heat 20 minutes to blend flavors. Season to taste. Sprinkle with ground nutmeg and additional chopped parsley, if desired. *Makes 8 servings*

Favorite recipe from **North Dakota Wheat Commission**

Bouillabaisse

California Turkey Chili

1¼ cups chopped onion
1 cup chopped green bell pepper
2 cloves garlic, minced
3 tablespoons vegetable oil
1 can (28 ounces) kidney beans, drained
1 can (28 ounces) stewed tomatoes, undrained
1 cup red wine or water
3 cups cubed cooked California-grown turkey
1 tablespoon chili powder
1 tablespoon chopped fresh cilantro *or* 1 teaspoon dried coriander
1 teaspoon crushed red pepper
½ teaspoon salt
Shredded Cheddar cheese (optional)
Additional chopped onion (optional)
Additional chopped fresh cilantro (optional)

Cook and stir onion, green pepper, garlic and oil in large saucepan over high heat until tender. Add beans, tomatoes with liquid, wine, turkey, chili powder, cilantro, red pepper and salt. Cover; simmer 25 minutes or until heated through. Top with cheese, onion or cilantro, if desired. *Makes 6 servings*

Favorite recipe from **California Poultry Federation**

French Onion Soup

2 tablespoons butter
3 medium onions, thinly sliced and separated into rings
1 package (1.0 ounce) LAWRY'S® Au Jus Gravy Mix
3 cups water
4 thin slices sourdough French bread Unsalted butter, softened
4 slices Swiss or Gruyère cheese

In large skillet, heat 2 tablespoons butter. Add onions and cook over medium-high heat until golden. In small bowl, combine Au Jus Gravy Mix and water; add to onions. Bring to a boil over medium-high heat. Reduce heat to low; cover and simmer 15 minutes, stirring occasionally. Broil bread on one side until lightly toasted. Turn bread slices over; spread with unsalted butter. Top with cheese; broil until cheese melts. *Makes 4 servings*

Hint: If using individual, ovenproof bowls, pour soup into bowls; top with a slice of untoasted bread. Top with cheese. Place under broiler just until cheese is melted.

Ham and Beer Cheese Soup

1 cup chopped onion
½ cup sliced celery
2 tablespoons butter or margarine
1 cup hot water
1 HERB-OX® chicken flavor bouillon cube *or* 1 teaspoon instant chicken bouillon
3 cups half-and-half
3 cups (18 ounces) diced CURE 81® ham
1 (16-ounce) loaf pasteurized process cheese spread, cubed
1 (12-ounce) can beer
3 tablespoons all-purpose flour
Popcorn (optional)

In Dutch oven over medium-high heat, sauté onion and celery in butter until tender. In small liquid measuring cup, combine water and bouillon; set aside. Add half-and-half, ham, cheese, beer and ¾ cup broth to onion and celery mixture. Cook, stirring constantly, until cheese melts. Combine remaining ¼ cup broth and flour; stir until smooth. Add flour mixture to soup, stirring constantly. Cook, stirring constantly, until slightly thickened. Sprinkle individual servings with popcorn, if desired. *Makes 8 servings*

California Turkey Chili

Pasta e Fagioli

½ cup chopped onion
½ cup sliced carrot
½ cup sliced celery
4 tablespoons extra-virgin olive oil
2 cloves garlic, finely chopped
2 cups reduced-sodium chicken broth or
    more as needed
1 can (15 ounces) cannellini beans,
    rinsed and drained
1 can (14½ ounces) Italian plum
    tomatoes with juices
1 cup BARILLA® Ditalini or other small
    pasta shape
1 cup cut green beans (fresh or frozen)
1 cup frozen small lima beans
2 cups packed dark leaves of escarole or
    Swiss chard, cut into small pieces
    Salt and pepper
¼ cup grated Romano cheese, plus more
    to taste

1. Combine onion, carrot, celery, olive oil and garlic in large broad saucepan. Cover and cook over low heat about 10 minutes until vegetables are tender but not browned.

2. Stir in broth, beans and tomatoes with liquid. Cover and cook about 15 minutes until flavors are blended.

3. Add ditalini, green beans, lima beans and escarole to saucepan. Cook, uncovered, 10 to 12 minutes or until vegetables are very tender and mixture is thick. Add salt and pepper to taste. Stir in cheese. Ladle into bowls; serve with additional cheese.

Makes 4 to 6 servings

Country Cream of Chicken Chowder

¼ cup CRISCO® Oil*
¼ cup finely chopped onion
¼ cup all-purpose flour
4 cups chicken broth
2 cups skim milk
1 bay leaf
3 cups frozen hash brown potatoes
1 package (10 ounces) frozen whole
    kernel corn
1 package (10 ounces) frozen cut green
    beans
1 package (10 ounces) frozen peas
1 package (10 ounces) frozen sliced
    carrots
1½ cups finely chopped cooked chicken
⅛ teaspoon pepper
2 tablespoons chopped fresh parsley *or*
    chives

Use your favorite Crisco Oil product.

1. Heat oil in large saucepan on medium heat. Add onion. Cook and stir until tender. Stir in flour. Cook until bubbly. Stir in broth and milk gradually. Cook and stir until mixture is bubbly and slightly thickened. Add bay leaf.

2. Add potatoes, corn, beans, peas and carrots. Increase heat to medium-high. Bring mixture back to a boil. Reduce heat to low. Simmer 5 minutes or until beans are tender. Stir in chicken and pepper. Heat thoroughly. Remove bay leaf. Serve sprinkled with parsley.

Makes 10 servings

Arizona Pork Chili

1 tablespoon vegetable oil
1½ pounds boneless pork, cut into ¼-inch cubes
    Salt and black pepper (optional)
1 can (15 ounces) black, pinto or kidney beans, drained
1 can (14½ ounces) DEL MONTE® Diced Tomatoes with Garlic & Onion, undrained
1 can (4 ounces) diced green chiles, drained
1 teaspoon ground cumin
    Tortillas and sour cream (optional)

1. Heat oil in large skillet over medium-high heat. Add pork; cook until browned. Season with salt and pepper to taste, if desired.

2. Add beans, tomatoes, chiles and cumin. Simmer 10 minutes, stirring occasionally. Serve with tortillas and sour cream, if desired.

Makes 6 servings

Prep Time: 10 minutes
Cook Time: 25 minutes

Kaleidoscope Chowder

3 cups water
3 large potatoes, peeled and diced
1 (26-ounce) jar NEWMAN'S OWN® Diavolo Sauce
2 large carrots, peeled and thinly sliced
1½ to 2 pounds assorted seafood, such as fish fillets, bay scallops, shrimp or clams
½ cup dry white wine
2 cups shredded fresh spinach leaves
1 yellow bell pepper, seeded and diced
    Freshly grated Parmesan cheese

In large stockpot, bring water to a boil. Add potatoes; cook 5 minutes. Stir in Newman's Own® Diavolo Sauce and carrots. Bring to a boil; reduce heat and simmer 5 minutes.

Cut fish fillets into bite-size pieces. Peel and devein shrimp. Add seafood and wine to soup. Cook over medium-high heat, stirring often, until fish is opaque, 3 to 4 minutes. Add spinach and bell pepper; cover. Remove from heat and let stand until spinach and pepper are heated through, about 2 minutes. Serve with Parmesan cheese.   *Makes 4 servings*

Note: This chowder is also excellent with diced cooked chicken breast.

Turkey, Corn and Sweet Potato Soup

½ cup chopped onion
1 small jalapeño pepper,* minced
1 teaspoon margarine
5 cups turkey broth or reduced sodium chicken bouillon
1½ pounds sweet potatoes, peeled and cut into 1-inch cubes
2 cups cooked turkey, cut into ½-inch cubes
½ teaspoon salt
1½ cups frozen corn
    Fresh cilantro (optional)

Jalapeño peppers can sting and irritate the skin; wear rubber or plastic gloves when handling peppers and do not touch eyes. Wash hands after handling.

In 5-quart saucepan over medium-high heat, cook and stir onion and jalapeño pepper in margarine 5 minutes or until onion is soft. Add broth, potatoes, turkey and salt; bring to a boil. Reduce heat to low, cover and simmer 20 to 25 minutes or until potatoes are tender. Stir in corn. Increase heat to medium and cook 5 to 6 minutes.

To serve, spoon 1 cup soup into bowl and garnish with cilantro, if desired.

Makes 8 servings

*Favorite recipe from **National Turkey Federation***

Easy Ham & Veg•All® Chowder

2 cans (15 ounces each) VEG•ALL®
    Original Mixed Vegetables, with
    liquid
1 can (10¾ ounces) cream of potato
    soup
1 cup cooked ham, cubed
½ teaspoon dried basil
¼ teaspoon black pepper

In medium saucepan, combine Veg•All, soup,
ham, basil and black pepper. Heat until hot;
serve.   *Makes 4 to 6 servings*

Prep Time: 7 minutes

Hearty and Heart-Healthy Idaho Potato Soup/Stew

1 tablespoon olive oil
2 (10-ounce) packages frozen chopped
    onions
2 pounds Idaho Potatoes, scrubbed and
    cut into ½ inch cubes (about 5 cups)
1 (14½-ounce) can low-sodium chicken
    broth
¼ cup chopped sun-dried tomatoes
3 cups packaged shredded
    cabbage/carrot (coleslaw mixture)
2 cups shredded cooked turkey
1 (10-ounce) package chopped frozen
    mixed vegetables, thawed

1. In heavy soup pot, heat oil on high and
stir in onions. Cook, stirring occasionally,
about 20 minutes or until well browned.

2. Add potatoes, broth and tomatoes. Bring
to a boil and cook, covered, 10 minutes or
until tender.

3. Add cabbage mixture, turkey and
vegetables; return to a boil and cook 6 to
8 minutes. Top with freshly ground pepper, if
desired.   *Makes 8 servings (about 12 cups)*

Favorite recipe from **Idaho Potato Commission**

Seafood Gumbo

½ cup chopped onion
½ cup chopped green pepper
½ cup (about 2 ounces) sliced fresh
    mushrooms
1 clove garlic, minced
2 tablespoons margarine
1 can (28 ounces) whole tomatoes,
    undrained
2 cups chicken broth
½ to ¾ teaspoon ground red pepper
½ teaspoon dried thyme leaves
½ teaspoon dried basil leaves
1 package (10 ounces) frozen cut okra,
    thawed
¾ pound white fish, cut into 1-inch
    pieces
½ pound peeled, deveined shrimp
3 cups hot cooked rice

Cook onion, green pepper, mushrooms and
garlic in margarine in large saucepan or Dutch
oven over medium-high heat until tender-
crisp. Stir in tomatoes and juice, broth, red
pepper, thyme and basil. Bring to a boil.
Reduce heat; simmer, uncovered, 10 to
15 minutes. Stir in okra, fish and shrimp;
simmer until fish flakes with fork, 5 to
8 minutes. Serve rice on top of gumbo.
                        Makes 6 servings

Favorite recipe from **USA Rice Federation**

Easy Ham & Veg•All® Chowder

Zucchini-Tomato-Noodle Soup

10 cups cubed zucchini
¾ cup water
4 cups chopped onion
½ cup butter
8 cups quartered tomatoes
4 chicken bouillon cubes
3 cloves garlic, chopped
1 teaspoon Beau Monde seasoning*
1 teaspoon salt
1 teaspoon black pepper
4 cups uncooked 100% durum noodles,
　　hot, cooked and drained
　Garlic bread (optional)

*A seasoning salt available in most supermarkets.
Celery salt can be substituted.

Combine zucchini and water in Dutch oven.
Cook over medium heat until crisp-tender.
Cook and stir onion in hot butter in small
skillet over medium heat until tender. Add
onion mixture, tomatoes, bouillon cubes,
garlic, seasoning, salt and pepper to zucchini
mixture. Simmer until tender. Add noodles;
heat through. Serve with garlic bread, if
desired.　　　　　　　　*Makes 8 servings*

Favorite recipe from **North Dakota Wheat Commission**

Cheesy Vegetable Soup

2 teaspoons CRISCO® Oil*
¼ cup chopped green or red bell pepper
¼ cup chopped onion
2 tablespoons all-purpose flour
½ teaspoon dry mustard
⅛ teaspoon cayenne pepper
1 cup chicken broth
½ cup skim milk
1 package (10 ounces) mixed vegetables
　　(broccoli, cauliflower and carrots) in
　　cheese flavor sauce, thawed
1 package (9 ounces) frozen cut green
　　beans, thawed
½ teaspoon salt

Use your favorite Crisco Oil product.

1. Heat oil in large saucepan on medium
heat. Add green pepper and onion. Cook and
stir 2 to 3 minutes or until crisp-tender.
Remove from heat.

2. Stir in flour, dry mustard and cayenne. Stir
in broth and milk gradually. Return to heat.
Cook and stir until mixture thickens.

3. Stir in vegetables in cheese sauce and
green beans. Simmer 5 minutes or until
vegetables are tender.　　*Makes 4 servings*

Pork and Wild Rice Chili

1 pound boneless pork loin, cut into
　　½-inch cubes
1 onion, chopped
1 teaspoon vegetable oil
2 cans (14½ ounces each) chicken broth
1 can (18 ounces) white kernel corn,
　　drained
2 cans (4 ounces each) chopped green
　　chilies, drained
¾ cup uncooked California wild rice,
　　rinsed
1 teaspoon ground cumin
½ teaspoon salt
½ teaspoon dried oregano leaves
1½ cups shredded Monterey Jack cheese
　　(optional)
6 sprigs fresh cilantro (optional)

Cook and stir pork and onion in oil in large
saucepan over high heat until onion is soft and
pork is lightly browned. Add chicken broth,
corn, green chilies, wild rice, cumin, salt and
oregano. Cover and simmer 45 minutes or
until rice is tender and grains have puffed
open. Garnish with cheese and cilantro, if
desired.　　　　　　　　*Makes 6 servings*

Favorite recipe from **California Wild Rice Advisory Board**

Shrimp Bisque

1 pound medium uncooked shrimp,
    peeled and deveined
½ cup chopped onion
½ cup chopped celery
½ cup chopped carrot
2 tablespoons butter or margarine
2 cans (14 ounces each) chicken broth
1 can (14½ ounces) DEL MONTE®
    Stewed Tomatoes - Original Recipe,
    undrained
¼ teaspoon dried thyme
1 cup half-and-half

1. Cut shrimp into small pieces; set aside. In large saucepan, cook onion, celery and carrot in butter until onion is tender. Add shrimp; cook 1 minute. Add broth, tomatoes and thyme; simmer 10 minutes.

2. Ladle ⅓ of soup into blender container or food processor. Cover and process until smooth. Repeat for remaining soup. Return to saucepan. Add half-and-half. Heat through. *Do not boil.*

*Makes 6 servings (approximately
1 cup each)*

Variation: Substitute 2 cans (6 ounces each) of crab for shrimp.

Prep Time: 15 minutes
Cook Time: 20 minutes

Chili Corn Soup

2 tablespoons vegetable oil
2 medium potatoes, diced
1 medium onion, diced
1 tablespoon chili powder
1 (16-ounce) can red kidney beans,
    drained and rinsed
1 (15¼-ounce) can corn, drained
1 (13¾-ounce) can vegetable broth
1½ teaspoons TABASCO® brand Pepper
    Sauce
1 teaspoon salt

Heat oil in 4-quart saucepan over medium heat. Add potatoes and onion; cook about 5 minutes, stirring occasionally. Add chili powder; cook 1 minute, stirring frequently.

Stir in beans, corn, vegetable broth, TABASCO® Sauce and salt. Heat to boiling over high heat. Reduce heat to low; cover and simmer 15 to 20 minutes or until potatoes are tender, stirring occasionally.

Makes 6 servings

Tortilla Soup

1 tablespoon butter or margarine
½ cup chopped green bell pepper
½ cup chopped onion
½ teaspoon ground cumin
3½ cups (two 14½-ounce cans) chicken
    broth
1 jar (16 ounces) ORTEGA® Salsa-Thick
    & Chunky
1 cup whole-kernel corn
1 tablespoon vegetable oil
6 corn tortillas, cut into ½-inch strips
¾ cup (3 ounces) shredded 4 cheese
    Mexican blend
Sour cream (optional)

MELT butter in medium saucepan over medium heat. Add bell pepper, onion and cumin; cook for 3 to 4 minutes or until tender. Stir in broth, salsa and corn. Bring to a boil. Reduce heat to low; cook for 5 minutes.

HEAT vegetable oil in medium skillet over medium-high heat. Add tortilla strips; cook for 3 to 4 minutes or until tender.

SERVE in soup bowls. Top with tortilla strips, cheese and a dollop of sour cream.

Makes 6 servings

Italian Rustico Soup

1 cup BARILLA® Elbows
2 tablespoons olive or vegetable oil
1 pound fresh escarole or spinach, chopped
1 small onion, chopped
2 teaspoons minced garlic
4 cups water
2 cans (14½ ounces each) chicken broth
1 jar (26 ounces) BARILLA® Lasagna & Casserole Sauce or Marinara Pasta Sauce
1 can (15 ounces) white beans, drained
2 teaspoons balsamic or red wine vinegar
Grated Parmesan cheese (optional)

1. Cook elbows according to package directions; drain.

2. Heat oil in 4-quart Dutch oven or large pot. Add escarole, onion and garlic; cook over medium heat, stirring occasionally, about 5 minutes or until onion is tender.

3. Stir in cooked elbows and remaining ingredients except cheese; heat to boiling. Reduce heat; cook, uncovered, 15 minutes, stirring occasionally. Serve with cheese, if desired. *Makes 12 servings*

Stick-to-Your-Ribs Hearty Beef Stew

1½ pounds lean beef stew meat, cut into bite-size pieces
¼ cup all-purpose flour
½ teaspoon seasoned salt
⅓ cup WESSON® Vegetable Oil
2 medium onions, cut into 1-inch pieces
1 (14.5-ounce) can beef broth
1 (8-ounce) can HUNT'S® Tomato Sauce
4 medium potatoes, peeled and cubed
5 stalks celery, cut into 1-inch pieces
6 carrots, peeled and cut into 1-inch pieces
1½ teaspoons salt
½ teaspoon Italian seasoning
½ teaspoon pepper
1 tablespoon cornstarch plus 2 tablespoons water

In a bag, toss beef with flour and seasoned salt until well coated. In a large Dutch oven, in hot Wesson® Oil, brown beef with onions until tender. Add *remaining* ingredients *except* cornstarch mixture; stir until well blended. Bring to a boil; reduce heat and simmer, covered, for 1 hour 15 minutes or until beef is tender. Stir cornstarch mixture; whisk into stew. Continue to cook an additional 10 minutes, stirring occasionally.

Makes 6 to 8 servings

Tip: For a fancier stew, reduce beef broth by ½ cup and add ½ cup red wine.

Italian Rustico Soup

Wisconsin Sausage Soup

½ cup butter
1 onion, chopped
1 carrot, chopped
1 teaspoon minced garlic
1 cup all-purpose flour
2 cups chicken broth
2 cups milk
¾ cup beer
1 teaspoon Worcestershire sauce
½ teaspoon salt
½ teaspoon dry mustard
1 bay leaf
7 ounces Cheddar cheese, shredded
3 ounces Swiss cheese, shredded
½ pound HILLSHIRE FARM® Smoked
    Sausage

Melt butter in medium saucepan over medium heat. Add onion, carrot and garlic; sauté until softened. Add flour; cook 5 minutes, stirring often. Add chicken broth, milk, beer, Worcestershire sauce, salt, mustard and bay leaf. Reduce heat to low; cook until soup has thickened, whisking often. Remove and discard bay leaf.

Slowly whisk cheeses into soup until combined and smooth. Cut Smoked Sausage lengthwise into quarters, then slice into ½-inch pieces. Sauté sausage in small skillet over medium-high heat until heated through. Blot excess grease with paper towels; add sausage to soup.   *Makes 8 to 10 servings*

Country Stew

2 bags SUCCESS® Brown Rice
1 pound ground turkey
1 small onion, chopped
2 cans (14½ ounces each) tomatoes,
    cut up, undrained
1 teaspoon pepper
½ teaspoon dried basil leaves, crushed
½ teaspoon garlic powder
1 can (16 ounces) whole kernel corn,
    drained

Prepare rice according to package directions.

Brown ground turkey with onion in large skillet, stirring occasionally to separate turkey. Add tomatoes, pepper, basil and garlic powder; simmer 20 minutes, stirring occasionally. Stir in rice and corn; heat thoroughly, stirring occasionally. Garnish, if desired.   *Makes 8 servings*

Hearty Corn & Cheese Chowder

4 thick slices bacon, diced
¾ cup chopped onion
2 cups chicken broth or water
2 cups milk
1 (6.2-ounce) package PASTA RONI®
    Shells & White Cheddar
1 cup frozen or canned corn, drained
½ cup finely diced red bell pepper
¼ cup chopped chives or green onions

1. In large saucepan over medium heat, cook bacon 5 minutes. Add onion; cook 5 minutes or until bacon is crisp, stirring occasionally. Remove from saucepan; drain. Set aside.

2. In same saucepan, add chicken broth, milk, pasta, corn and bell pepper; bring to a boil. Reduce heat to medium. Boil, uncovered, 12 minutes or until pasta is tender.

3. Stir in bacon mixture and Special Seasonings. Return to a boil; boil 2 to 3 minutes. Ladle into bowls; top with chives.
          Makes 4 servings

Prep Time: 10 minutes
Cook Time: 25 minutes

Wisconsin Sausage Soup

Texas Beef Stew

1 pound lean ground beef
1 small onion, chopped
1 can (28 ounces) crushed tomatoes
  with roasted garlic
1½ cups BIRDS EYE® frozen Farm Fresh
  Mixtures Broccoli, Cauliflower &
  Carrots
1 can (14½ ounces) whole new potatoes,
  halved
1 cup BIRDS EYE® frozen Sweet Corn
1 can (4½ ounces) chopped green
  chilies, drained
½ cup water

• In large saucepan, cook beef and onion over medium-high heat until beef is well browned, stirring occasionally.

• Stir in tomatoes, vegetables, potatoes with liquid, corn, chilies and water; bring to a boil.

• Reduce heat to medium-low; cover and simmer 5 minutes or until heated through.

Makes 4 servings

Serving Suggestion: Serve over rice with warm crusty bread.

Birds Eye® Idea: The smell of onions and garlic can penetrate your cutting boards. Keep a separate cutting board exclusively for these vegetables.

Prep Time: 5 minutes
Cook Time: 15 minutes

Vegetable Chili

2 cans (15 ounces each) chunky chili
  tomato sauce
1 bag (16 ounces) BIRDS EYE® frozen
  Farm Fresh Mixtures Broccoli, Corn
  and Red Peppers
1 can (15½ ounces) red kidney beans
1 can (4½ ounces) chopped green chilies
½ cup shredded Cheddar cheese

• Combine tomato sauce, vegetables, beans and chilies in large saucepan; bring to a boil.

• Cook, uncovered, over medium heat 5 minutes.

• Sprinkle individual servings with cheese.

Makes 4 to 6 servings

Prep Time: 5 minutes
Cook Time: 10 minutes

West Coast Bouillabaisse

1 cup sliced onion
2 stalks celery, cut diagonally into slices
2 cloves garlic, minced
1 tablespoon vegetable oil
4 cups chicken broth
1 can (28 ounces) tomatoes with juice,
  cut up
1 can (6½ ounces) minced clams with
  juice
½ cup dry white wine
1 teaspoon Worcestershire sauce
½ teaspoon dried thyme, crushed
¼ teaspoon bottled hot pepper sauce
1 bay leaf
1 cup frozen cooked bay shrimp, thawed
1 (7-ounce) pouch of STARKIST®
  Premium Albacore or Chunk Light
  Tuna
Salt and pepper to taste
6 slices lemon
6 slices French bread

In Dutch oven sauté onion, celery and garlic in oil for 3 minutes. Stir in broth, tomatoes with juice, clams with juice, wine, Worcestershire, thyme, hot pepper sauce and bay leaf. Bring to a boil; reduce heat. Simmer for 15 minutes. Stir in shrimp and tuna; cook for 2 minutes to heat. Remove bay leaf. Season with salt and pepper. Garnish with lemon slices and serve with bread. *Makes 6 servings*

Chicken Tortilla Soup

6 boneless, skinless chicken thighs, cut
    into 1-inch pieces
2 tablespoons plus 2 teaspoons vegetable
    oil, divided
4 corn tortillas, halved, cut into ¼-inch
    strips
1 cup chopped onions
2 cloves garlic, minced
2 cans (14½ ounces each) fat free
    chicken broth
1 can (10 ounces) diced tomatoes with
    green chilies
½ cup water
1 cup frozen whole kernel corn
¼ cup chopped cilantro
1 tablespoon fresh lime juice
1 teaspoon ground cumin

In Dutch oven, place 2 tablespoons oil and
heat to medium-high temperature. Add tortilla
strips; cook 3 to 4 minutes or until crisp.
Remove with slotted spoon; drain on paper
towels. In same Dutch oven, add remaining
2 teaspoons oil and heat to medium-high
temperature. Add chicken, onions and garlic;
cook, stirring, 5 to 7 minutes or until chicken
is lightly browned. Add broth, tomatoes and
water; heat to boiling. Reduce heat to
medium-low; cover and cook 10 minutes. Add
corn, cilantro, lime juice and cumin; cook
5 minutes. Spoon into bowls; top with tortilla
strips.   *Makes 4 servings*

Favorite recipe from **Delmarva Poultry Industry, Inc.**

Minestrone

3 slices bacon, diced
½ cup chopped onion
1 large clove garlic, minced
2 cans (10½ ounces each) beef broth
1½ cups water
2 cans (15½ ounces each) Great
    Northern white beans, undrained
1 can (6 ounces) CONTADINA® Tomato
    Paste
1 teaspoon Italian herb seasoning
¼ teaspoon ground black pepper
2 medium zucchini, sliced
1 package (10 ounces) frozen mixed
    vegetables
½ cup elbow macaroni, uncooked
½ cup (2 ounces) grated Parmesan
    cheese (optional)

1. Sauté bacon in large saucepan until crisp.
Add onion and garlic; sauté until onion is
tender.

2. Add broth, water, beans and liquid, tomato
paste, Italian seasoning and pepper.

3. Reduce heat to low; simmer, uncovered,
for 10 minutes. Add zucchini, mixed
vegetables and macaroni. Return to a boil over
high heat, stirring to break up vegetables.

4. Reduce heat to low; simmer for 8 to
10 minutes or until vegetables and macaroni
are tender. Sprinkle with Parmesan cheese just
before serving, if desired.   *Makes 8 cups*

Prep Time: 7 minutes
Cook Time: 28 minutes

Easy Slow-Cooked Chili

2 pounds lean ground beef
2 tablespoons chili powder
1 tablespoon ground cumin
1 can (28 ounces) crushed tomatoes in purée, undrained
1 can (15 ounces) red kidney beans, drained and rinsed
1 cup water
2 cups *French's*® French Fried Onions, divided
¼ cup *Frank's*® *RedHot*® Cayenne Pepper Sauce
    Sour cream and shredded Cheddar cheese

Slow Cooker Directions

1. Cook ground beef, chili powder and cumin in large nonstick skillet over medium heat until browned, stirring frequently; drain. Transfer to slow cooker.

2. Stir in tomatoes with juice, beans, water, *½ cup* French Fried Onions and **Frank's RedHot** Sauce. Cover and cook on LOW setting for 6 hours (or on HIGH for 3 hours).

3. Serve chili topped with sour cream, cheese and remaining onions.   *Makes 8 servings*

Variation: For added Cheddar flavor, substitute *French's*® new **Cheddar French Fried Onions** for the original flavor.

Prep Time: 10 minutes
Cook Time: 6 hours

Carnival Pork Stew

3 pounds lean boneless pork loin, cut into 2-inch pieces
    Salt and black pepper
2 tablespoons oil
8 ounces smoked ham, cut into ½-inch chunks
2 medium onions, chopped
2 stalks celery, chopped
2 green bell peppers, chopped
6 cloves garlic, minced
½ teaspoon dried thyme
1 (28-ounce) can whole tomatoes, undrained, cut up
¾ cup SMUCKER'S® Peach Preserves
1 cup water
1 tablespoon hot pepper sauce
1 cup uncooked long-grain rice
½ cup chopped fresh parsley
½ cup chopped green onions

Sprinkle pork with salt and black pepper. Heat oil in large Dutch oven. Add pork; cook 5 to 8 minutes or until well browned. Remove pork with slotted spoon; set aside.

Add ham, onions, celery, green peppers, garlic and thyme. Cook and stir over medium-high heat until vegetables are wilted, about 6 minutes. Add browned pork, tomatoes, preserves, water and hot pepper sauce. Cover and simmer for 45 minutes.

Add rice, parsley and green onions; stir to blend well. Cover and simmer 20 to 25 minutes or until rice is tender. Season to taste with salt and black pepper.

Makes 8 servings

Easy Slow-Cooked Chili

Italian Bow Tie Vegetable Soup

3 cans (14½ ounces each) chicken broth
1 can (14½ ounces) Italian-style or regular stewed tomatoes
½ teaspoon Italian seasoning
1½ cups (4 ounces) uncooked bow tie pasta (farfalle)
1 package (about 1 pound) small frozen precooked meatballs
1 medium zucchini, cut into ¼-inch slices
½ cup diced red or green bell pepper
1½ cups *French's®* French Fried Onions

1. Combine broth, tomatoes and Italian seasoning in large saucepan. Bring to a boil.

2. Stir in pasta, meatballs, zucchini and bell pepper. Simmer for 12 minutes or until pasta is cooked al dente and meatballs are heated through, stirring occasionally. Spoon soup into serving bowls; top with French Fried Onions.

Makes 6 servings

Prep Time: 5 minutes
Cook Time: 12 minutes

Burgundy Beef Stew

¾ pound beef sirloin steak, cut into 1-inch cubes
1 cup diagonally sliced carrots
1 teaspoon minced garlic
¼ cup Burgundy or other dry red wine
2⅓ cups canned beef broth
1 can (14½ ounces) diced tomatoes, undrained
1 box UNCLE BEN'S® COUNTRY INN® Rice Pilaf
1 jar (15 ounces) whole pearl onions, drained

1. Generously spray large saucepan or Dutch oven with nonstick cooking spray. Heat over high heat until hot. Add beef; cook 2 to 3 minutes or until no longer pink. Stir in carrots, garlic and wine; cook 2 minutes.

2. Add broth, tomatoes, rice and contents of seasoning packet. Bring to a boil. Cover; reduce heat and simmer 10 minutes, stirring occasionally. Add onions; cook 10 minutes more or until rice is tender. Remove from heat and let stand, covered, 5 minutes.

Makes 4 servings

Variation: One 15-ounce can of drained sweet peas and pearl onions can be substituted for the pearl onions.

Gazpacho

3 cups tomato juice
4 tomatoes, chopped
1 green bell pepper, chopped
1 cucumber, chopped
1 cup chopped celery
1 cup chopped green onions
3 tablespoons red wine vinegar
2 tablespoons FILIPPO BERIO® Olive Oil
1 tablespoon chopped fresh parsley
1 to 2 teaspoons salt
1 clove garlic, finely minced
Freshly ground black pepper or hot pepper sauce

In large bowl, combine tomato juice, tomatoes, bell pepper, cucumber, celery, green onions, vinegar, olive oil, parsley, salt and garlic. Cover; refrigerate several hours or overnight before serving. Season to taste with black pepper or hot pepper sauce. Serve cold.

Makes 10 to 12 servings

Italian Bow Tie Vegetable Soup

Dining In

Why dine out when you can dine in?
More and more people are staying home and cooking great meals so they
can dine like royalty without ever having to leave their castle.

Chicken Jambalaya

2 tablespoons vegetable oil
¾ pound boneless chicken thighs or
    breasts, cut into cubes
1 cup ham, cut into very thin strips
    (about 5 ounces)
1 can (14½ to 16 ounces) seasoned
    diced tomatoes in juice, undrained
1½ cups water
1 can (4 ounces) diced green chilies,
    undrained
1 package KNORR® Recipe Classics™
    Vegetable Soup, Dip and Recipe Mix
1 cup uncooked rice

• In large skillet, heat oil over medium-high heat and brown chicken and ham.

• Stir in tomatoes, water, chilies and recipe mix. Bring to a boil over high heat. Stir in rice.

• Reduce heat to low and simmer, covered, stirring occasionally, 20 minutes or until rice is tender.   *Makes 4 servings*

Prep Time: 15 minutes
Cook Time: 25 minutes

Fish Broccoli Casserole

1 package (10 ounces) frozen broccoli
    spears, thawed, drained
1 cup cooked flaked Florida whitefish
1 can (10¾ ounces) condensed cream of
    mushroom soup
½ cup milk
¼ teaspoon salt
⅛ teaspoon freshly ground black pepper
½ cup crushed potato chips

Preheat oven to 425°F. Grease 1½-quart casserole. Layer broccoli in prepared casserole. Combine fish, soup, milk, salt and pepper in large bowl.

Spread fish mixture over broccoli. Sprinkle with potato chips. Bake 12 to 15 minutes or until golden brown.   *Makes 4 servings*

Favorite recipe from **Florida Department of Agriculture and Consumer Services, Bureau of Seafood and Aquaculture**

Chicken Jambalaya

Broccoli & Cheddar Noodle Casserole

1 package (12 ounces) dry wide egg noodles
3 tablespoons margarine or butter, divided
2 cups chopped onions
4 cups broccoli flowerets
1 can (14.5 ounces) CONTADINA® Stewed Tomatoes, undrained
1 can (6 ounces) CONTADINA Tomato Paste
1 package (1½ ounces) spaghetti sauce seasoning mix
2 cups water
1 teaspoon garlic salt
1½ cups (6 ounces) shredded Cheddar cheese
½ cup CONTADINA Seasoned Italian Bread Crumbs

1. Cook noodles according to package directions; drain.

2. Meanwhile, melt 2 tablespoons margarine in 5-quart saucepan; sauté onions until tender.

3. Stir in broccoli, undrained tomatoes, tomato paste, seasoning mix, water and garlic salt. Bring to a boil. Reduce heat; simmer, uncovered, for 10 minutes, stirring occasionally. Stir in cooked noodles.

4. Layer half of the noodle mixture in 13×9×2-inch baking dish. Sprinkle with cheese. Layer with remaining noodle mixture.

5. Melt remaining 1 tablespoon margarine; stir in crumbs. Sprinkle over casserole; cover and bake in preheated 350°F oven 20 minutes. Uncover; bake 5 minutes.

Makes 6 servings

Prep Time: 25 minutes
Cook Time: 25 minutes

Lasagna Florentine

2 tablespoons BERTOLLI® Olive Oil
3 medium carrots, finely chopped
1 package (8 to 10 ounces) sliced mushrooms
1 medium onion, finely chopped
2 cloves garlic, finely chopped
1 jar (1 pound 10 ounces) RAGÚ® Robusto! Pasta Sauce
1 container (15 ounces) ricotta cheese
2 cups shredded mozzarella cheese, divided
1 box (10 ounces) frozen chopped spinach, thawed and squeezed dry
¼ cup grated Parmesan cheese
2 eggs
1 teaspoon salt
1 teaspoon dried Italian seasoning
16 lasagna noodles, cooked and drained

Preheat oven to 375°F. In 12-inch skillet, heat oil over medium heat and cook carrots, mushrooms, onion and garlic until carrots are almost tender, about 5 minutes. Stir in Ragú® Robusto! Pasta Sauce; heat through.

Meanwhile, in medium bowl, combine ricotta cheese, 1½ cups mozzarella cheese, spinach, Parmesan cheese, eggs, salt and Italian seasoning; set aside.

In 13×9-inch baking dish, evenly spread ½ cup sauce mixture. Arrange 4 lasagna noodles lengthwise over sauce, overlapping edges slightly. Spread ⅓ of the ricotta mixture over noodles; repeat layers, ending with noodles. Top with remaining sauce and ½ cup mozzarella cheese. Cover with foil and bake 40 minutes. Remove foil and continue baking 10 minutes or until bubbling.

Makes 8 servings

Chicken Biscuit Bake

Base
　1 tablespoon CRISCO® Oil*
　1 cup chopped onion
　¼ cup all-purpose flour
　½ teaspoon salt
　¼ teaspoon pepper
　¼ teaspoon dried basil leaves
　¼ teaspoon dried thyme leaves
2½ cups skim milk
　1 tablespoon Worcestershire sauce
　1 chicken flavor bouillon cube *or*
　　1 teaspoon chicken flavor bouillon
　　granules
　2 cups chopped cooked chicken
　1 bag (16 ounces) frozen mixed
　　vegetables
　2 tablespoons grated Parmesan cheese

Biscuits
　1 cup all-purpose flour
　1 tablespoon sugar
1½ teaspoons baking powder
　1 tablespoon chopped fresh parsley
　⅛ teaspoon salt
　⅓ cup skim milk
　3 tablespoons CRISCO® Oil*

Use your favorite Crisco Oil product.

1. Heat oven to 375°F.

2. For base, heat oil in large saucepan on medium-high heat. Add onion. Cook and stir until tender. Remove from heat. Stir in flour, salt, pepper, basil and thyme. Add milk, Worcestershire sauce and bouillon cube. Return to medium-high heat. Cook and stir until mixture comes to a boil and is thickened. Stir in chicken, vegetables and cheese. Heat thoroughly, stirring occasionally. Pour into 2-quart casserole.

3. For biscuits, combine flour, sugar, baking powder, parsley and salt in medium bowl. Add milk and oil. Stir with fork until dry ingredients are just moistened. Drop dough by well-rounded measuring tablespoonfuls onto hot chicken mixture to form 8 biscuits.

4. Bake at 375°F for 35 to 45 minutes or until chicken mixture is bubbly and biscuits are golden brown.　　*Makes 8 servings*

No-Fuss Tuna Quiche

　1 unbaked 9-inch deep-dish pastry shell
1½ cups low-fat milk
　3 extra-large eggs
　⅓ cup chopped green onions
　1 tablespoon chopped drained pimiento
　1 teaspoon dried basil leaves, crushed
　½ teaspoon salt
　1 (3-ounce) pouch of STARKIST®
　　Premium Albacore or Chunk Light
　　Tuna
　½ cup (2 ounces) shredded low-fat
　　Cheddar cheese
　8 spears (4 inches each) broccoli

Preheat oven to 450°F. Bake pastry shell for 5 minutes; remove to rack to cool. *Reduce oven temperature to 325°F.* For filling, in large bowl, whisk together milk and eggs. Stir in onions, pimiento, basil and salt. Fold in tuna and cheese. Pour into prebaked pastry shell. Bake at 325°F for 30 minutes.

Meanwhile, in saucepan, steam broccoli spears over simmering water for 5 minutes. Drain; set aside. After 30 minutes baking time, arrange broccoli spears, spoke-fashion, over quiche. Bake 25 to 35 minutes more or until knife inserted 2 inches from center comes out clean. Let stand for 5 minutes. Cut into 8 wedges, centering broccoli spear in each wedge.

Makes 8 servings

Note: If desired, 1 cup chopped broccoli can be added to the filling before baking.

Italian-Glazed Pork Chops

1 tablespoon olive oil
8 bone-in pork chops
1 medium zucchini, thinly sliced
1 medium red bell pepper, chopped
1 medium onion, thinly sliced
3 cloves garlic, finely chopped
¼ cup dry red wine or beef broth
1 jar (1 pound 10 ounces) RAGÚ®
    Chunky Gardenstyle Pasta Sauce

1. In 12-inch skillet, heat oil over medium-high heat and brown chops. Remove chops and set aside.

2. In same skillet, cook zucchini, red bell pepper, onion and garlic, stirring occasionally, 4 minutes. Stir in wine and Ragú Pasta Sauce.

3. Return chops to skillet, turning to coat with sauce. Simmer, covered, 15 minutes or until chops are tender and barely pink in the center. Serve, if desired, over hot cooked couscous or rice.   *Makes 8 servings*

Prep Time: 10 minutes
Cook Time: 25 minutes

Linguine with Mixed Sweet Peppers, Dried Tomatoes, Feta, Walnuts and Basil

1 each red, green and yellow bell pepper
1 bunch fresh basil
¼ cup olive oil, plus extra
4 cloves garlic, minced
½ yellow onion, chopped finely
¼ cup SONOMA® Dried Tomato Bits
    Salt and pepper
1 pound dried linguine
6 ounces feta cheese
½ cup walnut pieces, coarsely chopped

Halve peppers through the stem end. Cut away stem, core and ribs. Slice peppers thinly. Pick basil leaves from their stems and set aside.

In large skillet, heat ¼ cup oil over moderate heat. Add garlic and onion; sauté 1 minute, just enough to release their fragrance. Stir in peppers, basil, tomatoes, 2 pinches salt, 1 pinch black pepper, and a tablespoon or two of water. Cover; reduce heat to low and cook peppers until soft but not completely tender, 10 to 15 minutes.

Meanwhile, cook the pasta in 4 quarts boiling water. Add a little olive oil for flavor and to reduce sticking. Check peppers occasionally to make sure they don't burn. When pasta is done, drain and transfer to a large bowl. Add contents of skillet, feta, and walnuts to bowl; toss well, adding more salt and pepper to taste and a drizzle of olive oil.

Makes 4 servings

Prep Time: 15 minutes
Cook Time: 15 minutes

Cajun Chicken Bayou

2 cups water
1 can (10 ounces) diced tomatoes and
    green chilies, undrained
1 box UNCLE BEN'S CHEF'S RECIPE®
    Traditional Red Beans & Rice
2 boneless, skinless chicken breasts
    (about 8 ounces)

1. In large skillet, combine water, tomatoes, beans & rice and contents of seasoning packet; mix well.

2. Add chicken. Bring to a boil. Cover; reduce heat and simmer 20 minutes or until chicken is no longer pink in center.

Makes 2 servings

Tip: If you prefer a spicier dish, add hot pepper sauce just before serving.

Italian-Glazed Pork Chop

Sonoma® Pot Pie

2 cans (10½ ounces each) chicken gravy
3 cups cooked chicken or turkey chunks
1 package (10 ounces) frozen mixed
    vegetables
⅔ cup SONOMA® Dried Tomato Bits
1 can (3 ounces drained weight) sliced
    mushrooms
¼ cup water
1½ teaspoons dried thyme leaves, divided
2¼ cups reduced-fat buttermilk baking
    mix
¾ cup plus 2 tablespoons lowfat milk

Preheat oven to 450°F. In 3-quart saucepan combine gravy, chicken, vegetables, tomato bits, mushrooms, water and ½ teaspoon thyme. Stir occasionally over medium-low heat until mixture comes to a boil. Meanwhile, in large bowl combine baking mix, milk and remaining 1 teaspoon thyme; mix just to blend thoroughly. Pour chicken mixture into shallow 2-quart casserole or 9-inch square baking dish. Top with large spoonfuls baking mix mixture, making equal-sized mounds. Place casserole on baking sheet and bake about 20 minutes or until chicken mixture is bubbly and topping is golden brown.   *Makes 4 to 6 servings*

Cheesy Broccoli Bake

1 (10-ounce) package frozen chopped
    broccoli
1 (10¾-ounce) can condensed Cheddar
    cheese soup
½ cup sour cream
2 cups (12 ounces) chopped CURE 81®
    ham
2 cups cooked rice
½ cup soft, torn bread crumbs
1 tablespoon butter or margarine, melted

Heat oven to 350°F. Cook broccoli according to package directions; drain. Combine soup and sour cream. Stir in broccoli, ham and rice. Spoon into 1½-quart casserole.

Combine bread crumbs and butter; sprinkle over casserole. Bake 30 to 35 minutes or until thoroughly heated.   *Makes 4 to 6 servings*

Surimi Seafood-Zucchini Frittata with Fresh Tomato Sauce

2 tablespoons vegetable oil
1 zucchini, thinly sliced
½ cup chopped onion
¼ cup chopped green bell pepper
3 eggs
6 egg whites
2 teaspoons finely chopped fresh basil *or*
    ½ teaspoon dried basil
½ teaspoon salt, optional
¼ teaspoon black pepper
6 ounces crab or lobster-flavored surimi
    seafood, chunk style
2 tablespoons butter or margarine
3 cups tomato sauce

Preheat oven to 375°F. Heat oil in 10-inch heavy metal skillet over medium heat. Add zucchini, onion and green pepper; cook 5 minutes, stirring often. Place in medium bowl; set aside to cool slightly. In large bowl, beat eggs and egg whites with basil, salt and black pepper until well blended. Add zucchini mixture and surimi seafood; beat well. Meanwhile, melt butter in same skillet over medium heat, swirling skillet to coat evenly with butter. Pour in egg-surimi seafood mixture and place skillet on middle shelf of oven. Bake 12 to 15 minutes or until eggs are set throughout. Loosen around edges with metal spatula; cut into wedges. Serve hot with ½ cup tomato sauce over each frittata slice.
        Makes 6 servings

*Favorite recipe from **National Fisheries Institute***

Sonoma® Pot Pie

Turkey-Olive Ragoût en Crust

½ pound boneless white or dark turkey meat, cut into 1-inch cubes
1 clove garlic, minced
1 teaspoon vegetable oil
¼ cup (about 10) small whole frozen onions
½ cup reduced-sodium chicken bouillon or turkey broth
½ teaspoon dried parsley flakes
⅛ teaspoon dried thyme leaves
1 small bay leaf
1 medium red potato, skin on, cut into ½-inch cubes
10 frozen snow peas
8 whole small pitted ripe olives
1 can (4 ounces) refrigerated crescent rolls
½ teaspoon dried dill weed

1. Preheat oven to 375°F.

2. In medium skillet over medium heat, cook and stir turkey in garlic and oil 3 to 4 minutes or until no longer pink; remove and set aside. Add onions to skillet; cook and stir until lightly browned. Add bouillon, parsley, thyme, bay leaf and potato. Bring mixture to a boil. Reduce heat; cover and simmer 10 minutes or until potato is tender. Remove and discard bay leaf.

3. Combine turkey mixture with potato mixture. Stir in snow peas and olives. Divide mixture between 2 (1¾-cup) individual ovenproof casseroles.

4. Divide crescent rolls into 2 rectangles; press perforations together to seal. If necessary, roll out each rectangle to make dough large enough to cover top of each casserole. Sprinkle dough with dill weed, pressing lightly into dough. Cut small decorative shape from each dough piece; discard cutouts or place on baking sheet and bake in oven with casseroles. Place dough over turkey-vegetable mixture in casseroles. Trim dough to fit; press dough to

edge of each casserole to seal. Bake 7 to 8 minutes or until pastry is golden brown.
Makes 2 individual deep-dish pies

Lattice Crust Variation: With pastry wheel or knife, cut each rectangle lengthwise into 6 strips. Arrange strips, lattice-fashion, over turkey-vegetable mixture; trim dough to fit. Press ends of dough to edge of each casserole to seal.

Note: For more golden crust, brush top of dough with beaten egg yolk before baking.

*Favorite recipe from **National Turkey Federation***

Wisconsin Cheese Pasta Casserole

1 pound uncooked spaghetti or fettuccine, broken into 3-inch pieces
1 quart (4 cups) prepared spaghetti sauce
½ cup plus ⅓ cup grated Wisconsin Romano cheese, divided
1¾ cups (7 ounces) sliced or shredded Wisconsin Colby cheese
1½ cups (6 ounces) shredded Wisconsin Mozzarella cheese

Prepare pasta according to package instructions; drain. Toss warm pasta with prepared spaghetti sauce to coat. Add ½ cup Romano cheese to mixture and mix well. Spread half of sauced pasta into bottom of 13×9×2-inch baking dish. Cover with 1 cup Colby cheese. Spread remaining pasta over cheese. Top with remaining ¾ cup Colby cheese. Sprinkle with remaining ⅓ cup Romano cheese and Mozzarella cheese. Bake at 350°F for 35 to 40 minutes or until top is lightly browned and casserole is bubbly. Remove from heat and let stand at least 10 minutes before serving.

Makes 6 to 8 servings

*Favorite recipe from **Wisconsin Milk Marketing Board***

Sausage Ham Jambalaya

6 ounces spicy smoked sausage links,
    sliced
6 ounces cooked ham, diced
2 cans (14½ ounces each) DEL MONTE®
    Stewed Tomatoes - Original Recipe
1 cup uncooked long grain white rice
1 large clove garlic, minced
1 tablespoon chopped fresh parsley
1 bay leaf

1. Brown sausage and ham in heavy 4-quart saucepan. Drain tomatoes, reserving liquid; pour liquid into measuring cup. Add water to measure 1½ cups.

2. Add reserved liquid, tomatoes and remaining ingredients to sausage mixture.

3. Cover and simmer 30 to 35 minutes, stirring occasionally. Remove bay leaf. Garnish with additional chopped parsley, if desired.

Makes 4 to 6 servings

Prep Time: 10 minutes
Cook Time: 40 minutes

Texas-Style Deep-Dish Chili Pie

1 tablespoon vegetable oil
1 pound beef stew meat, cut into ½-inch
    cubes
2 cans (14½ ounces each) Mexican-style
    stewed tomatoes, undrained
1 medium green bell pepper, diced
1 package (1.0 ounce) LAWRY'S® Taco
    Spices & Seasonings
1 tablespoon yellow cornmeal
1 can (15¼ ounces) kidney beans,
    drained
1 package (15 ounces) flat refrigerated
    pie crusts
½ cup (2 ounces) shredded cheddar
    cheese, divided

In Dutch oven, heat oil. Add beef and cook over medium-high heat until browned; drain fat. Add stewed tomatoes, bell pepper, Taco Spices & Seasonings and cornmeal. Bring to a boil over medium-high heat; reduce heat to low and cook, uncovered, 20 minutes. Add kidney beans; mix well. In 10-inch pie plate, unfold 1 crust and fill with chili mixture and ¼ cup cheese. Top with remaining crust, fluting edges. Bake, uncovered, in 350°F oven 30 minutes. Sprinkle remaining cheese over crust; return to oven and bake 10 minutes longer.   *Makes 6 servings*

Serving Suggestion: Serve with a tossed green salad.

Chicken Penne with Gorgonzola and Peas

1 (10-ounce) package penne pasta
4 boneless skinless chicken breast halves
1 clove garlic, minced
1 tablespoon olive oil
1 (10-ounce) package frozen peas
1 cup whipping cream
½ teaspoon salt
¼ teaspoon black pepper
1 cup crumbled BELGIOIOSO®
    Gorgonzola Cheese
    BELGIOIOSO® Parmesan Cheese,
    grated

In large saucepan, cook pasta according to directions. Meanwhile, cut chicken into ¼-inch strips. In large skillet, cook and stir garlic in hot oil over medium-high heat. Add chicken and cook 10 minutes or until chicken is no longer pink. Add peas and cook 3 minutes. Stir in cream, salt and pepper; gently boil, stirring constantly until mixture thickens, about 2 minutes. Drain pasta and toss with chicken, sauce and BelGioioso Gorgonzola Cheese. Sprinkle with BelGioioso Parmesan Cheese and serve immediately.

Makes 4 servings

Three Bean and Franks Bake

1 tablespoon vegetable oil
1 medium onion, chopped
2 cloves garlic, minced
1 red bell pepper, seeded and coarsely chopped
1 green bell pepper, seeded and coarsely chopped
1 can (16 ounces) vegetarian baked beans
1 can (16 ounces) butter or lima beans, drained
1 can (16 ounces) red or kidney beans, drained
½ cup ketchup
½ cup packed light brown sugar
2 tablespoons cider vinegar
1 tablespoon HEBREW NATIONAL® Deli Mustard
1 package (12 ounces) HEBREW NATIONAL® Beef Franks, Reduced Fat Beef Franks or 97% Fat Free Beef Franks, cut into 1-inch pieces

Preheat oven to 350°F. Heat oil in large saucepan over medium heat; add onion and garlic and cook 8 minutes, stirring occasionally. Add red and green bell peppers; cook 5 minutes, stirring occasionally. Stir in baked beans, butter beans, red beans, ketchup, brown sugar, vinegar and mustard; bring to a boil. Stir franks into bean mixture.

Transfer mixture to 2-quart casserole or 8- or 9-inch square baking dish. Bake 40 to 45 minutes or until hot and bubbly.
   Makes 6 main-dish or 10 side-dish servings

Wisconsin Swiss Linguine Tart

½ cup butter, divided
2 cloves garlic, minced
30 thin French bread slices
3 tablespoons flour
1 teaspoon salt
¼ teaspoon white pepper
   Dash nutmeg
2½ cups milk
¼ cup grated Wisconsin Parmesan cheese
2 eggs, beaten
2 cups (8 ounces) shredded Wisconsin Baby Swiss cheese
8 ounces fresh linguine, cooked, drained
⅓ cup green onion slices
2 tablespoons minced fresh basil *or*
   2 teaspoons dried basil, crushed
2 plum tomatoes

Melt ¼ cup butter. Add garlic; cook 1 minute. Brush 10-inch pie plate with butter mixture; line bottom and side with bread, allowing bread to come 1 inch over side. Brush bread with remaining butter mixture. Bake at 350°F for 5 minutes or until lightly browned. Set aside.

Melt remaining butter in saucepan over low heat. Blend in flour and seasonings. Gradually add milk; cook, stirring constantly, until thickened. Remove from heat; add Parmesan cheese. Stir small amount of sauce into eggs; mix well. Stir in remaining sauce.

Toss 1¼ cups Swiss cheese with linguine, green onions and basil. Pour sauce over linguine mixture; mix well. Pour into crust. Cut each tomato lengthwise into eight slices; place on tart. Sprinkle with remaining ¾ cup Swiss cheese. Bake at 350°F for 25 minutes or until warm. Let stand 5 minutes.
   Makes 8 servings

Favorite recipe from **Wisconsin Milk Marketing Board**

Three Bean and Franks Bake

Manicotti Marinara

1 package (8 ounces) BARILLA®
    Manicotti *or* ½ package (8 ounces)
    BARILLA® Jumbo Shells
2 jars (26 ounces each) BARILLA®
    Marinara Pasta Sauce, divided
2 eggs
1 container (15 ounces) ricotta cheese
4 cups (16 ounces) shredded mozzarella
    cheese, divided
1 cup (4 ounces) grated Parmesan
    cheese, divided
¼ cup chopped fresh parsley *or*
    1 tablespoon dried parsley

1. Cook manicotti shells according to package directions; drain. Preheat oven to 350°F. Spray bottom of 15×10×2-inch glass baking dish with nonstick cooking spray. Spread 1 jar marinara sauce over bottom of baking dish.

2. Beat eggs in large bowl. Stir in ricotta, 3 cups mozzarella, ¾ cup Parmesan and parsley. Fill each cooked shell with ricotta mixture. Arrange filled shells in baking dish over sauce. Top with second jar of marinara sauce, remaining 1 cup mozzarella and ¼ cup Parmesan.

3. Cover with foil and bake about 45 minutes or until bubbly. Uncover and continue baking about 5 minutes or until cheese is melted. Let stand 5 minutes before serving.

Makes 6 servings

Note: One package (10 ounces) frozen chopped spinach, thawed and well drained, may be added to the ricotta mixture.

Saffron Chicken Risotto

1½ pounds boneless, skinless chicken
    breasts
¼ teaspoon salt
⅛ teaspoon white pepper
1 tablespoon olive oil
1 cup sliced fresh mushrooms
½ cup sliced green onions
½ cup chopped red bell pepper
½ cup chopped celery
1 tablespoon butter
1 cup uncooked rice
    Pinch of ground saffron
⅓ cup dry white wine
2 cups chicken broth
3 cups water
⅓ cup grated Parmesan cheese
⅓ cup sliced black olives
⅓ cup heavy cream

Cut chicken into 1-inch chunks; season with salt and white pepper. Heat oil in large skillet over medium-high heat until hot. Add chicken, mushrooms, onions, red pepper and celery. Cook and stir until chicken is no longer pink in center. Remove chicken and vegetables; set aside. Melt butter in skillet until hot. Add rice and saffron; cook 2 to 3 minutes, stirring constantly. Add wine; stir until absorbed. Stir in 1 cup broth; cook, uncovered, until broth is absorbed, stirring frequently. Continue stirring and adding remaining 1 cup broth and water, one cup at a time; allow each cup to be absorbed before adding another, until rice is tender and has creamy consistency, about 25 to 30 minutes. Stir in cheese, olives, cream and chicken mixture; heat thoroughly. Serve immediately. *Makes 4 servings*

Tip: Medium grain rice will yield the best consistency for risottos, but long grain rice may be used.

Favorite recipe from **USA Rice Federation**

Manicotti Marinara

Coq au Vin & Pasta

4 large or 8 small chicken thighs (2 to 2½ pounds), trimmed of excess fat
2 teaspoons rotisserie or herb chicken seasoning*
1 tablespoon margarine or butter
3 cups (8 ounces) halved or quartered mushrooms
1 medium onion, coarsely chopped
½ cup dry white wine or vermouth
1 (4.9-ounce) package PASTA RONI® Homestyle Chicken Flavor
½ cup sliced green onions

*1 teaspoon paprika and 1 teaspoon garlic salt can be substituted.

1. Sprinkle meaty side of chicken with rotisserie seasoning. In large skillet over medium-high heat, melt margarine. Add chicken, seasoned side down; cook 3 minutes. Reduce heat to medium-low; turn chicken over.

2. Add mushrooms, onion and wine. Cover; simmer 15 to 18 minutes or until chicken is no longer pink inside. Remove chicken from skillet; set aside.

3. In same skillet, bring 1 cup water to a boil. Stir in pasta, green onions and Special Seasonings. Place chicken over pasta. Reduce heat to medium-low. Cover; gently boil 6 to 8 minutes or until pasta is tender. Let stand 3 to 5 minutes before serving.

Makes 4 servings

Prep Time: 10 minutes
Cook Time: 30 minutes

Southwest Skillet

1 cup cubed cooked chicken breast
1 bag (16 ounces) BIRDS EYE® frozen Pasta Secrets Zesty Garlic
1 cup chunky salsa
½ teaspoon chili powder
½ cup chopped green or red bell pepper

• In large skillet, combine all ingredients.

• Cook over medium heat 10 to 15 minutes or until heated through.   *Makes 4 servings*

Cheesy Southwest Skillet: Stir in ½ cup shredded Cheddar cheese during last 5 minutes. Cook until cheese is melted.

Creamy Southwest Skillet: Remove skillet from heat. Stir in ¼ cup sour cream before serving.

Prep Time: 5 minutes
Cook Time: 15 minutes

Carolina Baked Beans & Pork Chops

2 cans (16 ounces each) pork and beans
½ cup chopped onion
½ cup chopped green bell pepper
¼ cup *French's®* Classic Yellow® Mustard
¼ cup packed light brown sugar
2 tablespoons *French's®* Worcestershire Sauce
1 tablespoon *Frank's®* RedHot® Cayenne Pepper Sauce
6 boneless pork chops (1 inch thick)

1. Preheat oven to 400°F. Combine all ingredients *except pork chops* in 3-quart shallow baking dish; mix well. Arrange chops on top, turning once to coat with sauce.

2. Bake, uncovered, 30 to 35 minutes or until pork is no longer pink in center. Stir beans around chops once during baking. Serve with green beans or mashed potatoes, if desired.

Makes 6 servings

Prep Time: 10 minutes
Cook Time: 30 minutes

Coq au Vin & Pasta

Pizza-Style Stuffed Potatoes

$\frac{1}{2}$ pound lean ground American lamb
4 large baking potatoes, scrubbed
$\frac{1}{3}$ cup finely chopped onion
$\frac{1}{3}$ cup chopped green bell pepper
$\frac{1}{4}$ cup chopped mushrooms
2 teaspoons dried parsley flakes
2 teaspoons Italian seasoning
$\frac{1}{2}$ teaspoon garlic powder
$\frac{1}{2}$ cup plain nonfat yogurt
$\frac{1}{2}$ teaspoon salt
$\frac{1}{4}$ teaspoon black pepper
1 cup (4 ounces) shredded reduced-fat mozzarella cheese, divided
$\frac{1}{2}$ cup pizza sauce
12 sliced black olives (optional)
2 tablespoons grated Parmesan cheese

Pierce potatoes several times with fork. Microwave on paper towel at HIGH 10 to 12 minutes or until potatoes are soft. Cool slightly.

Preheat oven to 400°F. Cook lamb in medium skillet over medium heat until no longer pink; drain. Remove to microwavable dish. Add onion, bell pepper and mushrooms; microwave at HIGH 2 minutes. Stir in parsley, Italian seasoning and garlic powder.

Make lengthwise slit in each potato. Scoop out pulp, leaving shells intact. Place pulp in medium bowl. Beat in yogurt, salt and black pepper. Add $\frac{2}{3}$ cup mozzarella cheese and ground lamb mixture; mix until blended. Spoon mixture into potato shells. Top each potato with pizza sauce, remaining $\frac{1}{3}$ cup mozzarella cheese, olives, if desired, and Parmesan cheese.* Bake 20 minutes or until hot and bubbly.   *Makes 4 servings*

*Stuffed potatoes can be wrapped in foil and frozen before baking. To serve, thaw in refrigerator and bake as directed.

Favorite recipe from **American Lamb Council**

Red Cloud Beef and Onions

$2\frac{1}{4}$ cups nonfat milk
$1\frac{1}{2}$ cups water
$1\frac{1}{2}$ cups yellow cornmeal
$\frac{1}{2}$ cup grated Parmesan cheese
1 tablespoon butter or margarine
4 medium yellow onions, sliced (1 pound 6 ounces)
2 teaspoons vegetable oil
1 pound lean ground beef or pork
2 to 3 teaspoons chili powder (or to taste)
$\frac{1}{2}$ cup canned whole pimientos or roasted red bell peppers, cut into $\frac{1}{2}$-inch strips
2 cans (4 ounces each) whole green chilies, cut into $\frac{1}{2}$-inch strips

For cornmeal base, combine milk, water and cornmeal in saucepan. Place over medium heat and cook, stirring, until mixture bubbles. Continue cooking 30 to 60 seconds or until mixture is consistency of soft mashed potatoes. Remove from heat; stir in cheese and butter. Spoon into $2\frac{1}{2}$-quart casserole. Sauté onions in oil in large skillet until soft. Spoon into casserole in ring around edge. In same skillet, sauté beef or pork until browned; stir in chili powder. Spoon meat mixture into center of casserole. Arrange pimientos and chilies in latticework pattern over top. Cover and bake at 400°F for 25 to 30 minutes or until hot in center. Serve with dollops of sour cream, if desired.   *Makes 6 servings*

Favorite recipe from **National Onion Association**

Pizza-Style Stuffed Potato

Jambalaya

1 pound uncooked large shrimp, shelled and deveined
½ pound kielbasa or smoked sausage, sliced
2 ribs celery, diagonally sliced
1 green bell pepper, cut into strips
1 can (14½ ounces) whole tomatoes, undrained
1 can (10½ ounces) condensed chicken broth
2 tablespoons *Frank's® RedHot®* Cayenne Pepper Sauce
½ teaspoon dried thyme leaves
1⅓ cups uncooked instant rice
1⅓ cups *French's®* French Fried Onions, divided

Generously spray large nonstick skillet with nonstick cooking spray; heat over high heat. Add shrimp and sausage; cook about 3 minutes or until shrimp are opaque.

Stir in celery, bell pepper, tomatoes with liquid, chicken broth, *Frank's RedHot* Sauce, thyme, rice and ⅔ *cup* French Fried Onions. Bring to a boil, stirring occasionally. Cover; remove from heat. Let stand 5 to 8 minutes or until all liquid is absorbed. Sprinkle with remaining ⅔ *cup* onions just before serving.

Makes 6 servings

Prep Time: 10 minutes
Cook Time: 10 minutes

Country Chicken and Biscuits

1 can (10¾ ounces) condensed cream of celery soup
⅓ cup milk or water
4 boneless, skinless chicken breast halves, cooked and cut into bite-sized pieces
1 can (14½ ounces) DEL MONTE® Cut Green Beans, drained
1 can (11 ounces) refrigerated biscuits

1. Preheat oven to 375°F.

2. Combine soup and milk in large bowl. Gently stir in chicken and green beans; season with pepper, if desired. Spoon into 11×7-inch or 2-quart microwavable dish.

3. Cover with plastic wrap; slit to vent. Microwave on HIGH 8 to 10 minutes or until heated through, rotating dish once. If using conventional oven, cover with foil and bake at 375°F, 20 to 25 minutes or until hot.

4. Separate biscuit dough into individual biscuits. Immediately arrange biscuits over hot mixture. Bake in conventional oven at 375°F about 15 minutes or until biscuits are golden brown and baked through.

Makes 4 servings

Easy Turkey and Rice

1 bag SUCCESS® Rice
Vegetable cooking spray
1 tablespoon olive oil
½ pound fresh mushrooms, sliced
¾ cup sliced celery
¼ cup chopped green onion
¼ cup chopped red bell pepper
2 cups chopped cooked turkey
1 can (10¾ ounces) condensed cream of chicken soup
½ cup fat-free mayonnaise
½ cup peanuts (optional)

Prepare rice according to package directions.

Preheat oven to 350°F.

Spray 1½-quart casserole with cooking spray; set aside. Heat oil in large skillet over medium heat. Add vegetables; cook and stir until crisp-tender. Add rice and all remaining ingredients except peanuts; mix lightly. Spoon into prepared casserole. Bake until thoroughly heated, about 25 minutes. Sprinkle with peanuts. Garnish, if desired.

Makes 4 servings

Fiesta Beef Pot Pie

Filling

- 1 tablespoon CRISCO® Stick or
  1 tablespoon CRISCO® all-vegetable shortening, melted
- 1 pound lean boneless beef chuck steak, cut into ¼-inch chunks*
- ½ cup chopped green bell pepper**
- ½ cup chopped onion**
- 1 (14½-ounce) can Mexican-style stewed tomatoes**
- 1 (8½-ounce) can whole kernel corn, drained
- 1 (4-ounce) can sliced mushrooms, drained
- ½ cup water
- ⅓ cup tomato paste
- 2 teaspoons sugar
- 1 teaspoon chili powder
- ½ teaspoon ground cumin
- ¼ teaspoon salt
- ⅛ teaspoon crushed red pepper (optional)
- ⅓ cup sliced ripe olives

Crust

- 1⅔ cups all-purpose flour
- ⅓ cup yellow cornmeal
- 2 tablespoons toasted wheat germ
- 1 teaspoon salt
- ¾ CRISCO® Stick or ¾ cup CRISCO® all-vegetable shortening
- ⅓ cup shredded Cheddar cheese
- 5 to 7 tablespoons cold water

Topping

- 1 egg, beaten
- ⅓ cup shredded Cheddar cheese

One pound ground round can be substituted for the cubed chuck, if desired.

** *If Mexican-style tomatoes are not available, substitute 14½-ounce can stewed tomatoes; increase green pepper and onion to ⅔ cup each and add one tablespoon diced jalapeño pepper and ¼ teaspoon garlic powder to filling.*

1. For filling, in 10-inch skillet over medium heat in hot shortening, cook meat until well browned; with slotted spoon, remove meat to bowl. In drippings remaining in skillet, cook bell pepper and onion until tender. Add stewed tomatoes, corn, mushrooms, water, tomato paste, sugar, chili powder, cumin, salt, crushed red pepper and cooked beef. Heat to boiling over high heat. Reduce heat to low; cover and simmer 30 minutes, stirring mixture occasionally. Remove skillet from heat; stir in sliced ripe olives.

2. Meanwhile, for crust, in bowl, combine flour, cornmeal, wheat germ and salt. Cut in shortening and cheese to resemble coarse crumbs. Stir in water, 1 tablespoon at a time, until dough forms ball. Divide dough in half.

3. On floured surface, roll half of dough 1½ inches larger all around than inverted 9-inch pie plate; ease into pie plate. Trim edge even with plate.

4. Heat oven to 425°F. Spoon hot filling into unbaked 9-inch pie shell. Roll remaining dough as for bottom crust. Moisten edge of bottom crust with water. Lift top crust onto filled pie. Cut slits or design in top crust to allow steam to escape while baking. Trim pastry edge, leaving ½ inch overhang. Fold top edge under bottom crust; flute or make rope edge.

5. For topping, brush egg over top crust. Place sheet of foil underneath pie plate; crimp edges to form rim to catch any drips during baking. Bake pie 35 minutes or until meat filling begins to bubble and crust is golden. *Do not overbake.* Sprinkle with ⅓ cup cheese.

Makes 6 servings

Turkey Enchilada Pie

¾ pound ground turkey
2 teaspoons vegetable oil
1 can (14½ ounces) DEL MONTE® Diced Tomatoes with Zesty Mild Green Chilies
1 package (1¼ ounces) taco seasoning mix
½ cup sliced green onions
1 can (2¼ ounces) sliced ripe olives, drained
6 corn tortillas
1½ cups shredded sharp Cheddar cheese

1. Brown meat in oil in large skillet over medium-high heat. Stir in tomatoes and taco seasoning mix.

2. Reduce heat; cover and cook 10 minutes, stirring occasionally. Stir in green onions and olives.

3. Place 1 tortilla in bottom of 2-quart baking dish; cover with about ½ cup meat sauce. Top with about ¼ cup cheese. Repeat, making a six-layer stack.

4. Pour ½ cup water down edge, into bottom of dish. Cover with foil and bake at 425°F, 30 minutes or until heated through. Cut into 4 wedges. Garnish with sour cream, if desired.
Makes 4 servings

Prep Time: 15 minutes
Cook Time: 48 minutes

Three Cheese Baked Ziti

1 container (15 ounces) part-skim ricotta cheese
2 eggs, beaten
¼ cup grated Parmesan cheese
1 box (16 ounces) ziti pasta, cooked and drained
1 jar (1 pound 10 ounces) RAGÚ® Chunky Gardenstyle Pasta Sauce
1 cup shredded mozzarella cheese (about 4 ounces)

Preheat oven to 350°F. In large bowl, combine ricotta cheese, eggs and Parmesan cheese; set aside.

In another bowl, thoroughly combine pasta and Ragú Chunky Gardenstyle Pasta Sauce.

In 13×9-inch baking dish, spoon ½ of the pasta mixture; evenly top with ricotta cheese mixture, then remaining pasta mixture. Sprinkle with mozzarella cheese. Bake 30 minutes or until heated through. Serve, if desired, with additional heated pasta sauce.
Makes 8 servings

Prep Time: 20 minutes
Cook Time: 30 minutes

Broccoli, Chicken and Rice Casserole

1 box UNCLE BEN'S CHEF'S RECIPE® Broccoli Rice Au Gratin Supreme
2 cups boiling water
4 boneless, skinless chicken breasts (about 1 pound)
¼ teaspoon garlic powder
2 cups frozen broccoli
1 cup (4 ounces) reduced-fat shredded Cheddar cheese

1. Heat oven to 425°F. In 13×9-inch baking pan, combine rice and contents of seasoning packet. Add boiling water; mix well. Add chicken; sprinkle with garlic powder. Cover and bake 30 minutes.

2. Add broccoli and cheese; continue to bake, covered, 8 to 10 minutes or until chicken is no longer pink in center.
Makes 4 servings

Turkey Enchilada Pie

Pork & Rice Provençal

4 well-trimmed boneless pork loin
   chops, ¾ inch thick (about 1 pound)
1 teaspoon dried basil
½ teaspoon dried thyme
½ teaspoon garlic salt
¼ teaspoon ground black pepper
2 tablespoons margarine or butter,
   divided
1 (6.8-ounce) package RICE-A-RONI®
   Beef Flavor
½ cup chopped onion
1 clove garlic, minced
1 (14½-ounce) can seasoned diced
   tomatoes, undrained
1 (2¼-ounce) can sliced ripe olives,
   drained *or* ⅓ cup sliced pitted
   kalamata olives

1. Sprinkle pork chops with basil, thyme,
garlic salt and pepper; set aside. In large skillet
over medium-high heat, melt 1 tablespoon
margarine. Add pork chops; cook 3 minutes.
Reduce heat to medium; turn pork chops over
and cook 3 minutes. Remove from skillet; set
aside.

2. In same skillet over medium heat, sauté
rice-vermicelli mix, onion and garlic with
remaining 1 tablespoon margarine until
vermicelli is golden brown.

3. Slowly stir in 1¾ cups water, tomatoes and
Special Seasonings; bring to a boil. Cover;
reduce heat to low. Simmer 10 minutes.

4. Add pork chops and olives. Cover; simmer
10 minutes or until rice is tender and pork
chops are no longer pink inside.

Makes 4 servings

Prep Time: 10 minutes
Cook Time: 40 minutes

Chicken and Sweet Potato Ragoût

2 tablespoons vegetable oil, divided
1 (3-pound) chicken, cut into 8 pieces
1 large onion, chopped
1 (14½-ounce) can chicken broth
3 small sweet potatoes, peeled and cut
   into ¼-inch slices
2 cups shredded green cabbage
1 tablespoon TABASCO® brand Pepper
   Sauce
1 teaspoon salt
¼ cup water
1 tablespoon flour
¼ cup peanut butter

Heat 1 tablespoon oil in 12-inch skillet over
medium heat. Add chicken; cook until well
browned. Remove to plate. Add remaining
1 tablespoon oil and onion to skillet; cook
5 minutes. Return chicken to skillet; add
broth, potatoes, cabbage, TABASCO® Sauce
and salt. Heat to boiling over high heat.
Reduce heat to low; cover and simmer
30 minutes or until tender, stirring
occasionally.

Combine water and flour in small cup.
Gradually stir into skillet with peanut butter.
Cook over high heat until mixture thickens.

Makes 4 servings

Pork & Rice Provençal

Vegetable Cobbler

Cobbler

PAM® No-Stick Cooking Spray

1 medium butternut squash, peeled and cut into 1½-inch pieces

3 medium red potatoes, unpeeled and cut into 1½-inch pieces

3 medium parsnips, peeled and cut into 1-inch pieces

1 medium red onion, cut into 6 wedges

¼ cup WESSON® Vegetable Oil

1 tablespoon chopped fresh dill weed

1 teaspoon salt

¾ cup homemade chicken stock or canned chicken broth

½ cup milk

1 (15-ounce) can pears, cut into 1-inch pieces, juice reserved

1 tablespoon cornstarch

4 cups broccoli florets

1 teaspoon grated fresh lemon peel

Topping

1¾ cups all-purpose baking mix

¾ cup shredded Cheddar cheese

½ cup cornmeal

1 tablespoon chopped fresh dill weed

¾ teaspoon coarsely ground pepper

¾ cup milk

Cobbler

Preheat oven to 400°F. Spray 13×9×2-inch baking dish with PAM® Cooking Spray. In prepared baking dish, toss *all* vegetables *except* broccoli with Wesson® Oil, 1 tablespoon dill and salt to coat. Bake, covered, 40 to 45 minutes. Meanwhile, in saucepan, combine stock, milk, reserved pear juice and cornstarch; blend well. Bring to a boil. Add broccoli and lemon peel and cook until slightly thick; set aside.

Topping

In small bowl, combine *all* topping ingredients; mix with fork until well blended.

Stir vegetables in baking dish. Add pears; gently mix. Pour broccoli sauce evenly over vegetables. Drop 12 heaping spoonfuls of topping evenly over vegetables. Bake, uncovered, for 15 minutes or until topping is golden.   *Makes 8 servings*

Mexican Lasagna

1 package (16 sheets) BARILLA® Oven Ready Lasagna Noodles (do not boil)

1 pound ground beef

1 package (1.5 ounces) taco seasoning

1 jar (26 ounces) BARILLA® Lasagna & Casserole Sauce or Marinara Pasta Sauce

2 eggs

1 container (15 ounces) ricotta cheese

4 cups (16 ounces) shredded Mexican-style cheese, divided

1. Preheat oven to 375°F. Spray 13×9×2-inch baking pan with nonstick cooking spray. Remove 12 lasagna noodles from package. Do not boil.

2. Cook ground beef and taco seasoning in large skillet, following directions on seasoning package. Remove from heat; stir in lasagna sauce.

3. Beat eggs in medium bowl. Stir in ricotta cheese and 2 cups Mexican-style cheese.

4. To assemble lasagna, spread 1 cup meat mixture over bottom of pan. Arrange 4 uncooked lasagna noodles over meat mixture, overlapping edges, if necessary, to fit pan. Top with half of ricotta mixture and 1 cup meat mixture. Repeat layers (4 uncooked lasagna noodles, remaining half of ricotta mixture and 1 cup meat mixture); top with remaining 4 uncooked lasagna noodles, remaining meat mixture and remaining 2 cups Mexican-style cheese.

5. Cover with foil and bake 45 to 55 minutes or until bubbly. Uncover and continue cooking about 5 minutes or until cheese is melted. Let stand 15 minutes before cutting.

Makes 12 servings

Spanish Rice and Meatballs

6 slices bacon
1 pound lean ground beef
½ cup soft bread crumbs
1 egg, slightly beaten
½ teaspoon salt
⅛ teaspoon pepper
½ cup chopped onion
½ cup sliced celery
⅔ cup uncooked white rice
1½ cups water
1 can (14½ ounces) whole peeled tomatoes, cut into bite-size pieces
⅓ cup HEINZ® 57 Sauce®
¼ teaspoon pepper
⅛ teaspoon hot pepper sauce
1 green bell pepper, cut into ¾-inch chunks

In large skillet, cook bacon until crisp; remove, coarsely crumble and set aside. Drain drippings, reserving 1 tablespoon. In large bowl, combine beef, bread crumbs, egg, salt and ⅛ teaspoon pepper. Form into 20 meatballs, using a rounded tablespoon for each. In same skillet, brown meatballs in reserved drippings; remove. In same skillet, sauté onion and celery until tender-crisp; drain excess fat. Add rice, water, tomatoes, 57 Sauce, ¼ teaspoon pepper and hot pepper sauce. Cover; simmer 20 minutes. Stir in bacon, meatballs and green pepper. Cover; simmer an additional 10 minutes or until rice is tender and liquid is absorbed, stirring occasionally.

Makes 4 servings (4 cups rice mixture)

Tomato, Basil & Broccoli Chicken

4 boneless, skinless chicken breast halves
 Salt and black pepper (optional)
2 tablespoons margarine or butter
1 package (6.9 ounces) RICE-A-RONI® Chicken Flavor
1 teaspoon dried basil leaves
2 cups broccoli florets
1 medium tomato, seeded, chopped
1 cup (4 ounces) shredded mozzarella cheese

1. Sprinkle chicken with salt and pepper, if desired.

2. In large skillet, melt margarine over medium-high heat. Add chicken; cook 2 minutes on each side or until browned. Remove from skillet; set aside, reserving drippings. Keep warm.

3. In same skillet, sauté rice-vermicelli mix in reserved drippings over medium heat until vermicelli is golden brown. Stir in 2½ cups water, Special Seasonings and basil. Place chicken over rice mixture; bring to a boil over high heat.

4. Cover; reduce heat. Simmer 15 minutes. Top with broccoli and tomato.

5. Cover; continue to simmer 5 minutes or until liquid is absorbed and chicken is no longer pink in center. Sprinkle with cheese. Cover; let stand a few minutes before serving.

Makes 4 servings

Classic Veg•All® Chicken Pot Pie

2 cans (15 ounces each) VEG•ALL® Original Mixed Vegetables, drained
1 can (10 ounces) cooked chicken, drained
1 can (10¾ ounces) cream of chicken soup
¼ teaspoon thyme
2 (9-inch) frozen ready-to-bake pie crusts

1. Preheat oven to 375°F. In medium bowl, combine Veg•All, chicken, soup, and thyme; mix well. Fit one pie crust into 9-inch pie pan; pour vegetable mixture into pie crust. Top with remaining crust; crimp edges to seal and prick top with fork.

2. Bake for 30 to 45 minutes or until crust is golden brown and filling is hot. Allow pie to cool slightly before cutting into wedges to serve. *Makes 4 servings*

Tex-Mex Ground Turkey Potato Boats

2 medium potatoes
½ pound ground turkey
½ cup chopped onion
1 clove garlic, minced
1 can (8 ounces) stewed tomatoes
1 teaspoon chili powder
¼ teaspoon salt
¼ teaspoon dried oregano leaves, crushed
¼ teaspoon ground cumin
¼ teaspoon red pepper flakes
½ cup (2 ounces) shredded reduced-fat Cheddar cheese

1. Preheat oven to 400°F. Pierce potatoes several times with fork. Bake 50 to 60 minutes or until soft. Cool slightly. Reduce oven temperature to 375°F.

2. Slice potatoes in half lengthwise. Scoop out pulp with spoon, leaving ¼-inch shell. (Reserve potato pulp for other use.) Place potato shells on jelly-roll pan or baking sheet.

3. Place turkey, onion and garlic in medium skillet. Cook over medium-high heat 5 minutes or until turkey is no longer pink; drain. Add tomatoes, chili powder, salt, oregano, cumin and red pepper flakes to turkey in skillet. Cook 15 minutes or until most of liquid has evaporated.

4. Spoon turkey mixture evenly into potato shells; sprinkle with cheese. Bake 15 minutes or until cheese melts. *Makes 4 servings*

Favorite recipe from **National Turkey Federation**

Pasta Alfredo

½ pound thin vegetable-flavored noodles, cooked and drained
½ cup grated Parmesan cheese
½ cup prepared HIDDEN VALLEY® The Original Ranch® Dressing
2 tablespoons chopped parsley
Additional Parmesan cheese and freshly ground black pepper, to taste

In large pot, toss noodles, cheese, salad dressing and parsley. Warm over medium heat until cheese melts. Sprinkle individual servings with additional cheese and black pepper.

Makes 4 servings

Classic Veg•All® Chicken Pot Pie

Paella

¼ cup FILIPPO BERIO® Olive Oil
1 pound boneless skinless chicken breasts, cut into 1-inch strips
½ pound Italian sausage, cut into 1-inch slices
1 onion, chopped
3 cloves garlic, minced
2 (14½-ounce) cans chicken broth
2 cups uncooked long grain white rice
1 (8-ounce) bottle clam juice
1 (2-ounce) jar chopped pimientos, drained
2 bay leaves
1 teaspoon salt
¼ teaspoon saffron threads, crumbled (optional)
1 pound raw shrimp, shelled and deveined
1 (16-ounce) can whole tomatoes, drained
1 (10-ounce) package frozen peas, thawed
12 littleneck clams, scrubbed
¼ cup water
Fresh herb sprig (optional)

Preheat oven to 350°F. In large skillet, heat olive oil over medium heat until hot. Add chicken; cook and stir 8 to 10 minutes or until brown on all sides. Remove with slotted spoon; set aside. Add sausage to skillet; cook and stir 8 to 10 minutes or until brown. Remove with slotted spoon; set aside. Add onion and garlic to skillet; cook and stir 5 to 7 minutes or until onion is tender. Transfer chicken, sausage, onion and garlic mixture to large casserole.

Add chicken broth, rice, clam juice, pimientos, bay leaves, salt and saffron, if desired, to chicken mixture. Cover; bake 30 minutes. Add shrimp, tomatoes and peas; stir well. Cover; bake an additional 15 minutes or until rice is tender, liquid is absorbed and shrimp are opaque. Remove bay leaves.

Meanwhile, combine clams and water in stockpot or large saucepan. Cover and cook over medium heat 5 to 10 minutes or until clams open; remove clams immediately as they open. Discard any clams with unopened shells. Place clams on top of paella. Garnish with herb sprig, if desired.

Makes 4 to 6 servings

Sweet Potato Turkey Pie

1 can (24 ounces) sweet potatoes, drained
2 tablespoons margarine, melted
¼ teaspoon pumpkin pie spice
Nonstick vegetable cooking spray
2 cups cubed cooked turkey (½- to ¾-inch cubes)
1 can (10¾ ounces) reduced-fat and reduced-sodium cream of mushroom soup
1 package (9 ounces) frozen French-style green beans, thawed and drained
1 can (2 ounces) mushroom stems and pieces, drained
½ teaspoon *each* salt and pepper
2 tablespoons crushed canned French fried onion rings
1 can (8 ounces) cranberry sauce (optional)

1. In medium bowl blend sweet potatoes, margarine and pumpkin pie spice until smooth. Spray 9-inch pie plate with nonstick vegetable cooking spray. Line pie plate with potato mixture to form a "pie shell"; set aside.

2. In medium bowl combine turkey, soup, beans, mushrooms, salt and pepper. Pour mixture into prepared shell. Sprinkle onions over top. Bake at 350°F 30 minutes or until hot. Serve with cranberry sauce, if desired.

Makes 6 servings

Favorite recipe from **National Turkey Federation**

Broccoli Lasagna Bianca

1 (15- to 16-ounce) container fat-free
　ricotta cheese
1 cup EGG BEATERS® Healthy Real Egg
　Product
1 tablespoon minced basil or 1 teaspoon
　dried basil leaves
½ cup chopped onion
1 clove garlic, minced
2 tablespoons FLEISCHMANN'S®
　Original Margarine
¼ cup all-purpose flour
2 cups fat-free (skim) milk
2 (10-ounce) packages frozen chopped
　broccoli, thawed and well drained
1 cup (4 ounces) shredded part-skim
　mozzarella cheese
9 lasagna noodles, cooked and drained
1 small tomato, chopped
2 tablespoons grated Parmesan cheese
　Fresh basil leaves, for garnish

In medium bowl, combine ricotta cheese, Egg Beaters® and minced basil; set aside.

In large saucepan over medium heat, sauté onion and garlic in margarine until tender-crisp. Stir in flour; cook for 1 minute. Gradually stir in milk; cook, stirring, until mixture thickens and begins to boil. Remove from heat; stir in broccoli and mozzarella cheese.

In lightly greased 13×9×2-inch baking dish, place 3 lasagna noodles; top with ⅓ each ricotta and broccoli mixtures. Repeat layers 2 more times. Top with tomato; sprinkle with Parmesan cheese. Bake at 350°F for 1 hour or until set. Let stand 10 minutes before serving. Garnish with basil leaves.
　　Makes 8 servings (3¼×4½ inches each)

Prep Time: 20 minutes
Cook Time: 90 minutes

Country Sausage Macaroni and Cheese

1 pound BOB EVANS® Special
　Seasonings Roll Sausage
1½ cups milk
12 ounces pasteurized processed Cheddar
　cheese, cut into cubes
½ cup Dijon mustard
1 cup diced fresh or drained canned
　tomatoes
1 cup sliced mushrooms
⅓ cup sliced green onions
⅛ teaspoon cayenne pepper
12 ounces uncooked elbow macaroni
2 tablespoons grated Parmesan cheese

Preheat oven to 350°F. Crumble and cook sausage in medium skillet until browned. Drain on paper towels. Combine milk, processed cheese and mustard in medium saucepan; cook and stir over low heat until cheese melts and mixture is smooth. Stir in sausage, tomatoes, mushrooms, green onions and cayenne pepper. Remove from heat.

Cook macaroni according to package directions; drain. Combine hot macaroni and cheese mixture in large bowl; toss until well coated. Spoon into greased shallow 2-quart casserole dish. Cover and bake 15 to 20 minutes. Stir; sprinkle with Parmesan cheese. Bake, uncovered, 5 minutes more. Let stand 10 minutes before serving. Refrigerate leftovers.
　　Makes 6 to 8 servings

Italian Beef Burrito

1½ pounds ground beef
2 medium onions, finely chopped
2 medium red and/or green bell peppers, chopped
1 jar (1 pound 10 ounces) RAGÚ® Robusto!™ Pasta Sauce
½ teaspoon dried oregano leaves, crushed
8 (10-inch) flour tortillas, warmed
2 cups shredded mozzarella cheese (about 8 ounces)

1. In 12-inch skillet, brown ground beef over medium-high heat.

2. Stir in onions and red bell peppers and cook, stirring occasionally, 5 minutes or until tender; drain. Stir in Ragú Pasta Sauce and oregano; heat through.

3. To serve, top each tortilla with 1 cup ground beef mixture and ¼ cup cheese; roll up and serve. *Makes 8 servings*

Prep Time: 15 minutes
Cook Time: 15 minutes

Veg•All® Beef & Cheddar Bake

2 cans (15 ounces each) VEG•ALL® Original Mixed Vegetables, drained
3 cups shredded Cheddar cheese
2 cups cooked elbow macaroni
1 pound extra-lean ground beef, cooked and drained
½ cup chopped onion
¼ teaspoon pepper

1. Preheat oven to 350°F.

2. In large mixing bowl, combine Veg•All, cheese, macaroni, ground beef, onion and pepper; mix well. Pour mixture into large casserole.

3. Bake for 30 to 35 minutes. Serve hot.
Makes 4 to 6 servings

Stacked Burrito Pie

½ cup GUILTLESS GOURMET® Mild Black Bean Dip
2 teaspoons water
5 low-fat flour tortillas (6 inches each)
½ cup nonfat sour cream or plain yogurt
½ cup GUILTLESS GOURMET® Roasted Red Pepper Salsa
1¼ cups (5 ounces) shredded low-fat Monterey Jack cheese
4 cups shredded iceberg or romaine lettuce
½ cup GUILTLESS GOURMET® Salsa (Roasted Red Pepper or Southwestern Grill)
Lime slices and chili pepper (optional)

Preheat oven to 350°F. Combine bean dip and 2 teaspoons water in small bowl; mix well. Line 7½-inch springform pan with 1 tortilla. Spread 2 tablespoons bean dip mixture over tortilla, then spread with 2 tablespoons sour cream and 2 tablespoons red pepper salsa. Sprinkle with ¼ cup cheese. Repeat layers 3 more times. Place remaining tortilla on top and sprinkle with remaining ¼ cup cheese.

Bake 40 minutes or until heated through. (Place sheet of foil under springform pan to catch any juices that may seep through the bottom.) Cool slightly before unmolding. To serve, cut into 4 quarters. Place 1 cup lettuce on 4 serving plates. Top each serving with 1 quarter burrito pie and 2 tablespoons salsa. Garnish with lime slices and pepper, if desired.
Makes 4 servings

Italian Beef Burrito

Skillet Franks and Potatoes

3 tablespoons vegetable oil, divided
4 HEBREW NATIONAL® Quarter Pound Dinner Beef Franks or 4 Beef Knockwurst
3 cups chopped cooked red potatoes
1 cup chopped onion
1 cup chopped seeded green bell pepper or combination of green and red bell peppers
3 tablespoons chopped fresh parsley (optional)
1 teaspoon dried sage leaves
½ teaspoon salt
¼ teaspoon freshly ground black pepper

Heat 1 tablespoon oil in large nonstick skillet over medium heat. Score franks; add to skillet. Cook franks until browned. Transfer to plate; set aside.

Add remaining 2 tablespoons oil to skillet. Add potatoes, onion and bell pepper; cook and stir about 12 to 14 minutes or until potatoes are golden brown. Stir in parsley, sage, salt and black pepper.

Return franks to skillet; push down into potato mixture. Cook about 5 minutes or until heated through, turning once halfway through cooking time. *Makes 4 servings*

Turkey Kielbasa with Cabbage, Sweet Potatoes and Apples

1 bottle (12 ounces) dark beer or ale
2 tablespoons Dijon mustard
½ teaspoon caraway seeds
6 cups coarsely shredded cabbage
1 pound fully cooked turkey kielbasa or smoked turkey sausage, cut into 2-inch pieces
1 Granny Smith apple, cut into ¼-inch wedges
1 can (16 ounces) sweet potatoes, cut into 1½-inch cubes

1. Combine beer, mustard and caraway seeds in large deep skillet. Bring to a boil over high heat. Add cabbage. Reduce heat to medium-low. Cover and cook 5 to 8 minutes or until cabbage is crisp-tender.

2. Add kielbasa, apple and sweet potatoes. Increase heat to high. Bring mixture to a boil. Reduce heat to medium-low. Cover and cook 3 to 5 minutes or until apple is crisp-tender. *Makes 6 servings*

*Favorite recipe from **National Turkey Federation***

Chicken Casserole Olé

12 boneless, skinless chicken tenders
2 cups water
1 can (15 ounces) mild chili beans, undrained
1 cup salsa
½ cup chopped green bell pepper
2 cups UNCLE BEN'S® Instant Rice
2 cups (8 ounces) shredded Mexican cheese blend, divided
2 cups bite-size tortilla chips

1. Spray large skillet with nonstick cooking spray. Add chicken; cook over medium-high heat 12 to 15 minutes or until lightly browned on both sides and chicken is no longer pink in center.

2. Add water, beans with liquid, salsa and bell pepper. Bring to a boil; add rice and 1 cup cheese. Cover; remove from heat and let stand 5 minutes or until liquid is absorbed. Top with tortilla chips and remaining 1 cup cheese; let stand, covered, 3 to 5 minutes or until cheese is melted. *Makes 6 servings*

Skillet Franks and Potatoes

Chicken Tuscany

6 medium red potatoes, scrubbed and
  sliced ⅛ inch thick
12 ounces shiitake, cremini, chanterelle
  and/or button mushrooms, sliced
4 tablespoons olive oil, divided
4 tablespoons grated Parmesan cheese,
  divided
3 teaspoons minced garlic, divided
3 teaspoons minced fresh rosemary *or*
  1½ teaspoons dried rosemary leaves,
  divided
  Salt and ground pepper
1 package (about 3 pounds) PERDUE®
  Fresh Pick of the Chicken

Preheat oven to 425°F. Pat potatoes dry with
paper towels. Toss potatoes and mushrooms
with 2½ tablespoons oil, 2 tablespoons cheese,
2 teaspoons garlic, 2 teaspoons rosemary,
½ teaspoon salt and ¼ teaspoon pepper. In
13×9-inch baking dish, arrange potatoes in
one layer; top with remaining 2 tablespoons
cheese. Bake 15 minutes or until potatoes are
lightly browned; set aside.

Meanwhile, in large nonstick skillet over
medium heat, heat remaining 1½ tablespoons
oil. Add chicken pieces. Season lightly with
salt and pepper; sprinkle with remaining garlic
and rosemary. Cook chicken 5 to 6 minutes on
each side or until browned. (Do not crowd
pan; if necessary, brown chicken in two
batches.)

Arrange chicken on top of potato mixture;
drizzle with any oil from skillet and return to
oven. Bake 20 to 25 minutes longer or until
chicken is no longer pink in center. Serve
chicken, potatoes and mushrooms with green
salad, if desired.   *Makes 6 servings*

Stuffed Shells Florentine

1 cup (about 4 ounces) coarsely chopped
  mushrooms
½ cup chopped onion
1 clove garlic, minced
1 teaspoon Italian seasoning
¼ teaspoon ground black pepper
1 tablespoon FLEISCHMANN'S®
  Original Margarine
1 (16-ounce) container fat-free cottage
  cheese
1 (10-ounce) package frozen chopped
  spinach, thawed and well drained
½ cup EGG BEATERS® Healthy Real Egg
  Product
24 jumbo pasta shells, cooked in unsalted
  water and drained
1 (15¼-ounce) jar reduced-sodium
  spaghetti sauce

In large skillet, over medium-high heat, sauté
mushrooms, onion, garlic, Italian seasoning
and pepper in margarine until tender. Remove
from heat; stir in cottage cheese, spinach and
Egg Beaters®. Spoon mixture into shells.

Spread ½ cup spaghetti sauce in bottom of
13×9×2-inch baking dish; arrange shells over
sauce. Top with remaining sauce; cover. Bake
at 350°F for 35 minutes or until hot.

Makes 7 servings

Prep Time: 30 minutes
Cook Time: 40 minutes

Chicken Tuscany

Sunflower Wheat-Beef Pot Pie

Crust

1¾ cups all-purpose flour
¼ cup fine whole wheat flour
1 teaspoon salt
⅛ teaspoon baking powder
⅔ Butter Flavor CRISCO® Stick or ⅔ cup Butter Flavor CRISCO® all-vegetable shortening
5 to 6 tablespoons cold water

Filling

¼ cup chopped celery
¼ cup chopped potatoes
¼ cup chopped carrots
¼ cup frozen corn
¼ cup frozen peas
3 tablespoons minced onion
1 teaspoon minced fresh parsley
3 tablespoons salted sunflower seeds
1½ cups water, divided
¾ cup beef broth
1 tablespoon plus 1½ teaspoons cornstarch
½ teaspoon instant beef flavor bouillon granules
½ teaspoon instant chicken flavor bouillon granules
¼ teaspoon black pepper
⅛ teaspoon salt
1 tablespoon plus 1½ teaspoons ketchup
1 cup cubed cooked roast beef
¾ cup condensed Cheddar cheese soup
1 tablespoon butter or margarine
¼ cup shredded American cheese

1. Heat oven to 400°F.

2. For crust, combine all-purpose flour, whole wheat flour, 1 teaspoon salt and baking powder in bowl. Cut in shortening, using pastry blender (or 2 knives), until flour is blended to form pea-size pieces.

3. Sprinkle with water, 1 tablespoon at a time. Toss lightly with fork until dough forms a ball. Divide dough in half. Press each half between hands to form 5- to 6-inch "pancake."

4. Flour rolling surface and rolling pin lightly. Roll dough for bottom crust into circle and trim 1 inch larger than inverted 9-inch pie plate. Loosen dough carefully. Fold into quarters. Unfold and press into pie plate. Trim edge even with pie plate. Moisten pastry edge with water.

5. For filling, combine celery, potatoes, carrots, corn, peas, onion, parsley, sunflower seeds and 1¼ cups water in large saucepan. Bring to a boil. Reduce heat. Simmer 10 minutes.

6. Heat beef broth in separate large saucepan. Combine cornstarch, beef bouillon granules, chicken bouillon granules, pepper, salt, ketchup and remaining ¼ cup water in small bowl. Stir into beef broth. Cook and stir until thickened. Add beef, cooked vegetables with liquid, and soup. Spoon into unbaked pie shell. Dot with butter. Sprinkle with cheese.

7. Roll top crust same as bottom and lift onto filled pie. Trim ½ inch beyond edge of pie plate. Fold top edge under bottom crust. Flute with fingers or fork. Cut slits or design in top crust or prick with fork for steam to escape.

8. Bake at 400°F for 15 minutes. *Reduce oven temperature to 350°F.* Bake for 20 to 25 minutes. *Do not overbake.* Serve hot.

Makes one 9-inch pie

Zesty Seafood Lasagna

2 packages (1.8 ounces each) white
    sauce mix
4½ cups milk
1 teaspoon dried basil leaves
½ teaspoon dried thyme leaves
½ teaspoon garlic powder
¾ cup grated Parmesan cheese, divided
3 tablespoons *Frank's® RedHot®* Cayenne
    Pepper Sauce
9 oven-ready lasagna pasta sheets
2 packages (10 ounces each) frozen
    chopped spinach, thawed and
    squeezed dry
½ pound cooked shrimp
½ pound raw bay scallops or flaked
    imitation crabmeat
2 cups (8 ounces) shredded mozzarella
    cheese, divided

1. Preheat oven to 400°F. Prepare white sauce according to package directions, using milk and adding basil, thyme and garlic powder in large saucepan. Stir in ½ cup Parmesan cheese and *Frank's RedHot* Sauce.

2. Spread 1 cup sauce in bottom of greased 13×9×2-inch casserole. Layer 3 pasta sheets crosswise over sauce. (Do not let edges touch.) Layer half of the spinach and seafood over pasta. Spoon 1 cup sauce over seafood; sprinkle with ¾ cup mozzarella cheese. Repeat layers a second time. Top with final layer of pasta sheets, remaining sauce and cheeses.

3. Cover pan with greased foil. Bake 40 minutes. Remove foil; bake 10 minutes or until top is browned and pasta is fully cooked. Let stand 15 minutes before serving.

Makes 8 servings

Tip: Splash *Frank's RedHot* Sauce on foods after cooking, instead of salt and black pepper. *Frank's RedHot* Sauce perks up the flavor of all foods!

Prep Time: 30 minutes
Cook Time: 50 minutes

Johnnie Marzetti

1 tablespoon CRISCO® Oil*
1 cup chopped celery
1 cup chopped onion
1 medium green bell pepper, chopped
1 pound ground beef round
1 can (14½ ounces) Italian-style stewed
    tomatoes, undrained
1 can (8 ounces) tomato sauce
1 can (6 ounces) tomato paste
1 cup water
1 bay leaf
1½ teaspoons dried basil leaves
1¼ teaspoons salt
¼ teaspoon black pepper
1 package (12 ounces) egg noodles,
    cooked and well drained
½ cup plain dry bread crumbs
1 cup (4 ounces) shredded sharp
    Cheddar cheese

Use your favorite Crisco Oil product.

1. Heat oven to 375°F. Oil 12½×8½×2-inch baking dish lightly. Place cooling rack on countertop.

2. Heat oil in large skillet on medium heat. Add celery, onion and green pepper. Cook and stir until tender. Remove vegetables from skillet. Set aside. Add meat to skillet. Cook until browned, stirring occasionally. Return vegetables to skillet. Add tomatoes, tomato sauce, tomato paste, water, bay leaf, basil, salt and black pepper. Reduce heat to low. Simmer 5 minutes, stirring occasionally. Remove bay leaf.

3. Place noodles in baking dish. Spoon meat mixture over noodles. Sprinkle with bread crumbs and cheese.

4. Bake at 375°F for 15 to 20 minutes or until cheese melts. *Do not overbake.* Remove baking dish to cooling rack. Garnish, if desired.

Makes 8 servings

Savory Chicken and Biscuits

1 pound boneless, skinless chicken thighs or breasts, cut into 1-inch pieces
1 medium potato, cut into 1-inch pieces
1 medium yellow onion, cut into 1-inch pieces
8 ounces fresh mushrooms, quartered
1 cup fresh baby carrots
1 cup chopped celery
1 (14½-ounce) can chicken broth
3 cloves garlic, minced
1 teaspoon dried rosemary leaves
1 teaspoon salt
1 teaspoon black pepper
3 tablespoons cornstarch blended with ½ cup cold water
1 cup frozen peas, thawed
1 (4-ounce) jar sliced pimentos, drained
1 package BOB EVANS® Frozen Buttermilk Biscuit Dough

Preheat oven to 375°F. Combine chicken, potato, onion, mushrooms, carrots, celery, broth, garlic, rosemary, salt and pepper in large saucepan. Bring to a boil over high heat. Reduce heat to low and simmer, uncovered, 5 minutes. Stir in cornstarch mixture; cook 2 minutes. Stir in peas and pimentos; return to a boil. Transfer chicken mixture to 2-quart casserole dish; arrange frozen biscuits on top. Bake 30 to 35 minutes or until biscuits are golden brown. Refrigerate leftovers.

Makes 4 to 6 servings

Lasagna Primavera

1 (8-ounce) package lasagna noodles
3 carrots, cut into ¼-inch slices
1 cup broccoli flowerets
1 cup zucchini, cut into ¼-inch slices
1 crookneck squash, cut into ¼-inch slices
2 (10-ounce) packages frozen chopped spinach, thawed
1 (8-ounce) package ricotta cheese
1 (26-ounce) jar NEWMAN'S OWN® Marinara Sauce with Mushrooms
3 cups (12 ounces) shredded mozzarella cheese
½ cup (2 ounces) grated Parmesan cheese

Bring 3 quarts water to a boil in a 6-quart saucepan over high heat. Add lasagna noodles and cook 5 minutes. Add carrots; cook 2 more minutes. Add broccoli, zucchini and crookneck squash and cook the final 2 minutes or until pasta is tender. Drain well.

Squeeze liquid out of spinach. Combine spinach with ricotta cheese. In a 3-quart rectangular baking pan, spread ⅓ of the Newman's Own® Marinara Sauce with Mushrooms. Line pan with lasagna noodles. Layer ½ each of the vegetables, spinach mixture and mozzarella cheese over the noodles; top with ½ of the remaining Newman's Own® Marinara Sauce with Mushrooms. Repeat layers. Sprinkle with Parmesan cheese.

Place baking pan on 10×15-inch baking sheet which has been lined with foil. Bake uncovered in a 400°F oven about 30 minutes or until hot in the center. Let stand 10 minutes before serving. (Casserole may be prepared up to 2 days before baking. Refrigerate, covered, until 1 hour before baking. If cold, bake for 1 hour at 350°F.)

Makes 8 servings

Savory Chicken and Biscuits

Quick Beef Bourguignonne

3 tablespoons all-purpose flour
½ teaspoon dried thyme
½ teaspoon ground black pepper
¾ pound boneless sirloin or top round steak, cut into 1-inch pieces
2 tablespoons vegetable oil, divided
3 cups (8 ounces) halved or quartered cremini or white mushrooms
⅓ cup thinly sliced shallots or chopped onion
1 (14½-ounce) can beef broth
¼ cup water
¼ cup dry red wine or water
1 (4.8-ounce) package PASTA RONI® Garlic Alfredo
¾ cup thinly sliced carrots

1. Combine flour, thyme and pepper in resealable plastic food storage bag. Add steak; shake to coat evenly with flour mixture.

2. In large skillet over medium-high heat, heat 1 tablespoon oil. Add steak; cook 3 minutes or until lightly browned on all sides. Remove from skillet; set aside.

3. In same skillet over medium heat, heat remaining 1 tablespoon oil. Add mushrooms and shallots; cook 3 minutes, stirring occasionally.

4. Add beef broth, ¼ cup water and wine; bring to a boil. Add pasta, steak, carrots and Special Seasonings. Reduce heat to medium. Simmer 5 minutes or until pasta is tender. Let stand 5 minutes before serving.

Makes 4 servings

Prep Time: 15 minutes
Cook Time: 20 minutes

Tangy Shrimp with Angel Hair Pasta

2 tablespoons olive oil
2 teaspoons minced garlic
1 pound uncooked large shrimp, peeled and deveined
1⅓ cups *French's*® French Fried Onions, divided
1 cup chicken broth
¼ cup chopped parsley
3 tablespoons lemon juice
½ teaspoon salt
¼ teaspoon ground black pepper
1 package (9 ounces) uncooked fresh angel hair or capellini pasta (or 1 pound dry pasta)

1. Heat oil in 12-inch nonstick skillet over high heat. Add garlic and sauté about 30 seconds or until golden.

2. Add shrimp and cook 2 minutes. Stir in ⅔ *cup* French Fried Onions, broth, parsley, lemon juice, salt and pepper. Cook 2 minutes or until shrimp turn pink.

3. Meanwhile, cook pasta according to package directions using shortest cooking time; drain. Toss with shrimp mixture. Transfer to serving platter and sprinkle with remaining onions. *Makes 4 servings*

Prep Time: 10 minutes
Cook Time: about 5 minutes

Quick Beef Bourguignonne

Skillet Spaghetti Pizza

1 pound bulk Italian sausage
1 tablespoon minced garlic
½ pound uncooked thin spaghetti, broken into 2-inch lengths
1 jar (26 ounces) spaghetti sauce
1½ cups water
1 cup (4 ounces) shredded mozzarella cheese
½ cup diced green bell pepper
1⅓ cups *French's®* French Fried Onions

1. Cook sausage and garlic in large nonstick skillet over medium heat until browned, stirring frequently; drain.

2. Stir in uncooked spaghetti, spaghetti sauce and water. Bring to a boil; reduce heat to medium-low. Cover and simmer 15 minutes or until spaghetti is cooked, stirring occasionally.

3. Top spaghetti mixture with cheese, bell pepper and French Fried Onions; remove from heat. Cover and let stand 3 minutes until cheese is melted. Serve immediately.

Makes 8 servings

Tip: You may substitute link sausage; remove from casing before cooking.

Variation: Substitute other pizza toppings such as mushrooms, eggplant, olives or pepperoni for green pepper.

Prep Time: 10 minutes
Cook Time: 23 minutes

Cheesy Chicken Pot Pie

1 pound boneless, skinless chicken breast halves, cut into ½-inch chunks
1 tablespoon all-purpose flour
1 jar (1 pound) RAGÚ® Cheese Creations!® Double Cheddar Sauce
1 bag (16 ounces) frozen mixed vegetables, thawed
1 prepared pastry for single-crust pie

Preheat oven to 425°F. In 2-quart casserole, toss chicken with flour. Stir in Ragú Cheese Creations! Sauce and vegetables. Cover casserole with prepared pastry. Press pastry around edge of casserole to seal; trim excess pastry, then flute edges. Cover with aluminum foil and bake 20 minutes. Remove foil and continue baking 20 minutes or until crust is golden and chicken is thoroughly cooked. Let stand 5 minutes before serving.

Makes 6 servings

Recipe Tip: This is the perfect dish for leftovers. Substitute cooked pork roast, turkey breast or even roast beef for the chicken.

SPAM™ Fajitas

Nonstick cooking spray
1 green bell pepper, cut into julienne strips
½ onion, cut into ¼-inch slices
1 (12-ounce) can SPAM® Classic, cut into julienne strips
¾ cup CHI-CHI'S® Salsa
8 (8-inch) flour tortillas, warmed
2 cups shredded lettuce
½ cup (2 ounces) shredded hot pepper Monterey Jack or Cheddar cheese
½ cup nonfat plain yogurt
Additional CHI-CHI'S® Salsa (optional)

Spray large nonstick skillet with cooking spray. Heat skillet over medium-high heat. Add green pepper and onion; sauté 2 minutes. Add SPAM®; sauté 2 minutes. Stir in salsa and heat thoroughly. Spoon about ½ cup SPAM™ mixture onto each flour tortilla. Top each with ¼ cup lettuce, 1 tablespoon cheese, 1 tablespoon yogurt and salsa, if desired.

Makes 8 servings

Skillet Spaghetti Pizza

Heartland Shepherd's Pie

¾ pound ground beef
1 medium onion, chopped
1 can (14½ ounces) DEL MONTE®
    Stewed Tomatoes-Original Recipe
1 can (8 ounces) DEL MONTE Tomato
    Sauce
1 can (14½ ounces) DEL MONTE Mixed
    Vegetables, drained
    Instant mashed potato flakes plus
    ingredients to prepare (enough for
    6 servings)
3 cloves garlic, minced (optional)

1. Preheat oven to 375°F. In large skillet, brown meat and onion over medium-high heat; drain.

2. Add tomatoes and tomato sauce; cook over high heat until thickened, stirring frequently. Stir in mixed vegetables. Season with salt and pepper, if desired.

3. Spoon into 2-quart baking dish; set aside. Prepare 6 servings mashed potatoes according to package directions, first cooking garlic in specified amount of butter.

4. Top meat mixture with potatoes. Bake 20 minutes or until heated through. Garnish with chopped parsley, if desired.

Makes 4 to 6 servings

Prep Time: 5 minutes
Cook Time: 30 minutes

Rigatoni with Four Cheeses

3 cups milk
1 tablespoon chopped carrot
1 tablespoon chopped celery
1 tablespoon chopped onion
1 tablespoon fresh parsley sprigs
¼ teaspoon black peppercorns
¼ teaspoon hot pepper sauce
½ bay leaf
    Dash nutmeg
¼ cup Wisconsin butter
¼ cup flour
½ cup (2 ounces) grated Wisconsin
    Parmesan cheese
¼ cup (1 ounce) grated Wisconsin
    Romano cheese
12 ounces rigatoni, cooked, drained
1½ cups (6 ounces) shredded Wisconsin
    Cheddar cheese
1½ cups (6 ounces) shredded Wisconsin
    Mozzarella cheese
¼ teaspoon chili powder

In a 2-quart saucepan, combine milk, carrot, celery, onion, parsley, peppercorns, hot pepper sauce, bay leaf and nutmeg. Bring to boil. Reduce heat to low; simmer 10 minutes. Strain, reserving liquid. Melt butter in 2-quart saucepan over low heat. Blend in flour. Gradually add reserved liquid; cook, stirring constantly, until thickened. Remove from heat. Add Parmesan and Romano cheeses; stir until blended. Pour over pasta; toss well. Combine Cheddar and Mozzarella cheese. In buttered 2-quart casserole, layer ½ of pasta mixture, Cheddar cheese mixture and remaining pasta mixture. Sprinkle with chili powder. Bake at 350°F for 25 minutes or until hot.

Makes 6 servings

Favorite recipe from **Wisconsin Milk Marketing Board**

Heartland Shepherd's Pie

Sausage and Broccoli Noodle Casserole

1 jar (1 pound) RAGÚ® Cheese
   Creations!® Classic Alfredo Sauce
⅓ cup milk
1 pound sweet Italian sausage, cooked
   and crumbled
1 package (9 ounces) frozen chopped
   broccoli, thawed
8 ounces egg noodles, cooked and
   drained
1 cup shredded Cheddar cheese (about
   4 ounces)
¼ cup chopped roasted red peppers

1. Preheat oven to 350°F. In large bowl, combine Ragú Cheese Creations! Sauce and milk. Stir in sausage, broccoli, noodles, ¾ cup cheese and roasted peppers.

2. In 13×9-inch baking dish, evenly spread sausage mixture. Sprinkle with remaining ¼ cup cheese.

3. Bake 30 minutes or until heated through.
Makes 6 servings

Tip: Substitute sausage with equal amount of vegetables for a hearty vegetarian entrée.

Prep Time: 15 minutes
Cook Time: 30 minutes

Lemon-Garlic Chicken & Rice

4 skinless, boneless chicken breast
   halves
1 teaspoon paprika
   Salt and pepper (optional)
2 tablespoons margarine or butter
2 cloves garlic, minced
1 package (6.9 ounces) RICE-A-RONI®
   Chicken Flavor
1 tablespoon lemon juice
1 cup chopped red or green bell pepper
½ teaspoon grated lemon peel

1. Sprinkle chicken with paprika, salt and pepper.

2. In large skillet, melt margarine over medium-high heat. Add chicken and garlic; cook 2 minutes on each side or until browned. Remove from skillet; set aside, reserving drippings. Keep warm.

3. In same skillet, sauté rice-vermicelli mix in reserved drippings over medium heat until vermicelli is golden brown. Stir in 2¼ cups water, lemon juice and Special Seasonings. Top rice with chicken; bring to a boil over high heat.

4. Cover; reduce heat. Simmer 10 minutes. Stir in red pepper and lemon peel. Cover; continue to simmer 10 minutes or until liquid is absorbed, rice is tender and chicken is no longer pink inside. *Makes 4 servings*

String Pie

1 pound ground beef
½ cup chopped onion
¼ cup chopped green bell pepper
1 jar (15½ ounces) spaghetti sauce
8 ounces spaghetti, cooked and drained
⅓ cup grated Parmesan cheese
2 eggs, beaten
2 teaspoons butter, melted
1 cup cottage cheese
½ cup (2 ounces) shredded mozzarella
   cheese

Preheat oven to 350°F. Cook beef, onion and green pepper in large skillet over medium-high heat until meat is browned. Drain fat. Stir in spaghetti sauce. Combine spaghetti, Parmesan cheese, eggs and butter in large bowl; mix well. Place in bottom of 13×9-inch baking pan. Spread cottage cheese over top; cover with sauce mixture. Sprinkle with mozzarella cheese. Bake until mixture is thoroughly heated and cheese is melted, about 20 minutes. *Makes 6 to 8 servings*

Favorite recipe from **North Dakota Beef Commission**

Broccoli Lasagna

1 tablespoon CRISCO® Oil* plus
   additional for oiling
1 cup chopped onion
3 cloves garlic, minced
1 can (14½ ounces) no salt added
   tomatoes, undrained and chopped
1 can (8 ounces) no salt added tomato
   sauce
1 can (6 ounces) no salt added tomato
   paste
1 cup thinly sliced fresh mushrooms
¼ cup chopped fresh parsley
1 tablespoon red wine vinegar
1 teaspoon dried oregano leaves
1 teaspoon dried basil leaves
1 bay leaf
½ teaspoon salt
¼ teaspoon crushed red pepper
1½ cups lowfat cottage cheese
1 cup (4 ounces) shredded low moisture
   part-skim mozzarella cheese, divided
6 lasagna noodles, cooked (without salt
   or fat) and well drained
3 cups chopped broccoli, cooked and
   well drained
1 tablespoon grated Parmesan cheese

Use your favorite Crisco Oil product.

1. Heat oven to 350°F. Oil 11¾×7½×2-inch baking dish lightly.

2. Heat 1 tablespoon oil in large saucepan on medium heat. Add onion and garlic. Cook and stir until tender. Stir in tomatoes, tomato sauce, tomato paste, mushrooms, parsley, vinegar, oregano, basil, bay leaf, salt and crushed red pepper. Bring to a boil. Reduce heat to low. Cover. Simmer 30 minutes, stirring occasionally. Remove bay leaf.

3. Combine cottage cheese and ½ cup mozzarella cheese in small bowl. Stir well.

4. Place 2 lasagna noodles in bottom of baking dish. Layer with one cup broccoli, one-third of the tomato sauce and one-third of the cottage cheese mixture. Repeat layers. Cover with foil.

5. Bake at 350°F for 25 minutes. Uncover. Sprinkle with remaining ½ cup mozzarella cheese and Parmesan cheese. Bake, uncovered, 10 minutes or until cheese melts. *Do not overbake.* Let stand 10 minutes before serving.

Makes 8 servings

Layered Mexican Tortilla Cheese Casserole

1 can (14½ ounces) salsa-style or
   Mexican-style stewed tomatoes,
   undrained
½ cup chopped fresh cilantro, divided
2 tablespoons fresh lime juice
   Nonstick vegetable cooking spray
6 (6-inch) corn tortillas, torn into
   1½-inch pieces
1 can (15 ounces) black beans, rinsed
   and drained
1 can (8 ounces) whole kernel corn,
   drained, or 1 cup frozen whole
   kernel corn, thawed
2 cups (8 ounces) SARGENTO® Mexican
   Blend Shredded Cheese

1. In small bowl, combine tomatoes, ¼ cup cilantro and lime juice; set aside.

2. Coat 8-inch square baking dish with cooking spray. Arrange ¼ of tortillas in bottom of dish; spoon ¼ of tomato mixture over tortillas. Top with ¼ of beans, ¼ of corn and ¼ of cheese. Repeat layering 3 more times with remaining tortillas, tomato mixture, beans, corn and cheese.

3. Bake uncovered at 375°F 25 minutes or until cheese is melted and sauce is bubbly. Sprinkle with remaining ¼ cup cilantro. Let stand 10 minutes before serving.

Makes 4 servings

Scalloped Chicken & Pasta

¼ cup margarine or butter, divided
1 package (6.2 ounces) PASTA RONI®
    Shells & White Cheddar
2 cups frozen mixed vegetables
⅔ cup milk
2 cups chopped cooked chicken or ham
¼ cup dry bread crumbs

1. Preheat oven to 450°F.

2. In 3-quart saucepan, combine 2¼ cups water and 2 tablespoons margarine. Bring just to a boil. Stir in pasta and frozen vegetables. Reduce heat to medium.

3. Boil, uncovered, stirring frequently, 12 to 14 minutes or until most of water is absorbed. Add Special Seasonings, milk and chicken. Continue cooking 3 minutes.

4. Meanwhile, melt remaining 2 tablespoons margarine in small saucepan; stir in bread crumbs.

5. Transfer pasta mixture to 8- or 9-inch glass baking dish. Sprinkle with bread crumbs. Bake 10 minutes or until bread crumbs are browned and edges are bubbly.   *Makes 4 servings*

Easy Three Cheese Tuna Soufflé

4 cups large croutons*
2½ cups milk
4 large eggs
1 can (10¾ ounces) cream of celery soup
3 cups shredded cheese (use a
    combination of Cheddar, Monterey
    Jack and Swiss)
1 (7-ounce) pouch of STARKIST®
    Premium Albacore or Chunk Light
    Tuna
1 tablespoon butter or margarine
½ cup chopped celery
½ cup finely chopped onion
¼ pound mushrooms, sliced

Use garlic and herb or ranch-flavored croutons.

In bottom of lightly greased 13×9-inch baking dish, arrange croutons. In medium bowl, beat together milk, eggs and soup; stir in cheeses and tuna. In small skillet, melt butter over medium heat. Add celery, onion and mushrooms; sauté until onion is soft.

Spoon sautéed vegetables over croutons; pour egg-tuna mixture over top. Cover; refrigerate overnight. Remove from refrigerator 1 hour before baking; bake in 325°F oven 45 to 50 minutes or until hot and bubbly.
Makes 8 servings

Ham and Potato au Gratin

3 tablespoons butter or margarine
3 tablespoons all-purpose flour
2 cups milk
1½ cups (6 ounces) shredded Cheddar
    cheese
1 tablespoon Dijon mustard
2 cups HILLSHIRE FARM® Lean &
    Hearty Ham, cut into thin strips
1 package (24 ounces) frozen shredded
    hash brown potatoes, thawed
1 package (10 ounces) frozen chopped
    spinach, thawed and drained

Preheat oven to 350°F.

Melt butter in large saucepan over medium heat; stir in flour. Add milk. Cook and stir until bubbly; cook 1 minute more. Remove from heat. Stir in cheese and mustard; set aside.

Place ½ of Ham in ungreased medium casserole. Top ham with ½ of potatoes and ½ of milk mixture. Spoon spinach over top. Repeat layers with remaining ham, potatoes and milk mixture.

Bake, uncovered, 30 minutes or until heated through.   *Makes 8 servings*

Scalloped Chicken & Pasta

The Old Country

Grandma might have an unorthodox style in the kitchen, but she's the only one that can make that old family recipe really come alive. How about a little taste of the old country?

Mostaccioli per la Pasqua

1 package (16 ounces) BARILLA®
    Mostaccioli
¼ cup (½ stick) unsalted butter
1 large onion, chopped
1 pound asparagus, trimmed and cut
    into 1-inch pieces
8 ounces ham, diced
½ cup heavy cream
½ teaspoon salt
½ teaspoon pepper

1. Cook mostaccioli according to package directions; drain.

2. Meanwhile, melt butter in large skillet over medium heat. Add onion; cook and stir 5 minutes or until tender. Add asparagus; cook and stir 5 minutes or until tender. Stir in ham, cream, salt and pepper; heat to boiling. Reduce heat and simmer 1 minute.

3. Add hot drained mostaccioli to skillet and toss with sauce. Serve immediately.

Makes 6 to 8 servings

Tip: Asparagus is best cooked the day that it is purchased, but it can be stored in the refrigerator for up to three days. Stand the asparagus in about one inch of water (in a container) and cover it with a plastic bag. Do not wash it until just before you're ready to use it.

Minted Orzo

1 package (12 ounces) orzo*
2 tablespoons chopped fresh mint
2 teaspoons grated lemon peel
    Salt and pepper to taste

*Orzo is a Greek, rice-shaped pasta found in the pasta or specialty aisles in most supermarkets.

Cook orzo in boiling water about 5 minutes. Drain and toss with remaining ingredients.

*Favorite recipe from **American Lamb Council***

Mostaccioli per la Pasqua

Mediterranean Cornish Hens

1 cup UNCLE BEN'S® Instant Rice
¾ cup chopped fresh spinach
¼ cup chopped sun-dried tomatoes in oil, drained
2 Cornish hens, thawed (about 1 pound each)
1 tablespoon butter or margarine, melted
1 clove garlic, minced

1. Heat oven to 425°F. Cook rice according to package directions. Stir in spinach and sun-dried tomatoes; cool.

2. Spoon ½ rice mixture into cavity of each hen. Tie drumsticks together with cotton string. Place hens on rack in roasting pan. Combine butter and garlic; brush each hen with garlic butter.

3. Roast 45 to 50 minutes* or until juices run clear, basting occasionally with drippings.

Makes 2 servings

*If hens weigh over 18 ounces each, roast 60 to 70 minutes.

Tip: Do not store garlic in the refrigerator. Garlic heads will keep up to two months if stored in an open container in a dark, cool place. Unpeeled cloves will keep for up to two weeks.

Garden Ranch Linguine with Chicken

8 ounces linguine, cooked & drained
2 cups cooked mixed vegetables, such as broccoli, cauliflower and bell peppers
2 cups cubed cooked chicken
1 cup prepared HIDDEN VALLEY® The Original Ranch® Dressing
1 tablespoon grated Parmesan cheese

Combine all ingredients except cheese in a large saucepan; toss well. Heat through; sprinkle with cheese before serving.

Makes 4 servings

Baja Fish Tacos

½ cup sour cream
½ cup mayonnaise
¼ cup chopped fresh cilantro
1 package (1.25 ounces) ORTEGA® Taco Seasoning Mix, *divided*
1 pound (about 4) cod or other white fish fillets, cut into 1-inch pieces
2 tablespoons vegetable oil
2 tablespoons lemon juice
1 package (12) ORTEGA® Taco Shells, warmed

Toppings
Shredded cabbage, chopped tomato, lime juice, ORTEGA® Thick & Smooth Taco Sauce

COMBINE sour cream, mayonnaise, cilantro and 2 *tablespoons* seasoning mix in small bowl.

COMBINE cod, vegetable oil, lemon juice and *remaining* seasoning mix in medium bowl; pour into large skillet. Cook, stirring constantly, over medium-high heat for 4 to 5 minutes or until fish flakes easily when tested with fork.

FILL taco shells with fish mixture. Top with sour cream sauce and desired toppings.

Makes 6 servings

Tip: Try a variety of fish and seafood, such as shark, shrimp, crab or lobster, in these fresh-tasting tacos.

Mediterranean Cornish Hen

California Tamale Pie

1 pound ground beef
1 cup yellow cornmeal
2 cups milk
2 eggs, beaten
1 package (1.48 ounces) LAWRY'S® Spices & Seasonings for Chili
2 teaspoons LAWRY'S® Seasoned Salt
1 can (17 ounces) whole kernel corn, drained
1 can (14½ ounces) whole tomatoes, cut up
1 can (2¼ ounces) sliced ripe olives, drained
1 cup (4 ounces) shredded cheddar cheese

In medium skillet, cook ground beef until browned and crumbly; drain fat. In 2½-quart casserole dish, combine cornmeal, milk and eggs; mix well. Add ground beef and remaining ingredients except cheese; stir to mix. Bake, uncovered, in 350°F oven 1 hour and 15 minutes. Add cheese and continue baking until cheese melts. Let stand 10 minutes before serving. *Makes 6 to 8 servings*

Microwave Directions: In 2½-quart glass casserole dish, microwave ground beef on HIGH 5 to 6 minutes; drain fat and crumble beef. Mix in cornmeal, milk and eggs; blend well. Add remaining ingredients except cheese. Cover with plastic wrap, venting one corner. Microwave on HIGH 15 minutes, stirring after 8 minutes. Sprinkle cheese over top and microwave on HIGH 2 minutes. Let stand 10 minutes before serving.

Serving Suggestion: Serve with mixed green salad flavored with kiwi and green onion.

Hint: Substitute 1 package (1.25 ounces) LAWRY'S® Taco Spices & Seasonings for Spices & Seasonings for Chili Seasoning Mix, if desired.

Seafood Marinara with Linguine

1 pound dry linguine
2 tablespoons olive or vegetable oil, divided
1 cup chopped onion
3 large cloves garlic, minced
1 can (14.5 ounces) CONTADINA® Recipe Ready Diced Tomatoes, undrained
1 can (14.5 ounces) chicken broth
1 can (12 ounces) CONTADINA Tomato Paste
½ cup dry red wine or water
1 tablespoon chopped fresh basil *or* 2 teaspoons dried basil leaves, crushed
2 teaspoons chopped fresh oregano *or* ½ teaspoon dried oregano leaves, crushed
1 teaspoon salt
8 ounces fresh or frozen medium shrimp, peeled, deveined
8 ounces fresh or frozen bay scallops

1. Cook pasta according to package directions; drain and keep warm.

2. Meanwhile, heat 1 tablespoon oil in large skillet. Add onion and garlic; sauté for 2 minutes.

3. Add undrained tomatoes, broth, tomato paste, wine, basil, oregano and salt. Bring to a boil. Reduce heat to low; simmer, uncovered, for 10 minutes.

4. Heat remaining oil in small skillet. Add shrimp and scallops; sauté for 3 to 4 minutes or until shrimp turn pink.

5. Add shrimp and scallops to sauce; simmer for 2 to 3 minutes or until heated through. Serve over pasta. *Makes 6 servings*

Prep Time: 12 minutes
Cook Time: 20 minutes

Zesty Mexican Stir-Fry Fajitas

1 pound beef sirloin, flank or round steak, thinly sliced
1 large red bell pepper, thinly sliced
1 medium onion, sliced
1 jar (12 ounces) prepared beef gravy
2 tablespoons *Frank's® RedHot®* Cayenne Pepper Sauce
1 teaspoon garlic powder
1 teaspoon dried oregano leaves
1 teaspoon ground cumin
8 flour tortillas, heated

1. Heat *2 tablespoons oil* in large skillet over high heat until hot. Stir-fry beef in batches 5 minutes or until browned.

2. Add pepper and onion; cook 2 minutes. Add remaining ingredients except tortillas. Stir-fry an additional 2 minutes. Spoon mixture into tortillas; roll up. Splash on more **Frank's RedHot** Sauce to taste.   *Makes 4 servings*

Prep Time: 10 minutes
Cook Time: 10 minutes

Penne with Red Pepper Alfredo Sauce

1 jar (7.25 ounces) roasted red peppers, drained
1 jar (1 pound) RAGÚ® Cheese Creations!® Classic Alfredo Sauce
8 ounces penne or ziti pasta, cooked and drained

1. In blender or food processor, purée roasted peppers.

2. In 2-quart saucepan, heat Ragú Cheese Creations! Sauce over medium heat. Stir in puréed roasted peppers; heat through. Toss with hot pasta and garnish, if desired, with chopped fresh basil leaves.

Makes 4 servings

Prep Time: 10 minutes
Cook Time: 10 minutes

Rice, Cheese & Bean Enchiladas

1 (2-cup) bag UNCLE BEN'S® Boil-in-Bag Rice
4 cups shredded zucchini, drained (2 medium)
1 tablespoon reduced-sodium taco sauce mix
1 can (15 ounces) pinto beans, rinsed and drained
1 can (10 ounces) reduced-fat, reduced-sodium cream of mushroom soup
1 can (8 ounces) diced green chilies
12 (8-inch) flour tortillas
2 cups (8 ounces) reduced-fat Mexican cheese blend, divided

1. Prepare rice following package directions.

2. Combine zucchini and taco sauce mix in large nonstick skillet. Cook and stir zucchini 5 minutes. Add beans, soup, chilies and rice. Bring to a boil.

3. Spray 13×9-inch microwavable baking dish with nonstick cooking spray. Spoon about ½ cup of rice mixture onto center of each tortilla. Top with 2 tablespoons cheese. Roll up to enclose filling; place in baking dish. Sprinkle remaining cheese over enchiladas. Microwave at HIGH 4 minutes or until cheese is melted.   *Makes 6 servings*

Serving Suggestion: Serve with sliced mango or orange sections.

Original Ortega® Taco Recipe

1 pound ground beef
1 package (1.25 ounces) ORTEGA® Taco
  Seasoning Mix
¾ cup water
1 package (12) ORTEGA Taco Shells,
  warmed

Suggested Toppings
  Shredded lettuce, chopped tomatoes,
  shredded cheddar cheese, ORTEGA
  Thick & Smooth Taco Sauce

BROWN beef; drain. Stir in seasoning mix and
water; bring to a boil. Reduce heat to low;
cook, stirring occasionally, for 5 to 6 minutes
or until mixture is thickened.

FILL taco shells with beef mixture. Top with
desired toppings.   *Makes 6 servings*

Fettuccine Carbonara

1 box (12 ounces) fettuccine noodles
1 cup frozen green peas
1 jar (1 pound) RAGÚ® Cheese
  Creations!® Light Parmesan Alfredo
  Sauce
4 slices turkey bacon, crisp-cooked and
  crumbled

1. Cook fettuccine according to package
directions, adding peas during last 2 minutes
of cooking; drain and set aside.

2. In 2-quart saucepan, heat Ragú Cheese
Creations! Sauce over medium heat; stir in
bacon.

3. To serve, toss sauce with hot fettuccine
and peas. Sprinkle, if desired, with ground
black pepper and grated Parmesan cheese.
      Makes 6 servings

Prep Time: 5 minutes
Cook Time: 15 minutes

Italian Sausage and Rice Frittata

 7 large eggs
 ¾ cup milk
 ½ teaspoon salt
 ½ pound mild or hot Italian sausage,
   casing removed and sausage broken
   into small pieces
1½ cups uncooked UNCLE BEN'S® Instant
   Brown Rice
 1 can (14½ ounces) Italian-style stewed
   tomatoes
 ¼ teaspoon Italian herb seasoning
1½ cups (6 ounces) shredded Italian
   cheese blend, divided

1. Whisk together eggs, milk and salt in
medium bowl. Set aside.

2. Preheat oven to 325°F. Cook sausage about
7 minutes in 11-inch ovenproof nonstick
skillet over high heat until no longer pink.

3. Reduce heat to medium-low. Stir in rice,
stewed tomatoes with their juices, breaking up
any large pieces, and Italian seasoning.
Sprinkle evenly with 1 cup cheese.

4. Pour egg mixture into skillet; stir gently to
distribute egg. Cover and cook 15 minutes or
until eggs are just set.

5. Remove from heat. Sprinkle remaining
½ cup cheese over frittata. Bake about
10 minutes or until puffed and cheese is
melted.

6. Remove skillet from oven. Cover and let
stand 5 minutes. Cut into 6 wedges before
serving.   *Makes 6 servings*

Tip: Choose a blend of shredded mozzarella
and provolone for this frittata, or a blend of
your choice.

Original Ortega® Taco Recipe

Greek Lamb Braised with Vegetables

¼ cup FILIPPO BERIO® Olive Oil
2½ pounds lean boneless lamb, cut into 1½-inch cubes
1 cup chicken broth
½ cup dry white wine
2 medium carrots, diagonally cut into 1-inch pieces
2 ribs celery, diagonally cut into 1-inch pieces
½ medium bulb fennel, cut into ¼-inch-thick slices lengthwise through stem
1 (14-ounce) can artichoke hearts, drained and cut into quarters lengthwise
3 green onions, trimmed and cut into 1½-inch pieces
Salt and freshly ground black pepper
8 ounces uncooked orzo pasta
Chopped fresh parsley

In Dutch oven, heat olive oil over medium-high heat until hot. Add lamb; cook and stir 5 minutes or until lightly browned. Add broth and wine; cover. Bring mixture to a boil. Reduce heat to low; simmer 1½ hours. Add carrots, celery, fennel, artichokes and green onions. Simmer 15 to 20 minutes or until lamb and vegetables are tender.

Season to taste with salt and pepper. Meanwhile, cook orzo according to package directions until al dente (tender but still firm). Drain. Serve lamb mixture over orzo. Top with parsley.

Makes 6 servings

Yucatan Snapper

½ cup orange juice
¼ cup lime juice
¼ cup soy sauce
½ teaspoon LAWRY'S® Garlic Powder with Parsley
4 red snapper or halibut fillets (1 to 1½ pounds)
1 tablespoon vegetable oil
½ cup chopped onion
½ cup diced red bell pepper
1 cup diced fresh or canned papaya or mango
⅔ cup diced orange segments
2 teaspoons finely diced jalapeño pepper
1 tablespoon lime juice
1 teaspoon finely chopped cilantro
Orange slices (garnish)
Fresh cilantro (garnish)

In small bowl, combine first four ingredients; mix well. In glass baking dish, place fish. Pour ½ cup marinade over fish. Cover and refrigerate 1 to 6 hours to marinate. In medium skillet, heat oil. Add onion and bell pepper and cook over medium-high heat until tender. Add ½ cup marinade, papaya, oranges, jalapeño, lime juice and cilantro; cook over low heat 5 to 7 minutes. Remove fish from marinade; discard used marinade. Cook fish on grill or bake in oven until fish flakes easily when tested with fork. To serve, arrange fish fillets on plate. Top with papaya citrus salsa.

Makes 4 servings

Serving Suggestion: Garnish with orange slices and fresh cilantro.

Greek Lamb Braised with Vegetables

Chicken Satay

1 pound boneless skinless chicken
    breast halves
1 recipe Peanut Dip (recipe follows),
    divided
    Cucumber slices
    Chopped fresh cilantro

1. Soak 8 (6-inch) bamboo skewers in hot water 20 minutes. Cut chicken lengthwise into 1-inch-wide strips; thread onto skewers.

2. Place skewers in large shallow glass dish. Pour ½ cup Peanut Dip over chicken, turning to coat evenly. Cover and marinate in refrigerator 30 minutes.

3. Place skewers on oiled grid and discard any remaining marinade. Grill over high heat 5 to 8 minutes or until chicken is no longer pink, turning once. Place on serving platter. Serve with cucumber, cilantro and remaining Peanut Dip.

Makes 4 main-dish servings

Prep Time: 15 minutes
Marinate Time: 30 minutes
Cook Time: 5 minutes

Peanut Dip

⅓ cup peanut butter
⅓ cup *French's*® Napa Valley Style Dijon
    Mustard
⅓ cup orange juice
1 tablespoon chopped peeled fresh
    ginger
1 tablespoon honey
1 tablespoon *Frank's*® *RedHot*® Cayenne
    Pepper Sauce
1 tablespoon teriyaki baste and glaze
    sauce
2 cloves garlic, minced

Combine peanut butter, mustard, juice, ginger, honey, **Frank's RedHot** Sauce, teriyaki sauce

and garlic in large bowl. Refrigerate until ready to serve. *Makes 1 cup dip*

Prep Time: 10 minutes

Yucatan Chicken Stir-Fry

4 boneless skinless chicken breast halves
    (about 1½ pounds)
1½ teaspoons olive or vegetable oil
1 tablespoon chili powder
1 bag (16 ounces) BIRDS EYE® frozen
    Farm Fresh Mixtures Broccoli, Corn
    & Red Peppers, thawed
½ cup tomato sauce
1½ teaspoons salt
    Hot cooked rice (optional)

• Cut chicken into strips or chunks.

• In wok or large skillet, heat oil over medium-high heat 2 minutes.

• Meanwhile, coat chicken with chili powder. Add chicken to wok; stir-fry 3 to 5 minutes or until browned.

• Stir in vegetables, tomato sauce and salt. Reduce heat to low; cook 5 to 7 minutes or until vegetables are crisp-tender and chicken is no longer pink in center.

• Serve with rice, if desired.

Makes 4 servings

Prep Time: 10 minutes
Cook Time: 10 to 12 minutes

Chicken Satay with Peanut Dip

Picadillo Chicken

1 broiler-fryer chicken, cut up (about
   3½ pounds)
1½ tablespoons all-purpose flour
½ teaspoon salt
2 tablespoons vegetable oil
1 large onion, coarsely chopped
2 cloves garlic, minced
1 can (14½ ounces) stewed tomatoes
1 can (8 ounces) tomato sauce
⅓ cup raisins
⅓ cup sliced pickled jalapeños, drained
1 teaspoon ground cumin
¼ teaspoon cinnamon
⅓ cup toasted slivered almonds
   Hot cooked rice (optional)
1 cup (4 ounces) SARGENTO® Nacho
   & Taco Blend Shredded Cheese

Rinse chicken; pat dry. Dust with flour and
salt. In large skillet, brown chicken, skin side
down, in hot oil over medium heat, about
5 minutes; turn. Add onion and garlic; cook
5 minutes more. Add stewed tomatoes, tomato
sauce, raisins, jalapeños, cumin and cinnamon;
heat to a boil. Reduce heat; cover and simmer
15 minutes. Uncover and simmer 5 to
10 minutes more or until chicken is tender
and sauce is thickened.* Stir in almonds; serve
over rice. Sprinkle with cheese.

Makes 6 servings

*At this point, chicken may be covered and refrigerated
up to 2 days before serving. Reheat before adding
almonds.*

Calzone Italiano

Pizza dough for one 14-inch pizza
1 can (15 ounces) CONTADINA® Pizza
   Sauce, divided
3 ounces sliced pepperoni *or* ½ pound
   crumbled Italian sausage, cooked,
   drained
2 tablespoons chopped green bell pepper
1 cup (4 ounces) shredded mozzarella
   cheese
1 cup (8 ounces) ricotta cheese

1. Divide dough into 4 equal portions. Place
on lightly floured large, rimless cookie sheet.
Press or roll out dough to 7-inch circles.

2. Spread 2 tablespoons pizza sauce onto half
of each circle to within ½ inch of edge; top
with ¼ each pepperoni, bell pepper and
mozzarella cheese.

3. Spoon ¼ cup ricotta cheese onto
remaining half of each circle; fold dough over.
Press edges together tightly to seal. Cut slits in
top of dough to allow steam to escape.

4. Bake in preheated 350°F oven for 20 to
25 minutes or until crusts are golden brown.
Meanwhile, heat remaining pizza sauce; serve
over calzones.   *Makes 4 servings*

Note: If desired, 1 large calzone may be made
instead of 4 individual calzones. To prepare,
shape dough into 1 (13-inch) circle. Spread
½ cup pizza sauce onto half of dough; proceed
as above. Bake for 25 minutes.

Prep Time: 15 minutes
Cook Time: 25 minutes

Hungarian Goulash Stew

¾ pound lean ground beef (80% lean)
½ cup chopped onion
1 clove garlic, minced
1 package (4.8 ounces) PASTA RONI®
    Angel Hair Pasta with Herbs
1 can (14½ ounces) diced tomatoes,
    undrained
1 cup frozen corn *or* 1 can (8 ounces)
    whole kernel corn, drained
1½ teaspoons paprika
⅛ teaspoon black pepper
    Sour cream (optional)

1. In 3-quart saucepan, brown ground beef, onion and garlic; drain.

2. Add 1⅓ cups water, pasta, Special Seasonings, tomatoes, frozen corn, paprika and black pepper. Bring just to a boil.

3. Reduce heat to medium.

4. Boil uncovered, stirring frequently, 5 to 6 minutes or until pasta is tender.

5. Let stand 3 minutes or until desired consistency. Stir before serving. Serve with sour cream, if desired. *Makes 4 servings*

Layered Mexican Casserole

8 ounces ground beef
1 (12-ounce) can whole kernel corn,
    drained
1 (12-ounce) jar chunky salsa
1 (2¼-ounce) can sliced pitted ripe
    olives, drained
1 cup cream-style cottage cheese
1 (8-ounce) carton dairy sour cream
5 cups tortilla chips (7 to 8 ounces)
2 cups (8 ounces) shredded Wisconsin
    Cheddar cheese, divided
½ cup chopped tomato

Brown ground beef in large skillet; drain. Add corn and salsa; cook until thoroughly heated. Reserve 2 tablespoons olives; stir remaining olives into beef mixture. Combine cottage cheese and sour cream in bowl.

In 2-quart casserole, layer 2 cups chips, half of meat mixture, ¾ cup Cheddar cheese and half of cottage cheese mixture. Repeat layers; cover. Bake in preheated 350°F oven 35 minutes. Line edge of casserole with remaining 1 cup chips; top with tomato, reserved 2 tablespoons olives and remaining ½ cup Cheddar cheese. Bake 10 minutes or until cheese is melted and chips are hot. *Makes 4 to 6 servings*

Favorite recipe from **Wisconsin Milk Marketing Board**

Salsa Chicken & Rice Skillet

1 (6.9-ounce) package RICE-A-RONI® Chicken Flavor
2 tablespoons margarine or butter
1 pound boneless, skinless chicken breasts, cut into 1-inch pieces
1 cup salsa
1 cup frozen or canned corn, drained
1 cup (4 ounces) shredded Cheddar cheese
1 medium tomato, chopped (optional)

1. In large skillet over medium heat, sauté rice-vermicelli mix with margarine until vermicelli is golden brown.

2. Slowly stir in 2 cups water, chicken, salsa and Special Seasonings. Bring to a boil. Reduce heat to low. Cover; simmer 15 minutes.

3. Stir in corn. Cover; simmer 5 minutes or until rice is tender and chicken is no longer pink inside. Top with cheese and tomato, if desired. Cover; let stand 5 minutes for cheese to melt. *Makes 4 servings*

Prep Time: 5 minutes
Cook Time: 30 minutes

Albacore Salad Puttanesca with Garlic Vinaigrette

2 cups cooked angel hair pasta, chilled
2 cups chopped peeled plum tomatoes
1 can (4¼ ounces) chopped* ripe olives, drained
1 cup Garlic Vinaigrette Dressing (recipe follows)
1 (3-ounce) pouch of STARKIST® Premium Albacore Tuna
¼ cup chopped fresh basil leaves

If you prefer, the olives can be sliced rather than chopped.

In large bowl, combine chilled pasta, tomatoes, olives and 1 cup Garlic Vinaigrette Dressing. Add tuna and basil leaves; toss. Serve immediately. *Makes 2 servings*

Garlic Vinaigrette Dressing

⅓ cup red wine vinegar
2 tablespoons lemon juice
1 to 2 cloves garlic, minced or pressed
1 teaspoon freshly ground black pepper
Salt to taste
1 cup olive oil

In small bowl, whisk together vinegar, lemon juice, garlic, pepper and salt. Slowly add oil, whisking continuously, until well blended. Refrigerate leftover dressing.

Prep Time: 10 minutes

Black Bean Sausage Skillet

2 tablespoons olive oil
1 cup chopped red onion
1 cup chopped green bell pepper
1 pound BOB EVANS® Special Seasonings Roll Sausage
3 (15-ounce) cans black beans, undrained
1 teaspoon dried oregano leaves
½ teaspoon garlic powder
¼ teaspoon ground cumin
⅛ teaspoon ground cinnamon
Salt and black pepper to taste
Cooked rice
Flour tortillas, cut into wedges (optional)
Sour cream and salsa for garnish

Heat olive oil in deep skillet; cook and stir onion and bell pepper until tender. Remove from skillet. Crumble sausage into skillet and cook until browned. Drain off any drippings. Return onion and bell pepper to skillet with beans, oregano, garlic, cumin, cinnamon, salt and pepper; simmer 20 minutes. Serve over rice with tortillas, if desired. Garnish with sour cream and salsa. Refrigerate leftovers.

Makes 6 servings

Salsa Chicken & Rice Skillet

Old Naples Style Penne

1 dozen mussels, debearded and well
    scrubbed
1 dozen small clams, well scrubbed
¼ cup water
1 package (16 ounces) BARILLA® Penne
3 tablespoons olive oil
2 large cloves garlic, minced
8 ounces green beans, trimmed and cut
    into 1-inch pieces
2 large ripe tomatoes, seeded and diced
½ teaspoon salt
½ teaspoon pepper

1. Combine mussels, clams and water in large skillet with cover. Cover and cook 3 to 5 minutes over medium-high heat or until shells open. Remove shells and discard. Strain broth to remove sand. Place mussels, clams and strained broth in bowl; set aside. Clean and dry skillet.

2. Cook penne according to package directions; drain.

3. Meanwhile, heat olive oil in same skillet over medium-high heat. Add garlic; cook and stir 30 seconds. Add green beans and strained liquid from clams and mussels; cover and cook 5 minutes, stirring once. Add tomatoes, salt and pepper; cover and cook 6 to 8 minutes or until beans are tender. Add clams and mussels; heat through.

4. Place hot drained penne in serving bowl. Add clam and mussel sauce; toss to coat. Serve immediately. *Makes 6 servings*

Crunchy Layered Beef & Bean Salad

1 pound ground beef or turkey
2 cans (15 to 19 ounces each) black
    beans or pinto beans, rinsed and
    drained
1 can (14½ ounces) stewed tomatoes,
    undrained
1⅓ cups *French's®* French Fried Onions,
    divided
1 tablespoon *Frank's® RedHot®* Cayenne
    Pepper Sauce
1 package (1¼ ounces) taco seasoning
    mix
6 cups shredded lettuce
1 cup (4 ounces) shredded Cheddar or
    Monterey Jack cheese

1. Cook beef in large nonstick skillet over medium heat until thoroughly browned; drain well. Stir in beans, tomatoes, ⅔ cup French Fried Onions, **Frank's RedHot** Sauce and taco seasoning. Heat to boiling. Cook over medium heat 5 minutes, stirring occasionally.

2. Spoon beef mixture over lettuce on serving platter. Top with cheese.

3. Microwave remaining ⅔ cup onions 1 minute on HIGH. Sprinkle over salad.
Makes 6 servings

Prep Time: 10 minutes
Cook Time: 6 minutes

Old Naples Style Penne

Corned Beef and Cabbage with Parsley Dumplings

1 (4-pound) corned beef brisket, rinsed and trimmed
2 tablespoons TABASCO® brand Green Pepper Sauce
1 small green cabbage, coarsely shredded

Parsley Dumplings
    2 cups flour
    1 tablespoon baking powder
    ¼ teaspoon salt
    1 cup milk
    1 egg, beaten
    2 tablespoons chopped fresh parsley
    1 tablespoon butter or margarine, melted
    2 teaspoons TABASCO® brand Green Pepper Sauce

Place corned beef in large saucepan with enough cold water to cover by 2 inches; add TABASCO® Green Pepper Sauce. Heat to boiling over high heat. Reduce heat to low; cover and simmer 2 hours, occasionally skimming surface.

During last 10 minutes of cooking corned beef, add cabbage to cooking liquid; return to boil over high heat. Reduce heat, cover and simmer 10 minutes or until cabbage is tender. Remove corned beef and cabbage to warm serving platter; keep warm. Reserve liquid in saucepan.

For Parsley Dumplings, combine flour, baking powder and salt in large bowl. Whisk milk, egg, parsley, butter and TABASCO® Green Pepper Sauce in small bowl until blended. Stir milk mixture into dry ingredients just until blended. Form dumplings by dropping tablespoonfuls of batter into reserved simmering liquid. Cover and simmer 10 minutes or until dumplings are cooked in center. Using slotted spoon, transfer dumplings to platter with corned beef and cabbage.   *Makes 6 to 8 servings*

Fish Cakes with Thai Salsa

2 cans (14½ ounces each) DEL MONTE® Diced Tomatoes with Garlic & Onion, undrained
¾ cup sliced green onions
1 tablespoon minced ginger root
¼ teaspoon crushed red pepper flakes
⅓ cup chopped cilantro
3½ cups cooked, flaked fish (1¾ to 2 pounds uncooked halibut, salmon or snapper)
2 eggs, beaten
½ cup Italian-seasoned dry bread crumbs
¼ cup mayonnaise
1 to 2 tablespoons butter

1. Combine tomatoes with ½ cup green onions, ginger and red pepper flakes in medium saucepan. Cook, uncovered, over high heat until thickened, stirring occasionally. Stir in cilantro. Cool.

2. Combine fish, eggs, crumbs, mayonnaise, remaining ¼ cup green onions and ⅓ cup tomato salsa mixture in medium bowl. Season with black pepper, if desired. Form into 16 patties.

3. Melt butter in large skillet over high heat. Reduce heat to medium-low; cook patties about 3 minutes on each side or until golden brown on both sides. Serve over salad greens, if desired. Top with salsa. Drizzle with Oriental sesame oil and garnish, if desired.
                    Makes 16 (2½-inch) cakes

Note: To cook fish, place in microwavable dish; cover. Microwave at HIGH 7 to 9 minutes or until fish flakes easily when tested with a fork, rotating twice during cooking; drain.

Prep and Cook Time: 35 minutes

Corned Beef and Cabbage with Parsley Dumplings

Greek Beef & Rice

1 bag SUCCESS® Rice
1 pound lean ground beef
2 medium zucchini, sliced
½ cup chopped onion
1 medium clove garlic, minced
1 can (14½ ounces) tomato sauce
¾ teaspoon dried basil leaves, crushed
¾ teaspoon salt
¼ teaspoon pepper

Prepare rice according to package directions.

Brown beef in large skillet, stirring occasionally to separate beef. Pour off all but 2 tablespoons drippings. Add zucchini, onion and garlic to skillet; cook and stir until crisp-tender. Add all remaining ingredients *except* rice; cover. Simmer 10 minutes, stirring occasionally. Add rice; heat thoroughly, stirring occasionally. Garnish, if desired.   *Makes 6 servings*

Huevos Rancheros Tostados

1 can (8 ounces) tomato sauce
⅓ cup prepared salsa or picante sauce
¼ cup chopped fresh cilantro or thinly
    sliced green onions
4 large eggs
    Butter or margarine
4 (6-inch) corn tortillas, crisply fried,
    or 4 prepared tostada shells
1 cup (4 ounces) SARGENTO® Taco
    Blend Shredded Cheese

Combine tomato sauce, salsa and cilantro; heat in microwave oven or in saucepan over medium-high heat until hot. Fry eggs in butter, sunny side up. Place one egg on each tortilla; top with sauce. Sprinkle with cheese.
          Makes 4 servings

Variation: Spread tortillas with heated refried beans before topping with eggs, if desired.

Thin-Sliced Panzanella

3 tablespoons extra-virgin olive oil
1 garlic clove, pressed or minced
1 package (about 1 pound) PERDUE®
    FIT 'N EASY® Fresh Skinless and
    Boneless Thin-Sliced Chicken Breast
1 teaspoon dried Italian herb seasoning
    Salt and ground pepper to taste
6 ripe Italian plum tomatoes, halved
1 tablespoon balsamic vinegar
10 to 12 fresh basil leaves, divided
8 ounces uncooked fettuccine
2 tablespoons grated Romano cheese
1 large bunch arugula, well rinsed

In small bowl, combine oil and garlic. Remove 2 teaspoons oil mixture and use to rub chicken. Reserve remaining oil mixture. Sprinkle chicken with Italian seasoning, salt and pepper; refrigerate until ready to cook.

Prepare outdoor grill for cooking or preheat broiler. In food processor, combine 1 tablespoon reserved oil mixture, tomatoes, vinegar and half the basil. Pulse on and off to chop tomatoes. Season sauce with salt and pepper and set aside.

Cook pasta according to package directions. Drain and toss with remaining oil mixture, cheese and salt and pepper.

Grill or broil chicken 3 to 6 inches from heat source 1½ to 2 minutes on each side until cooked through. To serve, spoon warm pasta over greens; top with chicken and tomato sauce and garnish with remaining basil leaves.
          Makes 4 servings

Greek Beef & Rice

Pork Tenderloin Mole

1½ pounds pork tenderloin (about 2 whole)
1 teaspoon vegetable oil
½ cup chopped onion
1 clove garlic, minced
1 cup Mexican-style chili beans,
    undrained
¼ cup chili sauce
¼ cup raisins
2 tablespoons water
1 tablespoon peanut butter
1 teaspoon unsweetened cocoa
    Dash each salt, ground cinnamon and
    ground cloves

Place tenderloin in shallow baking pan. Roast at 350°F for 30 minutes or until juicy and slightly pink in center.

Heat oil in medium saucepan. Cook onion and garlic over low heat for 5 minutes. Combine onion and garlic with remaining ingredients in food processor; process until almost smooth. Heat mixture in saucepan thoroughly over low temperature, stirring frequently. Serve over tenderloin slices.   *Makes 6 servings*

*Favorite recipe from **National Pork Board***

Salmon Vera Cruz

1 package UNCLE BEN'S® Long Grain
    & Wild Rice Original Recipe
2⅓ cups water
1 tablespoon margarine (optional)
3 salmon fillets, 6 to 8 ounces each,
    skinned
3 tablespoons honey
3 tablespoons pine nuts, chopped
¾ cup sun dried tomatoes, whole
½ cup green olives, sliced lengthwise
½ cup carrots, julienned
½ cup red onion, diced
1 medium jalapeño pepper, seeded and
    minced
1½ cups fresh spinach, cleaned, stems
    removed

1. In large skillet with cover, combine rice, seasoning, water and margarine. Bring to a boil; reduce heat, and simmer 10 minutes.

2. Combine honey and pine nuts. Coat tops of salmon fillets. Place salmon on rice; recover and simmer 8 minutes. Remove salmon; keep warm.

3. Stir in tomatoes, olives, carrots, onion and jalapeño pepper. Simmer 5 to 7 minutes. Remove from heat; stir in spinach.

4. Replace salmon on top of rice. Let stand 5 minutes. Garnish with chopped cilantro.
    Makes 3 to 4 servings

Preparation Time: 25 minutes

Scandinavian Chicken

3 tablespoons butter
6 boneless skinless chicken thighs, cut
    into 1-inch pieces
1 teaspoon salt
¼ teaspoon black pepper
⅔ cup finely chopped onion
1 cup mushrooms, sliced
¾ cup sour cream
½ cup (2 ounces) shredded Havarti
    cheese
¼ cup plain fresh bread crumbs
2 tablespoons chopped fresh parsley

In large skillet, melt butter over medium-high heat. Add chicken; cook, stirring occasionally, about 7 minutes or until browned. Sprinkle with salt and pepper. Add onion; cook and stir until onion is tender, about 5 minutes. Add mushrooms; cook 5 minutes, stirring occasionally, until chicken is no longer pink in center. Reduce heat to low; stir in sour cream and cheese. Cook until cheese melts, about 2 minutes. Stir in bread crumbs; sprinkle with fresh parsley.   *Makes 4 servings*

*Favorite recipe from **National Chicken Council***

Giardiniera Sauce

1 pound dry pasta
1 tablespoon olive or vegetable oil
2 cups sliced fresh mushrooms
1 cup chopped onion
½ cup sliced green bell pepper
2 cloves garlic, minced
1 can (14.5 ounces) CONTADINA®
    Stewed Tomatoes, undrained
½ cup chicken broth
1 can (6 ounces) CONTADINA Tomato
    Paste
2 teaspoons Italian herb seasoning
½ teaspoon salt (optional)

1. Cook pasta according to package directions; drain and keep warm.

2. Meanwhile, heat oil in large skillet. Add mushrooms, onion, bell pepper and garlic; sauté 3 to 4 minutes or until vegetables are tender.

3. Stir in undrained tomatoes, chicken broth, tomato paste, Italian seasoning and salt, if desired. Bring to a boil.

4. Reduce heat to low; simmer, uncovered, 10 minutes, stirring occasionally. Serve over pasta. *Makes 8 servings*

Prep Time: 8 minutes
Cook Time: 15 minutes

Penne with Sausage and Kalamata Olives

8 ounces uncooked penne pasta
1 pound sweet Italian sausage
½ cup ricotta cheese
1 large tomato, quartered
2 teaspoons TABASCO® brand Pepper
    Sauce
1 teaspoon salt
¼ cup sliced kalamata olives
2 tablespoons chopped fresh parsley

Heat 4 quarts salted water to boiling in large saucepan. Add penne; cook until tender. Drain.

Meanwhile, remove casing from sausage. Cook sausage in 10-inch skillet over medium-high heat until well browned, stirring to crumble. With slotted spoon, remove sausage to paper towels.

Combine ricotta cheese, tomato, TABASCO® Sauce and salt in food processor or blender; process until smooth. Toss penne with sausage, ricotta mixture, olives and chopped parsley in large bowl; mix well. *Makes 4 servings*

Tagliatelle with Creamy Sauce

7 to 8 ounces tagliatelle pasta, cooked,
    drained
1 cup GALBANI® Mascarpone cheese
1 package (10 ounces) frozen peas,
    cooked, drained
2 ounces (½ cup) finely chopped
    GALBANI® Prosciutto di Parma
1½ cups (6 ounces) shredded mozzarella
    cheese
Butter or margarine

Layer ½ of the tagliatelle in buttered 9×9-inch baking dish. Spoon ½ of the Mascarpone onto tagliatelle. Sprinkle with ½ of the peas and ½ of the prosciutto. Top with ½ of the mozzarella. Repeat layers. Dot with butter. Bake in preheated 350°F oven 20 minutes or until heated through.

Makes 4 to 6 servings

Mexican-Style Stuffed Peppers

8 medium green bell peppers, halved and seeded
3 cups cooked long-grain white rice
1 package (10 ounces) frozen peas and carrots
1 cup whole kernel corn
½ cup chopped green onions
1¾ cups ORTEGA® Salsa-Homestyle Recipe, divided
1½ cups 4-cheese Mexican blend, divided

PREHEAT oven to 375°F.

PLACE bell peppers in microwave-safe dish with 3 tablespoons water. Cover with plastic wrap. Microwave on HIGH (100%) power for 4 to 5 minutes or until slightly tender. Drain.

COMBINE rice, peas and carrots, corn, green onions, ¾ cup salsa and 1 cup cheese in large bowl. Fill each pepper with about ½ cup rice mixture. Place peppers in ungreased 13×9×2-inch baking dish; top with remaining salsa and cheese.

BAKE uncovered for 20 to 25 minutes. Uncover; bake for additional 5 minutes or until heated through and cheese is melted.

Makes 8 servings

Zesty Artichoke Pesto Sauce

1 jar (6 ounces) marinated artichoke hearts, chopped, marinade reserved
1 cup sliced onion
1 can (14.5 ounces) CONTADINA® Recipe Ready Diced Tomatoes, undrained
1 can (6 ounces) CONTADINA Italian Paste with Tomato Pesto
1 cup water
½ teaspoon salt
Hot cooked pasta

1. Heat reserved artichoke marinade in large saucepan over medium-high heat until warm.

2. Add onion; cook for 3 to 4 minutes or until tender. Add artichoke hearts, tomatoes and juice, tomato paste, water and salt.

3. Bring to a boil; reduce heat to low. Cook, stirring occasionally, for 10 to 15 minutes or until flavors are blended. Serve over pasta.

Makes 6 to 8 servings

Savory Caper and Olive Sauce:

Eliminate artichoke hearts. Heat 2 tablespoons olive oil in large saucepan over medium-high heat. Add onion; cook for 3 to 4 minutes or until tender. Add tomatoes and juice, tomato paste, water, salt, ¾ cup sliced and quartered zucchini, ½ cup (2¼-ounce can) drained sliced ripe olives and 2 tablespoons capers. Proceed as directed above.

Prep Time: 5 minutes
Cook Time: 19 minutes

Mexican-Style Stuffed Peppers

Spicy Thai Chicken

¾ cup canned cream of coconut
3 tablespoons lime juice
3 tablespoons soy sauce
3 large green onions, cut up
3 large cloves garlic
8 sprigs cilantro
3 anchovy fillets
1 teaspoon TABASCO® brand Pepper
   Sauce
2 whole boneless skinless chicken breasts,
   cut in half (about 1½ pounds)

Combine cream of coconut, lime juice, soy sauce, green onions, garlic, cilantro, anchovies and TABASCO® Sauce in container of blender or food processor. Cover; blend until smooth. Place chicken in large shallow dish or plastic bag; add marinade. Cover; refrigerate at least 2 hours, turning chicken occasionally.

Remove chicken from marinade; reserve marinade. Place chicken on grill about 5 inches from source of heat. Brush generously with marinade. Grill 5 minutes. Turn chicken; brush with marinade. Grill 5 minutes longer or until chicken is cooked. Heat any remaining marinade to a boil; boil 1 minute. Serve as a dipping sauce for chicken.

Makes 4 servings

Mexican Beef Stir-Fry

1 pound beef flank steak
2 tablespoons vegetable oil
1 teaspoon ground cumin
1 teaspoon dried oregano leaves
1 clove garlic, crushed
1 red or green bell pepper, cut into thin
   strips
1 medium onion, cut into thin wedges
1 to 2 jalapeño peppers,* thinly sliced
3 cups thinly sliced lettuce

Remove interior ribs and seeds if a milder flavor is desired. Jalapeño peppers can sting and irritate the skin; wear rubber gloves when handling peppers and do not touch eyes. Wash hands after handling peppers.

Cut beef steak into ⅛-inch-thick strips. Combine oil, cumin, oregano and garlic in small bowl. Heat ½ oil mixture in large nonstick skillet over medium-high heat. Add bell pepper, onion and jalapeño pepper; stir-fry 2 to 3 minutes or until crisp-tender. Remove and reserve. In same skillet, stir-fry beef strips (½ at a time) in remaining oil mixture 1 to 2 minutes. Return vegetables to skillet and heat through. Serve beef mixture over lettuce. *Makes 4 servings*

Tip: Recipe may also be prepared using beef top sirloin or top round steak cut 1 inch thick.

Serving Suggestion: Serve with corn bread.

Favorite recipe from **North Dakota Beef Commission**

Grilled Vegetable Rigatoni

8 ounces BARILLA® Rigatoni
1 medium eggplant, cut into large pieces
   for grilling
1 large zucchini, cut into large pieces for
   grilling
1 large yellow onion, peeled and cut into
   ½-inch slices
2 tablespoons olive or vegetable oil
1 jar (26 ounces) BARILLA® Mushroom
   and Garlic Pasta Sauce
   Grated Parmesan and Romano cheese
   blend

1. Cook rigatoni according to package directions; drain.

2. Meanwhile, brush eggplant, zucchini and onion with oil. Grill vegetables until crisp-tender. Coarsely chop vegetables.

3. Heat pasta sauce in saucepan; stir occasionally. Pour sauce over hot drained rigatoni; top with grilled vegetables. Serve with cheese. *Makes 6 to 8 servings*

Pasta Primavera

2 tablespoons butter or margarine
1 medium onion, finely chopped
1 clove garlic, minced
¾ pound asparagus, cut diagonally into 1½-inch pieces
½ pound fresh mushrooms, sliced
1 medium zucchini, sliced
1 carrot, sliced
1 cup half-and-half or light cream
½ cup chicken broth
1 tablespoon all-purpose flour
2 teaspoons dried basil leaves, crushed
1 pound uncooked fettuccine
¾ cup (3 ounces) SARGENTO® Parmesan & Romano Blend Shredded Cheese

In large skillet over medium heat, melt butter. Add onion and garlic; cook and stir until onion is tender. Add asparagus, mushrooms, zucchini and carrot; cook, stirring constantly, 2 minutes. Increase heat to high. Combine half-and-half, broth, flour and basil in small bowl; add to skillet. Bring mixture to a boil. Boil, stirring occasionally, until thickened.

Meanwhile, cook fettuccine according to package directions; drain. In serving bowl, place hot fettuccine, sauce and cheese; toss gently.   *Makes 8 servings*

Mediterranean Shrimp & Vegetable Linguine

1 pound uncooked medium shrimp, peeled and deveined
3 teaspoons BERTOLLI® Olive Oil
1 medium onion, finely chopped
1 large carrot, finely chopped
1 jar (1 pound 10 ounces) RAGÚ® Light Pasta Sauce
1 box (16 ounces) linguine, cooked and drained

1. Season shrimp, if desired, with salt and ground black pepper. In 12-inch skillet, heat 2 teaspoons oil over medium-high heat and cook shrimp, stirring occasionally, 3 minutes or until almost pink. Remove shrimp and set aside.

2. In same skillet, heat remaining 1 teaspoon oil over medium-high heat and cook onion and carrot, stirring occasionally, 5 minutes or until vegetables are tender.

3. Stir in Ragú Pasta Sauce and bring to a boil over high heat. Reduce heat to low and simmer 5 minutes. Return shrimp to skillet and simmer until shrimp turn pink. Serve over hot linguine.   *Makes 6 servings*

Prep Time: 15 minutes
Cook Time: 15 minutes

Smothered Mexican Pork Chops

1 tablespoon vegetable oil
4 boneless thin-cut pork chops (about ¾ pound)
1 can (14½ ounces) chunky tomatoes, salsa- or Cajun-style
1 can (16 ounces) black beans, drained
2 cups BIRDS EYE® frozen Farm Fresh Mixtures Broccoli, Corn and Red Peppers*

Or, substitute 2 cups Birds Eye® frozen Corn.

• Heat oil in large skillet over high heat. Add pork; cook until browned, about 4 minutes per side.

• Add tomatoes; reduce heat to medium. Cover and cook 5 minutes. Uncover and push pork to side of skillet.

• Add beans and vegetables. Place pork on top of vegetables. Increase heat to medium-high; cover and cook 5 minutes or until heated through.   *Makes about 4 servings*

Prep Time: 5 minutes
Cook Time: 20 minutes

Thai Stir Fry

1 package BUTTERBALL® Chicken
    Breast Tenders
1 tablespoon oil
½ cup red and yellow bell pepper strips
1 clove garlic, minced
1 tablespoon chopped fresh cilantro
1 teaspoon grated fresh ginger
2 tablespoons reduced sodium soy sauce
1 teaspoon brown sugar

Heat oil in large skillet over medium heat until hot. Cook and stir chicken about 6 minutes on each side or until golden brown. Add bell peppers, garlic, cilantro, ginger, soy sauce and brown sugar to skillet. Reduce heat to low; cover and simmer 4 minutes longer. Serve over rice or lo mein noodles, if desired.

Makes 4 servings

Preparation Time: 15 minutes

Mexicali Cornbread Casserole

2½ cups frozen mixed vegetables, thawed
1½ cups cubed HILLSHIRE FARM® Ham
1 package (10 ounces) cornbread
    stuffing mix
2 cups milk
3 eggs, lightly beaten
  Salt and black pepper to taste
½ cup (2 ounces) shredded taco-flavored
  cheese

Preheat oven to 375°F.

Combine mixed vegetables, Ham and stuffing mix in small casserole; set aside. Combine milk, eggs, salt and pepper in medium bowl; pour over ham mixture. Bake, covered, 45 minutes. Top with cheese; bake, uncovered, 3 minutes or until cheese is melted.

Makes 4 servings

Cellentani, Italian Sausage and Mushrooms in Tomato-Gorgonzola Sauce

1 package (16 ounces) BARILLA®
    Cellentani
1 small onion, minced
2 tablespoons minced garlic
2 tablespoons olive oil
12 ounces bulk Italian sausage
1½ cups (3 ounces) assorted fresh
    mushrooms, quartered
1 medium tomato, chopped
¾ cup red, green and yellow bell
    peppers, finely chopped
1 jar (26 ounces) BARILLA® Spicy
    Pepper Tomato Pasta Sauce
½ cup frozen peas
¼ cup heavy whipping cream
¼ cup red wine
1 tablespoon dried Italian seasoning
½ cup (3 ounces) crumbled Gorgonzola
    cheese

1. Cook cellentani according to package directions; drain.

2. Meanwhile, cook onion and garlic in olive oil in large skillet over medium heat until onion is transparent; do not let garlic brown. Add sausage; cook until no longer pink, stirring to break up sausage. Drain off excess fat from skillet. Add mushrooms, tomato and bell peppers; cook and stir 2 minutes. Stir in pasta sauce, peas, cream, wine and Italian seasoning. Add Gorgonzola; cook and stir 4 minutes.

3. Combine sauce with hot drained cellentani. Cover and let stand 1 minute.

Makes 8 servings

Thai Stir Fry

Grilled Panini Sandwiches

8 slices country Italian, sourdough or
  other firm-textured bread
8 slices SARGENTO® Deli Style Sliced
  Mozzarella Cheese
⅓ cup prepared pesto
4 large slices ripe tomato
2 tablespoons olive oil

1. Top each of 4 slices of bread with a slice of
cheese. Spread pesto over cheese. Arrange
tomatoes on top, then remaining slices of
cheese. Close sandwiches with remaining
4 slices bread.

2. Brush olive oil lightly over both sides of
sandwiches. Cook sandwiches over medium-
low coals or in a preheated ridged grill pan
over medium heat 3 to 4 minutes per side or
until bread is toasted and cheese is melted.

Makes 4 servings

Preparation Time: 5 minutes
Cooking Time: 8 minutes

Polish Reuben Casserole

2 (10-ounce) cans cream of mushroom
  soup
1⅓ cups milk
½ cup chopped onion
1 tablespoon prepared mustard
2 (16-ounce) cans sauerkraut, rinsed and
  drained
1 (8-ounce) package uncooked, medium-
  width noodles
1½ pounds Polish sausage, cut into ½-inch
  pieces*
2 cups (8 ounces) shredded Swiss
  cheese
¾ cup whole wheat bread crumbs
2 tablespoons butter, melted

*Country-style sausage can be substituted.

In a bowl, mix soup, milk, onion and mustard
until blended. Spread sauerkraut in a greased
13×9-inch baking dish. Top with uncooked
noodles. Spoon soup mixture evenly over
noodles. Sprinkle with sausage, then cheese. In
a small bowl, stir together crumbs and melted
butter; sprinkle over cheese layer. Cover tightly
with foil. Bake at 350°F for 1 hour or until
noodles are tender.

Makes 8 to 10 servings

Favorite recipe from **North Dakota Wheat Commission**

Quick Mediterranean Fish

1 medium onion, sliced
2 tablespoons olive oil
1 clove garlic, crushed
1 can (14½ ounces) DEL MONTE®
  Stewed Tomatoes - Italian Recipe
3 to 4 tablespoons medium salsa
¼ teaspoon ground cinnamon
1½ pounds firm fish (such as halibut, red
  snapper or sea bass)
12 stuffed green olives, halved crosswise

Microwave Directions

1. Combine onion, oil and garlic in 1½-quart
microwavable dish. Cover and microwave on
HIGH 3 minutes; drain.

2. Stir in tomatoes, salsa and cinnamon. Top
with fish and olives.

3. Cover and microwave on HIGH 3 to
4 minutes or until fish flakes easily with fork.
Garnish with chopped parsley, if desired.

Makes 4 to 6 servings

Prep Time: 7 minutes
Microwave Cook Time: 7 minutes

Grilled Panini Sandwich

Angel Hair Al Fresco

¾ cup skim milk
1 tablespoon margarine or butter
1 package (4.8 ounces) PASTA RONI®
  Angel Hair Pasta with Herbs
1 can (6⅛ ounces) white tuna in water,
  drained, flaked *or* 1½ cups chopped
  cooked chicken
2 medium tomatoes, chopped
⅓ cup sliced green onions
¼ cup dry white wine or water
¼ cup slivered almonds, toasted
  (optional)
1 tablespoon chopped fresh basil *or*
  1 teaspoon dried basil

1. In 3-quart saucepan, combine 1⅓ cups water, skim milk and margarine. Bring just to a boil.

2. Stir in pasta, Special Seasonings, tuna, tomatoes, onions, wine, almonds and basil. Return to a boil; reduce heat to medium.

3. Boil uncovered, stirring frequently, 6 to 8 minutes. Sauce will be thin, but will thicken upon standing.

4. Let stand 3 minutes or until desired consistency. Stir before serving.

Makes 4 servings

Simply Delicious Pasta Primavera

¼ cup margarine or butter
1 envelope LIPTON® RECIPE SECRETS®
  Vegetable Soup Mix
1½ cups milk
8 ounces linguine or spaghetti, cooked
  and drained
¼ cup grated Parmesan cheese (about
  1 ounce)

1. In medium saucepan, melt margarine over medium heat and stir in soup mix and milk. Bring just to a boil over high heat.

2. Reduce heat to low and simmer uncovered, stirring occasionally, 10 minutes or until vegetables are tender. Toss hot linguine with sauce and Parmesan cheese.

Makes 4 servings

Prep Time: 5 minutes
Cook Time: 12 minutes

Poached Seafood Italiano

1 tablespoon olive or vegetable oil
1 large clove garlic, minced
¼ cup dry white wine or chicken broth
4 (6-ounce) salmon steaks or fillets
1 can (14.5 ounces) CONTADINA®
  Recipe Ready Diced Tomatoes with
  Italian Herbs, undrained
2 tablespoons chopped fresh basil
  (optional)

1. Heat oil in large skillet. Add garlic; sauté 30 seconds. Add wine. Bring to boil.

2. Add salmon; cover. Reduce heat to medium; simmer 6 minutes.

3. Add undrained tomatoes; simmer 2 minutes or until salmon flakes easily when tested with fork. Sprinkle with basil just before serving, if desired. *Makes 4 servings*

Chicken and Vegetable Ragoût

  2 tablespoons olive or vegetable oil
½ cup chopped onion
  3 cloves garlic, minced
  1 pound (about 4) boneless, skinless
     chicken breast halves, cut into
     ½-inch pieces
  1 cup water or chicken broth
  1 can (14.5 ounces) CONTADINA®
     Recipe Ready Diced Tomatoes,
     undrained
  1 can (6 ounces) CONTADINA Italian
     Paste with Italian Seasonings
  1 cup sliced peeled carrots
  1 cup halved zucchini slices
  1 cup red or green bell pepper strips
  1 teaspoon Italian herb seasoning
½ teaspoon salt
⅛ teaspoon ground black pepper

1. Heat oil in large skillet. Add onion and garlic; sauté until tender. Add chicken; cook until browned, stirring frequently.

2. Add water, undrained tomatoes, tomato paste and carrots; cover. Simmer for 10 minutes.

3. Add zucchini, bell pepper, Italian seasoning, salt and pepper; cover.

4. Simmer for 15 to 20 minutes or until chicken is no longer pink in center and vegetables are tender. Serve over hot cooked rice or pasta, if desired.   *Makes 6 servings*

Prep Time: 15 minutes
Cook Time: 36 minutes

Pasta with Shrimp, Broccoli and Red Pepper

  8 ounces uncooked capellini, linguine or
     thin spaghetti
  2 tablespoons FILIPPO BERIO® Olive
     Oil
  1 medium onion, finely chopped
  1 clove garlic, minced
  1 bunch fresh broccoli, trimmed and
     separated into florets
½ cup chicken broth
  8 ounces cooked, peeled and deveined
     shrimp
  1 red bell pepper, seeded and thinly
     sliced
  2 tablespoons chopped fresh Italian
     parsley
  1 fresh jalapeño pepper, seeded and
     minced
     Salt and freshly ground black pepper

Cook pasta according to package directions until al dente (tender but still firm). Drain. Meanwhile, in large saucepan or Dutch oven, heat olive oil over medium heat until hot. Add onion and garlic; cook and stir 5 minutes or until onion is tender. Add broccoli and chicken broth. Cover; reduce heat to low. Simmer 8 to 10 minutes or until broccoli is tender-crisp. Add shrimp, bell pepper, parsley and jalapeño pepper; stir occasionally until heated through. Add pasta to broccoli mixture; toss until lightly coated. Season to taste with salt and black pepper.   *Makes 4 servings*

Grecian Lamb Kabobs

1 cup dry white wine
¼ cup olive oil
24 bay leaves
12 pieces lemon peel, about 3 inches, cut
    in half
2 medium onions, peeled, cut into
    9 wedges and wedges cut in half
½ teaspoon salt
¼ teaspoon black pepper
2 pounds boneless leg of American lamb,
    cut into 1-inch cubes
12 cherry tomatoes
2 green bell peppers, cut into 12 pieces,
    cut pieces in half
    Minted orzo (recipe follows)

Combine wine, olive oil, bay leaves, lemon peel, onions, salt and black pepper in large bowl. Pour into large resealable plastic food storage bag. Add lamb to marinade. Marinate overnight; turn lamb once.

Alternate lamb, bay leaves and lemon peel on skewers. On separate skewers, alternate bell peppers and onions; brush kabobs with marinade.

Boil remaining marinade 1 minute. Broil lamb kabobs and vegetable kabobs 5 to 7 minutes on each side. Add tomato to end of each lamb kabob during last 3 minutes of cooking. Baste with marinade throughout cooking. Serve with Minted Orzo. *Makes 6 servings*

Minted Orzo

1 package (12 ounces) orzo*
2 tablespoons chopped fresh mint
2 teaspoons grated lemon peel
    Salt and pepper to taste

Orzo is a Greek, rice-shaped pasta found in the pasta or specialty aisles in most supermarkets.

Cook orzo in boiling water about 5 minutes. Drain and toss with remaining ingredients.

*Favorite recipe from **American Lamb Council***

Sicilian Skillet Chicken

4 boneless, skinless chicken breast
    halves
6 tablespoons grated Parmesan cheese
3 tablespoons all-purpose flour
2 tablespoons olive oil
1 cup sliced mushrooms
½ medium onion, finely chopped
½ teaspoon dried rosemary, crushed
1 can (14½ ounces) DEL MONTE®
    Diced Tomatoes with Basil, Garlic
    & Oregano

1. Slightly flatten each chicken breast. Coat breasts with 4 tablespoons cheese and then flour. Season with salt and pepper, if desired.

2. Heat oil in large skillet over medium-high heat. Cook chicken until no longer pink, turning once. Remove to serving dish; keep warm.

3. Cook mushrooms, onion and rosemary in same skillet until tender. Add tomatoes; cook, uncovered, over medium-high heat until thickened.

4. Spoon sauce over chicken; top with remaining 2 tablespoons cheese. Serve with pasta and garnish with chopped parsley, if desired. *Makes 4 servings*

Prep Time: 5 minutes
Cook Time: 25 minutes

Grecian Lamb Kabobs

Pasta Fagioli

1 jar (1 pound 10 ounces) RAGÚ®
  Chunky Gardenstyle Pasta Sauce
1 can (19 ounces) white kidney beans,
  rinsed and drained
1 box (10 ounces) frozen chopped
  spinach, thawed
8 ounces ditalini pasta, cooked and
  drained (reserve 2 cups pasta water)

1. In 6-quart saucepot, combine Ragú Pasta
Sauce, beans, spinach, pasta and reserved
pasta water; heat through.

2. Season, if desired, with salt, ground black
pepper and grated Parmesan cheese.

Makes 4 servings

Prep Time: 10 minutes
Cook Time: 10 minutes

Roasted Red Pepper, Corn & Garbanzo Bean Salad

2 cans (15 ounces each) garbanzo beans
1 jar (16 ounces) GUILTLESS
  GOURMET® Roasted Red Pepper
  Salsa
1 cup frozen whole kernel corn, thawed
  and drained
2 green onions, thinly sliced
8 lettuce leaves
  Fresh tomato wedges and sunflower
  sprouts (optional)

Rinse and drain beans well; place in 2-quart
casserole dish. Add roasted red pepper salsa,
corn and onions; stir to combine. Cover and
refrigerate 1 hour or up to 24 hours.

To serve, line serving platter with lettuce.
Spoon bean mixture over top. Garnish with
tomatoes and sprouts, if desired.

Makes 8 servings

Chicken Paprikash

2 tablespoons CRISCO® Oil*
1 broiler-fryer, skin removed and cut
  into pieces (about 2½ pounds)
1 medium green bell pepper, chopped
1 medium onion, chopped
1 tablespoon *plus* 1¼ teaspoons paprika
2 cups chicken broth
2 to 3 parsley sprigs
1 container (16 ounces) nonfat sour
  cream alternative
1 tablespoon all-purpose flour
4 cups hot cooked noodles
  Salt and pepper (optional)

*Use your favorite Crisco Oil product.

1. Heat oil in large deep skillet on medium
heat. Add chicken. Cook until browned on all
sides. Remove chicken from skillet.

2. Add green pepper and onion to skillet.
Cook and stir until tender. Stir in paprika.
Cook one minute.

3. Return chicken to skillet. Add broth and
parsley. Reduce heat to low. Cover. Simmer
20 minutes or until chicken is no longer pink
in center, adding water as necessary. Remove
from heat. Remove chicken from skillet.

4. Combine "sour cream" and flour in small
bowl. Stir into hot broth in skillet. Place small
amount of "sour cream" mixture in food
processor or blender. Process until smooth.
Pour into small bowl. Repeat with remaining
"sour cream" mixture. Return chicken and
"sour cream" mixture to skillet. Heat
thoroughly, stirring occasionally. Serve over hot
noodles. Season with salt and pepper and
garnish, if desired. *Makes 4 servings*

Pasta Fagioli

Chicken and Black Bean Enchiladas

2 jars (16 ounces each) mild picante sauce

¼ cup chopped fresh cilantro

2 tablespoons chili powder

1 teaspoon ground cumin

2 cups (10 ounces) chopped cooked chicken

1 can (15 ounces) black beans, drained and rinsed

1⅓ cups *French's®* French Fried Onions, divided

1 package (about 10 ounces) flour tortillas (7 inches)

1 cup (4 ounces) shredded Monterey Jack cheese with jalapeño peppers

Preheat oven to 350°F. Grease 15×10-inch jelly-roll baking pan. Combine picante sauce, cilantro, chili powder and cumin in large saucepan. Bring to a boil. Reduce heat to low; simmer 5 minutes.

Combine 1½ cups sauce mixture, chicken, beans and ⅔ *cup* French Fried Onions in medium bowl. Spoon a scant ½ cup filling over bottom third of each tortilla. Roll up tortillas, enclosing filling, and arrange, seam-side down, in a single layer in bottom of prepared baking pan. Spoon remaining sauce evenly over tortillas.

Bake, uncovered, 20 minutes or until heated through. Sprinkle with remaining ⅔ *cup* onions and cheese. Bake 5 minutes or until cheese is melted and onions are golden. Serve immediately.

*Makes 5 to 6 servings
(4 cups sauce, 4½ cups filling)*

Tip: This is a great make-ahead party dish.

Prep Time: 45 minutes
Cook Time: 25 minutes

Angel Hair with Roasted Red Pepper Sauce

1 package (16 ounces) BARILLA® Angel Hair

1 jar (12 ounces) roasted red peppers with juice, divided

1 tablespoon olive or vegetable oil

3 cloves garlic, minced

2 cups heavy cream

1½ teaspoons salt

1 teaspoon pepper

½ cup (2 ounces) grated Romano cheese, divided

3 tablespoons fresh basil leaves, cut into thin strips (optional)

1. Cook angel hair according to package directions; drain.

2. Meanwhile, chop ¼ cup roasted peppers; set aside. Purée remaining peppers and juice in food processor or blender.

3. Heat oil in large nonstick skillet. Add garlic; cook and stir 2 minutes over medium-low heat. Add pepper purée, cream, salt and pepper; cook over medium heat, stirring frequently, about 6 minutes or until hot and bubbly. Stir in ¼ cup cheese.

4. Combine hot drained angel hair with pepper mixture. Top with reserved chopped peppers, ¼ cup cheese and basil, if desired.

Makes 6 to 8 servings

*Chicken and Black Bean
Enchiladas*

Stuffed Pork Loin Genoa Style

1 (4- to 5-pound) boneless pork loin
    roast
1¼ cups fresh parsley, chopped and
    divided
½ cup fresh basil leaves, chopped
½ cup pine nuts
½ cup grated Parmesan cheese
6 cloves garlic, peeled and chopped
½ pound ground pork
½ pound Italian sausage
1 cup dry bread crumbs
¼ cup milk
1 egg
1 teaspoon ground black pepper

In food processor or blender, blend 1 cup
parsley, basil, pine nuts, Parmesan cheese and
garlic. Set aside.

Mix together ground pork, Italian sausage,
bread crumbs, milk, egg, remaining ¼ cup
parsley and pepper.

Place roast fat-side down on cutting board.
Spread with the herb-cheese mixture; place
ground pork mixture along center of loin. Fold
in half; tie with kitchen string. Roast on rack
in shallow baking pan at 350°F for 1½ hours
or until internal temperature reaches 155°F.
Slice to serve.   *Makes 10 servings*

Prep Time: 15 minutes
Cook Time: 90 minutes

Favorite recipe from **National Pork Board**

Greens and Gemelli

8 ounces BARILLA® Gemelli
1 tablespoon olive oil
1 bag (10 ounces) spinach, washed and
    trimmed
1 jar (26 ounces) BARILLA® Green
    & Black Olive Pasta Sauce
8 ounces Italian sausage, cooked and
    crumbled
¼ cup crumbled feta cheese

1. Cook gemelli according to package
directions; drain.

2. Meanwhile, add olive oil to large skillet.
Add spinach; cook and stir 1 minute over
medium-high heat.

3. Reduce heat; stir in pasta sauce and
cooked sausage. Cook 5 minutes.

4. Pour sauce over hot drained gemelli;
sprinkle with cheese.

Makes 4 to 6 servings

Penne with Fresh Herb Tomato Sauce

1 pound uncooked penne pasta
4 ripe large tomatoes, peeled and
    seeded*
½ cup tomato sauce
¼ cup FILIPPO BERIO® Olive Oil
1 to 2 tablespoons lemon juice
2 teaspoons minced fresh parsley *or*
    1 teaspoon dried parsley
1 teaspoon minced fresh rosemary,
    oregano or thyme *or* 1 teaspoon
    dried Italian seasoning
Salt and freshly ground black pepper
Shavings of Parmesan cheese

**For chunkier sauce, reserve 1 peeled, seeded tomato.
Finely chop; stir into sauce.*

Cook pasta according to package directions
until al dente (tender but still firm). Drain;
transfer to large bowl. Process tomatoes in
blender container or food processor until
smooth. Add tomato sauce. While machine is
running, very slowly add olive oil. Add lemon
juice, parsley and herbs. Process briefly at high
speed. Spoon sauce over hot or room
temperature pasta. Season to taste with salt
and pepper. Top with cheese.

Makes 4 servings

Stuffed Pork Loin Genoa Style

Portofino Primavera

1 pound dry pasta
2 tablespoons olive oil
1 small onion, chopped
1 large clove garlic, minced
1 can (14.5 ounces) CONTADINA®
    Recipe Ready Diced Tomatoes,
    undrained
1 can (6 ounces) CONTADINA Tomato
    Paste
1 cup chicken broth or water
1 cup quartered sliced zucchini
½ cup sliced pitted ripe olives, drained
2 tablespoons capers
½ teaspoon salt

1. Cook pasta according to package directions; drain and keep warm.

2. Heat oil in medium saucepan. Add onion and garlic; sauté for 1 minute.

3. Add undrained tomatoes, tomato paste, broth, zucchini, olives, capers and salt.

4. Bring to a boil. Reduce heat to low; simmer, uncovered, for 15 to 20 minutes or until heated through. Serve over pasta.

Makes 8 servings

Prep Time: 6 minutes
Cook Time: 22 minutes

Florentine Strata

8 ounces BARILLA® Spaghetti or
    Linguine
1 jar (26 ounces) BARILLA® Roasted
    Garlic and Onion Pasta Sauce,
    divided
1 package (12 ounces) frozen spinach
    soufflé, thawed
2 cups (8 ounces) shredded mozzarella
    cheese, divided
¼ cup (1 ounce) grated Parmesan cheese,
    divided

1. Cook spaghetti according to package directions until partially done but still firm, 5 to 8 minutes. Drain.

2. Meanwhile, coat microwave-safe 13×9×2-inch baking dish with nonstick cooking spray. Pour 1½ cups pasta sauce into baking dish; top with half of drained spaghetti, half of spinach soufflé, 1 cup mozzarella cheese and 2 tablespoons Parmesan. Repeat layers of spaghetti, pasta sauce and cheeses.

3. Cover with plastic wrap and microwave on HIGH, turning every 4 minutes, until strata is bubbly and cheese is melted, 8 to 10 minutes. Let stand 3 minutes before serving.

Makes 8 servings

Tip: When preparing pasta that will be used in a casserole, it's important to reduce the suggested cooking time on the package by about one third. The pasta will continue to cook and absorb liquid while the casserole is cooking.

Citrus Chicken and Bell Pepper Fajitas

1 teaspoon CRISCO® Oil*
4 boneless, skinless chicken breast halves, cut into strips (about 1 pound)
2 medium green bell peppers, cut into strips
1 large onion, cut into 1-inch pieces
2 cloves garlic, minced
½ cup fresh lime juice
1 teaspoon ground cumin
1 teaspoon dried oregano leaves
⅛ teaspoon black pepper
8 (7- to 8-inch) flour tortillas
   Salt (optional)
½ cup salsa
¼ cup chopped green onions with tops

Use your favorite Crisco Oil product.

1. Heat oil in large skillet on medium-high heat. Add chicken, green peppers, onion and garlic. Cook and stir 2 minutes.

2. Reduce heat to low. Add lime juice, cumin, oregano and black pepper. Simmer 7 minutes or until chicken is no longer pink in center.

3. Warm tortillas, 15 seconds per side, in nonstick skillet on medium heat. Place on serving plate. Use slotted spoon to transfer chicken mixture to tortillas. Season with salt, if desired. Top with salsa and green onions. Fold up bottom, then fold in sides to enclose.

Makes 4 servings

Skillet Chicken Alfredo

4 boneless, skinless chicken breast halves (about 1¼ pounds)
1 egg, lightly beaten
½ cup Italian seasoned dry bread crumbs
2 tablespoons olive oil
1 jar (1 pound) RAGÚ® Cheese Creations!® Classic Alfredo Sauce
1 small tomato, cut into 4 slices
4 slices mozzarella cheese or ½ cup shredded mozzarella cheese (about 2 ounces)

1. Dip chicken in egg, then bread crumbs. In 12-inch nonstick skillet, heat oil over medium-high heat and lightly brown chicken. Remove chicken and set aside.

2. In same skillet, stir in Ragú Cheese Creations! Sauce and bring to a boil. Reduce heat to low. Return chicken to skillet; arrange 1 tomato slice on each chicken breast half. Cover and simmer 5 minutes.

3. Evenly top chicken with cheese and simmer, covered, an additional 2 minutes or until chicken is thoroughly cooked. Serve, if desired, over hot cooked pasta and garnish with chopped fresh basil or parsley.

Makes 4 servings

Prep Time: 5 minutes
Cook Time: 25 minutes

Hot Mediterranean Chicken Salad

4 cups chicken broth
6 boneless skinless chicken breast halves
⅓ cup FILIPPO BERIO® Extra Virgin Olive Oil
1 medium onion, cut into thin strips
1 clove garlic, crushed
1 tablespoon chopped fresh oregano *or* 1½ teaspoons dried oregano leaves
1 cup cooked small green beans
1 cup quartered cherry tomatoes
¾ cup pitted ripe olives
2 teaspoons grated lemon peel
1 to 2 tablespoons white wine vinegar
Juice of 1 lemon
Salt and freshly ground black pepper
6 cups finely shredded lettuce
Additional lemon juice
Chopped fresh parsley

In large saucepan or Dutch oven, bring chicken broth to a boil over high heat. Add chicken. Cover; reduce heat to low and simmer about 20 minutes or until chicken is no longer pink in center. Drain; let cool slightly. Coarsely chop.

In large skillet, heat olive oil over medium heat until hot. Add onion and garlic; cook and stir 5 minutes. Sprinkle with oregano; cook and stir an additional 5 to 10 minutes or until onion is almost transparent. Add green beans, tomatoes, olives and lemon peel; cook and stir until heated through. Add chicken. Season to taste with vinegar, juice of 1 lemon, salt and pepper. Heat briefly.

In large bowl, toss lettuce with additional lemon juice. Season to taste with salt and pepper. Divide equally among 6 plates. Spoon hot chicken salad over lettuce; garnish with parsley. *Makes 6 servings*

Italian Stir-Fried Lamb

12 ounces boneless American lamb, leg or sirloin, thinly bias-sliced into strips about 3 inches long
¾ cup chicken broth
¼ cup dry white wine or water
2 tablespoons pesto
4 teaspoons cornstarch
½ teaspoon dried oregano leaves
1 tablespoon vegetable oil
1 (9-ounce) package frozen Italian-style green beans, thawed
½ cup thinly sliced carrots
1 cup sliced fresh mushrooms
1 cup cherry tomato halves
4 ounces linguine or fettuccine, cooked
2 tablespoons grated Parmesan cheese

In small bowl, stir together chicken broth, wine, pesto, cornstarch and oregano; set aside. Preheat wok or large skillet over high heat; add oil. Stir-fry green beans and carrots 4 minutes. Add mushrooms; stir-fry 1 to 2 minutes or until vegetables are crisp-tender. Remove vegetables from wok; set aside.

Add lamb strips to wok. Stir-fry about 3 minutes or until slightly pink. Remove lamb from wok; add to reserved vegetable mixture. Return vegetable mixture and meat to wok. Stir cornstarch mixture; add to wok. Cook and stir until thickened and bubbly. Stir in tomatoes. Cook 1 minute. Serve over hot cooked pasta; sprinkle with cheese.

Makes 4 servings

Prep Time: 15 minutes
Cook Time: 20 minutes

*Favorite recipe from **American Lamb Council***

Hot Mediterranean Chicken Salad

Thai-Style Beef & Rice

1 (6.2-ounce) package RICE-A-RONI®
    Fried Rice
2 tablespoons margarine or butter
1 pound boneless sirloin or top round
    steak, cut into thin strips
2 cloves garlic, minced
¼ teaspoon crushed red pepper flakes
1 tablespoon sesame oil or vegetable oil
2 cups fresh or frozen snow peas, halved
    if large
½ cup red and/or yellow bell pepper
    strips
3 tablespoons soy sauce
1 tablespoon peanut butter
¼ cup chopped cilantro (optional)

1. In large skillet over medium heat, sauté rice-vermicelli mix with margarine until vermicelli is golden brown.

2. Slowly stir in 2 cups water and Special Seasonings; bring to a boil. Reduce heat to low. Cover; simmer 15 to 20 minutes or until rice is tender. Let stand 3 minutes.

3. Meanwhile, toss steak with garlic and red pepper flakes; set aside. In another large skillet or wok over medium-high heat, heat oil until hot. Add snow peas and bell pepper; stir-fry 2 minutes. Add meat mixture; stir-fry 2 minutes. Add soy sauce and peanut butter; stir-fry 1 minute or until meat is barely pink inside and vegetables are crisp-tender. Serve meat mixture over rice; sprinkle with cilantro, if desired.   *Makes 4 servings*

Prep Time: 15 minutes
Cook Time: 30 minutes

Shepherd's Pie

2 cups diced cooked leg of American
    lamb
2 large potatoes, cubed and cooked
1 cup cooked peas
1 cup cooked carrot slices
3 green onions, sliced
1 clove garlic, minced
1 teaspoon black pepper
2 cups prepared brown gravy
2 sheets refrigerated pie crust sheets

In large bowl, combine lamb, potatoes, peas, carrots, green onions, garlic, black pepper and brown gravy.

Press 1 pie crust sheet into 9-inch pie plate; fill with lamb mixture. Cover with second pie crust sheet.* Pinch edges; cut slits in top to allow steam to escape.

Bake 30 minutes at 350°F or until pie crust is golden brown.   *Makes 4 to 6 servings*

*Or, use mashed potatoes in place of second crust.

*Favorite recipe from **American Lamb Council***

Salsa Macaroni & Cheese

1 jar (1 pound) RAGÚ® Cheese
    Creations!® Double Cheddar Sauce
1 cup prepared mild salsa
8 ounces elbow macaroni, cooked and
    drained

1. In 2-quart saucepan, heat Ragú Cheese Creations! Sauce over medium heat. Stir in salsa; heat through.

2. Toss with hot macaroni. Serve immediately.
          Makes 4 servings

Prep Time: 5 minutes
Cook Time: 15 minutes

Thai-Style Beef & Rice

Chicken Primavera

2 tablespoons CRISCO® Oil*
6 boneless, skinless chicken breast
    halves, cut into 1-inch pieces
    (about 1½ pounds chicken)
1 clove garlic, minced
3 cups broccoli flowerets
2 cups sliced fresh mushrooms
1 fresh tomato, chopped
1 package (8 ounces) spaghetti or
    linguine, cooked and well drained
¾ cup grated Parmesan cheese
1 tablespoon dried basil leaves
½ teaspoon salt
¼ teaspoon pepper
¾ cup evaporated skimmed milk

Use your favorite Crisco Oil product.

1. Heat oil in large skillet on medium-high
heat. Add chicken and garlic. Cook and stir
5 minutes or until chicken is no longer pink
in center. Remove to serving plate.

2. Add broccoli, mushrooms and tomato to
skillet. Cook and stir 3 to 5 minutes or until
broccoli is crisp-tender. Return chicken to
skillet to heat. Transfer mixture to large serving
bowl. Add spaghetti, Parmesan cheese, basil,
salt and pepper. Toss to mix. Add milk. Mix
lightly. Serve immediately on spinach-covered
plates, if desired.   *Makes 6 servings*

Italian Vegetable Farfalle

8 ounces BARILLA® Farfalle
1 tablespoon olive oil
1 pound boneless skinless chicken
    breasts, cubed
  Salt and pepper
1 medium zucchini, coarsely chopped
1 medium yellow squash, coarsely
    chopped
1 jar (26 ounces) BARILLA® Tomato and
    Basil Pasta Sauce
  Grated Parmesan cheese

1. Cook farfalle according to package
directions; drain.

2. Meanwhile, heat olive oil in large skillet.
Add chicken; cook and stir over medium-high
heat until cooked through. Add salt and
pepper to taste. Add zucchini and yellow
squash to skillet; cook and stir 5 minutes.

3. Reduce heat; stir in pasta sauce. Cook
5 minutes. Pour sauce over hot drained
farfalle. Sprinkle with cheese.
    Makes 6 to 8 servings

Note: Nonstick cooking spray can be used as
an alternative to olive oil.

Tip: When purchasing zucchini and yellow
squash, look for firm squash that are brightly
colored and free of spots or bruises. Store
them in a plastic bag in the refrigerator for up
to five days.

Sicilian Caponata

5 tablespoons olive or vegetable oil,
    divided
8 cups (1½ pounds) cubed unpeeled
    eggplant
2½ cups onion slices
1 cup chopped celery
1 can (14.5 ounces) CONTADINA®
    Recipe Ready Diced Tomatoes with
    Roasted Garlic, undrained
⅓ cup chopped pitted ripe olives,
    drained
¼ cup balsamic or red wine vinegar
2 tablespoons capers
2 teaspoons granulated sugar
½ teaspoon salt
  Dash of ground black pepper

1. Heat 3 tablespoons oil in medium skillet.
Add eggplant; sauté 6 minutes. Remove
eggplant from skillet.

2. Heat remaining oil in same skillet. Add
onion and celery; sauté 5 minutes or until
vegetables are tender.

3. Stir in undrained tomatoes and eggplant; cover. Simmer 15 minutes or until eggplant is tender.

4. Stir in olives, vinegar, capers, sugar, salt and pepper; simmer, uncovered, 5 minutes, stirring occasionally. Serve with toasted bread slices, if desired. *Makes 4½ cups*

El Dorado Rice Casserole

1 can (14½ ounces) whole peeled
    tomatoes, cut up
1½ cups chicken broth
1 tablespoon vegetable oil
1 medium onion, chopped
1 cup long-grain rice
1 teaspoon LAWRY'S® Garlic Salt
1 cup sour cream
1 can (4 ounces) diced green chiles
1½ cups (6 ounces) shredded Monterey
    Jack cheese

Drain tomatoes, reserving juice. Add reserved juice to broth to make 2½ cups liquid; set aside. In medium saucepan, heat oil. Add onion and cook over medium-high heat until tender. Add tomato-broth mixture, tomatoes, rice and Garlic Salt. Bring to a boil over medium-high heat. Reduce heat to low; cover and simmer 25 minutes or until liquid is absorbed. In small bowl, combine sour cream and chiles. In 1½-quart casserole, layer ½ of prepared rice, ½ of sour cream mixture and ½ of cheese. Repeat. Bake at 350°F 20 minutes or until bubbly. *Makes 6 servings*

Serving Suggestion: Top casserole with avocado and pimiento slices.

Pepperonata

8 ounces dry pasta
3 tablespoons olive or vegetable oil
1 *each:* red, yellow and green bell
    pepper, thinly sliced
3 cups thinly sliced red or yellow onion
2 large cloves garlic, minced
2 cans (14.5 ounces each) CONTADINA®
    Recipe Ready Diced Tomatoes,
    drained
2 tablespoons chopped fresh parsley *or*
    2 teaspoons dried parsley flakes
1 tablespoon plus 1½ teaspoons
    balsamic or red wine vinegar
1 teaspoon salt
½ teaspoon dried thyme leaves, crushed
¼ teaspoon ground black pepper
1 tablespoon chopped parsley (optional)

1. Cook pasta according to package directions; drain and keep warm.

2. Heat oil in large skillet. Add bell peppers, onion and garlic; sauté for 6 to 8 minutes or until vegetables are tender.

3. Stir in tomatoes, parsley, vinegar, salt, thyme and black pepper; simmer, uncovered, for 12 to 15 minutes or until heated through, stirring occasionally.

4. Serve over pasta. Sprinkle with parsley, if desired. *Makes 4 servings*

Prep Time: 12 minutes
Cook Time: 25 minutes

Gemelli with Baby Shrimp and Sweet Peas

1 package (16 ounces) BARILLA®
    Gemelli
2 tablespoons unsalted butter
2 tablespoons thinly sliced green onion
1 cup heavy cream
    Salt and pepper
1½ cups (about 8 ounces) small frozen
    shelled and deveined shrimp, thawed
1 cup frozen baby peas, thawed

1. Cook gemelli according to package directions; drain.

2. Meanwhile, melt butter in large broad saucepan or deep skillet. Add green onion; cook and stir about 2 minutes or until wilted. Add cream and heat to boiling. Boil about 5 minutes or until slightly thickened and reduced to about ¾ cup. Add salt and pepper to taste.

3. Add hot drained gemelli to saucepan with shrimp and peas; cook and stir over low heat until heated through.

Makes 6 to 8 servings

Family Swiss Steak and Potatoes

½ cup all-purpose flour
1½ teaspoons salt
½ teaspoon pepper
2½ pounds beef round steak, about
    1½ inches thick
2 tablespoons CRISCO® Oil*
2 cups sliced onion
1 can (14½ ounces) whole tomatoes,
    undrained and cut up
½ cup water
½ teaspoon dried thyme leaves
1 bay leaf
8 medium potatoes, peeled, cut in half

*Use your favorite Crisco Oil product.

1. Combine flour, salt and pepper in shallow dish. Add meat. Coat both sides with flour mixture. Pound flour into meat.

2. Heat oil in large deep skillet or Dutch oven on medium heat. Add meat. Brown on both sides, adding onion during last 2 to 3 minutes.

3. Add tomatoes, water, thyme and bay leaf. Bring to a boil. Reduce heat to low. Cover. Simmer 1 hour 15 minutes. Turn meat over. Add potatoes. Simmer until meat and potatoes are tender.

4. Arrange meat and potatoes on platter. Remove bay leaf from sauce. Pour sauce over meat and potatoes. *Makes 8 servings*

Nacho Salad

3 ounces (about 60) GUILTLESS
    GOURMET® Unsalted Baked Tortilla
    Chips
2 teaspoons water
½ cup GUILTLESS GOURMET® Black
    Bean Dip (Spicy or Mild)
4 cups shredded romaine lettuce
2 medium tomatoes (red or yellow),
    chopped
½ cup (2 ounces) grated Cheddar cheese
½ cup GUILTLESS GOURMET® Salsa
    (Roasted Red Pepper or
    Southwestern Grill)

Divide and spread tortilla chips among 4 plates. Stir water into bean dip in small microwave-safe bowl or small saucepan. Microwave bean dip on HIGH (100% power) 2 to 3 minutes or heat over medium heat until warm. Evenly drizzle heated dip over tortilla chips. Sprinkle lettuce, tomatoes and cheese evenly over tortilla chips. To serve, spoon 2 tablespoons salsa over each salad.

Makes 4 servings

Gemelli with Baby Shrimp and Sweet Peas

Everything Veggie

If vegetables are your preference, try one of these vegetarian dishes that still feature your favorites from grocery store shelves. There won't be any taste sacrifices here.

Paris Pasta

2 tablespoons margarine or butter
2 cloves garlic, minced
½ cup milk
2 cups 1-inch asparagus pieces or very thin green beans
¼ teaspoon ground black pepper
1 (4.7-ounce) package PASTA RONI® Parmesano
½ cup diced roasted red bell peppers
½ cup chopped Muenster cheese
¼ cup chopped Fresh basil or parsley

1. In large saucepan over medium-high heat, melt margarine. Add garlic; sauté 1 minute.

2. Stir in 1⅓ cups water, milk, asparagus and black pepper. Bring to a boil.

3. Stir in pasta and Special Seasonings. Reduce heat to low. Gently boil, uncovered, 5 to 6 minutes or until pasta is tender, stirring occasionally.

4. Stir in bell peppers and cheese. Let stand 3 minutes or until cheese is melted. Top with basil.
Makes 4 servings

Penne with Creamy Tomato Sauce

1 tablespoon olive or vegetable oil
½ cup diced onion
2 tablespoons dry vermouth, white wine or chicken broth
1 can (14.5 ounces) CONTADINA® Recipe Ready Diced Tomatoes with Italian Herbs, undrained
½ cup heavy whipping cream
8 ounces dry penne or rigatoni, cooked, drained, kept warm
1 cup pitted ripe olives, drained, sliced
½ cup (2 ounces) grated Parmesan cheese
¼ cup sliced green onions

1. Heat oil in large skillet. Add diced onion; sauté 2 to 3 minutes or until onion is tender.

2. Add vermouth; cook 1 minute.

3. Stir in undrained tomatoes, cream, pasta, olives and Parmesan cheese; heat thoroughly, stirring occasionally. Sprinkle with green onions.
Makes 4 servings

Paris Pasta

Farmers' Market Salad

Dressing
- ½ cup chopped peperoncini
- ⅓ cup seasoned rice vinegar
- 3 tablespoons country Dijon mustard
- 2 tablespoons chopped fresh dill
- 1½ teaspoons sugar
- 1½ teaspoons garlic salt
- 1½ teaspoons fresh lemon juice
- 1½ teaspoons grated fresh lemon peel
- ½ teaspoon coarsely ground pepper
- ⅔ cup WESSON® Best Blend Oil

Salad
- 1 pound baby red potatoes, unpeeled
- 1 pound baby asparagus
- 1 pound mixed salad greens or spinach leaves, washed and drained
- 1 basket cherry tomatoes, halved, or baby teardrop yellow tomatoes
- 1 large orange bell pepper, thinly sliced
- 4 hard-boiled eggs, quartered

Dressing

In blender or food processor, add *all dressing* ingredients *except* Wesson® Oil. Pulse ingredients and slowly add Wesson® Oil until dressing is partially smooth; refrigerate.

Salad

In a saucepan of water, cook potatoes until tender. Drain potatoes; immerse in ice water for 5 minutes to stop cooking process. Cool completely; drain well. In large pot of boiling water, cook asparagus until crisp-tender. Repeat cooling procedure with asparagus. In a large bowl, toss salad greens with ⅓ dressing. Evenly divide salad greens among 4 plates. Arrange potatoes, asparagus, tomatoes, bell pepper and eggs in sections over salad greens. Drizzle half the remaining dressing over arranged vegetables and eggs. Serve salad with remaining dressing, if desired.

Makes 4 servings

Baked Eggplant with Cheese

- 6 or 7 small eggplants, sliced into ½-inch-thick slices
- 1 egg, beaten
- 1 cup bread crumbs
- 2 tablespoons olive oil
  Salt and ground black pepper to taste
- 1 tablespoon dried parsley
- 1 can (5 ounces) sliced mushrooms, drained
- 1 can (15 ounces) chunky tomato sauce
- 6 thin slices tomato
- 8 ounces shredded Wisconsin Scamorze or Mozzarella cheese
- 1 teaspoon grated onion
  Fresh basil leaves for garnish

Preheat oven to 375°F. Dip eggplant slices in egg, then in bread crumbs. Heat olive oil in skillet; brown eggplant lightly on both sides. Arrange in buttered baking dish. Season to taste with salt and pepper; sprinkle with parsley and sliced mushrooms. Pour tomato sauce over eggplant. Top with tomato slices and cheese. Sprinkle grated onion over cheese. Bake 30 minutes or until cheese is melted.

Makes 8 servings

Favorite recipe from **Wisconsin Milk Marketing Board**

Farmers' Market Salad

Fire & Ice Brunch Skillet

1 (6.8-ounce) package RICE-A-RONI®
    Spanish Rice
2 tablespoons margarine or butter
1 (16-ounce) jar salsa
⅓ cup sour cream
¼ cup thinly sliced green onions
4 large eggs
1 cup (4 ounces) shredded Cheddar
    cheese
Chopped cilantro (optional)

1. In large skillet over medium heat, sauté rice-vermicelli mix with margarine until vermicelli is golden brown.

2. Slowly stir in 2 cups water, salsa and Special Seasonings; bring to a boil. Reduce heat to low. Cover; simmer 15 to 20 minutes or until rice is tender.

3. Stir in sour cream and green onions. Using large spoon, make 4 indentations in rice mixture. Break 1 egg into each indentation. Reduce heat to low. Cover; cook 8 minutes or until eggs are cooked to desired doneness.

4. Sprinkle cheese evenly over eggs and rice. Cover; let stand 3 minutes or until cheese is melted. Sprinkle with cilantro, if desired.

Makes 4 servings

Tip: A twist on Mexican-style huevos rancheros, this dish is perfect for brunch or a light dinner.

Prep Time: 5 minutes
Cook Time: 30 minutes

Vegetable Stir-Fry in Spicy Black Bean Sauce

1 teaspoon vegetable oil
1 medium onion, chopped
1 medium-size green bell pepper, cut
    into strips
3 carrots, cut into julienne strips
    (matchstick size)
3 cups shredded cabbage (green, red or
    napa)
1 cup tofu, crumbled
4 cups cooked rice, kept warm
Fresh chives and radishes (optional)

Black Bean Sauce
1 cup GUILTLESS GOURMET® Spicy
    Black Bean Dip
2 teaspoons water
¼ cup low-sodium soy sauce
¼ cup cooking sherry
1 tablespoon minced peeled fresh ginger
1 clove garlic, minced

Heat oil in wok or large skillet over medium-high heat until hot. Add onion, pepper, carrots, cabbage and tofu; stir-fry until crisp-tender.

To prepare Black Bean Sauce, combine bean dip and water in small bowl; mix well. Stir in remaining Black Bean Sauce ingredients; pour over stir-fried vegetables. Stir-fry over high heat 2 minutes more. Reduce heat to low; cook 2 to 4 minutes more or until heated through, stirring often. Serve over hot rice. Garnish with chives and radishes, if desired.

Makes 6 servings

Fire & Ice Brunch Skillet

Acorn Squash Filled with Savory Spinach

4 small acorn squash
2 tablespoons FILIPPO BERIO® Olive Oil
1 (10-ounce) package frozen chopped spinach, thawed and drained
1 (8-ounce) container ricotta cheese
1 tablespoon grated Parmesan cheese
¼ teaspoon freshly ground black pepper
⅛ teaspoon salt
⅛ teaspoon ground nutmeg

Preheat oven to 325°F. Cut squash crosswise in half. Scoop out seeds and fibers; discard. Brush insides and outsides of squash halves with olive oil. Place in large shallow roasting pan. Bake, uncovered, 35 to 40 minutes or until tender when pierced with fork.

In medium bowl, combine spinach, ricotta cheese, Parmesan cheese, pepper, salt and nutmeg. Spoon equal amounts of spinach mixture into squash halves. Bake, uncovered, an additional 10 to 15 minutes or until heated through.   *Makes 8 servings*

To Microwave: Prepare squash as directed above. Place in large shallow microwave-safe dish. Cover with vented plastic wrap. Microwave on HIGH (100% power) 10 to 12 minutes or until squash are softened, rotating dish halfway through cooking. Prepare filling; spoon into squash halves. Cover with vented plastic wrap; microwave on HIGH 6 to 8 minutes or until filling is hot and squash are tender when pierced with fork.

Vegetarian Tacos

1 can (16 ounces) refried beans
1 onion, chopped
1 package (1.0 ounce) LAWRY'S® Taco Spices & Seasonings
1 large zucchini, coarsely grated
1 package (18 count) LAWRY'S® Taco Shells
1 can (2¼ ounces) sliced black olives, drained
2 medium tomatoes, chopped
    Shredded lettuce
2 cups (8 ounces) shredded cheddar or Monterey Jack cheese

In medium saucepan, combine refried beans, onion, Taco Spices & Seasonings and ½ of zucchini; mix well. Bring to a boil over medium-high heat; reduce heat to low and simmer, uncovered, 3 minutes. Fill each Taco Shell with 2 to 3 tablespoons mixture. Place filled shells on baking sheet. Bake in 350°F oven 5 minutes. Top with olives, tomatoes, lettuce, remaining zucchini and cheese.
        Makes 18 tacos

Serving Suggestion: Serve with a mixture of salsa and chopped avocado.

Acorn Squash Filled with Savory Spinach

Eggplant, Tomato & Cheese Casserole

1 small eggplant, peeled
5 tablespoons olive oil
2 medium onions, thinly sliced
½ teaspoon LAWRY'S® Garlic Powder
    with Parsley
½ teaspoon LAWRY'S® Seasoned Salt
¼ teaspoon LAWRY'S® Seasoned Pepper
¼ teaspoon red pepper flakes
2 to 2½ teaspoons dried basil
3 medium tomatoes, cored and thinly
    sliced
½ cup (4 ounces) farmer's cheese
¾ cup heavy cream

Slice eggplant crosswise into ¼-inch slices. Sprinkle with salt and layer on paper towels to remove moisture. Let stand 30 minutes, then rinse and pat dry. In large skillet, heat 1 tablespoon olive oil. Add onions, Garlic Powder with Parsley, Seasoned Salt, Seasoned Pepper and red pepper flakes and cook over medium-high heat until onions are soft. Add 1 teaspoon basil. Place 2 tablespoons olive oil in 11-inch au gratin dish or shallow casserole. Layer ½ onion mixture in bottom of dish, then overlap slices of ½ eggplant and ½ tomatoes. Top with remaining onion mixture, then remaining eggplant and tomatoes. Bake in 400°F oven, covered, 10 minutes. Drizzle with remaining 2 tablespoons olive oil and continue baking another 30 minutes; basting from time to time with accumulated pan juices. Remove from oven and let stand at room temperature for several hours. (Can be refrigerated at this point; however, return to room temperature before completing and serving.) In blender or food processor fitted with steel knife, beat together farmer's cheese and heavy cream. Add remaining basil. Spread over eggplant-tomato mixture. Place under broiler until cheese is melted and slightly browned, about 5 minutes.

Makes 6 servings

Penne with Arrabiatta Sauce

½ pound uncooked penne or other
    tube-shaped pasta
2 tablespoons olive oil or oil from
    sun-dried tomatoes
8 cloves garlic
1 can (28 ounces) crushed tomatoes in
    purée
¼ cup chopped sun-dried tomatoes
    packed in oil
3 tablespoons *Frank's® RedHot®* Cayenne
    Pepper Sauce
8 kalamata olives, pitted and chopped*
6 fresh basil leaves *or* 1½ teaspoons
    dried basil leaves
1 tablespoon capers

*To pit olives, place olives on cutting board. Press with side of knife until olives split. Remove pits.

1. Cook pasta according to package directions; drain.

2. Heat oil in large nonstick skillet over medium heat. Add garlic; cook until golden, stirring frequently. Add remaining ingredients. Bring to a boil. Simmer, partially covered, 10 minutes. Stir occasionally.

3. Toss pasta with half of the sauce mixture. Spoon into serving bowl. Pour remaining sauce mixture over pasta. Garnish with fresh basil or parsley, if desired.

Makes 4 servings (3 cups sauce)

Prep Time: 15 minutes
Cook Time: 20 minutes

Grilled Vegetable Fettuccine

1 large zucchini
1 large yellow squash
1 medium red bell pepper
1 medium yellow or green bell pepper
$\frac{1}{4}$ cup non-creamy Italian salad dressing
$\frac{2}{3}$ cup milk
1 tablespoon margarine or butter
1 (4.7-ounce) package PASTA RONI®
    Fettuccine Alfredo
$\frac{3}{4}$ cup (3 ounces) crumbled goat cheese
    or feta cheese
$\frac{1}{4}$ cup julienned fresh basil leaves

1. Preheat grill or broiler. Cut zucchini and squash lengthwise into quarters. Cut bell peppers lengthwise into quarters; discard stems and seeds. Brush dressing over all surfaces of vegetables. Grill over medium coals 10 to 12 minutes or broil on top rack 10 to 12 minutes or until vegetables are tender, turning occasionally.

2. Meanwhile, in medium saucepan, bring 1¼ cups water, milk, margarine, pasta and Special Seasonings to a boil. Reduce heat to medium-low. Gently boil, uncovered, 5 to 6 minutes or until pasta is slightly firm, stirring occasionally.

3. Cut grilled vegetables into ½-inch chunks; stir into pasta mixture. Let stand 3 minutes. Top with cheese and basil.

Makes 4 servings

Tip: Speed up preparation by using leftover grilled veggies from your weekend barbecue.

Prep Time: 15 minutes
Cook Time: 20 minutes

Ratatouille

1 large onion, thinly sliced into rings
2 zucchini, sliced
2 green bell peppers, cut into strips
1 small eggplant, peeled and cut into
    ¾-inch cubes
¾ teaspoon LAWRY'S® Garlic Powder
    with Parsley
½ teaspoon (to taste) LAWRY'S®
    Seasoned Salt
½ teaspoon (to taste) LAWRY'S®
    Seasoned Pepper
5 tomatoes, seeded and chopped
1 tablespoon capers (optional)

In 3-quart glass casserole, combine onion, zucchini, green pepper, eggplant and seasonings. Cover with plastic wrap, venting one corner. Microwave on HIGH (100%) 8 minutes. Stir in tomatoes; cover and microwave on HIGH 3 to 4 minutes, just until vegetables are tender-crisp and remain colorful. Add capers, if desired.

Makes 6 to 8 servings

Serving Suggestion: Serve hot or cold with warm pita bread wedges as a relish accompaniment or as a side dish.

Creamy Shells with Spinach and Mushrooms

1 package (16 ounces) BARILLA®
    Medium or Large Shells
1 can (12 ounces) evaporated milk
1 cup (4 ounces) grated Parmesan
    cheese, divided
4 ounces brick cheese, cubed (about
    ¾ cup)
4 tablespoons butter or margarine
2 tablespoons olive or vegetable oil
1 small onion, chopped
3 cloves garlic, minced
2 packages (10 ounces each) frozen
    chopped spinach, thawed and well
    drained
1½ cups (4 ounces) sliced mushrooms

1. Cook pasta shells according to package directions; drain.

2. Meanwhile, heat evaporated milk, Parmesan (reserving 2 tablespoons for topping) and brick cheese in small saucepan over medium heat until cheeses melt, stirring frequently. Set aside.

3. Heat butter and oil in large skillet over medium-high heat. Add onion and garlic; cook about 5 minutes, stirring occasionally, until onion is transparent. Add spinach and mushrooms; cook 5 minutes, stirring occasionally.

4. Stir cheese mixture into skillet; mix well. Pour over hot drained pasta shells on platter; sprinkle with reserved Parmesan.

Makes 8 servings

Stewed Mushrooms on Asparagus with Vegetarian Oyster Sauce

7 ounces asparagus, trimmed
  Salt
  Vegetable oil
2 slices ginger
4 ounces fresh black mushrooms
4 ounces baby corn
3 tablespoons LEE KUM KEE®
    Vegetarian Oyster Flavored Sauce
¼ teaspoon sugar
1 teaspoon cornstarch mixed with
    1 tablespoon water
¼ teaspoon LEE KUM KEE® Sesame Oil

1. Cook asparagus in boiling water with salt and vegetable oil 3 minutes. Remove and arrange on plate.

2. Heat 2 tablespoons vegetable oil in wok. Sauté ginger until fragrant. Add mushrooms and baby corn. Stir-fry 1 minute.

3. Combine Vegetarian Oyster Flavored Sauce, ⅔ cup water and sugar in small bowl; add to wok. Simmer 5 minutes. Add cornstarch mixture; simmer until thickened. Place mixture over asparagus and sprinkle with Sesame Oil. *Makes 4 to 6 servings*

Creamy Shells with Spinach and Mushrooms

Creole Beans and Rice

2 cans (14½ ounces *each*) peeled no salt
    added tomatoes, undrained
1 cup uncooked rice
2 tablespoons CRISCO® Oil*
½ cup chopped onion
4 cloves garlic, minced
1 cup chopped celery
1 cup chopped carrots
1 cup chopped green bell pepper
1 tablespoon ground cumin
1 tablespoon chili powder
1 teaspoon dried basil leaves
½ teaspoon cayenne pepper
2 cans (15½ ounces *each*) kidney beans,
    drained
1 can (6 ounces) no salt added tomato
    paste
3 tablespoons vinegar
1 tablespoon Worcestershire sauce
1 teaspoon sugar

Use your favorite Crisco Oil product.

1. Drain tomatoes, reserving liquid. Add
enough water to reserved liquid to measure
2 cups. Pour into medium saucepan. Add rice.
Bring to a boil on medium-high heat. Reduce
heat to low. Simmer 20 minutes or until rice is
tender.

2. Heat oil in large saucepan on medium
heat. Add onion and garlic. Cook and stir until
tender. Add celery and carrots. Cook and stir
until crisp-tender. Add green pepper, cumin,
chili powder, basil and cayenne. Cook and stir
until green pepper is tender.

3. Add tomatoes. Break up with spoon. Stir
in rice, beans, tomato paste, vinegar,
Worcestershire sauce and sugar. Reduce heat to
low. Heat thoroughly, stirring occasionally.
Garnish, if desired.   *Makes 8 servings*

Moroccan Supper

1 (7.2-ounce) package RICE-A-RONI®
    Rice Pilaf
½ cup chopped onion
2 cloves garlic, minced
2 tablespoons margarine or olive oil
1 teaspoon ground cumin
¼ teaspoon ground cinnamon
1 (15-ounce) can garbanzo beans or
    chick peas, rinsed and drained
1½ cups broccoli flowerets
¼ cup dried apricots, slivered, or raisins
⅓ cup slivered or sliced almonds, toasted
¼ cup chopped cilantro (optional)

1. In large skillet over medium heat, sauté
rice-pasta mix, onion and garlic with
margarine until pasta is light golden brown.

2. Slowly stir in 2 cups water, cumin,
cinnamon and Special Seasonings; bring to a
boil. Cover; reduce heat to low. Simmer
10 minutes.

3. Stir in beans, broccoli and apricots. Cover;
simmer 10 to 12 minutes or until rice is
tender. Serve topped with almonds and
cilantro, if desired.   *Makes 4 servings*

Tip: For a Southwestern flair, use black
beans, 1½ cups corn and ¼ teaspoon chili
powder instead of garbanzo beans, apricots
and cinnamon.

Prep Time: 10 minutes
Cook Time: 30 minutes

Creole Beans and Rice

Vegetable-Stuffed Baked Potatoes

1 jar (1 pound) RAGÚ® Cheese Creations!® Roasted Garlic Parmesan Sauce or Double Cheddar Sauce
1 bag (16 ounces) frozen assorted vegetables, cooked and drained
6 large baking potatoes, unpeeled and baked

In 2-quart saucepan, heat Ragú Cheese Creations! Sauce. Stir in vegetables; heat through.

Cut a lengthwise slice from top of each potato. Lightly mash pulp in each potato. Evenly spoon sauce mixture onto each potato. Sprinkle, if desired, with ground black pepper.

Makes 6 servings

Tomato-Bread Casserole

½ pound loaf French bread, sliced
3 tablespoons butter or margarine, softened
1½ pounds tomatoes, thinly sliced
1 cup lowfat cottage or ricotta cheese
1 can (14½ ounces) diced tomatoes, drained (reserving liquid)
¾ teaspoon LAWRY'S® Seasoned Salt
½ teaspoon oregano
¼ cup olive oil
¾ teaspoon LAWRY'S® Garlic Powder with Parsley
½ cup shredded Parmesan cheese
¼ cup chopped parsley (garnish)

Spread bread slices with butter; cut into large cubes. Arrange on baking sheet. Toast in 350°F oven until golden. Place ½ of cubes in greased 13×9×2-inch baking dish. Top bread cubes with ½ of fresh tomato slices, ½ of cottage cheese, ½ of canned tomatoes, ½ reserved tomato liquid, ½ of Seasoned Salt, ½ of oregano, ½ of oil, and ½ of Garlic Powder with Parsley. Layer again, ending with

oil. Sprinkle on Parmesan cheese. Cover and bake in 350°F oven for 40 minutes. Uncover and bake, 5 minutes longer to brown top. Garnish with parsley.

Makes 6 to 8 servings

Meal Idea: Serve with marinated mushrooms.

Prep Time: 15 minutes
Cook Time: 45 minutes

Vegetable & Cheese Platter

1 cup water
2 cups DOLE® Broccoli or Cauliflower, cut into florets
1½ cups DOLE® Peeled Mini Carrots
1 cup DOLE® Sugar Peas or green beans
2 medium DOLE® Red, Yellow or Green Bell Peppers, cut into 2-inch pieces
1 package (8 ounces) mushrooms, stems trimmed
3 cups hot cooked brown or white rice
1 cup (4 ounces) shredded low-fat Cheddar cheese
⅓ cup crumbled feta cheese

• Pour water into large pot; bring to a boil. Add broccoli and carrots. Reduce heat to low; cover and cook 5 minutes. Add sugar peas, bell peppers and mushrooms; cook 5 minutes more or until vegetables are tender-crisp. Drain vegetables.

• Spoon hot rice onto large serving platter; top with vegetables. Sprinkle with cheeses.

• Cover with aluminum foil; let stand 3 minutes or until cheeses melt.

Makes 4 servings

Prep Time: 15 minutes
Cook Time: 15 minutes

Vegetable-Stuffed Baked Potato

On Holiday

From festive feasts to scrumptious holiday desserts, this chapter has it all. Jam-packed with roasted poultry, baked hams and cool ice cream sandwiches.

Roasted Turkey Breast with Cherry & Apple Rice Stuffing

3¾ cups water
  3 boxes UNCLE BEN'S® Long Grain & Wild Rice Butter & Herb Fast Cook Recipe
  ½ cup butter or margarine, divided
  ½ cup dried red tart cherries
  1 large apple, peeled and chopped (about 1 cup)
  ½ cup sliced almonds, toasted*
  1 bone-in turkey breast (5 to 6 pounds)

*To toast almonds, place them on a baking sheet. Bake 10 to 12 minutes in preheated 325°F oven or until golden brown, stirring occasionally.

1. In large saucepan, combine water, rice, contents of seasoning packets, 3 tablespoons butter and cherries. Bring to a boil. Cover; reduce heat to low and simmer 25 minutes or until all water is absorbed. Stir in apple and almonds; set aside.

2. Preheat oven to 325°F. Place turkey breast, skin side down, on rack in roasting pan. Loosely fill breast cavity with rice stuffing. (Place any remaining stuffing in greased baking dish; cover and refrigerate. Bake alongside turkey for 35 to 40 minutes or until heated through.)

3. Place sheet of heavy-duty foil over stuffing, molding it slightly over sides of turkey. Carefully invert turkey, skin side up, on rack. Melt remaining 5 tablespoons butter; brush some of butter over surface of turkey.

4. Roast turkey, uncovered, 1 hour; baste with melted butter. Continue roasting 1¼ to 1¾ hours more, basting occasionally with melted butter, until meat thermometer inserted into center of thickest part of turkey breast, not touching bone, registers 170°F. Let turkey stand, covered, 15 minutes before carving.

Makes 6 to 8 servings

Roasted Turkey Breast with Cherry & Apple Rice Stuffing

French Yule Log

Powdered sugar
4 eggs, separated
¾ cup sugar, divided
¾ cup ground blanched almonds
⅓ cup all-purpose flour
⅓ cup HERSHEY'S Cocoa
½ teaspoon baking soda
¼ teaspoon salt
¼ cup water
1 teaspoon vanilla extract
¼ teaspoon almond extract
  Whipped Cream Filling (recipe follows)
  Creamy Cocoa Log Frosting (recipe follows)

1. Heat oven to 375°F. Line 15×10½-inch jelly-roll pan with foil; generously grease foil. Sift powdered sugar onto clean towel.

2. Beat egg yolks in medium bowl 3 minutes on medium speed of mixer. Gradually add ½ cup sugar, beating another 2 minutes until thick and lemon-colored. Combine almonds, flour, cocoa, baking soda and salt; add alternately with water to egg yolk mixture, beating on low speed just until blended. Stir in vanilla and almond extracts.

3. Beat egg whites in large bowl until foamy. Gradually add ¼ cup sugar, beating until stiff peaks form. Carefully fold chocolate mixture into beaten egg whites. Spread batter evenly into prepared pan.

4. Bake 16 to 18 minutes or until top springs back when lightly touched. Cool in pan on wire rack 10 minutes; remove from pan to prepared towel. Carefully remove foil. Cool completely.

5. Cut into four equal rectangles approximately 3½×10 inches. Chill layers while preparing filling and frosting. Place one cake layer on serving plate. Spread one-third (about 1 cup) Whipped Cream Filling evenly over cake layer; top with another cake layer. Repeat with remaining cake and filling, ending with cake

layer. Refrigerate about 1 hour before frosting. Generously frost loaf with Creamy Cocoa Log Frosting. Swirl frosting with spatula, or score with fork to resemble bark. Refrigerate at least 4 hours before serving. Garnish with shaved chocolate and holly, if desired. Cover; refrigerate leftover dessert.

Makes 10 to 12 servings

Whipped Cream Filling

1½ cups cold whipping cream
⅓ cup powdered sugar
1 teaspoon vanilla extract

Combine whipping cream, powdered sugar and vanilla in large bowl. Beat until cream is stiff. (Do not overbeat.)

Makes about 3 cups filling

Creamy Cocoa Log Frosting

3½ cups powdered sugar
½ cup HERSHEY'S Cocoa
½ cup (1 stick) butter or margarine, softened
2 tablespoons light corn syrup
2 teaspoons vanilla extract
⅓ cup milk

Combine powdered sugar and cocoa. Beat butter, ½ cup cocoa mixture, corn syrup and vanilla in medium bowl until smooth. Add remaining cocoa mixture alternately with milk, beating until smooth and of spreading consistency. *Makes 2½ cups frosting*

French Yule Log

Holiday Chicken Pinwheels

4 boneless, skinless chicken breast
   halves
3 ounces cream cheese, softened
¼ cup oil-packed, sun-dried tomatoes,
   minced
1 clove garlic, minced
1 tablespoon fresh basil, minced
2 teaspoons small capers, rinsed
¼ teaspoon salt
⅛ teaspoon ground black pepper
1 tablespoon olive oil
⅛ teaspoon paprika
2 tablespoons Dijon mustard
18 slices homemade-style bread
9 small parsley sprigs

Preheat oven to 350°F.

Place chicken breast halves between sheets of waxed paper. Lightly pound each breast until about ¼ inch thick; set aside. In medium bowl, combine cream cheese, sun-dried tomatoes, garlic, basil, capers, salt and pepper. Spread generous tablespoon of cream cheese mixture onto each chicken breast. Beginning at long edge, roll up each piece of chicken similar to a jelly roll. Secure each breast with toothpick.

Lightly coat chicken rolls with olive oil; sprinkle with paprika. Place chicken, seam side down in shallow baking dish. Bake 25 minutes; *do not overcook.* Cool, wrap and refrigerate until needed. At serving time, cut each chicken roll into ½-inch slices.

Cut 2½-inch circles from each bread slice; spread each bread circle with mustard. Top each piece of bread with chicken pinwheel; garnish with parsley. Arrange on platter to serve.   *Makes 36 appetizers*

Favorite recipe from **National Chicken Council**

Hoppin' John Skillet

1 (7.2-ounce) package RICE-A-RONI®
   Rice Pilaf
1 small onion, chopped
2 cloves garlic, minced
2 tablespoons margarine or butter
1½ cups fresh or frozen cut green beans or
   sliced fresh okra
1 (15-ounce) can black-eyed peas, rinsed
   and drained
¾ teaspoon hot pepper sauce
1 small tomato, chopped

1. In large skillet over medium heat, sauté rice-pasta mix, onion and garlic with margarine until pasta is light golden brown.

2. Slowly stir in 2 cups water, green beans and Special Seasonings; bring to a boil. Cover; reduce heat to low. Simmer 10 minutes.

3. Stir in black-eyed peas and hot pepper sauce. Cover; simmer 10 to 12 minutes or until rice is tender. Stir in tomato. Let stand 3 minutes.   *Makes 4 servings*

Prep Time: 5 minutes
Cook Time: 25 minutes

Wine and Herb Roaster with Ham and Oyster Stuffing

1 PERDUE® OVEN STUFFER® Roaster
   (5 to 8 pounds)
  Salt
½ teaspoon pepper
¼ cup butter or margarine
¼ cup chopped onion
2 tablespoons chopped celery
½ cup water
6 cooked oysters, diced
3 cups herb stuffing mix (4 ounces)
½ cup diced lean ham
  Wine and Herb Baste (recipe follows)
  Madeira Gravy (recipe follows)

Remove giblets and reserve for gravy. Rinse roaster, if desired; pat dry with paper towel. Season with salt and pepper. In medium skillet, melt butter and sauté onion and celery 5 minutes. Mix in water, oysters, stuffing mix and ham. Stuff roaster and close cavity with skewers or string. Tie legs together and fold wings back.

Place roaster in large roasting pan. Roast at 350°F for 2 to 2¾ hours. After 1 hour, brush with Wine and Herb Baste; repeat occasionally. Roaster is done when Bird-Watcher® thermometer pops up and juices are clear when thigh is pierced. Remove to serving platter and allow to rest 10 minutes while preparing gravy. Serve with Madeira Gravy.

Makes 6 servings

Wine and Herb Baste

¼ cup butter
1 clove garlic, minced
1 tablespoon chopped fresh parsley
1 teaspoon dried thyme leaves
½ teaspoon dried rosemary leaves, crumbled
¼ cup dry red wine

Combine all ingredients in small saucepan over low heat, stirring until butter is melted.

Madeira Gravy

  Oven Stuffer® Roaster giblets, except liver
4 cups water
½ cup Madeira wine
¼ cup flour

While roaster is cooking, place giblets in small saucepan with water and simmer, uncovered, until 2 cups liquid remain. Strain and reserve liquid.

When roaster is done, pour off all but 2 tablespoons drippings. Add reserved liquid from giblets to pan and stir to remove brown bits from bottom of pan. Combine wine and flour to make a smooth paste. Add to pan and cook over medium heat, whisking frequently, until gravy is thickened. Serve with roaster.

East Meets West Cocktail Franks

1 cup prepared sweet and sour sauce
1½ tablespoons rice vinegar or cider vinegar
1 tablespoon grated fresh ginger *or*
  1 teaspoon dried ginger
1 tablespoon dark sesame oil
½ teaspoon chile oil (optional)
1 package (12 ounces) HEBREW NATIONAL® Cocktail Beef Franks
2 tablespoons chopped cilantro or chives

Combine sweet and sour sauce, vinegar, ginger, sesame oil and chile oil in medium saucepan. Bring to a boil over medium heat. Cook 5 minutes or until thickened. Add cocktail franks; cover and cook until heated through. Transfer to chafing dish; sprinkle with cilantro. Serve with frilled wooden picks.

Makes 12 appetizer servings (2 cocktail franks per serving)

Brownie Peanut Butter Cupcakes

18 REYNOLDS® Foil Baking Cups
⅓ cup creamy peanut butter
¼ cup light cream cheese
2 tablespoons sugar
1 egg
1 package (about 19 ounces) fudge brownie mix
½ cup candy-coated peanut butter candies

PREHEAT oven to 350°F. Place Reynolds Foil Baking Cups in muffin pans or on cookie sheet; set aside. Beat peanut butter, cream cheese, sugar and egg in bowl with electric mixer; set aside.

PREPARE brownie mix, following package directions; set aside. Place 1 heaping teaspoon of peanut butter mixture in center of each baking cup. With spoon or small ice cream scoop, fill baking cups half full with brownie batter. Sprinkle each brownie cupcake with peanut butter candies.

BAKE 25 minutes; do not overbake. Cool.

Makes 18 brownie cupcakes

Crème de Brie® Heart Tarts

1 (15-ounce) package ready-to-bake 9-inch pie crusts
½ cup chopped onion
⅓ cup thinly sliced mushrooms
1 tablespoon butter
2 tablespoons white wine
1 tablespoon chopped fresh parsley
1 (5-ounce) package CRÈME DE BRIE®
2 eggs
½ cup light cream
  Dash pepper

Preheat oven to 375°F. Cut pie crust to fit into four 4-inch heart-shaped or round tart molds. Prick pie crust with a fork; cover and refrigerate. Over medium heat, sauté onion and mushrooms in butter until soft, about 8 minutes. Add wine and parsley and cook 1 minute until wine evaporates. Set aside. In small bowl, combine Crème de Brie, eggs, cream and pepper, whisking gently until blended. Add onion and mushrooms and mix well. Spoon into tart molds and bake 12 to 15 minutes or until lightly browned. Serve warm.

Makes 4 servings

East Meets West Cocktail Franks

Chocolate Sundae Cupcakes

24 REYNOLDS® Baking Cups
 1 package (about 18 ounces) devil's food cake mix
 1 container (16 ounces) ready-to-spread chocolate frosting
 ½ cup caramel ice cream topping
 1½ cups frozen whipped topping, thawed
 24 maraschino cherries with stems, drained

PREHEAT oven to 350°F. Place Reynolds Baking Cups in muffin pans; set aside. Prepare cake mix, following package directions for 24 cupcakes. Spoon batter into baking cups. Bake as directed. Cool.

FROST cupcakes. Top each cupcake with 1 teaspoon caramel topping and 1 tablespoon whipped topping. Garnish each cupcake with a cherry. Refrigerate until serving time.

Makes 24 cupcakes

Eastertime Leg of Lamb

 1 leg of American lamb (6 to 9 pounds)
 2 cloves garlic, cut into slivers
   Juice of 1 lemon
 2 teaspoons fresh basil, chopped*
 2 teaspoons fresh rosemary, chopped, or fresh summer savory*
   Salt, to taste
   Coarse black pepper, to taste

*Substitute ½ teaspoon dried crumbled herbs if fresh are not available.

Place lamb, fat side up, in shallow roasting pan. With sharp knife, cut slits in surface of lamb. Insert garlic slivers in slits.

Gently squeeze lemon juice over lamb, rubbing surface. Sprinkle with basil, rosemary, salt and pepper. Rub seasonings into lamb surface.

Roast in preheated 325°F oven 20 to 25 minutes per pound, or until meat thermometer registers 150°F for medium rare, 160°F for medium, or to desired degree of doneness.

Allow lamb to stand in warm place 15 to 20 minutes before carving.

Makes 8 to 12 servings

Favorite recipe from **American Lamb Council**

Maple Cider Basted Turkey

 1 PERDUE® Fresh Whole Turkey Breast (4 to 7 pounds)
 1 to 2 tablespoons canola oil
 1 tablespoon grainy, "country-style" mustard
   Salt and ground pepper to taste
 1 apple, cored but unpeeled, sliced thinly
 ¼ cup maple syrup
 2 tablespoons cider vinegar
   Dash Worcestershire sauce

Preheat oven to 350°F. Pat breast dry with paper towel. In small bowl, mix oil and mustard; rub over breast and under skin from neck end. Do not detach skin at base. Season with salt and pepper. Slide apple slices between skin and meat. If necessary, reinsert BIRD-WATCHER® Thermometer to original location. Place breast in roasting pan and roast, uncovered, 1½ to 1¾ hours, until BIRD-WATCHER Thermometer pops up and meat thermometer inserted into thickest part of breast registers 170°F.

Meanwhile, combine syrup, vinegar and Worcestershire sauce. During last 20 minutes of roasting, baste breast with mixture. If skin is browning too quickly, tent with foil. Remove breast to serving platter and let rest 10 to 15 minutes before carving.

Makes 6 to 8 servings

Chocolate Sundae Cupcakes

Holiday Bread Pudding

16 slices bread, cubed
1 cup dried cranberries or raisins
2 cans (12 fluid ounces *each*) NESTLÉ®
   CARNATION® Evaporated Milk
4 large eggs, lightly beaten
4 tablespoons butter, melted
¾ cup packed brown sugar
1 tablespoon vanilla extract
1 teaspoon ground cinnamon
½ teaspoon ground nutmeg
   Caramel sauce (optional)

PREHEAT oven to 350°F. Grease 12×8-inch baking dish.

COMBINE bread and cranberries in large bowl. Combine evaporated milk, eggs, butter, sugar, vanilla extract, cinnamon and nutmeg in medium bowl. Pour egg mixture over bread mixture; combine well. Pour mixture into prepared baking dish. Let stand for 10 minutes.

BAKE for 35 to 45 minutes or until knife inserted into center comes out clean. Top with caramel sauce. Garnish as desired.

Makes 8 servings

Pork Roast with Corn Bread & Oyster Stuffing

1 (5- to 7-pound) pork loin roast*
2 tablespoons butter or margarine
½ cup chopped onion
½ cup chopped celery
2 cloves garlic, minced
½ teaspoon fennel seeds, crushed
1 teaspoon TABASCO® brand Pepper
   Sauce
½ teaspoon salt
2 cups packaged corn bread stuffing mix
1 (8-ounce) can oysters, undrained,
   chopped

Have butcher crack backbone of pork loin roast.

Preheat oven to 325°F. Make a deep slit in back of each chop on pork loin.

Melt butter in large saucepan; add onion, celery, garlic and fennel seeds. Cook 5 minutes or until vegetables are tender; stir in TABASCO® Sauce and salt. Add stuffing mix, oysters and oyster liquid; toss to mix well.

Stuff corn bread mixture into slits in pork. (Any leftover stuffing may be baked in covered baking dish during last 30 minutes of roasting.) Place meat in shallow roasting pan. Cook 30 to 35 minutes per pound or until meat thermometer inserted into pork roast registers 170°F. Remove to heated serving platter. Allow meat to stand 15 minutes before serving.   *Makes 12 servings*

Holiday Bread Pudding

Turkey Breast with Southwestern Corn Bread Dressing

5 cups coarsely crumbled prepared corn bread

4 English muffins, coarsely crumbled

3 Anaheim chilies,* roasted, peeled, seeded and chopped

1 red bell pepper, roasted, peeled, seeded and chopped

¾ cup pine nuts, toasted

1 tablespoon chopped fresh cilantro

1 tablespoon chopped fresh parsley

1½ teaspoons chopped fresh basil *or* 1 teaspoon dried basil leaves

1½ teaspoons chopped fresh thyme *or* 1 teaspoon dried thyme leaves

1½ teaspoons chopped fresh oregano *or* 1 teaspoon dried oregano leaves

1 pound Italian turkey sausage

3 cups chopped celery

1 cup chopped onions

2 to 4 tablespoons chicken or turkey broth

1 bone-in turkey breast (5 to 6 pounds)

2 tablespoons minced garlic

½ cup chopped fresh cilantro

Canned mild green chilies can be substituted.

1. Preheat oven to 325°F. In large bowl, combine corn bread, muffins, chilies, bell pepper, pine nuts, 1 tablespoon cilantro, parsley, basil, thyme and oregano; set aside.

2. In large skillet, over medium-high heat, cook and stir turkey sausage, celery and onions 8 to 10 minutes or until sausage is no longer pink and vegetables are tender. Add to corn bread mixture. Add broth if mixture is too dry; set aside.

3. Loosen skin on both sides of turkey breast, being careful not to tear skin, and leaving it connected at breast bone. Spread 1 tablespoon garlic under loosened skin over each breast half. Repeat procedure, spreading ¼ cup cilantro over each breast half.

4. Place turkey breast in 13×9×2-inch roasting pan lightly coated with nonstick cooking spray. Spoon half of stuffing mixture under breast cavity. Spoon remaining stuffing into 2-quart casserole lightly coated with nonstick cooking spray; set aside. Roast turkey breast, uncovered, 2 to 2½ hours or until meat thermometer registers 170°F in deepest portion of breast. Bake remaining stuffing, uncovered, during last 45 minutes.

Makes 12 servings

Favorite recipe from **National Turkey Federation**

Holiday Appetizer Quiche

Crust

    2 cups all-purpose flour
    1 teaspoon salt
    ¾ cup Butter Flavor CRISCO® Stick or
        ¾ cup Butter Flavor CRISCO®
        all-vegetable shortening plus
        additional for shortening
    5 tablespoons cold water

Filling

    2 cups (8 ounces) shredded Swiss
        cheese
    ⅔ cup chopped ham, crumbled cooked
        sausage, diced pepperoni or
        crumbled cooked bacon
    ¾ cup thinly sliced green onions
        (including tops)
    ¼ cup snipped fresh parsley
    1 jar (4 ounces) diced pimientos, well
        drained
    5 eggs
    1 cup whipping cream
    1 cup half-and-half
    1 teaspoon salt
    ¼ teaspoon pepper

1. Heat oven to 400°F.

2. For crust, combine flour and salt in medium bowl. Cut in ¾ cup shortening, using pastry blender (or 2 knives), until all flour is blended in to form pea-size chunks. Sprinkle with water, 1 tablespoon at a time. Toss lightly with fork until dough forms ball.

3. Roll out dough to fit 15×10-inch jelly-roll pan. Place dough in greased pan, folding edges under. Flute edges. Prick crust with fork.

4. For filling, sprinkle cheese, ham, onions, parsley and pimientos evenly over crust. Beat eggs, cream, half-and-half, salt and pepper in medium bowl. Pour over filled crust.

5. Bake at 400°F for 25 to 30 minutes or until set. *Do not overbake.* Cool 5 to 10 minutes. Cut into 2×1½-inch pieces. Serve warm.

Makes about 50 appetizers

Note: Crust may bubble during baking and may need to be pricked with fork again.

Holiday Baked Ham

    1 bone-in smoked ham (8½ pounds)
    1 can (20 ounces) DOLE® Pineapple
        Slices
    1 cup apricot preserves
    1 teaspoon dry mustard
    ½ teaspoon ground allspice
        Whole cloves
        Maraschino cherries

• Preheat oven to 325°F. Remove rind from ham. Place ham on rack in open roasting pan, fat side up. Insert meat thermometer with bulb in thickest part away from fat or bone. Roast ham in oven about 3 hours.

• Drain pineapple slices; reserve syrup. In small saucepan, combine syrup, preserves, mustard and allspice. Bring to a boil; continue boiling, stirring occasionally, 10 minutes. Remove ham from oven, but keep oven hot. Stud ham with cloves; brush with glaze. Using wooden picks, secure pineapple slices and cherries to ham. Brush again with glaze. Return ham to oven. Roast 30 minutes longer or until thermometer registers 160°F (about 25 minutes per pound total cooking time). Brush with glaze 15 minutes before done. Let ham stand 20 minutes before slicing.

Makes 8 to 10 servings

Cranberry Orange Game Hens with Vegetable Stuffing

Game Hens
- 4 small Cornish game hens (16 ounces each)
- 1 carrot, finely diced
- 1 stalk celery, finely diced
- 2 cups bread stuffing mix
- 1 teaspoon poultry seasoning
- 1 cup chicken stock or broth
  Salt and pepper

Sauce
- 1 cup fresh or frozen cranberries, chopped
- 1 cup (12-ounce jar) SMUCKER'S® Orange Marmalade
- ¼ cup water
- 1 teaspoon lemon juice
  Lemon wedges for garnish (optional)

Remove as much fat as possible from game hens. Combine carrot, celery, stuffing mix, poultry seasoning and chicken stock. Season with salt and pepper. Fill cavity of each hen with stuffing; place on roasting pan. Bake at 400°F for 45 minutes.

Meanwhile, prepare sauce. In medium saucepan, combine all sauce ingredients. Cook over medium-high heat for 5 to 8 minutes until cranberries have released their juice. Set aside.

Remove game hens from oven. Spread sauce over top and sides of hens. Reserve any extra sauce to serve later with hens. Return hens to oven and continue baking 10 to 15 minutes.

To serve, place game hens on 4 serving plates. Spoon some of stuffing onto each plate. Spoon additional sauce over hens. Garnish with lemon wedges, if desired.

Makes 4 servings

Berry Striped Pops

- 2 cups strawberries
- ¾ cup honey,* divided
- 12 (3-ounce) paper cups or popsicle molds
- 6 kiwifruit, peeled and sliced
- 2 cups sliced peaches
- 12 popsicle sticks

*Honey should not be fed to infants under one year of age. Honey is a safe and wholesome food for older children and adults.

Purée strawberries with ¼ cup honey in blender or food processor. Divide mixture evenly between 12 cups or popsicle molds. Freeze about 30 minutes or until firm. Meanwhile, rinse processor; purée kiwifruit with ¼ cup honey. Repeat process with peaches and remaining ¼ cup honey. When strawberry layer is firm, pour kiwifruit purée into molds. Insert popsicle sticks and freeze about 30 minutes or until firm. Pour peach purée into molds and freeze until firm and ready to serve. *Makes 12 servings*

Favorite recipe from **National Honey Board**

Cranberry Orange Game Hen with Vegetable Stuffing

Color-Bright Ice Cream Sandwiches

¾ cup (1½ sticks) butter or margarine, softened
¾ cup creamy peanut butter
1¼ cups firmly packed light brown sugar
1 large egg
1 teaspoon vanilla extract
1½ cups all-purpose flour
1 teaspoon baking soda
¼ teaspoon salt
1¾ cups "M&M's"® Chocolate Mini Baking Bits, divided
2 quarts vanilla or chocolate ice cream, slightly softened

Preheat oven to 350°F. In large bowl cream butter, peanut butter and sugar until light and fluffy; beat in egg and vanilla. In medium bowl combine flour, baking soda and salt; blend into creamed mixture. Stir in 1⅓ cups "M&M's"® Chocolate Mini Baking Bits. Shape dough into 1¼-inch balls. Place about 2 inches apart on ungreased cookie sheets. Gently flatten to about ½-inch thickness with fingertips. Place 7 or 8 of the remaining "M&M's"® Chocolate Mini Baking Bits on each cookie; press in lightly. Bake 10 to 12 minutes or until edges are light brown. *Do not overbake.* Cool about 1 minute on cookie sheets; cool completely on wire racks. Assemble cookies in pairs with about ⅓ cup ice cream; press cookies together lightly. Wrap each sandwich in plastic wrap; freeze until firm.

Makes about 24 ice cream sandwiches

Vegetable-Stuffed Turkey Breast

¾ cup chopped onion
2 tablespoons FLEISCHMANN'S® Original Margarine, divided
1 cup cooked regular long-grain rice
1 cup shredded carrots
1 cup sliced mushrooms
½ cup chopped fresh parsley
¼ cup EGG BEATERS® Healthy Real Egg Product
½ teaspoon poultry seasoning
1 whole turkey breast (about 5 pounds)

In small skillet, over medium heat, sauté onion in 1 tablespoon margarine until tender; set aside.

In large bowl, combine rice, carrots, mushrooms, parsley, Egg Beaters® and poultry seasoning; stir in onion. Remove skin from turkey breast. Place rice mixture into cavity of turkey breast; cover cavity with foil.

Place turkey, breast-side up, on rack in roasting pan. Melt remaining margarine; brush over turkey. Roast at 350°F according to package directions or until meat thermometer registers 170°F. If necessary, tent breast with foil after 30 minutes to prevent overbrowning. Let turkey stand 15 minutes before carving. Portion 3 ounces sliced turkey and ½ cup stuffing per serving. (Freeze remaining turkey for another use.) *Makes 8 servings*

Prep Time: 30 minutes
Cook Time: 2 hours

Color-Bright Ice Cream Sandwiches

Jingle Bells Chocolate Pretzels

    1 cup HERSHEY₀S Semi-Sweet Chocolate Chips
    1 cup HERSHEY₀S Premier White Chips, divided
    1 tablespoon plus ½ teaspoon shortening (do not use butter, margarine, spread or oil), divided
    About 24 salted or unsalted pretzels (3×2 inches)

1. Cover tray or cookie sheet with wax paper.

2. Place chocolate chips, ⅔ cup white chips and 1 tablespoon shortening in medium microwave-safe bowl. Microwave at HIGH (100%) 1 minute; stir. Microwave at HIGH an additional 1 to 2 minutes, stirring every 30 seconds, until chips are melted when stirred.

3. Using fork, dip each pretzel into chocolate mixture; tap fork on side of bowl to remove excess chocolate. Place coated pretzels on prepared tray.

4. Place remaining ⅓ cup white chips and remaining ½ teaspoon shortening in small microwave-safe bowl. Microwave at HIGH 15 to 30 seconds or until chips are melted when stirred. Using tines of fork, drizzle chip mixture across pretzels. Refrigerate until coating is set. Store in airtight container in cool, dry place.

Makes about 24 coated pretzels

White Dipped Pretzels: Cover tray with wax paper. Place 1⅔ cups (10-ounce package) HERSHEY₀S Premier White Chips and 2 tablespoons shortening (do not use butter, margarine, spread or oil) in medium microwave-safe bowl. Microwave at HIGH 1 to 2 minutes or until chips are melted when stirred. Dip pretzels as directed above. Place ¼ cup HERSHEY₀S Semi-Sweet Chocolate Chips and ¼ teaspoon shortening (do not use butter, margarine, spread or oil) in small microwave-safe bowl. Microwave at HIGH 30 seconds to 1 minute or until chips are melted when stirred. Drizzle melted chocolate across pretzels, using tines of fork. Refrigerate and store as directed above.

Hidden Herb Grilled Turkey Breast

    1 (3- to 9-pound) BUTTERBALL® Breast of Young Turkey, thawed
    ¼ cup coarsely chopped fresh parsley
    2 tablespoons chopped mixed fresh herbs such as thyme, oregano and marjoram
    2 tablespoons grated Parmesan cheese
    1 teaspoon olive oil
    ½ teaspoon lemon juice
    ½ teaspoon salt
    ¼ teaspoon garlic powder
    ¼ teaspoon black pepper
    Vegetable oil

Prepare grill for indirect-heat grilling. Combine parsley, herbs, Parmesan cheese, oil, lemon juice, salt, garlic powder and pepper in medium bowl. Gently loosen and lift turkey skin from surface of meat. Spread herb blend evenly over breast meat. Replace skin over herb blend. Brush skin with vegetable oil. Place turkey breast, skin side up, on prepared grill. Cover grill and cook 1½ to 2½ hours for a 3- to 9-pound breast or until internal temperature reaches 170°F and meat is no longer pink in center.

Number of servings varies

Prep Time: 15 minutes plus grilling time

Jingle Bells Chocolate Pretzels

Holiday Hens with Sherry Gravy

4 teaspoons butter or margarine
2 teaspoons lemon juice
1 teaspoon Worcestershire sauce
3 packages (3 pounds each) PERDUE®
    Fresh Whole Cornish Hens (6 hens)
    Salt and ground black pepper to taste
    Scallion greens (optional)
6 sprigs fresh rosemary (optional)
3 tablespoons all-purpose flour
1 can (about 14 ounces) chicken broth
½ cup dry sherry

Preheat oven to 350°F. In large skillet over low heat, melt butter. Stir in lemon juice and Worcestershire sauce. Brush hens with butter mixture; sprinkle with salt and pepper, and tie legs together with kitchen string.

Place hens in large, shallow roasting pan. Roast 1 to 1¼ hours until skin is crisp and golden brown, juices run clear and no hint of pink remains when thigh is pierced. Remove to warm serving platter and discard string. Tie legs with scallion greens; garnish with rosemary.

To prepare gravy, stir flour into pan drippings. Cook over medium-low heat 4 to 5 minutes until flour is brown, stirring constantly. Gradually whisk in chicken broth and sherry; cook 3 to 4 minutes longer, until gravy is smooth and thickened, stirring often. Strain gravy into a sauce dish and serve with hens.

Makes 8 to 12 servings

Chocolate Glazed Pears

3 cups water
½ cup sugar
1 (2-inch) lemon peel twist
6 Northwest Bosc pears
6 ounces semi-sweet baking chocolate
2 tablespoons shortening

Combine water, sugar and lemon twist in large saucepan; bring to a boil. Pare pears and trim slightly to level bottom; remove core from blossom end, leaving stem intact. Add pears to poaching liquid; reduce heat. Cover and simmer gently about 8 to 10 minutes or until tender when pierced with tip of sharp knife; turn and baste occasionally. Remove pears from liquid; stand on flat dish. Cool. Melt chocolate and shortening in small saucepan over very low heat. Dry pears with paper towels. Holding each pear carefully by stem, spoon chocolate mixture over pear to coat. Let stand in cool place to set chocolate. Arrange pears on serving dish. *Makes 6 servings*

Favorite recipe from **Pear Bureau Northwest**

Holiday Hens with Sherry Gravy

Stuffed Cornish Hens for Christmas

4 PERDUE® Fresh Cornish Game Hens
1 tablespoon butter or margarine
1 tablespoon prepared mustard,
    preferably Pommery
  Corn oil for frying
2 medium potatoes, peeled and cut into
    ½-inch cubes
½ pound (1 large) chayote, peeled and
    cut into ½-inch cubes *or* 3 to
    4 carrots, cut into ½-inch cubes
½ cup chopped onion
2 cloves garlic, chopped
  Livers from Cornish Hens, sliced
½ cup coarsely chopped red or green bell
    pepper
¼ cup chopped ripe tomato
1 tablespoon raisins
1 teaspoon salt or to taste
¼ teaspoon black pepper
12 stuffed green olives
1 tablespoon cider vinegar
1 teaspoon dried thyme leaves, crushed
½ cup red wine

Remove giblets from hens (reserving livers). Rinse hens; pat dry with paper towel. Rub inside and out with mixture of butter and mustard. In heavy skillet, heat 1 tablespoon oil over medium heat. Brown hens lightly and remove.

In small saucepan, cook potatoes and chayote in boiling water for 5 minutes. Pour off water and drain vegetables on paper towels. Heat 2 tablespoons oil in skillet. Add potatoes, chayote, onion, garlic, livers, bell pepper, tomato, raisins, salt, black pepper and olives. Stir-fry 5 minutes over moderate heat, adding vinegar during last minute.

Preheat oven to 350°F. Stuff hens firmly with potato mixture, folding skin over cavity or closing with skewer. Place hens in large roasting pan, breast side up; surround with remaining potato mixture. Sprinkle hens with thyme and pour wine over all. Roast, uncovered, about 1 hour or until meat thermometer inserted into thigh registers 180°F and juices run clear when thigh is pierced, basting occasionally.

Makes 4 servings

Pumpkin Gingerbread Surprise

2 tablespoons butter
½ (6¼-ounce) bag miniature
    marshmallows
1 cup gingersnaps
1 quart DREYER'S® or EDY'S® Grand
    Pumpkin Ice Cream*
  Pumpkin pie spice or ground nutmeg

Available September through November.

• Melt butter in saucepan over low heat; slowly add marshmallows, stirring constantly until melted.

• Divide gingersnaps among 4 serving bowls or dessert plates; top each serving with 1 scoop DREYER'S® or EDY'S® Grand Pumpkin Ice Cream.

• Spoon marshmallow mixture over ice cream; sprinkle with pumpkin pie spice.

Makes 4 servings

Frizzy the Clown Cupcakes

24 REYNOLDS® Baking Cups
 1 package (about 18 ounces) cake mix
 1 container (16 ounces) vanilla
    ready-to-spread frosting
   Orange food coloring
   Powdered sugar
12 gummy fruit-flavored ring candies
24 small gumdrops
48 mini candy-coated plain chocolate
    candies
   Red string licorice

PREHEAT oven to 350°F. Place Reynolds Baking Cups in muffin pans; set aside. Prepare cake mix following package directions for 24 cupcakes. Spoon batter into baking cups. Bake as directed. Cool.

FROST cupcakes; set aside.

TINT a small amount of frosting with orange food coloring for Frizzy's hair. Add powdered sugar to frosting until it is no longer sticky (has consistency of cookie dough). Press frosting through garlic press or fine strainer. Pinch strands of frosting together and press on cupcake. For mouth, cut a section of a gummy fruit-flavored ring candy and add to cupcake. Add gumdrop for the nose, chocolate candies for eyes and red string licorice for eyebrows.

Makes 24 cupcakes

Cranberry Peach Tart with Almonds

Crust
   Prepared frozen or refrigerated pastry
    for one-crust 9-inch pie

Filling
 3 cups frozen sliced peaches (20-ounce
    package), thawed
 1 cup fresh or frozen cranberries,
    thawed
 ½ cup DOMINO® Granulated Sugar
 ¼ cup all-purpose flour
 ½ teaspoon nutmeg
 ¼ teaspoon salt

Topping
 ⅔ cup all-purpose flour
 ½ cup firmly packed DOMINO® Light
    Brown Sugar
 ½ teaspoon cinnamon
 ⅓ cup butter or margarine, softened
 ½ cup slivered almonds

Heat oven to 425°F. Line 9-inch tart pan or pie pan with pastry; trim edges until pastry is even with top edge of pan. Prick bottom of pastry with fork. Bake 10 minutes. Remove from oven. Reduce oven temperature to 375°F.

Combine filling ingredients in large bowl, tossing gently until well mixed. Spread evenly into partially-baked crust.

For crust, combine ⅔ cup flour, ½ cup brown sugar and cinnamon in small bowl. Cut in butter; stir in almonds. Sprinkle evenly over filling. Bake 40 to 50 minutes or until filling is bubbly. Cover pie loosely with foil during last 15 to 20 minutes of baking to prevent over-browning.   *Makes 6 to 8 servings*

Variation: For Blueberry Peach Tart with Almonds, substitute fresh or frozen blueberries, thawed, for the cranberries. Proceed as directed.

Preparation Time: 30 minutes
Bake Time: 1 hour

Gingerbread

½ cup packed brown sugar
⅓ cup Dried Plum Purée (recipe follows)
   or prepared dried plum butter or
   1 jar (2½ ounces) first-stage baby
   food dried plums
1 egg
2 tablespoons vegetable shortening
2 teaspoons vanilla
1 cup molasses
2⅓ cups all-purpose flour
2 teaspoons baking soda
1½ teaspoons ground ginger
1 teaspoon ground cinnamon
½ teaspoon ground cloves
½ teaspoon dry mustard
½ teaspoon salt
1 cup boiling water

Preheat oven to 375°F. Coat 9-inch square baking pan with vegetable cooking spray. In mixer bowl, beat brown sugar, dried plum purée, egg, shortening and vanilla at high speed 1 minute; beat in molasses until well blended. In medium bowl, combine flour, baking soda, spices and salt; mix into sugar mixture in three additions, alternating with water. Pour batter evenly into prepared pan. Bake in center of oven 35 to 40 minutes until springy to the touch. Cool completely in pan on wire rack. Sprinkle with powdered sugar, if desired. *Makes 16 servings*

Dried Plum Purée: Combine 1⅓ cups (8 ounces) pitted dried plums and 6 tablespoons hot water in container of food processor or blender. Pulse on and off until dried plums are finely chopped and smooth. Store leftovers in a covered container in the refrigerator for up to two months. Makes 1 cup.

Favorite recipe from **California Dried Plum Board**

Heartland Crown Roast of Pork

1 (8- to 9-pound) crown roast of pork
1 pound ground pork, cooked, drained
5 cups dry bread cubes
1 can (14½ ounces) chicken broth
1 cup walnut halves, toasted
½ cup chopped onion
½ cup chopped celery
1 teaspoon salt
¼ teaspoon *each* ground cinnamon and
   allspice
⅛ teaspoon pepper
2 cups sliced fresh or thawed frozen
   rhubarb
½ cup sugar

Place roast in shallow pan. Roast at 350°F until temperature on meat thermometer reaches 155°F, about 1½ hours. Remove roast from oven. Let stand 10 minutes before slicing to serve.

Meanwhile, combine ground pork, bread cubes, broth, walnuts, onion, celery and seasonings; mix well. Combine rhubarb and sugar in medium saucepan; bring to a boil. Pour over bread mixture; mix lightly. Spoon into buttered 2-quart casserole. Cover; bake at 350°F for 1½ hours. Serve with pork roast.
Makes 16 servings

Prep Time: 20 minutes
Cook Time: 1½ hours

Favorite recipe from **National Pork Board**

Gingerbread

Cornish Hens with Citrus Chutney Glaze

Grated peel and juice of 1 SUNKIST® orange
Grated peel and juice of 1 SUNKIST® lemon
¼ cup bottled mango chutney
1 tablespoon margarine or butter
4 Rock Cornish game hens (1¼ to 1½ pounds each), thawed if frozen (giblets and necks removed)

For glaze, in small saucepan combine citrus peel and juices, chutney and margarine. Simmer 5 minutes to blend flavors, breaking up any mango pieces with back of spoon. Tie legs of each hen together with string and turn wing tips under back of each hen. Brush hens lightly with glaze and arrange, breast side up, in shallow baking pan lined with aluminum foil. Bake at 350°F for 1 hour to 1 hour and 15 minutes or until hens are tender, brushing occasionally with remaining glaze. (Cover legs and wings with small pieces of foil if they start to become too brown.) Do not baste during last 10 minutes of baking. Remove string before serving. *Makes 4 servings*

Pumpkin Cheesecake Bars

1 (16-ounce) package pound cake mix
3 eggs, divided
2 tablespoons butter or margarine, melted
4 teaspoons pumpkin pie spice, divided
1 (8-ounce) package cream cheese, softened
1 (14-ounce) can EAGLE BRAND® Sweetened Condensed Milk (NOT evaporated milk)
1 (15-ounce) can pumpkin
½ teaspoon salt
1 cup chopped nuts

1. Preheat oven to 350°F. In large mixing bowl, beat cake mix, 1 egg, butter and

2 teaspoons pumpkin pie spice on low speed of electric mixer until crumbly. Press onto bottom of ungreased 15×10×1-inch jelly-roll pan.

2. In large mixing bowl, beat cream cheese until fluffy. Gradually beat in Eagle Brand until smooth. Beat in remaining 2 eggs, pumpkin, remaining 2 teaspoons pumpkin pie spice and salt; mix well. Pour over crust; sprinkle with nuts.

3. Bake 30 to 35 minutes or until set. Cool. Chill; cut into bars. Store covered in refrigerator. *Makes 4 dozen bars*

Creamy Holiday Tarts

1 (4-serving-size) package vanilla flavor instant pudding and pie filling mix
1 (14-ounce) can sweetened condensed milk
¾ cup raisins
¾ cup cold water
1 teaspoon ground nutmeg
1 teaspoon brandy extract
1 cup whipping cream, whipped, divided
2 (4-ounce) packages READY CRUST® Mini-Graham Cracker Crusts
Additional raisins and ground nutmeg, for garnish

1. Mix together pudding mix, sweetened condensed milk, raisins, water, nutmeg and brandy extract in large bowl. Chill 15 minutes.

2. Fold 1 cup whipped cream into pudding mixture. Spoon into crusts.

3. Garnish with remaining whipped cream. Sprinkle with additional raisins and nutmeg. Refrigerate leftovers. *Makes 12 servings*

Prep Time: 10 minutes

Cornish Hen with Citrus Chutney Glaze

Merry Santa Cupcakes

24 REYNOLDS® Holly Baking Cups
1 package (about 18 ounces) white cake mix
1 container (16 ounces) vanilla ready-to-spread frosting
    Red sugar crystals
    Mini candy-coated plain chocolate candies
    Mini marshmallows
    REYNOLDS® Holiday Prints® Printed Plastic Wrap

PREHEAT oven to 350°F. Place Reynolds Holly Baking Cups in muffin pans; set aside. Prepare cake mix, following package directions for 24 cupcakes. Spoon batter into baking cups. Bake as directed. Cool.

FROST cupcakes. Decorate each cupcake to look like Santa. For hat, sprinkle top third and halfway down one side of cupcake with red sugar crystals. Place chocolate candies on frosting for eyes and nose. Cut 2 marshmallows in half lengthwise, place at edge of red sugar for hat brim. Place a marshmallow at end of red sugar on side for the hat tassel. For beard, place about 9 marshmallows over bottom third of frosting.

WRAP cupcakes in Reynolds Holiday Prints Plastic Wrap or place cupcakes in a gift box lined with plastic wrap.

Makes 24 cupcakes

Side by Side Southern Stuffing and Turkey

1 (3-pound) BUTTERBALL® Boneless Breast of Young Turkey with Gravy Packet, thawed
    Vegetable oil
1 can (14½ ounces) chicken broth
½ cup chopped onion
½ cup chopped celery
4 tablespoons butter or margarine
4 cups packaged cornbread stuffing
1 can (16 ounces) sliced peaches, drained and coarsely chopped
½ cup chopped pecans

Spray small roasting pan with nonstick cooking spray. Place boneless breast on one side of roasting pan. Brush with vegetable oil. Combine chicken broth, onion, celery and butter in large saucepan; simmer 5 minutes over low heat. Add stuffing, peaches and pecans; lightly toss mixture. Place stuffing alongside boneless breast. Cover stuffing with foil. Bake in preheated 325°F oven 1 hour and 45 minutes or until internal temperature reaches 170°F. Let boneless breast stand 10 minutes for easy carving. Prepare gravy according to package directions. Serve turkey with gravy and stuffing.   *Makes 6 servings*

Preparation Time: 15 minutes plus roasting time

Merry Santa Cupcakes

Marbled Pumpkin Cheesecake Squares

¼ cup reduced-fat cream cheese, softened
2 tablespoons granulated sugar
3 tablespoons egg substitute
1 cup packed brown sugar
½ cup Dried Plum Purée (recipe follows)
    or prepared dried plum butter
2 egg whites
1½ teaspoons vanilla
1 cup all-purpose flour
1 teaspoon baking powder
¾ teaspoon ground cinnamon
¼ teaspoon ground ginger
¼ teaspoon salt
⅛ teaspoon ground cloves
¾ cup canned pumpkin

Preheat oven to 350°F. Coat 8-inch square baking dish or pan with vegetable cooking spray. In small bowl, beat cream cheese and granulated sugar until blended. Gradually add egg substitute, beating until blended. Set aside. In large bowl, beat brown sugar, dried plum purée, egg whites and vanilla until well blended. In medium bowl, combine flour, baking powder, cinnamon, ginger, salt and cloves; stir into brown sugar mixture until well blended. Beat in pumpkin. Spread batter evenly into prepared baking dish. Drop heaping tablespoonfuls of cream cheese mixture over batter. Using knife, gently swirl cream cheese mixture into batter. Bake in center of oven 25 to 30 minutes or until pick inserted into center comes out clean. Cool in baking dish 15 minutes. Cut into squares. Serve warm with fat-free vanilla ice cream or frozen yogurt, if desired.   *Makes 9 servings*

Dried Plum Purée: Combine 1⅓ cups (8 ounces) pitted dried plums and 6 tablespoons hot water in container of food processor or blender. Pulse on and off until dried plums are finely chopped and smooth. Store leftovers in a covered container in the refrigerator for up to two months. Makes 1 cup.

Favorite recipe from **California Dried Plum Board**

Walnut Christmas Balls

1 cup California walnuts
⅔ cup powdered sugar, divided
1 cup butter or margarine, softened
1 teaspoon vanilla
1¾ cups all-purpose flour
    Chocolate Filling (recipe follows)

In food processor or blender, process walnuts with 2 tablespoons of the sugar until finely ground; set aside. In large bowl, cream butter and remaining sugar. Beat in vanilla. Add flour and ¾ cup of the walnuts; mix until blended. Roll dough into about 3 dozen walnut-size balls. Place 2 inches apart on ungreased cookie sheets. Bake in preheated 350°F oven 10 to 12 minutes or until just golden around edges. Remove to wire racks to cool completely. Prepare Chocolate Filling. Place generous teaspoonful of filling on flat side of half the cookies. Top with remaining cookies, flat side down, forming sandwiches. Roll chocolate edges of cookies in remaining ground walnuts.
    Makes about 1½ dozen sandwich cookies

Chocolate Filling: Chop 3 squares (1 ounce each) semisweet chocolate into small pieces; place in food processor or blender with ½ teaspoon vanilla. In small saucepan, heat 2 tablespoons *each* butter or margarine and whipping cream over medium heat until hot; pour over chocolate. Process until chocolate is melted, turning machine off and scraping sides as needed. With machine running, gradually add 1 cup powdered sugar; process until smooth.

Favorite recipe from **Walnut Marketing Board**

Marbled Pumpkin Cheesecake Square

Bread Baking

There's nothing like freshly-baked bread, the crunchy crusts around warm bread. If you want that straight-from-the-oven taste, then these bakery recipes are for you.

Banana Pecan Braid

Dough
- 3 cups bread flour
- ½ cup chopped dates or pitted dates, snipped
- ½ cup chopped pecans, toasted
- ¼ cup sugar
- 2 teaspoons FLEISCHMANN'S® Bread Machine Yeast
- ½ teaspoon salt
- 3 tablespoons butter or margarine, cut up
- 3 tablespoons milk
- 3 tablespoons water (70° to 80°F)
- ½ cup mashed ripe banana
- 1 large egg

Topping
- 1 tablespoon sugar
- ½ teaspoon ground cardamom *or*
  - ¼ teaspoon ground allspice

Add dough ingredients to bread machine pan in the order suggested by manufacturer. Select dough/manual cycle. When cycle is complete, remove dough to floured surface. If necessary, knead in additional flour to make dough easy to handle.

Divide dough into 3 equal pieces; roll each to 15-inch rope. Braid 3 ropes together, pinching ends to seal. Place on greased baking sheet. Cover and let rise in warm, draft-free place until doubled in size, about 1 hour. In small bowl, combine topping ingredients; sprinkle over loaf. Bake at 375°F for 25 to 30 minutes or until done. Remove from baking sheet; cool on wire rack.   *Makes 1 loaf*

Note: Dough can be prepared in all size bread machines.

Banana Pecan Braid

Peanut Butter & Chocolate Pull-Apart Rolls

Dough

- ½ cup milk
- ⅓ cup water (70° to 80°F)
- ¼ cup creamy peanut butter, at room temperature
- ½ teaspoon salt
- 2¼ cups bread flour
- ¼ cup sugar
- 1½ teaspoons FLEISCHMANN'S® Bread Machine Yeast

Filling

- ½ cup (3 ounces) semisweet chocolate pieces
- 2 tablespoons creamy peanut butter

Icing

- ½ cup sifted powdered sugar
- 1 tablespoon creamy peanut butter or cocoa powder
- 2 to 4 teaspoons milk

To make dough, add dough ingredients to bread machine pan in the order suggested by manufacturer. Select dough/manual cycle.

To make filling, combine filling ingredients in small bowl; blend well. To shape and fill, when cycle is complete, remove dough to floured surface. If necessary, knead in additional flour to make dough easy to handle.

Roll dough into 14-inch circle. Cut into 6 wedges; place filling, dividing evenly, at wide end of each wedge. Beginning at wide end, roll up tightly; curve to form crescent. Arrange crescents, seam side down, in spoke fashion on greased large baking sheet. Pinch ends at center to seal. Cover and let rise in warm, draft-free place until doubled in size, about 30 to 45 minutes. Bake at 375°F for 15 to 20 minutes or until done. Remove from pan; cool on wire rack.

To make icing, combine icing ingredients in small bowl; stir until smooth. Drizzle on rolls.

Makes 6 rolls

Apples and Cheese Rolls

- 2 cups coarsely chopped Golden Delicious apples
- 2 tablespoons chopped onion
- 2 tablespoons margarine
- 2 teaspoons lemon juice
- ½ to ¾ teaspoon dried oregano leaves, crushed
- ½ teaspoon grated lemon peel
- ¼ teaspoon medium grind pepper
- 4 ounces shredded mozzarella cheese
- 1 loaf (14 to 16 ounces) frozen yeast bread dough, thawed

Sauté apples and onion in margarine until apples are barely tender. Add lemon juice, oregano, lemon peel and pepper; mix well. Cool mixture slightly; stir in cheese. Roll dough to 15×8-inch rectangle. Spread apple-cheese mixture over dough, leaving about 1-inch border on one (15-inch) side. Starting with opposite 15-inch side, tightly roll up dough jelly-roll fashion; moisten edge with water and seal. Cut into 1½-inch slices. Place slices on greased baking sheet about 1½ inches apart. Cover and let rise until doubled in size. Bake at 350°F 25 to 30 minutes or until lightly browned. Serve warm. *Makes 15 rolls*

Tip: Apples and Cheese Rolls are best served warm. To reheat one roll, loosely wrap in paper towel and microwave at HIGH (100%) 10 to 15 seconds.

Favorite recipe from **Washington Apple Commission**

Peanut Butter & Chocolate Pull-Apart Rolls

Bread Bowls

1¼ cups water
1 teaspoon salt
1½ teaspoons sugar
3 tablespoons white cornmeal
3¾ cups bread flour
2¼ teaspoons RED STAR® Active Dry
  Yeast

Bread Machine Method

Place room temperature ingredients in pan in order listed. Select dough cycle. At end of cycle, remove dough; follow shaping and baking instructions.

Traditional Method

Combine yeast, 1 cup flour and other dry ingredients. Heat water to 120° to 130°F; add to flour mixture. Beat 3 minutes on medium speed. By hand stir in enough remaining flour to make firm dough. Knead on floured surface 5 to 7 minutes until smooth and elastic. Use additional flour, if necessary. Place dough in lightly greased bowl. Cover; let rise until dough tests ripe.*

Shaping, Rising and Baking

Turn dough onto lightly floured surface; punch down to remove air bubbles. Divide and shape into three round balls. Place on greased cookie sheet covered with cornmeal. Cover; let rise until indentation remains after lightly touching sides of bowls. Bake in preheated 425°F oven 20 to 30 minutes. Spray or brush loaf with cold water several times during first 10 minutes of baking for a crisper crust. Remove from cookie sheet; cool.

To Make Bowls

Cut a thin slice off the top. Hollow out inside, leaving half-inch sides. Placing bowls in a 300°F oven for 10 minutes will dry sides and prevent premature soaking from the salads and soups.   *Makes 3 bread bowls*

Place two fingers into dough and then remove them. If the holes remain the dough is ripe and ready to punch down.

Cook's Notes: Fill bowls with your favorite thick soup, such as chili, hearty seafood, corn or potato chowder, or a crisp vegetable, seafood or fruit salad. Because of the thin bowl walls, they are not suitable for thin soups like chicken noodle or French onion. Fill bowls with favorite dip and use inside pieces as dunkers.

Focaccia with Dried Tomatoes and Fontina

1 tablespoon olive oil
1 loaf (1 pound) frozen bread dough,
  thawed according to package
  directions
1 jar (8 ounces) SONOMA® Marinated
  Dried Tomatoes, drained,
  2 tablespoons oil reserved
4 cloves garlic, minced
⅔ cup sliced black olives
1 tablespoon dried basil
1 teaspoon dried oregano
1 teaspoon dried rosemary
2 cups grated fontina cheese

Preheat oven to 425°F. Oil a 13×9×2-inch baking pan. Roll and stretch dough on lightly floured surface; fit dough into pan.

Combine reserved tomato oil with garlic; brush over dough. Sprinkle olives, basil, oregano and rosemary evenly over dough. Arrange tomatoes on top; cover with cheese.

Bake for 35 to 40 minutes until bread is springy to the touch and golden brown around the edges. (Cover loosely with foil during the last 10 minutes if becoming too brown.) Cut into squares while still warm.

Makes 16 squares

Bread Bowl

Holiday Rye Bread

3 to 3½ cups all-purpose flour, divided
2½ cups rye flour
⅓ cup sugar
2 envelopes FLEISCHMANN'S®
    RapidRise™ Yeast
2½ teaspoons salt
1 tablespoon grated orange peel
2 teaspoons fennel seed
1 cup beer or malt liquor
½ cup water
¼ cup light molasses
2 tablespoons butter or margarine
    Molasses Glaze (recipe follows)

In large bowl, combine 1½ cups all-purpose flour, rye flour, sugar, undissolved yeast, salt, orange peel and fennel seed. Heat beer, water, molasses and butter until very warm (120° to 130°F). Stir into dry ingredients. Beat 2 minutes at medium speed of electric mixer, scraping bowl occasionally. Stir in enough remaining flour to make soft dough. Knead on lightly floured surface until smooth and elastic, about 8 to 10 minutes. Cover; let rest 10 minutes.

Divide dough into 4 equal pieces. Roll each to 10×6-inch oval. Roll each up tightly from long side, as for jelly roll, tapering ends. Pinch seams to seal. Place on greased baking sheets. Cover; let rise in warm, draft-free place until doubled in size, about 1½ hours.

With sharp knife, make 3 diagonal cuts on top of each loaf. Brush with Molasses Glaze. Bake at 375°F for 15 minutes; brush loaves with Glaze. Bake additional 10 minutes or until done. Remove loaves from oven and brush again with Glaze. Cool on wire racks.

Makes 4 small loaves

Molasses Glaze: Combine 2 tablespoons molasses and 2 tablespoons water. Stir until well blended.

Cajun Bubble Bread

¼ cup (½ stick) unsalted butter
2 green onions, finely chopped
2 cloves garlic, minced
2 teaspoons Cajun seasoning spice
    blend*
4 tablespoons *Frank's® RedHot®* Cayenne
    Pepper Sauce
¼ cup chopped almonds, divided
2 pounds thawed frozen bread dough
⅔ cup (about 3 ounces) shredded
    Monterey Jack-Cheddar cheese
    blend, divided
2 tablespoons grated Parmesan cheese,
    divided

*If Cajun seasoning is unavailable, substitute ¾ teaspoon each Italian seasoning and chili powder, and ½ teaspoon celery seed.

1. Melt butter in small saucepan. Add onions, garlic and Cajun spice; cook over medium-low heat 3 minutes or just until tender. Remove from heat; stir in **Frank's RedHot** Sauce.

2. Grease 10-inch tube pan or 12-cup Bundt pan.** Sprinkle bottom of tube pan with 1 tablespoon almonds. Cut bread dough into 24 (1-inch) pieces; shape into balls. Dip dough balls, one at a time, into butter mixture. Place in single layer in bottom of tube pan. Sprinkle with ¼ cup Monterey Jack-Cheddar cheese, 1 tablespoon almonds and 2 teaspoons Parmesan.

3. Repeat layers twice with remaining ingredients. Cover with plastic wrap; let rise in warm place 1½ hours or until doubled in size.

4. Preheat oven to 375°F. Bake 35 minutes or until golden brown. (Loosely cover with foil during last 15 minutes if bread browns too quickly.) Loosen bread from sides of pan. Invert immediately onto serving plate; serve warm. *Makes 8 servings*

**You may substitute 2 (8×4-inch) loaf pans.

Prep Time: 30 minutes
Rise Time: 1½ hours
Cook Time: 35 minutes

Easy Apple Bread

2¾ cups bread or all-purpose flour
½ cup plus 2 tablespoons granulated
    sugar, divided
½ teaspoon salt
1 package active dry yeast
¼ cup warm water (110°F)
½ cup milk
½ cup margarine
1 egg, lightly beaten
½ teaspoon almond extract
2 cups drained canned apple slices*
½ cup slivered almonds (2¼ ounces)
1 teaspoon ground cinnamon
1 cup sifted powdered sugar
1½ tablespoons milk
¼ teaspoon vanilla extract

Or, use apples from 1 (20-ounce) can apple pie filling or canned peaches.

In large bowl, combine flour, 2 tablespoons granulated sugar and salt. In small bowl, add yeast to water; stir until dissolved. Combine milk and margarine in small saucepan; heat to 105° to 110°F. Add yeast mixture, egg and almond extract. Pour into flour mixture. Beat until well blended. Cover bowl with plastic wrap. Let rest 20 minutes.

Spread dough evenly in 2 greased 8-inch round cake pans. Arrange ½ of apple slices in circles over each pan of dough. Sprinkle with almonds. Cover loosely with waxed paper brushed with oil, then cover tightly with plastic wrap. Refrigerate 2 to 24 hours. When ready to bake, remove from refrigerator. Uncover dough. Let stand at room temperature 10 minutes.

Combine remaining ½ cup granulated sugar and cinnamon. Sprinkle ½ of mixture over each pan. Bake in preheated 350°F oven 40 to 45 minutes. Remove from pans and cool on wire racks.

In small bowl, combine powdered sugar, milk and vanilla; beat until smooth. Drizzle over bread.

Makes two 8-inch pans (8 servings each)

*Favorite recipe from **North Dakota Wheat Commission***

Idaho Potato Focaccia

2 medium Idaho Potatoes (5½ ounces
    each), washed and cut into cubes
Nonstick cooking spray
1 pound frozen white bread dough,
    thawed to room temperature
1 small onion, thinly sliced and
    separated into rings
2 cloves garlic, minced
2 tablespoons minced fresh herbs
    (chives, parsley, oregano, rosemary)
1 teaspoon Cajun seasoning

1. Spray large baking sheet with cooking spray. Pat thawed bread dough onto the pan, forming a 9-inch round. Spray dough with cooking spray and allow to rise in warm place until doubled in size.

2. Preheat oven to 425°F. Combine potatoes, onion, garlic, herbs and Cajun seasoning in medium bowl. Spray another baking sheet with cooking spray. Spread potato mixture in single layer on baking sheet. Bake 15 minutes; cool.

3. *Reduce heat to 350°F.* Spread cooled potato mixture on bread dough, being sure to include all browned bits from baking sheet. Gently press mixture onto bread dough, distributing evenly to edges of bread dough round. Bake 35 to 40 minutes or until golden brown. Serve warm or at room temperature.

Makes 8 servings

*Favorite recipe from **Idaho Potato Commission***

Donna's Heavenly Orange Chip Scones

4 cups all-purpose flour
1 cup granulated sugar
4 teaspoons baking powder
½ teaspoon baking soda
½ teaspoon salt
1 cup (6 ounces) NESTLÉ® TOLL HOUSE® Semi-Sweet Chocolate Mini Morsels
1 cup golden raisins
1 tablespoon grated orange peel
1 cup (2 sticks) unsalted butter, cut into pieces and softened
1 cup buttermilk
3 large eggs, *divided*
1 teaspoon orange extract
1 tablespoon milk
Icing (recipe follows)

PREHEAT oven to 350°F. Lightly grease baking sheets.

COMBINE flour, granulated sugar, baking powder, baking soda and salt in large bowl. Add morsels, raisins and orange peel; mix well. Cut in butter with pastry blender or two knives until mixture resembles coarse crumbs. Combine buttermilk, *2 eggs* and orange extract in small bowl. Pour buttermilk mixture into flour mixture; mix just until a sticky dough is formed. Do not overmix. Drop by ¼ cupfuls onto prepared baking sheets. Combine *remaining* egg and milk in small bowl. Brush egg mixture over top of dough.

BAKE for 18 to 22 minutes or until wooden pick inserted in center comes out clean. For best results, bake one baking sheet at a time. Cool on wire racks for 10 minutes. Drizzle scones with icing. Serve warm.

Makes 2 dozen scones

Icing: **COMBINE** 2 cups powdered sugar, ¼ cup orange juice, 1 tablespoon grated orange peel and 1 teaspoon orange extract in medium bowl. Mix until smooth.

Jamaican Cherry Bread

2½ teaspoons active dry yeast
3¼ cups bread flour
1 tablespoon grated lime peel
2 teaspoons minced fresh ginger *or* ¾ teaspoon ground ginger
1 teaspoon salt
1 cup milk
¼ cup firmly packed brown sugar
¼ cup lime juice
3 tablespoons butter, melted
⅔ cup toasted coconut*
½ cup dried tart cherries

To toast coconut: spread coconut on ungreased pan. Bake in preheated 350°F oven 5 to 7 minutes, stirring occasionally, or until golden brown.

Bread Machine Directions

1. Measure carefully, placing all ingredients except coconut and cherries in bread machine pan in order specified by owner's manual.

2. Program desired cycle; press start. Add coconut and cherries at the beep or at the end of the first kneading cycle. Remove baked bread from pan; cool on wire rack. Serve at room temperature.

Makes 1 loaf, about 16 slices

Favorite recipe from **Cherry Marketing Institute**

Donna's Heavenly Orange Chip Scones

Apple Cinnamon Rolls

5 to 5½ cups all-purpose flour
½ cup sugar
2 envelopes FLEISCHMANN'S®
    RapidRise™ Yeast
1 teaspoon salt
½ cup water
½ cup milk
¼ cup butter or margarine
3 large eggs
    Apple Filling (recipe follows)
    Cinnamon-Sugar Topping (recipe
    follows)

In large bowl, combine 1 cup flour, sugar, undissolved yeast and salt. Heat water, milk, and butter until very warm (120° to 130°F). Gradually add to dry ingredients. Beat 2 minutes at medium speed of electric mixer, scraping bowl occasionally. Add eggs and 1 cup flour; beat 2 minutes at high speed, scraping bowl occasionally. Stir in enough remaining flour to make soft dough. Knead on lightly floured surface until smooth and elastic, about 8 to 10 minutes. Cover; let rest 10 minutes.

Divide dough into 2 equal portions. Roll each portion into 12×8-inch rectangle. Spread Apple Filling evenly over dough. Beginning at long end of each, roll up tightly jelly-roll style. Pinch seams to seal. Cut each roll into 12 equal pieces. Place, cut sides up, in greased 9-inch round pans. Cover, let rise in warm, draft-free place until doubled in size, about 45 minutes. Sprinkle with Cinnamon-Sugar Topping.

Bake at 375°F for 25 to 30 minutes or until done. Remove from pans; serve warm.

Makes 24 rolls

Apple Filling: Combine 2 large cooking apples, chopped, 2 tablespoons all-purpose flour, ¾ cup sugar, and ¼ cup butter or margarine in medium saucepan; bring to a boil over medium high heat. Cook 3 minutes. Reduce heat to medium-low; cook 10 minutes, stirring constantly until thick. Stir in 1 teaspoon ground cinnamon and ½ teaspoon nutmeg. Cool completely.

Cinnamon-Sugar Topping: Combine ¾ cup sugar, 1 teaspoon ground cinnamon, and ½ teaspoon nutmeg. Stir until well blended.

Fruit-Filled Petal Rolls

1 package BOB EVANS® Frozen White
    Dinner Roll Dough
¼ cup spreadable fruit or fruit pie filling
1 cup powdered sugar
1 tablespoon orange juice

Thaw dough at room temperature 45 minutes to 1 hour; do not allow dough to begin rising. Knead dough until smooth. Stretch dough and roll into 12-inch square. Cut into 9 (4-inch) squares. Grease muffin pan; press dough squares into cups so that corners are standing up. Place 1 rounded teaspoon fruit filling in each cup. Allow rolls to rise according to package directions. Preheat oven to 350°F. Bake 15 minutes or until lightly browned; let cool slightly. For glaze, combine powdered sugar and orange juice until smooth. Brush tops of rolls with glaze. Serve warm or at room temperature with butter or margarine.

Makes 9 rolls

Golden Cheddar Batter Bread

1 package active dry yeast
¾ cup warm water (110° to 115°F)
3 cups unsifted all-purpose flour,
    divided
1½ cups finely chopped Golden Delicious
    apples
1 cup shredded Cheddar cheese
2 large eggs, lightly beaten
2 tablespoons vegetable shortening
2 tablespoons sugar
1 teaspoon salt
    Buttery Apple Spread (recipe follows)

1. In large bowl, combine yeast and water, stirring to dissolve yeast. Set aside until mixture begins to foam, about 5 minutes. Add 1½ cups flour, apples, cheese, eggs, shortening, sugar and salt to yeast mixture; beat with electric mixer at medium speed 2 minutes. Beat in remaining flour gradually with spoon. Cover with clean cloth and let rise 50 to 60 minutes or until doubled. Meanwhile, prepare Buttery Apple Spread.

2. Grease 9×5-inch loaf pan. Beat batter by hand 30 seconds. Spread batter evenly in prepared pan. Cover with cloth and let rise 40 minutes or until nearly doubled.

3. Heat oven to 375°F. Bake bread 45 to 55 minutes or until loaf sounds hollow when gently tapped. Remove from pan; cool on wire rack at least 15 minutes. Serve with Buttery Apple Spread.   *Makes 1 loaf*

Buttery Apple Spread: Peel, core and slice 1 Golden Delicious apple; place in small saucepan with 1 tablespoon water. Cover tightly and cook over medium heat until apple is very tender. Mash apple with fork; cool completely. In small bowl, beat ½ cup softened butter with electric mixer until light and fluffy. Gradually add mashed apple; beat until well combined. Makes about 1 cup.

Favorite recipe from **Washington Apple Commission**

Parker House Rolls

4¾ to 5¼ cups all-purpose flour, divided
⅓ cup sugar
2 envelopes FLEISCHMANN'S®
    RapidRise™ Yeast
1½ teaspoons salt
¾ cup milk
¾ cup water
¼ cup butter or margarine
1 large egg
¼ cup butter or margarine, melted

In large bowl, combine 2 cups flour, sugar, undissolved yeast and salt. Heat milk, water and ¼ cup unmelted butter until very warm (120° to 130°F). Stir into dry ingredients. Beat 2 minutes at medium speed of electric mixer, scraping bowl occasionally. Add egg and ½ cup flour; beat 2 minutes at high speed. Stir in enough remaining flour to make a soft dough. Knead on lightly floured surface until smooth and elastic, about 8 to 10 minutes. Cover;* let rest 10 minutes.

Divide dough in half; roll each half into 12-inch square, about ¼-inch thick. Cut each into 6 (12×2-inch) strips. Cut each strip into 3 (4×2-inch) rectangles. Brush each rectangle with melted butter. Crease rectangles slightly off center with dull edge of knife and fold at crease. Arrange rolls side by side in rows, slightly overlapping, on greased baking sheets, with shorter side of each roll facing down. Allow ¼ inch of space between each row. Cover; let rise in warm, draft-free place until doubled in size, about 30 minutes.

Bake at 400°F for 13 to 15 minutes or until done. Remove from sheets; cool on wire rack. Brush with remaining melted butter.
                              Makes 36 rolls

If desired, allow dough to rise in refrigerator 12 to 24 hours.

Dried Cherry-Almond Bread

1-Pound Loaf
- ¾ cup milk
- 1 tablespoon butter or margarine
- 1 large egg
- ¾ teaspoon salt
- 2 cups bread flour
- ⅓ cup dried tart red cherries or dried cranberries
- ¼ cup slivered almonds, toasted*
- 1 tablespoon sugar
- 1½ teaspoons FLEISCHMANN'S® Bread Machine Yeast

1½-Pound Loaf
- 1 cup plus 2 tablespoons milk
- 1 tablespoon butter or margarine
- 1 large egg
- 1 teaspoon salt
- 3 cups bread flour
- ½ cup dried tart red cherries or dried cranberries
- ⅓ cup slivered almonds, toasted*
- 4 teaspoons sugar
- 2 teaspoons FLEISCHMANN'S® Bread Machine Yeast

Toasting nuts brings out their full flavor and helps keep them crisp in breads. To toast nuts, spread the chopped nuts in a shallow baking pan large enough to accommodate a single layer. Bake the nuts at 350°F for 5 to 15 minutes or until lightly toasted, stirring several times and checking often. Be sure to cool the nuts before adding to the bread machine.

Use the 1-pound recipe if your machine pan holds 10 cups or less of water. Add ingredients to bread machine pan in the order suggested by manufacturer, adding dried tart red cherries and almonds with flour.

Recommended cycle: Basic/white bread cycle; light or medium/normal crust color setting. *Do not use delay cycle.*

Makes 1 loaf (8 or 12 slices)

Mexican Monkey Bread

- ½ cup (1 stick) butter, melted
- 2 tablespoons chili powder
- 1 tablespoon ground cumin
- 2 packages (about 16 ounces each) frozen bread dough, thawed and cut into 1-inch cubes
- 2 cups (8 ounces) shredded Monterey Jack or Mexican blend cheese, divided
- 2 cups *French's*® French Fried Onions, divided
- 1 can (4½ ounces) chopped green chilies, drained

1. Grease bottom and side of 10-inch tube pan. Combine melted butter and spices in small bowl. Dip bread cubes, one at a time, into butter mixture. Place ⅓ of bread cubes in bottom of prepared pan.

2. Sprinkle with ⅔ cup cheese, ⅔ *cup* French Fried Onions and half of chilies. Repeat layers. Top with remaining ⅓ of bread cubes. Cover pan with plastic wrap and place on baking sheet. Let rest in draft-free place for 1 hour or until doubled in size.

3. Preheat oven to 375°F. Bake 35 minutes or until golden. Sprinkle with remaining cheese and onions; bake 5 minutes or until cheese melts and onions are golden. Loosen edges of bread; invert onto baking rack. Immediately invert onto serving platter. Serve warm.

Makes 10 servings

Prep Time: 15 minutes
Stand Time: 1 hour
Cook Time: 40 minutes

Dried Cherry-Almond Bread

Chocolate Chip Coffeecake

   3 cups all-purpose flour
   ⅓ cup sugar
   2 envelopes FLEISCHMANN'S®
      RapidRise™ Yeast
   1 teaspoon salt
   ½ cup milk
   ½ cup water
   ½ cup butter or margarine
   2 large eggs
   ¾ cup semi-sweet chocolate morsels
      Chocolate Nut Topping (recipe
      follows)

In large bowl, combine 1 cup flour, sugar, undissolved yeast and salt. Heat milk, water and butter until very warm (120° to 130°F). Gradually add to dry ingredients. Beat 2 minutes at medium speed of electric mixer, scraping bowl occasionally. Add eggs and 1 cup flour; beat 2 minutes at high speed, scraping bowl occasionally. Stir in chocolate morsels and remaining flour to make a soft batter. Turn into greased 13×9×2-inch baking pan. Cover; let rise in warm, draft-free place until doubled in size, about 1 hour.

Bake at 400°F for 15 minutes; remove from oven and sprinkle with Chocolate Nut Topping. Return to oven and bake additional 10 minutes or until done. Cool in pan for 10 minutes. Remove from pan; cool on wire rack.   *Makes 1 cake*

Chocolate Nut Topping: In medium bowl, cut ½ cup butter into ⅔ cup all-purpose flour until crumbly. Stir in ⅔ cup sugar, 2 teaspoons ground cinnamon, 1 cup semi-sweet chocolate morsels and 1 cup chopped pecans.

Oatmeal Bread

   2¼ teaspoons quick-rising active dry yeast
      (one 1¼ ounce package)
   3 cups bread flour
   1 cup QUAKER® Oats (quick or old
      fashioned, uncooked)
   2 tablespoons granulated sugar
   1 teaspoon salt
   1¼ to 1⅓ cups milk or water
   2 tablespoons butter or margarine,
      melted or 1 tablespoon vegetable oil

Bring all ingredients to room temperature by letting them stand on the counter for about 30 minutes.* Place yeast in bread machine according to directions in manual. Combine flour, oats, sugar and salt in bowl; mix well. In separate bowl, combine milk and butter; mix well. Place into bread machine according to manual. When baking, use white bread and light crust setting.

Makes one 1½-pound loaf

*This can be done quickly by microwaving the ingredients for 15 to 20 seconds.

Maple Fruit Variation: Combine ⅓ cup pancake syrup with margarine and only 1 cup milk. Proceed as directed above. Add ½ cup dried fruit to bread dough partially through kneading cycle according to bread machine manual.

Whole Wheat Variation: Combine 1½ cups bread flour with 1½ cups whole wheat flour. Proceed as directed above.

Chocolate Chip Coffeecake

Pumpernickel Raisin Bread

3 tablespoons plus 1 teaspoon
GRANDMA'S® Gold Molasses,
divided
2 packages (¼ ounce each) active dry
yeast
1¼ cups warm water (105° to 115°F),
divided
2 cups all-purpose flour
1 cup rye flour
2 tablespoons unsweetened cocoa
powder
2 teaspoons salt
2 teaspoons caraway seeds
1½ cups golden raisins

Glaze:
1 tablespoon GRANDMA'S® Gold
Molasses
1 tablespoon water
2 tablespoons caraway seeds

1. Dissolve 1 teaspoon Grandma's® Gold Molasses and yeast in ¼ cup warm water in small bowl. Let stand until foamy, about 5 minutes.

2. Combine flours, cocoa, salt and 2 teaspoons caraway seeds in 12-cup food processor fitted with dough or steel blade. Add yeast mixture; mix well. Combine remaining 1 cup warm water and 3 tablespoons Grandma's® Gold Molasses in medium bowl.

3. With machine running, pour molasses mixture slowly through food tube. When dough forms a ball, process 1 minute. If dough sticks to side of bowl, add additional flour, 2 tablespoons at a time. If dough is too dry and does not stick together, add water, 1 tablespoon at a time.

4. Place dough in large greased bowl and turn to coat; cover with plastic wrap. Bring large shallow pot of water to a simmer. Remove from heat; place wire rack in pot. Place bowl with dough on rack; cover with towel. Let rise 1 to 1¼ hours or until doubled in bulk.

5. Punch dough down; flatten to ¼-inch thickness. Sprinkle with raisins; roll up dough and knead several times. Shape into 8-inch round; place on greased baking sheet. Place on rack over hot water as directed above; cover with towel. Let rise 1 to 1¼ hours or until doubled.

6. For glaze, combine 1 tablespoon Grandma's® Gold Molasses and 1 tablespoon water. Brush over loaf; sprinkle with 2 tablespoons caraway seeds.

7. Bake in 350°F oven 25 to 30 minutes until bread sounds hollow when tapped. Cool on rack 30 minutes.   *Makes 1 large loaf*

Roman Meal® Homemade Bread

2 cups ROMAN MEAL® Original Cereal
⅔ cup nonfat dry milk
1 tablespoon salt
2 packages active dry yeast
5½ cups all-purpose flour, divided
⅓ cup honey
¼ cup vegetable oil
1 tablespoon molasses
2½ cups very warm water (115° to 120°F)

In large bowl blend cereal, dry milk, salt, yeast and 3 cups flour. Add honey, oil, molasses and water. Stir to mix, beat 60 strokes. Blend in remaining 2½ cups flour. On lightly floured board, knead dough until it feels springy (about 5 minutes), adding just enough flour to hands and board to prevent sticking. Grease bowl; return dough to bowl, turning once to grease top. Cover and let rise in warm place until doubled (about 1 hour). Punch down dough and turn over. Cover and let rise 30 minutes. Form into 2 loaves and place in well-greased 9×5×3-inch loaf pans. Grease tops of loaves; cover and let rise until doubled (about 45 minutes). Bake at 400°F for about 40 minutes. Remove from pans and cool on racks.   *Makes 2 loaves*

European Wheat Bread

Medium

¾ cup plus 3 tablespoons water

1 egg white

3 tablespoons oil

3 tablespoons molasses

1½ teaspoons cinnamon

1½ teaspoons salt

3 cups whole wheat flour

3½ teaspoons RED STAR® Active Dry
Yeast *or* 2¼ teaspoons
QUICK•RISE™ Yeast

½ cup raisins

½ cup walnuts

Large

1 cup water

2 egg whites

¼ cup oil

¼ cup molasses

2 teaspoons cinnamon

2 teaspoons salt

4 cups whole wheat flour

4½ teaspoons RED STAR® Active Dry
Yeast *or* 3 teaspoons QUICK•RISE™
Yeast

⅔ cup raisins

⅔ cup walnuts

Bread Machine Method

Have liquid ingredients at 80°F and all others at room temperature. Place ingredients in pan in the order listed. Select basic cycle and medium/normal crust. Walnuts and raisins can be added 5 minutes before the end of the last kneading. Do not use the delay timer.

Mixer Methods

Using ingredient amounts listed for medium loaf, combine yeast, 1 cup whole wheat flour, and other dry ingredients, except walnuts and raisins. Combine liquids, except egg white, and heat to 120° to 130°F.

Hand-Held Mixer Method. Combine dry mixture and liquid ingredients in mixing bowl on low speed. Beat 2 to 3 minutes on medium speed. Add egg white; beat 1 minute. By hand, stir in walnuts, raisins and enough remaining flour to make a firm dough. Knead on floured surface 5 to 7 minutes or until smooth and elastic. Use additional flour if necessary.

Stand Mixer Method. Combine dry mixture and liquid ingredients in mixing bowl with paddle or beaters for 4 minutes on medium speed. Add egg white; beat 1 minute. Gradually add walnuts, raisins, and remaining flour and knead with dough hook(s) 5 to 7 minutes until smooth and elastic.

Food Processor Method. Put dry mixture in processing bowl with steel blade. While motor is running, add liquid ingredients, including egg white. Process until mixed. Continue processing, adding remaining flour until dough forms a ball. Add walnuts and raisins; pulse just until mixed.

Rising, Shaping and Baking

Place dough in lightly oiled bowl and turn to grease top. Cover; let rise until dough tests "ripe." (Gently stick two fingers in the risen dough up to the second knuckle and take them out. If the indentations remain, the dough is "ripe.") Turn dough onto lightly floured surface; punch down to remove air bubbles. Shape into a round loaf. Place on greased cookie sheet. Cover; let rise in warm place until indentation remains after touching. With a very sharp knife, make 3 or 4 slashes, ¼-inch deep on top of loaf; cut crosswise, to make a crisscross design. Bake in preheated 375°F oven 30 to 40 minutes. Remove from pan; cool.

Variation: Recipe will make 12 to 15 dinner rolls. Bake dinner rolls 12 to 15 minutes.

Cook's Note: Due to the low volume of this loaf, the medium recipe can be used in a small machine.

Fanfare Dinner Rolls

1 cup warm water (105° to 115°F)
2 envelopes quick-rising dry yeast
¼ teaspoon sugar
⅔ cup whole milk, room temperature
⅓ cup sugar
¼ cup WESSON® Canola Oil
1 large egg
1 tablespoon poppy seeds
2½ teaspoons salt
5⅓ cups all-purpose flour
1 cup (2 sticks) chilled unsalted butter,
    cut into thin slices
    PAM® No-Stick Cooking Spray
3 tablespoons unsalted butter, melted
    Poppy seeds

Pour water into a large bowl. Sprinkle yeast, then ¼ teaspoon sugar into water; stir well. Let stand 5 to 8 minutes or until mixture is slightly foamy. Meanwhile, in a small bowl, whisk milk, ⅓ cup sugar, Wesson® Oil, egg, poppy seeds and salt until well blended. Pour milk mixture into yeast mixture; mix well. Gradually add 1 cup flour to mixture and stir until batter is smooth. In a food processor, combine 4 cups flour and chilled butter; process until mixture resembles a coarse meal. Add to batter and stir until dry ingredients are moistened. Knead dough in bowl (about 5 minutes) until smooth. Add more flour if dough is sticky. Cover with towels and let rise in a warm place for 30 minutes or until dough nearly doubles in size.

Spray 24 muffin cups with PAM® Cooking Spray. Turn dough onto floured surface; knead about 4 minutes until dough is smooth and elastic. Evenly divide dough into 4 portions. Place 1 portion on floured surface; cover and refrigerate remaining portions. Roll dough to 13×12×⅛-inch rectangle. Cut rectangle lengthwise into six 2-inch strips. Stack strips on top of each other to form 6 layers. Cut stack into 6 equal individual small stacks. Place each stack, cut side down, into muffin cup. Repeat with remaining dough sections.

Cover with a towel; let rise in a warm place for 30 minutes or until nearly doubled in size.

Position one rack in the center of oven and the other rack above the first, allowing plenty of space for rolls to continue rising while baking. Preheat oven to 350°F. Brush rolls gently with melted butter; sprinkle with poppy seeds. Bake for 25 minutes until golden brown. Switch muffin pans halfway through bake time. Cool rolls 7 to 10 minutes. Remove rolls from pan; cool on wire rack. Serve warm.

Makes 2 dozen rolls

Tip: If you have any leftover dough, roll it into balls. Roll each ball lightly in Wesson® Oil and cinnamon-sugar. Place on a cookie sheet and bake until golden brown.

Onion-Herb Baked Bread

1 envelope LIPTON® RECIPE SECRETS®
    Golden Onion Soup Mix
1 medium clove garlic, finely chopped
1 teaspoon dried basil leaves
1 teaspoon dried oregano leaves
⅛ teaspoon pepper
½ cup butter or margarine, softened
1 loaf Italian or French bread (about
    16 inches long), halved lengthwise

Preheat oven to 375°F.

In small bowl, thoroughly blend all ingredients except bread; generously spread on bread halves. Arrange bread, cut-side up, on baking sheet. Bake 15 minutes or until golden. Serve warm.

Makes 1 loaf

Note: Store any remaining spread, covered, in refrigerator for future use.

Fanfare Dinner Rolls

Petit Pain au Chocolate

1 package (17.25 ounces) frozen puff
   pastry sheets, thawed
1 cup (6 ounces) NESTLÉ® TOLL
   HOUSE® Milk Chocolate Morsels,
   divided
1 large egg, beaten
1 bar (2 ounces *total*) NESTLÉ® TOLL
   HOUSE® Semi-Sweet Chocolate
   Baking Bars, broken into pieces
2 tablespoons butter or margarine
1 cup powdered sugar
2 tablespoons hot water

PREHEAT oven to 350°F. Grease 2 baking
sheets.

UNFOLD *1* pastry sheet on lightly floured
surface. Roll out to make 10-inch square. Cut
into 4 squares. Place *2 tablespoons* morsels in
center of each square. Brush edges lightly with
beaten egg and fold squares to form triangles.
Press edges to seal. Place on prepared baking
sheet about 2 inches apart. Repeat with
remaining pastry sheet. Brush top of each
pastry with beaten egg.

BAKE for 15 to 17 minutes or until puffed
and golden. Cool on baking sheets for
2 minutes; remove to wire racks to cool
completely.

MELT baking bar and butter in small,
microwave-safe bowl on HIGH (100%) power
for 30 seconds; stir. Microwave at additional
10- to 20-second intervals, stirring until
smooth. Stir in sugar. Add water, stirring until
icing is smooth, adding additional water, if
necessary. Drizzle icing over pastries.

Makes 8 pastries

Potato Rosemary Rolls

Dough
   1 cup plus 2 tablespoons water (70° to
      80°F)
   2 tablespoons olive oil
   1 teaspoon salt
   3 cups bread flour
   ½ cup instant potato flakes or buds
   2 tablespoons nonfat dry milk powder
   1 tablespoon sugar
   1 teaspoon SPICE ISLANDS® Rosemary,
      crushed
   1½ teaspoons FLEISCHMANN'S® Bread
      Machine Yeast

Topping
   1 egg, lightly beaten
   Sesame or poppy seeds or additional
      dried rosemary, crushed

Measure all dough ingredients into bread
machine pan in the order suggested by
manufacturer, adding potato flakes with flour.
Select dough/manual cycle. When cycle is
complete, remove dough to floured surface. If
necessary, knead in additional flour to make
dough easy to handle.

Divide dough into 12 equal pieces. Roll each
piece to 10-inch rope; coil each rope and tuck
end under coil. Place rolls 2 inches apart on
large greased baking sheet. Cover; let rise in
warm, draft-free place until doubled in size,
about 45 to 60 minutes. Brush tops with
beaten egg; sprinkle with sesame seeds. Bake
at 375°F for 15 to 20 minutes or until done.
Remove from pan; cool on wire rack.

Makes 12 rolls

Note: Dough can be prepared in 1½ and
2-pound bread machines.

Petit Pain au Chocolate

Southern Caramel Pecan Rolls

Topping
- ⅔ cup sifted powdered sugar
- ⅔ cup dark brown sugar
- ½ cup whipping cream
- 1 teaspoon vanilla
  PAM® No-Stick Cooking Spray
- 1 cup coarsely chopped pecans

Rolls
- 1 cup dark raisins
- ⅓ cup brandy
- 2 (1-pound) loaves frozen sweet or white bread dough, thawed, but not doubled in size
- ¼ cup WESSON® Best Blend Oil
- ½ cup packed dark brown sugar
- 1 tablespoon ground cinnamon
- ½ teaspoon ground nutmeg

Topping

In a medium bowl, stir together sugars, whipping cream and vanilla. Spray two 9×1½-inch round cake pans with PAM® Cooking Spray. Evenly divide mixture between pans and sprinkle with pecans; set aside pans.

Rolls

In a small bowl, soak raisins in brandy for 30 minutes; set aside and stir occasionally.

On floured surface, roll *each* loaf into 12×8×¼-inch rectangle. Generously brush *each* sheet of dough with Wesson® Oil. In a small bowl, mix together sugar, cinnamon and nutmeg. Sprinkle over dough; top with soaked raisins. Roll up rectangles jelly-roll style starting with long edge. Pinch dough to seal. Cut into 12 slices. Place rolls, spiral side down, in cake pans. Cover with towels and let rise in warm place for 30 minutes or until nearly double in size. Preheat oven to 375°F. Bake, uncovered, for 15 to 20 minutes. Cover pans with foil to prevent overbrowning and bake an additional 10 minutes. Cool in pans 7 minutes. Invert onto serving plate. Best when served warm.   *Makes 24 rolls*

Roasted Pepper-Olive Loaf

1-Pound Loaf
- ½ cup water
- 2 tablespoons drained diced roasted red bell peppers or pimientos
- 1 tablespoon sliced pitted ripe olives, drained
- 1 tablespoon butter or margarine
- ¾ teaspoon salt
- 2 cups bread flour
- 2 tablespoons nonfat dry milk powder
- 2 teaspoons sugar
- 1½ teaspoons FLEISCHMANN'S® Bread Machine Yeast

1½-Pound Loaf
- ¾ cup water
- 3 tablespoons drained diced roasted red bell peppers or pimientos
- 2 tablespoons sliced pitted ripe olives, drained
- 1 tablespoon butter or margarine
- 1 teaspoon salt
- 3 cups bread flour
- 3 tablespoons nonfat dry milk powder
- 1 tablespoon sugar
- 2 teaspoons FLEISCHMANN'S® Bread Machine Yeast

Use the 1-pound recipe if your machine pan holds 10 cups or less of water. Add ingredients to bread machine pan in the order suggested by manufacturer, adding roasted red bell peppers and olives with water. Recommended cycle: Basic/white bread cycle; medium/normal crust color setting. Timed-bake feature can be used.   *Makes 1 loaf (8 or 12 slices)*

Serving Suggestion: For elegant, yet easy hors d'oeuvres, cut slices of this colorful bread into triangles. Serve the triangles topped with your favorite Cheddar, Swiss or cream cheese spread.

Southern Caramel Pecan Rolls

Swiss/Olive Rye Bread

1-Pound Loaf
½ cup water
2 tablespoons vegetable oil
1¼ cups bread flour
¾ cup rye flour
½ cup shredded Swiss cheese
2 tablespoons sugar
¾ teaspoon salt
1½ teaspoons RED STAR® Active Dry
 Yeast *or* 1 teaspoon QUICK•RISE™
 Yeast
⅓ cup pimiento-stuffed olives (well-
 drained)

1½-Pound Loaf
¾ cup water
3 tablespoons vegetable oil
1⅞ cups bread flour
1 cup plus 2 tablespoons rye flour
¾ cup shredded Swiss cheese
3 tablespoons sugar
1 teaspoon salt
2¼ teaspoons RED STAR® Active Dry
 Yeast *or* 1½ teaspoons
 QUICK•RISE™ Yeast
½ cup pimiento-stuffed olives (well-
 drained)

2-Pound Loaf
1 cup water
¼ cup vegetable oil
2½ cups bread flour
1½ cups rye flour
1 cup shredded Swiss cheese
¼ cup sugar
1½ teaspoons salt
1 tablespoon RED STAR® Active Dry
 Yeast *or* 2 teaspoons QUICK•RISE™
 Yeast
¾ cup pimiento-stuffed olives (well-
 drained)

Bread Machine Method
Have water at 80°F and all other ingredients at room temperature. Place ingredients in pan in order listed. Select basic cycle and medium/normal crust. Do not use delay timer. To hand shape loaf, select dough/manual cycle.

Mixer Methods
Using ingredient amounts listed for medium loaf, combine yeast, 1 cup bread flour, sugar, and salt. Heat water and oil to 120° to 130°F.

Hand-Held Mixer Method. Combine dry mixture and liquid ingredients in mixing bowl on low speed. Beat 2 to 3 minutes on medium speed. By hand, stir in rye flour, Swiss cheese, olives, and enough remaining flour to make a firm dough. Knead on floured surface 5 to 7 minutes or until smooth and elastic. Use additional bread flour if necessary.

Stand Mixer Method. Combine dry mixture and liquid ingredients in mixing bowl with paddle or beaters for 4 minutes on medium speed. Gradually add rye flour, Swiss cheese, olives, and remaining flour and knead with dough hook(s) 5 to 7 minutes until smooth and elastic.

Food Processor Method. Place dry mixture and cheese in processing bowl with steel blade. While motor is running, add liquid ingredients. Process until mixed. Add rye flour and olives; process again. Continue processing, adding remaining bread flour until dough forms a ball.

continued on page 272

Swiss/Olive Rye Bread

Swiss/Olive Rye Bread, continued

Rising, Shaping, and Baking
Place dough in lightly oiled bowl and turn to grease top. Cover; let rise until dough tests ripe.* Turn dough onto lightly floured surface; punch down to remove air bubbles. Roll or pat into a 12×5-inch rectangle. Starting with shorter side, roll up tightly, pressing dough into roll. Pinch edges and taper ends to seal. Place on greased cookie sheet sprinkled with cornmeal. Cover; let rise until indentation remains after touching. With very sharp knife, make 2 or 3 diagonal slashes across top of loaf. Combine 1 egg and 1 tablespoon of water. Brush top of loaf. Bake in preheated 375°F oven for 30 to 40 minutes. Remove from pan; cool. *Makes 1 loaf*

*Stick two fingers into risen dough up to the second knuckle and take out. If the indentation remains, the dough is ripe and ready to punch down and shape.

Super Cinnamon Bun

Cinnamon Bun
    1 package (16 ounces) hot roll mix
    1 cup QUAKER® Oats (quick or old
        fashioned, uncooked)
    ¾ cup raisins
    ½ cup granulated sugar, divided
  2½ teaspoons ground cinnamon, divided
    1 cup hot water (120°F to 130°F)
    1 egg, lightly beaten
    5 tablespoons margarine or butter,
        melted, divided

Glaze
    ¾ cup powdered sugar
    3 to 4 teaspoons milk
    ½ teaspoon vanilla

Lightly grease large cookie sheet. In large bowl, combine hot roll mix, yeast packet, oats, raisins, ¼ cup sugar and 1½ teaspoons cinnamon. Stir in hot water, egg and 3 tablespoons melted margarine. Mix until dough pulls away from sides of bowl. Knead on lightly floured surface 5 minutes or until

smooth and elastic. Divide into 4 equal pieces; roll each piece into 12-inch rope on lightly floured surface. In center of prepared cookie sheet, form a coil with one rope. Attach a second rope to the coiled rope by pressing the rope ends together firmly; continue coiling around the first rope. Repeat with the third and fourth ropes to form one large bun.

Combine remaining ¼ cup sugar, 1 teaspoon cinnamon and 2 tablespoons melted margarine. Brush evenly over top and sides of bun. Cover loosely with plastic wrap; let rise in warm place 30 minutes or until about double in size.

Heat oven to 375°F. Bake 30 to 35 minutes or until golden brown. Carefully remove to wire rack; cool slightly. For glaze, combine all ingredients; mix until smooth. Drizzle over bun. Serve warm or at room temperature.
Makes 16 servings

Note: If hot roll mix is not available, combine 3 cups all-purpose flour, 1 cup oats, ¾ cup raisins, two ¼-ounce packages quick-rising yeast, ⅓ cup granulated sugar, 1½ teaspoons salt and 1½ teaspoons cinnamon. Continue as recipe directs.

Italian Herbed Oatmeal Focaccia

2 tablespoons cornmeal
1½ to 2¼ cups all-purpose flour
1 cup QUAKER® Oats (quick or old fashioned, uncooked)
2 tablespoons dried Italian seasoning, divided
1 package (¼ ounce, about 2¼ teaspoons) quick-rising yeast
2 teaspoons granulated sugar
1½ teaspoons garlic salt, divided
1 cup water
¼ cup plus 2 tablespoons olive oil, divided
4 to 6 sun-dried tomatoes packed in oil, drained and chopped
¼ cup grated Parmesan cheese

Lightly spray 13×9-inch baking pan with no-stick cooking spray; dust with cornmeal. In large bowl, combine 1 cup flour, oats, 1 tablespoon Italian seasoning, yeast, sugar and 1 teaspoon garlic salt; mix well. In small saucepan, heat water and ¼ cup olive oil until very warm (120° to 130°F); stir into flour mixture. Gradually stir in enough remaining flour to make a soft dough. Turn dough out onto lightly floured surface. Knead 8 to 10 minutes or until smooth and elastic. Cover and let rest 10 minutes.

Pat dough into prepared pan, pressing dough out to edges of pan. Using fingertips, poke indentations over surface of dough. Brush remaining 2 tablespoons oil over dough. Sprinkle with remaining 1 tablespoon Italian seasoning and ½ teaspoon garlic salt. Arrange dried tomatoes across top; sprinkle with cheese. Cover; let rise in warm place until doubled, about 30 minutes. Heat oven to 400°F. Bake 25 to 30 minutes or until golden brown. Cut into strips or squares. Serve warm.

Makes 12 servings

Last Minute Tomato Swirl Bread

2 loaves (16 ounces each) frozen bread dough, thawed according to package directions
2 large cloves garlic, pressed
1 jar (8 ounces) SONOMA® Marinated Tomatoes, drained and blotted with paper towels
3 tablespoons grated Parmesan cheese
2 tablespoons dried basil leaves
Cornmeal for baking sheets
1 egg, beaten

Preheat oven to 400°F. On lightly floured surface, roll and pat one loaf of dough into 12×7-inch rectangle. Gently sprinkle half of garlic over dough. Distribute half of tomatoes evenly over dough, leaving ½-inch border. Sprinkle with half of cheese and basil. Starting from one long edge, roll dough up tightly, jelly-roll style. Carefully pinch seam to seal. Repeat procedure with second loaf. Sprinkle baking sheets with cornmeal. Place loaves on baking sheets, seam sides down. Brush with egg. *Do not let rise.* Bake immediately 25 to 30 minutes or until loaves are browned and sound hollow when tapped. Remove to racks to cool before slicing. If desired, loaves can be wrapped well and frozen up to 1 month.

Makes 2 loaves (24 slices)

Tip: The flavorful oil from Marinated Tomatoes can be used for sautéing or for vinaigrettes.

Pan de Pueblo

1¼ cups warm water (100° to 110°F)
1 envelope FLEISCHMANN'S® Active
    Dry Yeast
2 teaspoons coarse salt
3¼ cups all-purpose flour
    Cornmeal

Egg White Mixture
1 egg white, lightly beaten with
    1 teaspoon water

Place ¼ cup warm water in large warm bowl. Sprinkle in yeast; stir until dissolved. Add remaining water, salt and 1 cup flour. Beat 2 minutes at medium speed of electric mixer, scraping bowl occasionally. Add ½ cup flour; beat 2 minutes at high speed. Stir in enough remaining flour to make a soft dough. Knead on lightly floured surface until smooth and elastic, about 8 to 10 minutes. Place in greased bowl, turning to grease top. Cover; let rise in warm, draft-free place until doubled in size, about 1½ hours.

Punch dough down. Remove dough to lightly floured surface; divide into 2 equal portions. Roll each piece into 20×5-inch oblong. Starting with long side, roll up tightly as for jelly roll. Pinch seam and ends to seal. Place seam side down and diagonally, on a baking sheet that has been sprinkled with cornmeal. Slit the tops several times diagonally with a sharp knife. Cover; let rise in warm, draft-free place until doubled in size, about 1 hour.

Bake at 450°F for 5 minutes with a pan of water on the oven floor. Remove the pan of water and continue baking the bread 5 minutes more. Brush bread with egg white mixture. Bake an additional 5 to 10 minutes or until brown and crusty. Remove from sheets; cool on wire racks. *Makes 2 loaves*

Poppy Seed Breadsticks

1 cup hot milk (about 120°F)
¼ CRISCO® Stick or ¼ cup CRISCO®
    all-vegetable shortening
1 tablespoon sugar
1 teaspoon salt
1 package active dry yeast
3 to 3½ cups all-purpose flour, divided
1 egg
2 tablespoons water
    Poppy seeds

1. Combine milk, ¼ cup shortening, sugar and salt. Cool slightly.

2. Combine yeast and 2½ cups flour in large bowl. Stir in milk mixture until well blended. Beat in enough remaining flour to make a stiff dough.

3. Turn dough onto lightly floured surface. Knead for 5 minutes or until smooth and elastic. Let rest for 5 minutes.

4. Cut dough into 72 equal pieces with sharp knife. Roll out each piece between palms of hands or on flat surface to make a 6-inch strip. Place on greased cookie sheets.

5. Combine egg and water. Brush breadsticks with egg mixture and sprinkle with poppy seeds. Cover; let rest for 20 minutes.

6. Heat oven to 300°F.

7. Bake at 300°F for 45 to 50 minutes or until golden brown. *Do not overbake.* Cool on racks. *Makes 72 breadsticks*

Pan de Pueblo

Delectable Chocolate Wreath

½ cup milk
¼ cup water (70° to 80°F)
3 tablespoons butter or margarine, cut up
1 large egg
⅓ cup sugar
¼ cup unsweetened cocoa powder
¾ teaspoon salt
2½ cups bread or all-purpose flour
2 teaspoons FLEISCHMANN'S® Bread Machine Yeast
White Chocolate, Raspberry and Pecan Filling (recipe follows)
Frosting (recipe follows)

Add all ingredients except filling and frosting to bread machine pan in the order suggested by manufacturer. Select dough/manual cycle. When cycle is complete, remove dough to lightly floured surface. If necessary, knead in enough flour to make dough easy to handle.

Roll dough to 22×6-inch rectangle. With sharp knife, cut in half lengthwise to make two 22×3-inch strips. Spread half of White Chocolate, Raspberry and Pecan Filling down center length of each strip. Fold long sides of dough over filling; pinch seams and ends to seal. Place ropes seam sides down on greased large baking sheet. Twist ropes together. Form into wreath; pinch ends to seal. Cover and let rise in warm, draft-free place until risen slightly, about 1 hour. Bake at 350°F for 35 to 40 minutes or until done. Remove from baking sheet; cool on wire rack. Drizzle with frosting. Garnish with candied fruit, if desired.

Makes 1 wreath

White Chocolate, Raspberry and Pecan Filling:
Combine ¾ cup white chocolate morsels, ½ cup chopped pecans, toasted, and 2 tablespoons seedless red raspberry jam.

Frosting:
Combine 1 cup sifted powdered sugar, 1 to 2 tablespoons milk and 1 teaspoon Spice Islands® Pure Vanilla Extract. Stir until smooth.

Wild Rice-Spinach-Feta Bread

¾ cup water
2 tablespoons honey
2 ounces frozen chopped spinach, thawed and squeezed dry
2½ cups bread flour
½ cup whole wheat flour
¾ teaspoon salt
1 tablespoon dried Italian seasoning
1 cup cooked wild rice
2 ounces crumbled feta cheese
2 teaspoons active dry yeast (not rapid-rise)

1. Measure carefully, placing ingredients in bread machine pan in order specified by owner's manual. Program dough cycle; press start.

2. Turn out dough onto lightly floured surface; shape into 2 to 3 baguettes. Place on greased baking sheet; cover and let rise in warm place 45 minutes or until doubled.

3. Bake in preheated 375°F oven 20 to 25 minutes or until browned and loaves sound hollow when lightly tapped.

Makes 2 to 3 baguettes

*Favorite recipe from **Minnesota Cultivated Wild Rice Council***

Delectable Chocolate Wreath

Soft Pretzels

2½ to 3 cups all-purpose flour, divided
 1 package RED STAR® Active Dry Yeast
    or QUICK•RISE™ Yeast
 1 tablespoon sugar
 ½ teaspoon salt
 1 cup warm water (120° to 130°F)
 2 tablespoons oil
 2 quarts water
 ⅓ cup baking soda
 1 egg white, slightly beaten
    Coarse salt

In large mixer bowl, combine 1¼ cups flour, yeast, sugar and salt; mix well. Add 1 cup warm water and oil. Blend at low speed until moistened; beat 3 minutes at medium speed. By hand, gradually stir in enough remaining flour to make a firm dough. Knead on floured surface until smooth and elastic, 5 to 8 minutes. Place in greased bowl, turning to grease top. Cover; let rise in warm place until light and doubled, about 1 hour (30 minutes for Quick•Rise™ Yeast).

Punch down dough. Divide into 4 parts. Divide each part into 3 pieces. On lightly floured surface, roll each piece into an 18-inch rope. Shape rope into a circle, overlapping about 4 inches from each end and leaving ends free. Take one end of dough in each hand and twist at the point where dough overlaps. Carefully lift ends across to the opposite edge of the circle. Tuck ends under edge to make a pretzel shape; moisten and press ends to seal. Place on greased cookie sheets. Let rise, uncovered, until puffy, about 20 minutes (10 minutes for Quick•Rise™ Yeast). In a 3-quart stainless or enameled saucepan, bring water and baking soda to a boil. Lower 1 or 2 pretzels into saucepan; simmer for 10 seconds on each side. Lift from water with slotted spoon or spatula; drain. Place on well greased cookie sheet. Let dry briefly. Brush with egg white; sprinkle with coarse salt. Bake at 425°F for 12 to 15 minutes until browned. Remove from cookie sheet. Serve warm with butter or mustard, if desired.

Makes 12 pretzels

White Bread

 2 packages active dry yeast
2¼ cups warm water (105° to 115°F),
    divided
 6 to 6½ cups bread flour
 ⅓ cup instant dry milk
 3 tablespoons sugar
 2 tablespoons oil
 1 tablespoon salt
    Butter or margarine, softened

Dissolve yeast in ½ cup water in large bowl. Stir in remaining 1¾ cups water, 3 cups flour, dry milk, sugar, oil and salt; beat until smooth. Mix in enough remaining flour to make soft dough. Turn dough onto lightly floured surface; knead until smooth and elastic, about 12 to 15 minutes. Place dough in greased bowl, turning once to coat. Cover and let rise in warm place until doubled in size, about 1 hour.

Punch down dough; divide into halves. Roll each half into 18×9-inch rectangle. Fold crosswise into thirds, overlapping the two sides. Roll dough tightly toward you, jelly-roll style, beginning at one of the open ends. Press with thumbs to seal after each turn. Pinch edge firmly to seal. Press each end with side of hand to seal. Fold ends under loaves.

Place loaves seam sides down in two 9×5×3-inch greased loaf pans. Brush lightly with butter. Let rise until doubled in size, 50 to 60 minutes.

Preheat oven to 450°F. Place loaves on low rack so that tops of pans are in center of oven. (Pans should not touch each other or sides of oven.) Bake 10 minutes; reduce heat to 350°F and bake 30 to 35 minutes until deep golden brown and loaves sound hollow when tapped. Remove from pans. Brush loaves with butter; cool on wire rack.　　*Makes 2 loaves*

Favorite recipe from **North Dakota Wheat Commission**

Apple Sauce Coffee Ring

Bread
- 1 package active dry yeast
- 1/3 cup plus 1 teaspoon granulated sugar, divided
- 1/4 cup warm water (105° to 115°F)
- 1/2 cup skim milk
- 1/2 cup MOTT'S® Natural Apple Sauce
- 1 egg
- 2 tablespoons margarine, melted and cooled
- 1 teaspoon salt
- 1 teaspoon grated lemon peel
- 5 cups all-purpose flour
- 1 teaspoon skim milk

Filling
- 1½ cups MOTT'S® Chunky Apple Sauce
- 1/2 cup raisins
- 1/3 cup firmly packed light brown sugar
- 1 teaspoon ground cinnamon

Glaze
- 1 cup powdered sugar
- 2 tablespoons skim milk
- 1 teaspoon vanilla extract

1. To prepare Bread, in large bowl, sprinkle yeast and 1 teaspoon granulated sugar over warm water; stir until yeast dissolves. Let stand 5 minutes or until mixture is bubbly. Stir in 1/2 cup milk, 1/2 cup apple sauce, remaining 1/3 cup granulated sugar, egg, margarine, salt and lemon peel.

2. Stir in flour, 1 cup at a time, until soft dough forms. Turn out dough onto floured surface; flatten slightly. Knead 5 minutes or until smooth and elastic, adding any remaining flour to prevent sticking if necessary. Shape dough into ball; place in large bowl sprayed with nonstick cooking spray. Turn dough over so that top is greased. Cover with damp towel; let rise in warm place 1 hour or until doubled in bulk.

3. Punch down dough. Roll out dough on floured surface into 15-inch square. Spray baking sheet with nonstick cooking spray.

4. To prepare Filling, in small bowl, combine 1½ cups chunky apple sauce, raisins, brown sugar and cinnamon. Spread filling over dough, to within 1/2 inch of edges. Roll up dough jelly-roll style. Moisten edge with water; pinch to seal seam. Moisten ends of dough with water; bring together to form ring. Pinch to seal seam. Place on prepared baking sheet. Make 1/8-inch-deep cuts across width of dough at 2-inch intervals around ring.

5. Let dough rise in warm place, uncovered, 30 minutes.

6. Preheat oven to 350°F. Brush top lightly with 1 teaspoon milk.

7. Bake 45 to 50 minutes or until lightly browned and ring sounds hollow when tapped. Remove from baking sheet; cool completely on wire rack.

8. To prepare Glaze, in small bowl, combine powdered sugar, 2 tablespoons milk and vanilla until smooth. Drizzle over top of ring. Cut into 24 slices.   *Makes 24 servings*

Cheese Pull-Apart Bread

- 3 packages frozen bread dough dinner rolls, thawed to room temperature
- 1/3 cup butter, melted
- 1 cup freshly grated BELGIOIOSO® Parmesan Cheese
- 1 cup shredded BELGIOIOSO® Provolone Cheese

Roll each dinner roll in butter, and then roll in BelGioioso Parmesan Cheese to coat. Arrange half of rolls in well-greased fluted tube pan. Sprinkle with BelGioioso Provolone Cheese. Top with remaining half of coated rolls. Sprinkle with any remaining Parmesan. Let rise until doubled in size, about 1 hour. Bake in preheated 375°F oven 35 to 45 minutes or until golden brown. Use table knife to loosen edge of bread; remove from pan. Serve warm.
Makes 12 servings

Pumpkin-Nut Bread

1-Pound Loaf
- ½ cup canned pumpkin
- ¼ cup milk
- 1 large egg
- 1 tablespoon butter or margarine
- ¾ teaspoon salt
- 1½ cups bread flour
- ½ cup whole wheat flour
- ⅓ cup coarsely chopped pecans or walnuts, toasted*
- 2 tablespoons packed brown sugar
- ¾ teaspoon SPICE ISLANDS® Pumpkin Pie Spice
- 1½ teaspoons FLEISCHMANN'S® Bread Machine Yeast

1½-Pound Loaf
- ¾ cup canned pumpkin
- ⅓ cup milk
- 1 large egg
- 1 tablespoon butter or margarine
- 1 teaspoon salt
- 2⅓ cups bread flour
- ⅔ cup whole wheat flour
- ½ cup coarsely chopped pecans or walnuts, toasted*
- 3 tablespoons packed brown sugar
- 1 teaspoon SPICE ISLANDS® Pumpkin Pie Spice
- 2 teaspoons FLEISCHMANN'S® Bread Machine Yeast

To toast nuts, spread chopped nuts in a shallow baking pan large enough to accommodate a single layer. Bake nuts at 350°F for 5 to 15 minutes or until lightly toasted, stirring several times and checking often. Be sure to cool nuts before adding to bread machine.

Use the 1-pound recipe if your machine pan holds 10 cups or less of water. Add ingredients to bread machine pan in the order suggested by manufacturer, adding pumpkin with milk and nuts with flours. (Pumpkin varies in moisture content. If dough is too dry or stiff or too soft or slack, adjust dough consistency—see Adjusting Dough Consistency tip below.)

Recommended cycle: Basic/white bread cycle; light or medium/normal crust color setting.

Makes 1 loaf (8 or 12 slices)

Adjusting Dough Consistency: Bread machine dough is slightly stickier than hand-kneaded dough. After mixing for a few minutes, the ingredients should turn into a dough that forms a soft, smooth ball around the blade. If your machine seems to be straining or if the dough appears too dry or stiff, add more liquid in 1-teaspoon increments to achieve the proper consistency. If the dough seems too soft or slack, add additional bread flour in 1-teaspoon increments until the proper consistency is reached. Do not add more than 3 to 4 tablespoons of liquid or flour. The machine cannot compensate for wide variations from the norm and may not bake the larger amount of dough thoroughly.

Savory French Bread

- 1 large loaf French bread
- ¼ cup butter or margarine, softened
- ½ teaspoon dried basil leaves
- ½ teaspoon dried dill weed
- ½ teaspoon chopped dried chives
- ¼ teaspoon garlic powder
- ¼ teaspoon paprika
- ½ teaspoon TABASCO® brand Pepper Sauce

Preheat oven to 400°F. Slice bread diagonally, but do not cut through bottom crust of loaf. Mix remaining ingredients in small bowl. Spread between bread slices; wrap bread in aluminum foil and heat in oven for 15 to 20 minutes. Serve warm.

Makes 6 to 8 servings

Pumpkin-Nut Bread

Creamy Cinnamon Rolls

2 (1-pound) loaves frozen bread dough, thawed

⅔ cup (one-half 14-ounce can) EAGLE BRAND® Sweetened Condensed Milk* (NOT evaporated milk), divided

1 cup chopped pecans

2 teaspoons ground cinnamon

1 cup sifted powdered sugar

½ teaspoon vanilla extract

Additional chopped pecans, if desired

Use remaining Eagle Brand as a dip for fruit. Pour into storage container and store tightly covered in refrigerator for up to 1 week.

1. On lightly floured surface, roll each bread dough loaf into 12×9-inch rectangle. Spread ⅓ cup Eagle Brand over dough rectangles. Sprinkle rectangles with 1 cup pecans and cinnamon. Roll up jelly-roll style starting from short side. Cut each log into 6 slices.

2. Generously grease 13×9-inch baking pan. Place rolls cut sides down in pan. Cover loosely with greased waxed paper and then with plastic wrap. Chill overnight. Cover and chill remaining Eagle Brand.

3. To bake, let pan of rolls stand at room temperature 30 minutes. Preheat oven to 350°F. Bake 30 to 35 minutes or until golden brown. Cool in pan 5 minutes; loosen edges and remove rolls from pan.

4. Meanwhile for frosting, in small mixing bowl, combine powdered sugar, remaining ⅓ cup Eagle Brand and vanilla. Drizzle frosting over warm rolls. Sprinkle with additional chopped pecans, if desired.

Makes 12 rolls

Prep Time: 20 minutes
Bake Time: 30 to 35 minutes
Chill Time: Overnight
Cool Time: 5 minutes

Wild Rice Three Grain Bread

1 package active dry yeast

⅓ cup warm water (105° to 115°F)

2 cups milk, scalded and cooled to 105° to 115°F

½ cup honey

2 tablespoons butter, melted

2 teaspoons salt

4 to 4½ cups bread flour or unbleached all-purpose flour

2 cups whole wheat flour

½ cup rye flour

½ cup uncooked rolled oats

1 cup cooked wild rice

1 egg, beaten with 1 tablespoon water

½ cup hulled sunflower seeds

In large bowl, dissolve yeast in water. Add milk, honey, butter and salt. Stir in 2 cups bread flour, whole wheat flour, rye flour and oats to make a soft dough. Add wild rice; cover and let rest 15 minutes. Stir in enough additional bread flour to make a stiff dough. Turn dough out onto board and knead 10 minutes. Add more flour as necessary to keep dough from sticking. Turn dough into lightly greased bowl; turn dough over to coat. Cover and let rise until doubled, about 2 hours. Punch down dough. Knead briefly on lightly oiled board. To shape dough, divide into 3 portions; roll into long strands. Braid strands and place on greased baking sheet in wreath shape, or divide in half and place each half in greased 9½×5½-inch loaf pans. Let rise until doubled, about 45 minutes. Brush tops of loaves with egg mixture; slash loaves if desired. Sprinkle with sunflower seeds. Bake at 375°F 45 minutes or until loaves sound hollow when tapped.

Makes 1 braided wreath or 2 loaves

*Favorite recipe from **Minnesota Cultivated Wild Rice Council***

Creamy Cinnamon Roll

Crispy Onion Crescent Rolls

1 can (8 ounces) refrigerated crescent
    dinner rolls
1⅓ cups *French's*® French Fried Onions,
    slightly crushed
1 egg, beaten

Preheat oven to 375°F. Line large baking sheet
with foil. Separate refrigerated rolls into
8 triangles. Sprinkle center of each triangle
with about 1½ tablespoons French Fried
Onions. Roll-up triangles from short side,
jelly-roll fashion. Sprinkle any excess onions
over top of crescents.

Arrange crescents on prepared baking sheet.
Brush with beaten egg. Bake 15 minutes or
until golden brown and crispy. Transfer to wire
rack; cool slightly. *Makes 8 servings*

Prep Time: 15 minutes
Cook Time: 15 minutes

Buttermilk Pan Rolls

1 cup cultured buttermilk
¼ cup water
¼ cup oil
2 tablespoons sugar
1 teaspoon salt
½ teaspoon baking soda
3 cups bread flour
2¼ teaspoons RED STAR® Active Dry
    Yeast or QUICK•RISE™ Yeast

Bread Machine Method
Have all ingredients at room temperature.
Place ingredients in the pan in the order listed.
Select dough/manual cycle. Do not use the
delay timer.

Mixer Methods
Combine yeast, 1 cup flour, and other dry
ingredients. Combine buttermilk and oil; heat
to 120° to 130°F.

Hand-Held Mixer Method. Combine dry
mixture and liquid ingredients in mixing bowl

on low speed. Beat 2 to 3 minutes on medium
speed. By hand stir in enough remaining flour
to make a soft dough. Knead on floured
surface until smooth, about 2 minutes.

Stand Mixer Method. Combine dry mixture
and liquid ingredients in mixing bowl with
paddle for 4 minutes on medium speed.
Gradually add remaining flour and knead with
dough hook(s) 5 minutes until smooth.

Food Processor Method. Put dry mixture in
processing bowl with steel blade. While motor
is running add liquid ingredients. Process until
mixed. Continue processing, adding remaining
flour until dough forms a ball.

Shaping and Baking
Press dough evenly into greased 9-inch square
cake pan. Sprinkle top of dough lightly with
flour. With sharp knife, cut dough into
12 rolls, cutting almost to bottom of pan.
Cover; let rise in warm place until indentation
remains after touching. Bake in preheated oven
400°F for 15 to 20 minutes until golden
brown. Remove from pan. Break apart into
rolls; serve warm. *Makes 12 servings*

Roman Meal® Cream of Rye Bread

1¼ teaspoons yeast
2 cups flour
⅔ cup ROMAN MEAL® Cream of Rye
    Cereal
2 tablespoons nonfat dry milk
1 teaspoon salt
2 teaspoons caraway seeds
1 tablespoon honey
2 teaspoons molasses
2 tablespoons shortening
1 cup water

Bread Machine Directions
Pour yeast to one side of inner pan. Add
remaining ingredients in order. Select white
bread and push "start." *Makes 1 loaf*

Crispy Onion Crescent Rolls

Challah

1-Pound Loaf

  ½ cup water
  1 large egg
  2 tablespoons margarine, cut up
  1 teaspoon salt
  2 cups bread flour
  4 teaspoons sugar
  1½ teaspoons FLEISCHMANN'S® Bread
    Machine Yeast
  1 yolk of large egg
  1 tablespoon water

1½-Pound Loaf

  ¾ cup water
  1 large egg
  3 tablespoons margarine, cut up
  1¼ teaspoons salt
  3 cups bread flour
  2 tablespoons sugar
  2 teaspoons FLEISCHMANN'S® Bread
    Machine Yeast
  1 yolk of large egg
  1 tablespoon water

Add water, egg, margarine, salt, bread flour, sugar and yeast to bread machine pan in the order suggested by manufacturer. Select dough/manual cycle. When cycle is complete, remove dough from machine to lightly floured surface. If necessary, knead in enough additional flour to make dough easy to handle. (For 1½-pound recipe, divide dough in half to make 2 loaves.)

For each loaf, divide dough into 2 pieces, one about ⅔ of the dough and the other about ⅓ of the dough. Divide larger piece into 3 equal pieces; roll into 12-inch ropes. Place ropes on greased baking sheet. Braid by bringing left rope under center rope; lay it down. Bring right rope under new center rope; lay it down. Repeat to end. Pinch ends to seal. Divide remaining piece into 3 equal pieces. Roll into 10-inch ropes; braid. Place small braid on top of large braid. Pinch ends firmly to seal and to secure to large braid. Cover and let rise in warm, draft-free place until almost doubled in size, 15 to 20 minutes. Lightly beat egg yolk and 1 tablespoon water; brush over braids.

Bake at 375°F for 25 to 30 minutes or until done, covering with foil after 15 minutes to prevent excess browning. (For even browning when baking two loaves, switch positions of baking sheets halfway through baking.) Remove from baking sheets; cool on wire racks.   *Makes 1 or 2 loaves*

Lawry's® Garlic Bread

  1 loaf (1 pound) French or sourdough
    bread
  ¼ to ½ cup margarine
  2 teaspoons LAWRY'S® Garlic Salt

Slice bread in half lengthwise and score each half into 10 sections; do not cut through bottom crust. Spread margarine evenly on cut sides of bread halves. Evenly sprinkle Lawry's Garlic Salt over both halves. Broil for 2 to 3 minutes or until golden brown. To serve, finish cutting through bread slices with kitchen scissors.   *Makes 20 slices*

Meal Idea: Serve with your favorite pasta, soup or entree and a crisp green salad. Also great prepared on French rolls and used with Italian sausage or smoked kielbasa sandwiches.

Variation: May use 1 teaspoon LAWRY'S® Garlic Powder with Parsley in place of Garlic Salt, if desired.

Prep Time: 5 minutes
Cook Time: 2 to 3 minutes

Apple and Raisin Fruit Braid

Sweet Bread
- ¼ cup granulated sugar
- 1 package active dry yeast
- ½ cup warm water (105°-115°F)
- 3 cups all-purpose flour, divided
- 2 egg whites
- ¼ cup MOTT'S® Natural Apple Sauce, at room temperature
- 3 tablespoons instant nonfat dry milk
- ¼ teaspoon salt

Apple and Raisin Filling
- 2½ cups MOTT'S® Chunky Apple Sauce
- ¾ cup raisins
- ¼ cup firmly packed light brown sugar
- ½ teaspoon ground cinnamon
- 2 tablespoons evaporated skim milk

Drizzle Icing
- ½ cup powdered sugar
- ¼ cup skim milk

1. To prepare Sweet Bread, in large bowl, sprinkle granulated sugar and yeast over warm water; stir until yeast dissolves. Let stand 5 minutes or until mixture is bubbly. Add 1½ cups flour, egg whites, ¼ cup apple sauce, dry milk and salt. Beat with electric mixer at medium speed until combined. Scrape down sides of bowl; continue beating 2 minutes.

2. Stir in enough remaining flour (about 1 cup) until soft dough forms. Turn out dough onto floured surface; flatten slightly. Knead 6 to 8 minutes or until smooth and elastic, adding remaining ½ cup flour to prevent sticking if necessary. Shape dough into ball; place in large bowl sprayed with nonstick cooking spray. Turn dough over so that top is greased. Cover with towel; let rise in warm place 45 to 60 minutes or until doubled in bulk.

3. To prepare Apple and Raisin Filling, while dough is rising, in medium saucepan, combine 2½ cups apple sauce, raisins, brown sugar and cinnamon. Cook over medium heat 10 to 15 minutes, stirring frequently. Allow to cool while dough rises.

4. Punch down dough; turn out onto lightly floured surface. Let rest 5 minutes. Spray baking sheet with nonstick cooking spray. Roll out dough into 14×9-inch rectangle; transfer to prepared baking sheet.

5. Spoon filling lengthwise down center of dough in 3-inch-wide strip. Make 2-inch cuts at 1-inch intervals on long sides of rectangle. Fold strips over filling, alternating from left and right and overlapping strips in center to form braided pattern. Tuck ends of last strips under braid.

6. Cover with towel; let rise in warm place about 30 minutes or until doubled in bulk. Preheat oven to 350°F. Uncover; brush top of braid with 2 tablespoons milk.

7. Bake 30 to 35 minutes or until lightly browned and braid sounds hollow when tapped. Immediately remove from baking sheet; cool completely on wire rack.

8. To prepare Drizzle Icing, in small bowl, combine powdered sugar and ¼ cup milk until smooth. Drizzle over bread. Cut into 18 slices. *Makes 18 servings*

Cajun Garlic Bread

- ¼ teaspoon garlic powder
- ⅛ teaspoon ground red pepper
- ⅛ teaspoon dried oregano or basil leaves
- 2 tablespoons butter, melted
- 1 loaf French bread, cut lengthwise into halves

Preheat oven to 350°F. Stir garlic powder, pepper and oregano into butter in small bowl. Drizzle butter mixture over cut sides of bread. Reassemble loaf; wrap in foil. Bake 10 minutes. *Makes 6 servings*

Apple Crumb Coffeecake

2¼ cups all-purpose flour
½ cup sugar
1 envelope FLEISCHMANN'S®
   RapidRise™ Yeast
½ teaspoon salt
¼ cup water
¼ cup milk
⅓ cup butter or margarine
2 large eggs
2 cooking apples, cored and sliced
   Crumb Topping (recipe follows)

In large bowl, combine 1 cup flour, sugar, undissolved yeast and salt. Heat water, milk, and butter until very warm (120° to 130°F). Gradually add to dry ingredients. Beat 2 minutes at medium speed of electric mixer, scraping bowl occasionally. Add eggs and ½ cup flour. Beat 2 minutes at high speed, scraping bowl occasionally. Stir in remaining flour to make stiff batter. Spread evenly in greased 9-inch square pan. Arrange apple slices evenly over batter. Sprinkle Crumb Topping over apples. Cover; let rise in warm, draft-free place until doubled in size, about 1 hour.

Bake at 375°F for 35 to 40 minutes or until done. Cool in pan 10 minutes. Remove from pan; cool on wire rack.

Makes 1 (9-inch) cake

Crumb Topping: Combine ⅓ cup sugar, ¼ cup all-purpose flour, 1 teaspoon ground cinnamon and 3 tablespoons cold butter or margarine. Mix until crumbly.

Note: For best results use a pastry blender to cut into the cold butter or margarine. Mix all ingredients until coarse crumbs form.

Cracked Wheat Bread

1-Pound Loaf
¾ cup plus 2 tablespoons water
½ cup cracked wheat
1 tablespoon plus 1 teaspoon margarine
1 tablespoon plus 1 teaspoon honey
2¼ cups bread flour
1 teaspoon salt
1½ teaspoons active dry yeast

1½-Pound Loaf
1¼ cups plus 1 tablespoon water
¾ cup cracked wheat
2 tablespoons margarine
2 tablespoons honey
3 cups bread flour
1½ teaspoons salt
2¼ teaspoons active dry yeast

2-Pound Loaf
1¾ cups water
1 cup cracked wheat
2 tablespoons plus 2 teaspoons
   margarine
3 tablespoons honey
4 cups bread flour
2 teaspoons salt
1 tablespoon active dry yeast

1. Bring water to a boil. In a small bowl, pour water over cracked wheat and let cool until 80°F.

2. Measure carefully, placing remaining ingredients and cracked wheat in bread machine pan in order specified by owner's manual.

3. Program desired cycle; press start. Remove baked bread from pan; cool on wire rack.

Makes 1 loaf

Favorite recipe from **North Dakota Wheat Commission**

Apple Crumb Coffeecake

Onion Buckwheat Bread

1 pound diced white onions
3 tablespoons olive oil
4½ teaspoons yeast
1½ cups water, at 90°F
½ cup milk
6½ cups unbleached bread flour
½ cup buckwheat flour
5 teaspoons sea salt
1 tablespoon finely chopped fresh
    rosemary
¾ cup (3 ounces) shredded Gouda or
    Cheddar cheese
Unbleached bread flour as needed for
    kneading
4 tablespoons poppy seeds or nigella
    seeds (onion seeds)

1. Sauté onions in olive oil in large skillet over medium-high heat until just browned, about 5 minutes. Set aside to cool.

2. Combine yeast with water in large bowl; let sit 10 minutes until bubbly.

3. Add milk to yeast mixture and stir to combine. Gradually add bread flour, buckwheat flour, salt, rosemary and onions to yeast mixture. When mixture is well combined, add cheese and blend. The dough will be slightly sticky.

4. Knead dough on lightly floured surface about 10 minutes, until smooth and elastic. Add additional bread flour as needed if dough is too soft.

5. Lightly oil clean bowl. Place dough in bowl; cover and let rise until doubled in bulk, 1½ to 2 hours.

6. Gently punch down dough and place on lightly floured surface. Cut dough in half and shape into round loaves. Spritz top of each loaf with water, and press on poppy seeds or nigella seeds. Place on lightly floured baking sheet; cover and let rise until almost doubled in bulk, 45 minutes to 1 hour.

7. Preheat oven to 450°F. Slash tops of loaves with razor and place in oven. Add steam by placing 2 ice cubes in pan on bottom of oven. Bake 10 minutes. *Reduce heat to 400°F* and bake an additional 35 to 40 minutes. Cool loaves completely on rack.

Makes 2 (10-inch) round loaves

Favorite recipe from **National Onion Association**

Mini-Sticky Pecan Buns

1 package BOB EVANS® Frozen White
    Dinner Roll Dough
½ cup packed brown sugar
2 teaspoons ground cinnamon
½ cup finely chopped pecans
½ cup melted butter

Thaw dough at room temperature 45 minutes to 1 hour; do not allow dough to begin rising. Divide each piece of dough into 4 equal pieces; roll each piece in tight circle to form a ball with smooth surface. Combine sugar, cinnamon and pecans in shallow dish. Dip dough balls in melted butter and roll in sugar mixture. Arrange in 2 layers in well-greased 10-inch tube pan, allowing space for dough to rise. Combine any remaining butter and sugar mixture; pour over rolls. Cover pan with damp towel; allow to rise at room temperature until doubled in bulk. Preheat oven to 350°F. Bake 30 minutes or until light golden in color. Let stand 10 to 15 minutes before turning out of pan onto serving plate. Serve warm.

Makes 8 to 10 servings

Spicy Buns

3½ to 4 cups all-purpose flour, divided
  2 packages RED STAR® Active Dry Yeast
    or QUICK•RISE™ Yeast
⅓ cup sugar
 1 teaspoon salt
½ teaspoon cinnamon
½ teaspoon nutmeg
¼ teaspoon mace
⅛ teaspoon ginger
⅔ cup water
½ cup butter
 3 eggs
 1 cup raisins or currants

In large mixer bowl, combine 2 cups flour, yeast, sugar, salt, cinnamon, nutmeg, mace and ginger; mix well. Heat water and butter until very warm (120° to 130°F—butter does not need to melt). Add to flour mixture. Add eggs; blend at low speed until moistened; beat 3 minutes at medium speed. By hand, stir in raisins and remaining flour to make a firm dough. Knead on floured surface until smooth and elastic, about 5 minutes. Place in greased bowl, turning to grease top. Cover; let rise in warm place until light and doubled, about 1 hour (30 minutes for Quick•Rise™ Yeast).

Punch down dough. On lightly floured surface, roll dough to ½-inch thickness. Cut out buns with 1½- to 2-inch round cutter. Place buns on greased cookie sheets 1½-inches apart. Cover; let rise in warm place until light and doubled, about 30 minutes (15 minutes for Quick•Rise™ Yeast). Bake at 350°F for 10 to 12 minutes until golden brown. Cool on racks. Drizzle with powdered sugar icing, if desired. Serve warm. *Makes 24 to 30 buns*

Jalapeño Cheese Bread

1-Pound Loaf
⅔ cup water
 1 tablespoon plus 1 teaspoon margarine,
  softened
 2 cups bread flour
¼ cup nonfat dry milk powder
 2 teaspoons sugar
¾ teaspoon salt
½ cup shredded Cheddar cheese
 1 tablespoon diced seeded jalapeño
  pepper
1¼ teaspoons active dry yeast

1½-Pound Loaf
 1 cup water
 2 tablespoons margarine, softened
 3 cups bread flour
⅓ cup nonfat dry milk powder
 1 tablespoon sugar
 1 teaspoon salt
⅔ cup shredded Cheddar cheese
1½ tablespoons diced seeded jalapeño
  pepper
 2 teaspoons active dry yeast

2-Pound Loaf
1⅓ cups water
 2 tablespoons plus 2 teaspoons
  margarine, softened
 4 cups bread flour
½ cup nonfat dry milk powder
 1 tablespoon plus 1 teaspoon sugar
1½ teaspoons salt
 1 cup shredded Cheddar cheese
 2 tablespoons diced seeded jalapeño
  pepper
2½ teaspoons active dry yeast

1. Measure carefully, placing all ingredients in bread machine pan in order specified by owner's manual.

2. Program desired cycle; press start. (*Do not use delay cycle.*) Remove baked bread from pan; cool on wire rack. *Makes 1 loaf*

Favorite recipe from **North Dakota Wheat Commission**

Festive Focaccia Pizza Bread

1 pound frozen bread dough, thawed
1½ teaspoons dried Italian herbs
¾ cup (3 ounces) pitted California ripe olives, sliced in thirds (rinse and pat dry before slicing)
¾ cup coarsely chopped California walnuts
1 cup (1 medium) thinly sliced onion
1½ cups (6 ounces) shredded JARLSBERG Cheese
1 tablespoon Lucini Premium Select extra virgin olive oil
Freshly ground pepper

Pat and stretch dough to fit 12-inch round baking pan. Cover with oiled waxed paper; let rise in warm place about 1 hour or until doubled in bulk.

Preheat oven to 375°F. Dimple dough with fingertips, making deep indentations. Sprinkle with herbs, then with olives, walnuts, onion and cheese. Drizzle with oil and sprinkle with pepper to taste.

Bake focaccia in lower third of oven 30 minutes or until golden brown. Serve warm or cool completely, wrap and refrigerate. Reheat before serving.

Makes 10 to 12 servings

Freezer Rolls

1¼ cups warm water (100° to 110°F)
2 envelopes FLEISCHMANN'S® Active Dry Yeast
½ cup warm milk (100° to 110°F)
⅓ cup butter or margarine, softened
½ cup sugar
1½ teaspoons salt
5½ to 6 cups all-purpose flour
2 large eggs

Place ½ cup warm water in large warm bowl. Sprinkle in yeast; stir until dissolved. Add remaining warm water, warm milk, butter, sugar, salt and 2 cups flour. Beat 2 minutes at medium speed of electric mixer. Add eggs and ½ cup flour. Beat at high speed for 2 minutes. Stir in enough remaining flour to make soft dough. Turn out onto lightly floured surface. Knead until smooth and elastic, about 8 to 10 minutes. Cover with plastic wrap; let rest for 20 minutes.

Punch dough down. Shape into desired shapes for dinner rolls. Place on greased baking sheets. Cover with plastic wrap and foil, sealing well. Freeze up to 1 week.*

Once frozen, rolls may be placed in plastic freezer bags.

Remove from freezer; place on greased baking sheets. Cover; let rise in warm, draft-free place until doubled in size, about 1½ hours.

Bake at 350°F for 15 minutes or until done. Remove from baking sheets; cool on wire racks. *Makes about 2 dozen rolls*

To bake without freezing: After shaping, let rise in warm, draft-free place, until doubled in size, about 1 hour. Bake according to above directions.

Shaping the Dough: **Crescents:** Divide dough in half. Roll each half to 14-inch circle. Cut each into 12 pie-shaped wedges. Roll up tightly from wide end. Curve ends slightly to form crescents; **Knots:** Divide dough into 24 equal pieces; roll each to 9-inch rope. Tie once loosely. **Coils:** Divide dough into 24 equal pieces; roll each to 9-inch rope. Coil each rope and tuck end under the coil. **Twists:** Divide dough into 24 equal pieces; roll each into 12-inch rope. Fold each rope in half and twist three to four times. Pinch ends to seal.

Festive Focaccia Pizza Bread

Banana-Chocolate Chip Bread

1-Pound Loaf
- ⅓ cup milk
- ⅓ cup mashed very ripe banana
- 1 large egg
- 1 tablespoon butter or margarine
- ¾ teaspoon salt
- 2 cups bread flour
- ¼ cup semisweet chocolate pieces
- 1½ teaspoons FLEISCHMANN'S® Bread Machine Yeast

1½-Pound Loaf
- ½ cup milk
- ½ cup mashed very ripe banana
- 1 large egg
- 1 tablespoon butter or margarine
- 1 teaspoon salt
- 3 cups bread flour
- ⅓ cup semisweet chocolate pieces
- 2 teaspoons FLEISCHMANN'S® Bread Machine Yeast

Use the 1-pound recipe if your machine pan holds 10 cups or less of water. Add ingredients to bread machine pan in the order suggested by manufacturer, adding mashed banana with milk, and semisweet chocolate pieces with flour. Recommended cycle: Basic/white bread cycle; medium/normal or light crust color setting. *Do not use delay cycle.*

Makes 1 loaf (8 or 12 slices)

Note: How this bread turns out depends on your machine. Some machines will make a smooth chocolate-colored bread. Others will leave bits of chocolate chips, and still others will give a marbled loaf.

Cherry Swirl Coffee Cake

- 1¼ cups milk
- ½ cup shortening or margarine
- ¼ cup sugar
- 1 teaspoon salt
- 1 package (¼-ounce) active dry yeast
- 3¼ cups all-purpose flour
- 2 eggs
- ½ teaspoon vanilla
- 1 cup (12-ounce jar) SMUCKER'S® Cherry Preserves
- 1 cup powdered sugar
  Milk
- ⅓ cup sliced almonds

In small saucepan, combine 1¼ cups milk, shortening, sugar and salt; bring just to a boil. Cool to lukewarm (105° to 115°F). Stir in yeast; transfer mixture to medium bowl.

Add 1 cup of the flour to milk mixture; beat well. Add eggs and vanilla; beat well. Stir in enough of the remaining flour to make a thick batter; beat until smooth. Cover and set in warm place until doubled in size, about 1 hour.

Stir batter down and pour into two greased 9-inch round cake pans; cover and set in warm place until doubled in size, about 1 hour. Make a swirl design on top of batter with a floured spoon; fill grooves with preserves, using ¼ cup for each coffee cake.

Bake at 375°F for 30 to 35 minutes or until golden brown. Remove from pans; cool slightly on wire racks. Fill grooves with remaining preserves.

Mix powdered sugar with enough milk to make a thin glaze consistency; drizzle over warm coffee cakes. Sprinkle with almonds.

Makes 2 coffee cakes

Banana-Chocolate Chip Bread

Braided Sandwich Ring

Dough

¾ cup buttermilk, at 80°F
2 large eggs, at room temperature
2 tablespoons vegetable oil
3 tablespoons sugar
1½ teaspoons salt
4 cups bread flour
2¼ teaspoons RED STAR® Active Dry Yeast

Glaze

1 egg
1 tablespoon milk
1 tablespoon sesame or poppy seeds

Filling

Mayonnaise, leaf lettuce, sliced tomatoes, onion rings, sliced black olives, thinly sliced deli meats (ham, roast beef, prosciutto, salami), sliced cheeses (brick, mozzarella, Swiss), Dijon mustard

Bread Machine Method

Place dough ingredients in pan in order listed. Select dough cycle. Check dough consistency after 5 minutes of kneading making adjustments if necessary.

Hand-Held Mixer Method

Combine 1 cup flour, sugar, yeast and salt. Heat buttermilk to 120° to 130°F. Combine flour mixture, buttermilk, 2 eggs and oil in mixing bowl on low speed. Beat 2 to 3 minutes on medium speed. By hand, stir in enough remaining flour to make firm dough. Knead on floured surface 5 to 7 minutes or until smooth and elastic. Use additional flour, if necessary.

Stand Mixer Method

Combine 1 cup flour, sugar, yeast and salt. Heat buttermilk to 120° to 130°F. Combine flour mixture, buttermilk, 2 eggs and oil in mixing bowl with paddle or beaters 4 minutes on medium speed. Gradually add remaining flour and knead with dough hook 5 to 7 minutes or until smooth and elastic. Use additional flour, if necessary.

Food Processor Method

Combine 1 cup flour, sugar, yeast and salt. Put flour mixture in processing bowl with steel blade. While motor is running, add buttermilk, oil and 2 eggs. Process until mixed. Continue processing, adding remaining flour until dough forms a ball.

Shaping and Baking

Place dough in lightly oiled bowl and turn to grease top. Cover; let rise until dough tests ripe.* Punch down dough. Divide into three parts. On lightly floured surface, roll each third into 24-inch rope. On greased cookie sheet lightly sprinkled with cornmeal, loosely braid ropes from center to ends. Shape into circle; fasten ends by pinching dough together. Cover; let rise until indentation remains after touching.

For glaze, combine remaining 1 egg and milk; gently brush risen dough. Sprinkle with sesame seeds. Bake in preheated 375°F oven 25 to 35 minutes or until golden brown; cool.

Using serrated knife, slice ring crosswise to create large sandwich. Spread bottom half with mayonnaise; arrange filling ingredients on top of mayonnaise. Spread top section with mustard; place on top of filling. Slice into serving portions.   *Makes 1 sandwich ring*

Place two fingers into the dough and then remove them. If the holes remain the dough is ripe and ready to punch down.

Shortcut "Sourdough" Corn Bread

1-Pound Loaf
- ½ cup plain low-fat yogurt
- ¼ cup milk
- 1 tablespoon butter or margarine
- ¾ teaspoon salt
- 1¾ cups bread flour
- ⅓ cup cornmeal
- 2 teaspoons sugar
- 1½ teaspoons FLEISCHMANN'S® Bread Machine Yeast

1½-Pound Loaf
- ⅔ cup plain low-fat yogurt
- ⅓ cup milk
- 1 tablespoon butter or margarine
- 1 teaspoon salt
- 2¾ cups bread flour
- ½ cup cornmeal
- 1 tablespoon sugar
- 2 teaspoons FLEISCHMANN'S® Bread Machine Yeast

Add ingredients to bread machine pan in the order suggested by manufacturer, adding yogurt with milk. (Yogurts vary in moisture content. If dough is too dry or stiff, or too soft or slack, adjust dough consistency—see Adjusting Dough Consistency tip below.) Recommended cycle: Basic/white bread cycle; medium/normal crust color setting.

Makes 1 loaf (8 or 12 slices)

Adjusting Dough Consistency: Check dough after 5 minutes of mixing; it should form a soft, smooth ball around the blade. If dough is too stiff or dry, add additional liquid, 1 teaspoon at a time, until dough is of the right consistency. If dough is too soft or sticky, add additional bread flour, 1 teaspoon at a time.

Wisconsin-Cheddar Jalapeño Bread

- 2 packages active dry yeast
- 1 teaspoon granulated sugar
- ½ cup warm water (110°F)
- 8¾ cups flour, divided
- 3 cups shredded extra-sharp cheddar cheese
- ¼ cup minced jalapeño pepper
- 1 tablespoon salt
- 2 teaspoons TABASCO® brand Pepper Sauce
- 2 cups milk
- 4 large eggs, lightly beaten

Stir yeast, sugar and warm water in small bowl. Let stand 5 minutes until foamy.

Meanwhile, combine 8 cups flour, cheddar cheese, jalapeño pepper, salt and TABASCO® Sauce in large bowl. Heat milk in small saucepan over low heat until warm (120° to 130°F). Stir milk into flour mixture. Set aside 1 tablespoon beaten egg to brush on dough before baking. Add remaining eggs to flour mixture; stir until mixture forms soft dough.

Knead dough on a lightly floured surface, 5 minutes or until smooth and elastic, kneading in remaining ¾ cup flour. Shape dough into a ball and place in large greased bowl, turning dough over to grease top. Cover with towel and let rise in warm place until doubled, about 1½ hours.

Grease two large cookie sheets. Punch down dough and divide in half. Shape each half into a ball; place on cookie sheets. Cover with towel and let rise in warm place until doubled, about 1½ hours.

Preheat oven to 375°F. Brush loaves with reserved beaten egg. Bake loaves about 45 minutes or until loaves sound hollow when lightly tapped. Remove to wire racks to cool.

Makes 2 loaves

Cinnamon Chip Filled Crescents

2 cans (8 ounces each) refrigerated quick crescent dinner rolls
2 tablespoons butter or margarine, melted
1⅔ cups (10-ounce package) HERSHEY'S® Cinnamon Chips, divided
Cinnamon Chips Drizzle (recipe follows)

1. Heat oven to 375°F. Unroll dough; separate into 16 triangles.

2. Spread melted butter on each triangle. Sprinkle 1 cup cinnamon chips evenly over triangles; gently press chips into dough. Roll from shortest side of triangle to opposite point. Place, point side down, on ungreased cookie sheet; curve into crescent shape.

3. Bake 8 to 10 minutes or until golden brown. Drizzle with Cinnamon Drizzle. Serve warm.   *Makes 16 crescents*

Cinnamon Chips Drizzle: Place remaining ⅔ cup chips and 1½ teaspoons shortening (do not use butter, margarine, spread or oil) in small microwave-safe bowl. Microwave at HIGH (100%) 1 minute; stir until chips are melted.

Almond Amaretto Loaf

1 cup milk
1 large egg
2 tablespoons butter or margarine
¼ cup amaretto liqueur
1 teaspoon lemon juice
¾ teaspoon salt
3 cups bread flour
½ cup chopped almonds, toasted
¼ cup sugar
2 teaspoons FLEISCHMANN'S® Bread Machine Yeast
Amaretto Glaze (recipe follows)
¼ cup sliced almonds, toasted

Add all ingredients except glaze and sliced almonds to bread machine pan in the order suggested by manufacturer, adding chopped almonds with flour. (If dough is too dry or stiff, or too soft or slack, adjust dough consistency). Recommended cycle: Basic/white bread cycle; light or medium/normal crust color setting. *Do not use delay cycle.*

Remove bread from pan; cool on wire rack. Drizzle with Amaretto Glaze and sprinkle with sliced almonds.   *Makes 1 (½ pound) loaf*

Amaretto Glaze: Combine 1 cup powdered sugar, sifted, 2 tablespoons amaretto liqueur and enough milk (1 to 2 teaspoons) to make glaze of drizzling consistency.

Barbecued French Bread

2 tablespoons butter
⅓ cup chopped onion
½ clove garlic, minced
⅓ cup chili sauce
2 tablespoons vinegar
1 tablespoon brown sugar
1 tablespoon prepared mustard
1½ teaspoons TABASCO® brand Pepper Sauce
1 large loaf French bread
Grated Parmesan cheese

Preheat oven to 400°F. Melt butter in medium saucepan over medium heat. Add onion and garlic; cook and stir about 3 minutes. Stir in chili sauce, vinegar, brown sugar, mustard and TABASCO® Sauce; simmer about 5 minutes or until mixture thickens.

Cut French bread diagonally into ¾-inch slices, almost but not through to bottom of loaf. Spread sauce between slices; sprinkle with Parmesan cheese. Wrap in aluminum foil and heat in oven 15 minutes.

Makes 1 loaf

Cinnamon Chip Filled Crescents

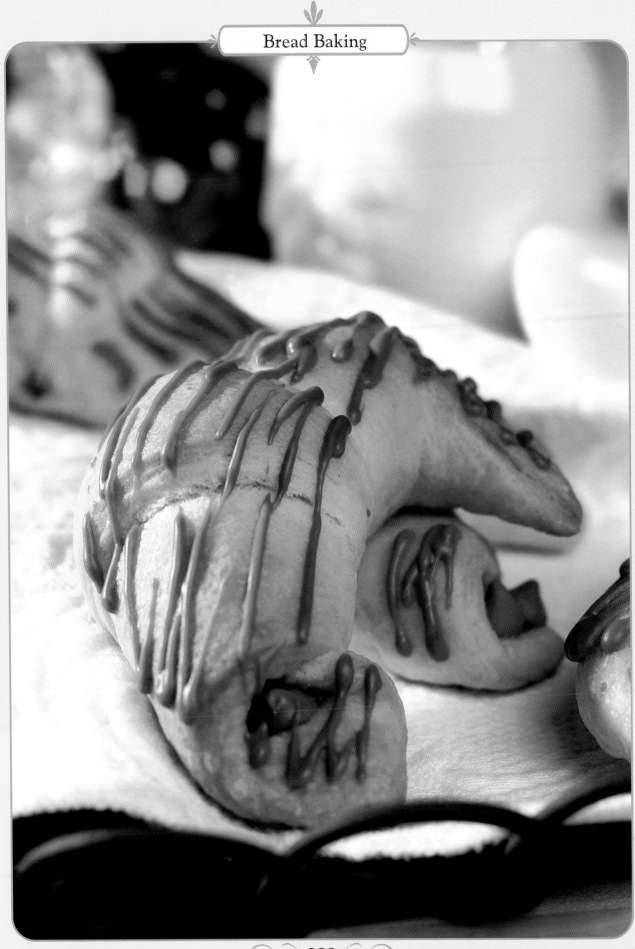

Harvest Stuffing Bread

3 cups all-purpose flour
1 tablespoon sugar
1 envelope FLEISCHMANN'S®
   RapidRise™ Yeast
2 tablespoons plus 1 teaspoon instant
   minced onions
1 tablespoon parsley flakes
1½ teaspoons poultry seasoning
1 teaspoon salt
1¼ cups water
1 tablespoon butter or margarine
1 egg, beaten
½ teaspoon whole celery seed

In large bowl, combine 2 cups flour, sugar, undissolved yeast, 2 tablespoons onions, parsley flakes, poultry seasoning and salt. Heat water and butter until very warm (120° to 130°F). Stir into dry ingredients. Beat 2 minutes at medium speed of electric mixer, scraping bowl occasionally. Stir in remaining flour to make stiff batter. Cover; let rest 10 minutes.

Turn batter into greased 1½-quart casserole. Smooth top of dough in casserole with floured hands. Cover; let rise in warm, draft-free place until doubled in size, about 30 minutes. Brush beaten egg on loaf. Sprinkle with remaining onions and celery seed. Bake at 375°F* for 35 minutes or until done. Remove from casserole; cool on wire rack.   *Makes 1 loaf*

*Bake at 350°F if glass casserole is used.

Black Pepper-Onion Bread

1-Pound Loaf
   ⅔ cup water
   1 tablespoon butter or margarine
   ¾ teaspoon salt
   2 cups bread flour
   2 tablespoons nonfat dry milk powder
   2 teaspoons sugar
   1 teaspoon SPICE ISLANDS® Minced
      Onions
   ½ teaspoon SPICE ISLANDS® Medium
      Grind Java Black Pepper*
   ⅛ teaspoon SPICE ISLANDS® Garlic
      Powder
   1½ teaspoons FLEISCHMANN'S® Bread
      Machine Yeast

1½-Pound Loaf
   1 cup water
   1 tablespoon butter or margarine
   1 teaspoon salt
   3 cups bread flour
   3 tablespoons nonfat dry milk powder
   1 tablespoon sugar
   1½ teaspoons SPICE ISLANDS® Minced
      Onions
   ¾ teaspoon SPICE ISLANDS® Medium
      Grind Java Black Pepper*
   ¼ teaspoon SPICE ISLANDS® Garlic
      Powder
   2 teaspoons FLEISCHMANN'S® Bread
      Machine Yeast

*If using a finer grind of pepper, reduce the amount to ¼ teaspoon for either loaf size.

Use the 1-pound recipe if your machine pan holds 10 cups or less of water. Add ingredients to bread machine pan in the order suggested by manufacturer. Recommended cycle: Basic/white bread cycle; medium/normal crust color setting. Timed-bake feature can be used.
       Makes 1 loaf (8 or 12 slices)

Harvest Stuffing Bread

Cranberry Pecan Wreath

3½ to 4 cups all-purpose flour
⅓ cup sugar
1 envelope FLEISCHMANN'S®
    RapidRise™ Yeast
¾ teaspoon salt
½ cup milk
⅓ cup butter or margarine
¼ cup water
2 large eggs
    Cranberry-Pecan Filling (recipe
    follows)
    Orange Glaze (recipe follows)

In large bowl, combine 1½ cups flour, sugar, undissolved yeast and salt. Heat milk, butter and water until very warm (120° to 130°F); stir into dry ingredients. Stir in eggs and enough remaining flour to make soft dough. Knead on lightly floured surface until smooth and elastic, about 8 to 10 minutes. Cover; let rest 10 minutes.

Roll dough to 30×6-inch rectangle; spread Cranberry-Pecan Filling over dough to within ½ inch of edges. Beginning at long end, roll up tightly, pinching seam to seal. Form into ring; join ends, pinching to seal. Transfer to greased large baking sheet. Cover; let rise in warm, draft-free place until doubled in size, about 45 to 60 minutes.

Bake at 350°F for 40 to 45 minutes or until done. Remove from pan; cool on wire rack. Drizzle with Orange Glaze. Decorate with additional cranberries, orange slices and pecan halves, if desired.

Makes 1 (10-inch) coffeecake

Cranberry-Pecan Filling: In medium saucepan, combine 1½ cups fresh or frozen cranberries, finely chopped; 1 cup firmly packed brown sugar; and ⅓ cup butter or margarine. Bring to a boil over medium-high heat. Reduce heat; simmer 5 to 7 minutes or until very thick, stirring frequently. Remove mixture from heat; stir in ¾ cup chopped pecans, toasted.

Orange Glaze: In small bowl, combine 1¼ cups sifted powdered sugar; 2 tablespoons butter or margarine, softened; 1 to 2 tablespoons milk; and 2 teaspoons freshly grated orange peel. Stir until smooth.

French Onion Bread Stix

1⅓ cups *French's*® French Fried Onions,
    crushed
¼ cup grated Parmesan cheese
1 container (11 ounces) refrigerated soft
    bread sticks
1 egg white, beaten

1. Preheat oven to 350°F. Combine French Fried Onions and cheese in pie plate. Separate dough into 12 pieces on sheet of waxed paper.

2. Brush one side of dough with egg white. Dip pieces, wet sides down, into crumbs, pressing firmly. Baste top surface with egg white and dip into crumbs.

3. Twist pieces to form spirals. Arrange on ungreased baking sheet. Bake 15 to 20 minutes or until golden brown.

Makes 12 bread sticks

Prep Time: 5 minutes
Cook Time: 15 minutes

Cranberry Pecan Wreath

Chocolate Chocolate Crescents

3¼ to 3½ cups all-purpose flour
¼ cup sugar
1 envelope FLEISCHMANN'S®
    RapidRise™ Yeast
1 teaspoon salt
¾ cup evaporated milk
¼ cup water
¼ cup butter or margarine
1 (1-ounce) square unsweetened
    chocolate
1 (1-ounce) square semisweet chocolate
1 large egg
    Powdered sugar
    Chocolate Filling (recipe follows)

In large bowl, combine 1 cup flour, sugar, undissolved yeast and salt. In saucepan, combine milk, water, butter, unsweetened and semisweet chocolate. Heat over medium-low heat until chocolate melts and temperature reaches 120° to 130°F. Stir into dry ingredients. Beat 2 minutes at medium speed of electric mixer, scraping bowl occasionally. Add egg and ½ cup flour; beat 2 minutes at high speed. Stir in enough remaining flour to make soft dough. Knead on lightly floured surface until smooth and elastic, about 8 to 10 minutes. Cover; let rest 10 minutes.

Divide dough into 12 pieces. Roll each piece into 8×4-inch oval. Spread Chocolate Filling evenly over each oval. Beginning at short end, roll up tightly. Pinch seams to seal. Place rolls, seam sides down, on heavily greased baking sheets. With sharp knife, make 5 slits on top of each roll, cutting halfway through. Curve ends to form crescents. Cover; let rise in warm, draft-free place until doubled in size, about 1 hour.

Bake at 375°F for 15 to 20 minutes or until done. Remove from sheet; cool on wire rack. Sprinkle with powdered sugar.

Makes 12 crescents

Chocolate Filling: In small bowl, combine 1 cup sugar, ½ cup cocoa powder and 3 tablespoons flour. With fork or pastry blender, cut in ¼ cup butter or margarine; blend well. Stir in 1 egg; add ½ cup finely chopped pecans. Stir well.

Honey Cloverleafs

1 package (16 ounces) hot roll mix
6 tablespoons honey, divided
¼ cup butter or margarine
1 teaspoon grated lemon peel
1 cup sliced almonds

Prepare hot roll mix in large bowl according to package directions, adding 2 tablespoons honey to liquid. Cover kneaded dough with bowl and let rest 5 minutes.

Melt butter in small saucepan over medium heat. Add remaining 4 tablespoons honey; stir in lemon peel.

Roll dough into 36 balls (about 1 to 1½ inch diameter each). Form clusters of three balls; dip each in honey mixture then in almonds. Place each cluster in well-greased muffin cup. Cover and set in warm place to rise about 30 minutes or until doubled in bulk.

Bake in preheated 350°F oven 15 to 20 minutes or until lightly browned. Brush with honey mixture, if desired. Remove from pan and cool slightly on wire rack. Serve warm or cool.
Makes 1 dozen rolls

Variation: Dough may be dipped in honey mixture then in chopped parsley, rosemary or other fresh herbs.

*Favorite recipe from **National Honey Board***

Ginger Bread

1-Pound Loaf
- ½ cup milk
- 2 tablespoons molasses
- 1 large egg
- 1 tablespoon butter or margarine, cut up
- ½ teaspoon salt
- 2 cups bread flour
- ¾ teaspoon SPICE ISLANDS® Ground Ginger
- ¼ teaspoon SPICE ISLANDS® Ground Cinnamon
- ¼ teaspoon SPICE ISLANDS® Ground Cloves
- 1½ teaspoons FLEISCHMANN'S® Bread Machine Yeast

1½-Pound Loaf
- ¾ cup milk
- 3 tablespoons molasses
- 1 large egg
- 2 tablespoons butter or margarine, cut up
- ¾ teaspoon salt
- 3 cups bread flour
- 1 teaspoon SPICE ISLANDS® Ground Ginger
- ½ teaspoon SPICE ISLANDS® Ground Cinnamon
- ¼ teaspoon SPICE ISLANDS® Ground Cloves
- 2 teaspoons FLEISCHMANN'S® Bread Machine Yeast

Add ingredients to bread machine pan in the order suggested by manufacturer. (If dough is too dry or stiff, or too soft or slack, adjust dough consistency—see Adjusting Dough Consistency tip below.) Recommended cycle: Basic/white bread cycle; light or medium/normal crust color setting. *Makes 1 loaf (8 or 12 slices)*

Note: Use the 1-pound recipe if your machine pan holds 10 cups or less of water. For large-capacity machines with glass domes, make the 1-pound loaf size only and cover dome with foil (do not cover vents) while baking to ensure complete baking.

Adjusting Dough Consistency: Check dough after 5 minutes of mixing; it should form a soft, smooth ball around the blade. If dough is too stiff or dry, add additional liquid, 1 teaspoon at a time, until dough is of the right consistency. If dough is too soft or sticky, add additional bread flour, 1 teaspoon at a time.

Miniature Biscuits

- 2 cups all-purpose flour
- 1 tablespoon baking powder
- ½ teaspoon baking soda
- ½ teaspoon salt
- 6 tablespoons CRISCO® Stick or 6 tablespoons CRISCO® all-vegetable shortening
- ⅔ cup buttermilk

1. Heat oven to 500°F. Place sheets of foil on countertop for cooling biscuits.

2. Combine flour, baking powder, baking soda and salt in large mixing bowl. Cut in shortening using a pastry blender or two knives until the mixture resembles coarse meal. Add buttermilk, and stir with fork just until mixture holds together.

3. Turn dough onto floured surface and knead 10 times. Roll or pat dough into rectangle ¾-inch thick. Cut with round cutter into 2-inch biscuits. Place biscuits 2 inches apart on ungreased baking sheet.

4. Bake one baking sheet at a time at 500°F for 8 to 12 minutes, or until browned and puffed. *Do not overbake.* Remove biscuits to foil. Bake remaining biscuits. Serve as soon as possible. *Makes 24 biscuits*

Apple-Cinnamon Granola Bread

1-Pound Loaf

⅔ cup water
⅓ cup unsweetened applesauce
1 tablespoon butter or margarine
½ teaspoon salt
1½ cups whole wheat flour
¾ cup bread flour
½ cup granola
¼ cup nonfat dry milk powder
1 tablespoon packed brown sugar
½ teaspoon SPICE ISLANDS® Ground Cinnamon
1¼ teaspoons FLEISCHMANN'S® Bread Machine Yeast

1½-Pound Loaf

1 cup water
½ cup unsweetened applesauce
1 tablespoon butter or margarine
¾ teaspoon salt
2¼ cups whole wheat flour
1¼ cups bread flour
¾ cup granola
⅓ cup nonfat dry milk powder
4 teaspoons packed brown sugar
¾ teaspoon SPICE ISLANDS® Ground Cinnamon
1½ teaspoons FLEISCHMANN'S® Bread Machine Yeast

Add ingredients to bread machine pan in the order suggested by manufacturer, adding applesauce with water, and granola with flours. (If dough is too dry or stiff, or too soft or slack, adjust dough consistency—see Adjusting Dough Consistency tip below.) Recommended cycle: Whole wheat/whole grain or basic/white bread cycle; light or medium/normal crust color setting. (If basic/white bread cycle is used, add 1 tablespoon gluten to either size recipe—see Adding Gluten tip below.) Timed-bake feature can be used. *Makes 1 loaf (8 or 12 slices)*

Note: For large-capacity machines with glass domes, make only 1-pound loaf size to ensure complete baking.

Checking Dough Consistency: Check dough after 5 minutes of mixing; it should form a soft, smooth ball around the blade. If dough is too stiff or dry, add additional liquid, 1 teaspoon at a time, until dough is of the right consistency. If dough is too soft or sticky, add additional bread flour, 1 teaspoon at a time.

Adding Gluten: Some bread machines have a whole wheat or whole grain cycle, which comes in handy when making whole grain breads. If your machine lacks this cycle, try adding gluten to whole wheat, whole grain and rye bread recipes to improve loaf height, texture, and structure. (If your supermarket doesn't carry gluten, check with a health food store.) Use 1 tablespoon gluten for both the 1-pound recipe and the 1½-pound recipe.

Painted Bread Knots

1 tablespoon *French's*® Classic Yellow® Mustard
1 tablespoon milk
1 container (11 ounces) refrigerated crusty French loaf dough
Coarse salt

1. Preheat oven to 350°F. Combine mustard and milk in small bowl. Cut bread dough into 12 (1-inch) slices. Roll each slice into 8-inch long piece. Tie each into knot.

2. Arrange knots on lightly greased baking sheet. Paint each with mustard mixture. Sprinkle with salt. Bake 20 minutes or until golden. Transfer baking sheet to wire rack and let knots stand on baking sheet until completely cool.

3. Serve with additional mustard.

Makes 12 servings

Prep Time: 10 minutes
Cook Time: 20 minutes

Apple-Cinnamon Granola Bread

Make a Cake

Many occasions call for a special cake and these classics will not disappoint. From shortcakes to spice cakes, there's something for every special affair.

Chocolate Squares with Nutty Caramel Sauce

1 cup sugar
¾ cup all-purpose flour
½ cup HERSHEY₅S Dutch Processed Cocoa or HERSHEY₅S Cocoa
½ teaspoon baking powder
½ teaspoon salt
¾ cup vegetable oil
¼ cup milk
3 eggs
½ teaspoon vanilla extract
1 bag (14 ounces) caramel candies
½ cup water
1 cup pecan pieces
Sweetened whipped cream (optional)

1. Heat oven to 350°F. Grease bottom only of 8-inch square baking pan.

2. Stir together sugar, flour, cocoa, baking powder and salt in medium bowl. Add oil, milk, eggs and vanilla; beat until smooth. Pour batter into prepared pan.

3. Bake 35 to 40 minutes or until wooden pick inserted in center comes out clean. Cool completely in pan on wire rack.

4. Remove wrappers from caramels. Combine caramels and water in small saucepan. Cook over low heat, stirring occasionally, until smooth and well blended. Stir in pecans; cool until thickened slightly. Cut cake into squares; serve with warm caramel nut sauce and sweetened whipped cream, if desired.

Makes 9 servings

Chocolate Square with Nutty Caramel Sauce

Red's Rockin' Rainbow Cupcakes

2¼ cups all-purpose flour
1 tablespoon baking powder
½ teaspoon salt
1⅔ cups granulated sugar
½ cup (1 stick) butter, softened
1 cup milk
2 teaspoons vanilla extract
3 large egg whites
Blue and assorted food colorings
1 container (16 ounces) white frosting
1½ cups "M&M's"® Chocolate Mini Baking Bits, divided

Preheat oven to 350°F. Lightly grease 24 (2¾-inch) muffin cups or line with paper or foil liners; set aside. In large bowl combine flour, baking powder and salt. Blend in sugar, butter, milk and vanilla; beat about 2 minutes. Add egg whites; beat 2 minutes. Divide batter evenly among prepared muffin cups. Place 2 drops desired food coloring into each muffin cup. Swirl gently with knife. Sprinkle evenly with ¾ cup "M&M's"® Chocolate Mini Baking Bits. Bake 20 to 25 minutes or until toothpick inserted in center comes out clean. Cool completely on wire racks. Combine frosting and blue food coloring. Spread frosting over cupcakes; decorate with remaining ¾ cup "M&M's"® Chocolate Mini Baking Bits to make rainbows. Store in tightly covered container.

Makes 24 cupcakes

Easy Egg Nog Pound Cake

1 (18.25-ounce) package yellow cake mix
1 (4-serving size) package instant vanilla pudding and pie filling mix
¾ cup BORDEN® Egg Nog
¾ cup vegetable oil
4 eggs
½ teaspoon ground nutmeg
Powdered sugar, if desired

1. Preheat oven to 350°F. In large mixing bowl, combine cake mix, pudding mix, Borden Egg Nog and oil; beat at low speed of electric mixer until moistened. Add eggs and nutmeg; beat at medium-high speed 4 minutes.

2. Pour into greased and floured 10-inch fluted or tube pan.

3. Bake 40 to 45 minutes or until wooden pick inserted near center comes out clean.

4. Cool 10 minutes; remove from pan. Cool completely. Sprinkle with powdered sugar, if desired.   *Makes one 10-inch cake*

Prep Time: 10 minutes
Bake Time: 40 to 45 minutes

Valentine's Cupcakes

24 REYNOLDS® Valentine Baking Cups
1 package (about 18 ounces) white cake mix
1 container (16 ounces) white or pink ready-to-spread frosting
Red cinnamon candies
Chocolate heart candies
REYNOLDS® CUT-RITE® Wax Paper

PREHEAT oven to 350°F. Place Reynolds Valentine Baking Cups in muffin pans; set aside. Prepare cake mix following package directions for 24 cupcakes. Spoon batter into baking cups. Bake as directed. Cool.

FROST cupcakes with white or pink frosting. Place red cinnamon candies around cupcake edges. Stand two chocolate heart candies in center of frosting or use a small cookie cutter to cut hearts from a chocolate candy bar. (To prevent chocolate candy bar from cracking, remove wrapper, place on a sheet of Reynolds Cut-Rite Wax Paper and soften in microwave on DEFROST (30% power) 15 to 30 seconds.)

Makes 24 cupcakes

Red's Rockin' Rainbow Cupcakes

Harvest Honey Spice Cake

1 cup honey
⅓ cup vegetable oil
⅓ cup strong brewed coffee
3 eggs
2½ cups all-purpose flour
1½ teaspoons baking soda
1½ teaspoons ground cinnamon
¾ teaspoon ground nutmeg
½ teaspoon salt
2 cups peeled chopped tart apples
½ cup toasted slivered almonds
½ cup dried cranberries
  Powdered sugar
  Toasted sliced almonds, for garnish

Using electric mixer beat together honey, oil and coffee. Beat in eggs.

Combine dry ingredients; gradually add to honey-egg mixture, mixing until well blended. Stir in apples, almonds and cranberries.

Pour into lightly greased and floured Bundt or tube pan. Bake at 350°F for 35 to 40 minutes or until toothpick inserted in center comes out clean. Remove from oven; cool on wire rack. Dust with powdered sugar; garnish with sliced almonds, if desired.   *Makes 12 servings*

Favorite recipe from **National Honey Board**

Raspberry Shortcakes

1½ cups frozen whole raspberries, divided
6 tablespoons sugar, divided
1 cup all-purpose flour
1 teaspoon baking powder
¼ teaspoon baking soda
1 tablespoon margarine
1 egg white
⅓ cup evaporated skim milk
¼ teaspoon almond extract
¾ cup low-fat cottage cheese
1 teaspoon lemon juice

Preheat oven to 450°F. Spray baking sheet with nonstick cooking spray.

Toss 1¼ cups raspberries with 2 tablespoons plus 1½ teaspoons sugar; set aside in refrigerator. Combine flour, 2 tablespoons sugar, baking powder and baking soda in medium bowl. Cut in margarine with pastry blender or 2 knives; set aside. Beat egg white, milk and almond extract in small bowl; add to flour mixture and mix lightly. Knead slightly on lightly floured board. Roll out to ½-inch thickness. Cut out 8 biscuits with 2½-inch biscuit cutter. Place biscuits on prepared baking sheet. Bake 10 minutes or until lightly browned on top.

Meanwhile, place cottage cheese, remaining 1½ teaspoons sugar and lemon juice in food processor or blender; process until smooth. Fold in remaining ¼ cup raspberries. To serve, split biscuits in half and place each bottom half on individual serving dish. Top each with 2 tablespoons reserved raspberries and 1 tablespoon cheese mixture. Cover with biscuit top. Spoon remaining reserved raspberries and cheese mixture over tops.
      Makes 8 servings

Favorite recipe from **The Sugar Association, Inc.**

Apricot Cream Cake

Filling
2 cups chopped dried apricots (¼- to ½-inch pieces)
⅔ cup sugar
⅓ cup chopped pecans

Topping
⅓ cup flake coconut
¼ cup sugar
¼ cup chopped pecans
1 tablespoon Butter Flavor CRISCO® Stick or 1 tablespoon Butter Flavor CRISCO® all-vegetable shortening, melted

Cake
1 package (8 ounces) light (Neufchâtel) cream cheese, softened
½ Butter Flavor CRISCO® Stick or ½ cup Butter Flavor CRISCO® all-vegetable shortening
1¼ cups sugar
2 eggs
1 teaspoon vanilla
2 cups sifted all-purpose flour
1 teaspoon baking powder
½ teaspoon baking soda
¼ teaspoon salt
⅓ cup milk

Decorations
10 pecan halves
SMUCKER'S® Caramel Topping
10 dried apricot halves
Nasturtiums (optional)

1. For filling, place chopped apricots in medium saucepan. Add water to cover (about 1 cup). Bring to a boil. Reduce heat. Cover. Simmer until tender. Stir in ⅔ cup sugar. Cool completely. Stir in ⅓ cup nuts.

2. For topping, combine coconut, ¼ cup sugar, ¼ cup nuts and melted shortening in small bowl. Stir to mix.

3. Heat oven to 350°F. Grease 10-inch springform pan. Flour lightly.

4. For cake, combine cream cheese and ½ cup shortening in large bowl. Beat at high speed of electric mixer until fluffy. Add 1¼ cups sugar gradually, beating until light and fluffy. Add eggs and vanilla. Beat 2 minutes.

5. Combine flour, baking powder, baking soda and salt in small bowl. Add to creamed mixture alternately with milk, beating at medium speed 1 minute after each addition. Spread half of batter (about 2¼ cups) into pan. Spoon filling over batter to within ½ inch of edge. Cover with remaining batter. Sprinkle with topping.

6. Bake at 350°F for 45 to 50 minutes or until cake begins to pull away from side of pan and toothpick inserted in center comes out clean. *Do not overbake.* Cool 30 minutes. Loosen cake from side of pan with knife or metal spatula. Remove side of pan. Invert cake on wire rack. Remove bottom of pan using thin metal spatula or pancake turner. Cool 30 minutes. Place cake, top side up, on serving plate. Cool completely.

7. For decorations, brush nut halves lightly with caramel topping. Place 1 nut half in center of each apricot half. Press apricot half around nut. Place filled apricots around edge of cake. Place nasturtiums in center of cake, if desired. *Makes 1 (10-inch) round cake (12 servings)*

Vermont Spice Cake

Cake

    3 cups all-purpose flour
 3½ teaspoons baking powder
    2 teaspoons pumpkin pie spice
    1 teaspoon baking soda
 ¾ teaspoon ground nutmeg
 ½ teaspoon salt
 1½ cups granulated sugar
 ¾ cup (1½ sticks) butter, softened
    3 large eggs
 1½ cups LIBBY'S® 100% Pure Pumpkin
 ½ cup NESTLÉ® CARNATION®
        Evaporated Milk
 ¼ cup water
 1½ teaspoons vanilla extract

Maple Frosting

    11 ounces cream cheese, softened
 ⅓ cup butter, softened
 3½ cups sifted powdered sugar
    2 to 3 teaspoons maple flavoring
        Orange peel twists, fresh mint,
            chopped nuts or nut halves
            (optional)

PREHEAT oven to 325°F. Grease and flour two 9-inch-round cake pans.

For Cake

COMBINE flour, baking powder, pumpkin pie spice, baking soda, nutmeg and salt in small bowl. Beat granulated sugar and butter in large mixer bowl until creamy. Add eggs; beat for 2 minutes. Beat in pumpkin, evaporated milk, water and vanilla extract. Gradually beat in flour mixture. Spread evenly into prepared cake pans.

BAKE for 35 to 40 minutes or until wooden pick inserted in center comes out clean. Cool in pans on wire racks for 15 minutes; remove to wire racks to cool completely.

For Maple Frosting

BEAT cream cheese, butter and powdered sugar in large mixer bowl until fluffy. Add maple flavoring; mix well.

To Assemble

CUT each layer in half horizontally with long, serrated knife. Frost between layers and on top of cake, leaving side unfrosted. Garnish as desired.   *Makes 12 servings*

Note: To make a 2-layer cake, frost between layers, over top and on side of cake.

Scrumptious Apple Cake

    3 egg whites
 1½ cups sugar
    1 cup unsweetened applesauce
    1 teaspoon vanilla
    2 cups all-purpose flour
    2 teaspoons ground cinnamon
    1 teaspoon baking soda
 ¼ teaspoon salt
    4 cups cored peeled tart apple slices
        (McIntosh or Crispin)
        Yogurt Glaze (recipe follows)

Preheat oven to 350°F. Beat egg whites until slightly foamy; add sugar, applesauce and vanilla. Combine flour, cinnamon, baking soda and salt in separate bowl; add to applesauce mixture. Spread apples in 13×9-inch pan or 9-inch round springform pan sprayed with nonstick cooking spray. Spread batter over apples. Bake 35 to 40 minutes or until wooden toothpick inserted in center comes out clean; cool on wire rack. Prepare Yogurt Glaze; spread over cooled cake.

Makes 15 to 20 servings

Yogurt Glaze: Combine 1½ cups plain or vanilla nonfat yogurt, 3 tablespoons brown sugar (or to taste) and 1 teaspoon vanilla or 1 teaspoon lemon juice. Stir together until smooth.

*Favorite recipe from **New York Apple Association, Inc.***

Vermont Spice Cake

Touchdown Brownie Cups

1 cup (2 sticks) butter or margarine
½ cup HERSHEY'S Cocoa or HERSHEY'S Dutch Processed Cocoa
1 cup packed light brown sugar
½ cup granulated sugar
3 eggs
1 teaspoon vanilla extract
1 cup all-purpose flour
1⅓ cups chopped pecans, divided

1. Heat oven to 350°F. Line 2½-inch muffin cups with paper or foil bake cups.

2. Place butter in large microwave-safe bowl; cover. Microwave at HIGH (100%) 1½ minutes or until melted. Add cocoa; stir until smooth. Add brown sugar and granulated sugar; stir until well blended. Add eggs and vanilla; beat well. Add flour and 1 cup pecans; stir until well blended. Fill prepared muffin cups about ¾ full with batter; sprinkle about 1 teaspoon remaining pecans over top of each.

3. Bake 20 to 25 minutes or until tops are beginning to dry and crack. Cool completely in cups on wire rack.

Makes about 17 cupcakes

Chocolate Raspberry Torte

1⅓ cups all-purpose flour
1 cup sugar, divided
1½ teaspoons baking powder
½ teaspoon salt
2 eggs, separated
1 cup (½ pint) cold whipping cream
½ teaspoon almond extract
  Chocolate Filling & Frosting (recipe follows)
½ cup sliced almonds
¼ cup seedless red raspberry preserves
  Sweetened whipped cream (optional)

1. Heat oven to 350°F. Grease and flour two 8- or 9-inch round baking pans.

2. Stir together flour, ½ cup sugar, baking powder and salt; set aside. Beat egg whites in large bowl until foamy; gradually add ¼ cup sugar, beating until stiff peaks form. Beat 1 cup whipping cream in small bowl until stiff; fold into beaten egg whites.

3. Combine egg yolks, remaining ¼ cup sugar and almond extract in clean small bowl; beat on medium speed of mixer 3 minutes until thick and lemon colored. Gently fold into whipped cream mixture. Gradually fold flour mixture into whipped cream mixture just until ingredients are blended (mixture will be thick). Divide batter evenly between prepared pans; smooth surface.

4. Bake 25 to 30 minutes or until cake springs back when touched lightly in center. Cool 5 minutes; remove from pans to wire racks. Cool completely.

5. Prepare Chocolate Filling & Frosting. Split each cake layer in half horizontally. Place one layer on serving plate; spread with ⅔ cup filling. Sprinkle with 1 tablespoon almonds; repeat with two more layers. Top with last layer; spread with raspberry preserves. Frost side of cake with remaining filling. Garnish top edge with whipped cream, if desired. Sprinkle edge and center with remaining almonds; refrigerate until ready to serve. Cover; refrigerate leftover torte.

Makes 16 servings

Chocolate Filling & Frosting: Stir together ⅔ cup sugar and ⅓ cup HERSHEY'S Cocoa in medium bowl. Add 1½ cups cold whipping cream and 1½ teaspoons vanilla extract; beat until stiff. Makes about three cups.

Touchdown Brownie Cups

Mocha Dream Cake

Cake
- 1½ cups hot water
- 1 tablespoon TASTER'S CHOICE® 100% Pure Instant Coffee
- 1 cup NESTLÉ® CARNATION® COFFEE-MATE® Powdered Coffee Creamer
- 2⅓ cups all-purpose flour, *divided*
- 1½ teaspoons baking soda
- 1⅓ cups (8 ounces) NESTLÉ® TOLL HOUSE® Premier White Morsels
- ⅓ cup vegetable oil
- 1⅔ cups granulated sugar
- 4 large eggs
- ⅔ cup (5 fluid-ounce can) NESTLÉ® CARNATION® Evaporated Milk
- 2 tablespoons white vinegar
- 1 teaspoon vanilla extract
- ⅔ cup NESTLÉ® TOLL HOUSE® Baking Cocoa

Frosting
- ⅔ cup NESTLÉ® TOLL HOUSE® Premier White Morsels
- ⅓ cup butter or margarine
- 1 tablespoon TASTER'S CHOICE® 100% Pure Instant Coffee
- 1½ teaspoons water
- 2 packages (3 ounces *each*) cream cheese, softened
- 4 to 4½ cups powdered sugar

PREHEAT oven to 350°F. Grease and flour two 9-inch-round cake pans.

For Cake
COMBINE water and Taster's Choice in medium bowl. Stir in Coffee-Mate with wire whisk. Combine *1⅔ cups* flour and baking soda in another medium bowl. Microwave 1⅓ cups morsels and vegetable oil in large, microwave-safe bowl on MEDIUM-HIGH (70%) power for 1 minute; stir. Microwave at additional 10- to 15-second intervals, stirring just until melted. Add coffee mixture, granulated sugar, eggs, evaporated milk, vinegar and vanilla extract to melted morsels;

mix with wire whisk. Gradually beat in flour mixture until combined. (Batter will be thin.) Pour *3¼ cups* batter into medium bowl; stir in *remaining* flour. Pour into prepared pans.

BLEND cocoa into *remaining* batter with wire whisk until blended. Slowly pour even amounts of cocoa batter into center of each pan. (Cocoa batter will spread evenly outward from center.)

BAKE for 40 to 45 minutes or until wooden pick inserted in center comes out clean. Cool in pans on wire racks for 10 minutes; remove to wire racks to cool completely. Frost cake with frosting between layers and on top and side of cake.

For Frosting
MICROWAVE ⅔ cup morsels and butter in large, microwave-safe bowl on MEDIUM-HIGH (70%) power for 1 minute; stir. Microwave at additional 10- to 15-second intervals, stirring just until melted. Combine Taster's Choice and water in small bowl. Beat cream cheese and coffee mixture into melted morsels. Gradually beat in powdered sugar until mixture reaches spreading consistency. Makes about 2½ cups.

Makes 10 to 12 servings

Mocha Dream Cake

Zesty Lemon Pound Cake

1 cup (6 ounces) NESTLÉ® TOLL
    HOUSE® Premier White Morsels or
    3 bars (6-ounce box) NESTLÉ®
    TOLL HOUSE® Premier White
    Baking Bars, broken into pieces
2½ cups all-purpose flour
1 teaspoon baking powder
½ teaspoon salt
1 cup (2 sticks) butter, softened
1½ cups granulated sugar
2 teaspoons vanilla extract
3 large eggs
3 to 4 tablespoons (about 3 medium
    lemons) grated lemon peel
1⅓ cups buttermilk
1 cup powdered sugar
3 tablespoons fresh lemon juice

PREHEAT oven to 350°F. Grease and flour
12-cup bundt pan.

MELT morsels in medium, microwave-safe
bowl on MEDIUM-HIGH (70%) power for
1 minute; stir. Microwave at additional 10- to
20-second intervals, stirring until smooth; cool
slightly.

COMBINE flour, baking powder and salt in
small bowl. Beat butter, granulated sugar and
vanilla extract in large mixer bowl until
creamy. Beat in eggs, one at a time, beating
well after each addition. Beat in lemon peel
and melted morsels. Gradually beat in flour
mixture alternately with buttermilk. Pour into
prepared bundt pan.

BAKE for 50 to 55 minutes or until wooden
pick inserted in cake comes out clean. Cool in
pan on wire rack for 10 minutes. Combine
powdered sugar and lemon juice in small
bowl. Make holes in cake with wooden pick;
pour *half* of lemon glaze over cake. Let stand
for 5 minutes. Invert onto plate. Make holes in
top of cake; pour *remaining* glaze over cake.
Cool completely before serving.

Makes 16 servings

Chocolate Cappuccino Cupcakes

24 REYNOLDS® Baking Cups
1 package (about 18 ounces) chocolate
    cake mix
¼ cup instant coffee, divided
2 teaspoons hot water
1 container (16 ounces) ready-to-spread
    cream cheese frosting
½ cup semi-sweet chocolate morsels
2 teaspoons vegetable oil

PREHEAT oven to 350°F. Place Reynolds
Baking Cups in muffin pans; set aside. Prepare
cake mix following package directions for
24 cupcakes, adding 2 tablespoons instant
coffee before mixing. Spoon batter into baking
cups. Bake as directed. Cool.

DISSOLVE remaining instant coffee in hot
water. Stir frosting into coffee mixture until
smooth. Frost cupcakes.

MICROWAVE chocolate morsels and oil on
HIGH power in a small microwave-safe dish,
1 to 1½ minutes, stirring once, until chocolate
is melted.

DRIZZLE melted chocolate over frosted
cupcakes. Let stand until chocolate sets.

Makes 24 cupcakes

Zesty Lemon Pound Cake

Arlington Apple Gingerbread Cake

Cake
- 2 cans (20 ounces each) sliced apples, drained*
- 1 cup plus 1 teaspoon granulated sugar, divided
- 2 teaspoons ground cinnamon, divided
- 2 teaspoons fresh lemon juice
- 1 teaspoon grated lemon peel
- ½ Butter Flavor CRISCO® Stick or ½ cup Butter Flavor CRISCO® all-vegetable shortening
- 1 cup light molasses
- 2 eggs
- 3 cups all-purpose flour
- 2 teaspoons ground ginger
- ½ teaspoon ground cloves
- 1 cup boiling water
- 2 teaspoons baking soda

Topping (Optional)
- Confectioners' sugar
- Prepared lemon pie filling
- Whipped cream

Substitute 4½ cups sliced, peeled, translucent Ida Red or Jonathan apples (about 1½ pounds or 4 to 5 medium apples) for canned, if desired. Combine with blended sugar and cinnamon, lemon juice and lemon peel in saucepan. Cook and stir until apples become softened. Transfer mixture to baking pan. Continue as directed in step 3.

1. Heat oven to 350°F.

2. For cake, arrange apple slices in bottom of ungreased 13×9×2-inch baking pan. Combine 1 teaspoon granulated sugar and 1 teaspoon cinnamon in small bowl. Sprinkle over apples along with lemon juice and lemon peel.

3. Combine shortening and remaining 1 cup granulated sugar in large bowl. Beat with spoon until blended. Add molasses and eggs. Beat until blended.

4. Combine flour, ginger, remaining 1 teaspoon cinnamon and cloves in medium bowl. Add to molasses mixture. Beat until blended.

5. Combine boiling water and baking soda. Stir into molasses mixture until blended. Pour over apple mixture.

6. Bake at 350°F for 50 to 60 minutes or until toothpick inserted in center comes out clean. *Do not overbake.* Cool completely in pan on wire rack.

7. For optional topping, sprinkle top of cake with confectioners' sugar. Place spoonfuls of pie filling and whipped cream on each serving.
Makes one 13×9×2-inch cake (12 to 16 servings)

Black Forest Chocolate Fudge Cake

- 2 cups cake flour
- 1 cup unsweetened cocoa powder
- 1 teaspoon baking powder
- ½ teaspoon salt
- 1½ cups packed brown sugar
- 2 eggs
- 1 egg white
- 1 cup Dried Plum Purée (recipe follows) or prepared dried plum butter
- ¾ cup nonfat milk
- 4 teaspoons vanilla
- 1 cup boiling water
- 2 tablespoons instant espresso coffee powder
- 2 teaspoons baking soda
- 2 cups frozen pitted unsweetened dark sweet cherries, coarsely chopped, thawed and well drained
- ½ cup chopped toasted walnuts
- Mocha Glaze (recipe follows)
- Chocolate Drizzle (optional, recipe follows)
- Fresh cherries or frozen cherries, thawed
- Mint sprigs for garnish

Preheat oven to 350°F. Coat 12- to 16-cup Bundt or other tube pan with vegetable cooking spray. In large bowl, combine flour, cocoa, baking powder and salt; mix in brown sugar. In medium bowl, whisk eggs, egg white, Dried Plum Purée, milk and vanilla. In 2-cup measure, combine boiling water, espresso powder and baking soda. Stir Dried Plum Purée and water mixtures into flour mixture; mix just until blended. Pour half the batter into prepared pan; sprinkle cherries and walnuts evenly over batter. Top with remaining batter. Bake in center of oven about 45 minutes until pick inserted into center comes out clean. Cool in pan on wire rack 15 minutes; remove from pan. Cool completely on wire rack. Prepare Mocha Glaze. Spoon over cake, allowing glaze to run down sides. Prepare Chocolate Drizzle, if desired. Drizzle over glaze. Fill cake center with additional cherries and garnish with mint.

Makes 16 servings

Dried Plum Purée: Combine 1⅓ cups (8 ounces) pitted dried plums and 6 tablespoons hot water in container of food processor or blender. Pulse on and off until dried plums are finely chopped and smooth. Store leftovers in covered container in refrigerator for up to two months. Makes 1 cup.

Mocha Glaze: Place 1 cup powdered sugar in small bowl. Dissolve ⅛ teaspoon instant espresso powder in 4 teaspoons water. Stir into sugar until smooth, adding 1 teaspoon water, if needed, for desired consistency.

Chocolate Drizzle: In top of double boiler or bowl set over simmering water, melt 2 tablespoons semisweet chocolate chips. Stir in 2 teaspoons hot water until blended. Cool until desired consistency.

Favorite recipe from **California Dried Plum Board**

Cool and Minty Party Cake

1 (14-ounce) can EAGLE BRAND® Sweetened Condensed Milk (NOT evaporated milk)
2 teaspoons peppermint extract
8 drops green food coloring, if desired
2 cups (1 pint) whipping cream, whipped (do not use non-dairy topping)
1 (18.25- or 18.5-ounce) package white cake mix
    Green crème de menthe liqueur
1 (8-ounce) container frozen non-dairy whipped topping, thawed

1. Line 9-inch round layer cake pan with aluminum foil. In large mixing bowl, combine Eagle Brand, peppermint extract and food coloring, if desired. Fold in whipped cream. Pour into prepared pan; cover. Freeze at least 6 hours or until firm.

2. Meanwhile, prepare and bake cake mix as package directs for two 9-inch round layers. Remove from pans; cool completely.

3. With fork, poke holes in cake layers, 1 inch apart, halfway through each layer. Spoon small amounts of liqueur into holes. Place one cake layer on serving plate; top with frozen Eagle Brand mixture, then second cake layer. Trim frozen layer to edge of cake layers.

4. Frost quickly with whipped topping. Return to freezer at least 6 hours before serving. Garnish as desired. Freeze leftovers.

Makes one 9-inch cake

Brownie Sundae Cake

1 (19- to 21-ounce) package fudge brownie mix, prepared according to package directions for cake-like brownies
1 cup "M&M's"® Semi-Sweet Chocolate Mini Baking Bits
½ cup chopped nuts, optional
1 quart vanilla ice cream, softened
¼ cup caramel or butterscotch ice cream topping

Line 2 (9-inch) round cake pans with aluminum foil, extending slightly over edges of pans. Lightly spray bottoms with vegetable cooking spray; set aside. Preheat oven as brownie mix package directs. Divide brownie batter evenly between pans; sprinkle ½ cup "M&M's"® Semi-Sweet Chocolate Mini Baking Bits and ¼ cup nuts, if desired, over each pan. Bake 23 to 25 minutes or until edges begin to pull away from sides of pan. Cool completely. Remove layers by lifting foil from pans.

To assemble cake, place one brownie layer, topping-side down, in 9-inch springform pan. Carefully spread ice cream over brownie layer; drizzle with ice cream topping. Place second brownie layer on top of ice cream layer, topping-side up; press down lightly. Wrap in plastic wrap and freeze until firm. Remove from freezer about 15 minutes before serving. Remove side of pan. Cut into wedges.

Makes 12 slices

Texas Peanut Butter Pound Cake

¾ cup butter
1 cup sugar
3 eggs
½ cup peanut butter
1 cup flour
2 tablespoons chopped peanuts

Combine butter and sugar in a medium bowl. Using low speed of mixer, cream mixture until light and fluffy. Add eggs, one at a time; beating well after each addition. Blend in peanut butter. Stir in flour. Turn batter into greased loaf pan. Bake at 325°F for 30 minutes. Sprinkle with chopped nuts and bake for 30 to 40 minutes more or until sharp knife inserted into center of loaf comes out clean.

Makes 1 loaf

Variation: Stir 1 cup chocolate chips into batter before baking.

Serving Suggestions:

Top a slice of pound cake with 1 scoop of vanilla ice cream, chocolate sauce, whipped cream and chopped peanuts.

Slice pound cake into ½-inch thick slices. Spread half of the slices with desired flavor of preserves. Top with remaining slices to make sandwiches. Cut into 4 triangles and serve.

Lightly toast or grill thick pound cake slices. Drizzle with Peanut Butter Chocolate Sauce: Combine ¼ cup chocolate syrup and 2 tablespoons smooth peanut butter; mix well. Top with a dollop of whipped cream, if desired, and serve.

Favorite recipe from **Texas Peanut Producers Board**

Brownie Sundae Cake

Easter Baskets and Bunnies Cupcakes

2 cups sugar
1¾ cups all-purpose flour
¾ cup HERSHEY'S Cocoa or HERSHEY'S Dutch Processed Cocoa
1½ teaspoons baking powder
1½ teaspoons baking soda
1 teaspoon salt
2 eggs
1 cup milk
½ cup vegetable oil
2 teaspoons vanilla extract
1 cup boiling water
Creamy Vanilla Frosting (recipe follows)
Green, red and yellow food color
3¾ cups (10-ounce package) MOUNDS® Sweetened Coconut Flakes, divided and tinted*
Suggested garnishes (marshmallows, HERSHEY'S MINI KISSES™ Milk Chocolates, licorice, jelly beans)

To tint coconut, combine ¾ teaspoon water with several drops green food color in small bowl. Stir in 1¼ cups coconut. Toss with fork until evenly tinted. Repeat with red and yellow food color and remaining coconut.

1. Heat oven to 350°F. Line muffin cups (2½ inches in diameter) with paper bake cups.

2. Stir together sugar, flour, cocoa, baking powder, baking soda and salt in large bowl. Add eggs, milk, oil and vanilla; beat on medium speed of mixer 2 minutes. Stir in boiling water (batter will be thin). Fill muffin cups ⅔ full with batter.

3. Bake 22 to 25 minutes or until wooden pick inserted in center comes out clean. Cool completely. Prepare Creamy Vanilla Frosting; frost cupcakes. Immediately press desired color tinted coconut onto each cupcake. Garnish as desired to resemble Easter basket or bunny. *Makes about 33 cupcakes*

Creamy Vanilla Frosting: Beat ⅓ cup softened butter or margarine in medium bowl. Add 1 cup powdered sugar and 1½ teaspoons vanilla extract; beat well. Add 2½ cups powdered sugar alternately with ¼ cup milk, beating to spreading consistency. Makes about 2 cups frosting.

Cherry Cupcakes

1 (18¾-ounce) box chocolate cake mix
3 eggs
1⅓ cups water
½ cup vegetable oil
1 (21-ounce) can cherry pie filling
1 (16-ounce) can vanilla frosting

Prepare cake mix according to package directions, adding eggs, water and oil. Pour batter into 24 paper-lined muffin-pan cups, filling two-thirds full.

Remove 24 cherries from cherry filling; set aside. Spoon a generous teaspoon of remaining cherry filling onto the center of each cupcake.

Bake in preheated 350°F oven 20 to 25 minutes. Cool in pans on wire racks 10 minutes. Remove from pan. Let cool completely. Frost cupcakes with vanilla frosting. Garnish cupcakes with reserved cherries. *Makes 24 cupcakes*

Favorite recipe from **Cherry Marketing Institute**

Easter Baskets and Bunnies Cupcakes

Glazed Cranberry Mini-Cakes

$\frac{1}{3}$ cup butter or margarine, softened
$\frac{1}{3}$ cup granulated sugar
$\frac{1}{3}$ cup packed light brown sugar
 1 egg
$1\frac{1}{4}$ teaspoons vanilla extract
$1\frac{1}{3}$ cups all-purpose flour
 $\frac{3}{4}$ teaspoon baking powder
 $\frac{1}{4}$ teaspoon baking soda
 $\frac{1}{4}$ teaspoon salt
 2 tablespoons milk
$1\frac{1}{4}$ cups coarsely chopped fresh
     cranberries
 $\frac{1}{2}$ cup coarsely chopped walnuts
$1\frac{2}{3}$ cups HERSHEY'S Premier White
     Chips, divided
   White Glaze (recipe follows)

1. Heat oven to 350°F. Lightly grease or paper-line small muffin cups ($1\frac{3}{4}$ inches in diameter).

2. Beat butter, granulated sugar, brown sugar, egg and vanilla in large bowl until fluffy. Stir together flour, baking powder, baking soda and salt; gradually blend into butter mixture. Add milk; stir until blended. Stir in cranberries, walnuts and $\frac{2}{3}$ cup white chips (reserve remaining chips for glaze). Fill muffin cups $\frac{7}{8}$ full with batter.

3. Bake 18 to 20 minutes or until wooden pick inserted in center comes out clean. Cool 5 minutes; remove from pans to wire rack. Cool completely. Prepare White Glaze; drizzle over top of mini-cakes. Refrigerate 10 minutes to set glaze.

Makes about 3 dozen mini-cakes

White Glaze: Place remaining 1 cup HERSHEY'S Premier White Chips in small microwave-safe bowl; sprinkle 2 tablespoons vegetable oil over chips. Microwave at HIGH (100% power) 30 seconds; stir. If necessary, microwave at HIGH additional 30 seconds or just until chips are melted when stirred.

Orange Carrot Cake

 1 cup margarine or butter, softened
 1 cup GRANDMA'S® Molasses
     Unsulphured
 4 eggs
 $\frac{1}{2}$ cup orange juice
 1 cup all-purpose flour
 1 cup whole wheat flour
 2 teaspoons baking soda
 1 teaspoon ground cinnamon
 $\frac{1}{2}$ teaspoon salt
 2 cups shredded carrots
 $\frac{1}{2}$ cup chopped walnuts

Frosting
 1 package (3 ounces) cream cheese,
     softened
 2 tablespoons margarine or butter,
     softened
$1\frac{1}{2}$ cups powdered sugar
 1 teaspoon grated orange peel

Heat oven to 350°F. Grease two 8- or 9-inch round cake pans. In large bowl, combine margarine, molasses, eggs and orange juice; mix well. Stir in flours, baking soda, cinnamon and salt; mix well. Stir in carrots and walnuts. Pour into prepared pans. Bake at 350°F 30 to 35 minutes or until toothpick inserted in centers comes out clean. Cool 15 minutes; remove from pans. Cool completely.

In small bowl, combine all frosting ingredients; beat until smooth. Place one cake layer on serving plate; spread top with frosting. Top with second layer; spread top with frosting. If desired, garnish with additional orange peel and walnuts.

Makes 12 servings

Pineapple-Coconut Party Cake

Cake

    2 cups granulated sugar
    1 Butter Flavor CRISCO® Stick or 1 cup
        Butter Flavor CRISCO® all-vegetable
        shortening plus additional for
        greasing
    3 eggs
    1 teaspoon vanilla
    1 teaspoon coconut extract
    3 cups sifted all-purpose flour
    1 tablespoon baking powder
    1 cup milk

Topping

    1 can (20 ounces) crushed pineapple or
        pineapple tidbits in unsweetened
        juice
    1 tablespoon cornstarch
    1 cup firmly packed light brown sugar
    1 cup shredded coconut
    1 cup chopped pecans
    ½ teaspoon rum extract
    ¼ teaspoon vanilla
    12 to 16 maraschino cherries, drained

1. Heat oven to 350°F. Grease 13×9×2-inch pan with shortening. Flour lightly.

2. For cake, combine granulated sugar and 1 cup shortening in large bowl. Beat at medium speed of electric mixer until light and fluffy. Add eggs, 1 at a time, beating well after each addition. Beat in 1 teaspoon vanilla and coconut extract until blended.

3. Combine flour and baking powder in medium bowl. Add to creamed mixture alternately with milk, beating at low speed after each addition until well blended. Beat at medium speed 2 minutes. Pour into pan. Spread evenly. (Batter will be very thick.)

4. Bake at 350°F for 35 to 45 minutes or until toothpick inserted in center comes out clean. *Do not overbake.* (Cake will rise above top of pan and then fall slightly. Cake may be slightly lower in center.) Cool completely in pan on wire rack.

5. For topping, drain 2 tablespoons juice from pineapple. Combine juice and cornstarch in small bowl. Stir to dissolve.

6. Combine pineapple, remaining juice and brown sugar in medium saucepan. Bring to a boil. Stir in cornstarch mixture. Boil and stir 1 minute or until mixture is thickened and clear. Remove from heat. Stir in coconut, nuts, rum extract and ¼ teaspoon vanilla.

7. Use large fork or skewer to poke holes in top of cake. Pour topping over cake, spreading to edges. Arrange cherries on top of cake so that when cake is cut, each slice will have cherry in center. Refrigerate at least 30 minutes before serving.

*Makes 1 (13×9×2-inch) cake
(12 to 16 servings)*

Note: Prepare cake and topping the day before serving, if desired.

Rich Chocolate Cake with Creamy Peanut Butter Milk Chocolate Frosting

Cake
    2 cups all-purpose flour
    1¾ cups granulated sugar
    ⅔ cup NESTLÉ® TOLL HOUSE® Baking
        Cocoa
    1½ teaspoons baking powder
    1½ teaspoons baking soda
    ½ teaspoon salt
    1 cup milk
    1 cup water
    ½ cup vegetable oil
    2 large eggs
    2 teaspoons vanilla extract
    1⅔ cups (11-ounce package) NESTLÉ®
        TOLL HOUSE® Peanut Butter &
        Milk Chocolate Morsels, *divided*

Creamy Peanut Butter Milk
Chocolate Frosting
    1 package (8 ounces) cream cheese,
        softened
    1 teaspoon vanilla extract
    ⅛ teaspoon salt
    3 cups powdered sugar

Garnish
    1 bar (2 ounces *total*) NESTLÉ® TOLL
        HOUSE® Semi-Sweet Chocolate
        Baking Bar, made into curls (see
        Tip)

For Cake
PREHEAT oven to 350°F. Grease and flour
two 9-inch-round cake pans.

COMBINE flour, granulated sugar, cocoa,
baking powder, baking soda and salt in large
mixer bowl. Add milk, water, vegetable oil,
eggs and vanilla extract; blend until
moistened. Beat for 2 minutes (batter will be
thin). Pour into prepared pans. Sprinkle ⅓ *cup*
morsels over each cake layer.

BAKE for 25 to 30 minutes or until wooden
pick inserted in center comes out clean. Cool
in pans on wire racks for 10 minutes; remove
to wire racks to cool completely. Frost with
Creamy Peanut Butter Milk Chocolate Frosting
between layers and on top and side of cake.
Garnish with chocolate curls before serving.

For Creamy Peanut Butter Milk
Chocolate Frosting
MICROWAVE *remaining* morsels in small,
microwave-safe bowl on MEDIUM-HIGH
(70%) power for 1 minute; stir. Microwave at
additional 10- to 20-second intervals, stirring
until smooth. Beat cream cheese, melted
morsels, vanilla extract and salt in small mixer
bowl until light and fluffy. Gradually beat in
powdered sugar.   *Makes 10 to 12 servings*

Tip: To make chocolate curls, carefully draw a
vegetable peeler across a bar of NESTLÉ®
TOLL HOUSE® Semi-Sweet Chocolate. Vary
the width of your curls by using different sides
of the chocolate bar.

Rich Chocolate Cake with
Creamy Peanut Butter Milk
Chocolate Frosting

Patriotic Cocoa Cupcakes

2 cups sugar
1¾ cups all-purpose flour
¾ cup HERSHEY'S Cocoa
2 teaspoons baking soda
1 teaspoon baking powder
1 teaspoon salt
2 eggs
1 cup buttermilk or sour milk*
1 cup boiling water
½ cup vegetable oil
1 teaspoon vanilla extract
Vanilla Frosting (recipe follows)
Chocolate stars or blue and red
decorating icing (in tube)

To sour milk: Use 1 tablespoon white vinegar plus milk to equal 1 cup.

1. Heat oven to 350°F. Grease and flour muffin cups (2½ inches in diameter) or line with paper bake cups.

2. Combine dry ingredients in large bowl. Add eggs, buttermilk, water, oil and vanilla; beat on medium speed of mixer 2 minutes (batter will be thin). Fill cups ⅔ full with batter.

3. Bake 15 minutes or until wooden pick inserted in center comes out clean. Remove cupcakes from pan. Cool completely. To make chocolate stars for garnish, if desired, cut several cupcakes into ½-inch slices; cut out star shapes from cake slices. Frost remaining cupcakes. Garnish with chocolate stars or with blue and red decorating icing.

Makes about 30 cupcakes

Vanilla Frosting: Beat ¼ cup (½ stick) softened butter, ¼ cup shortening and 2 teaspoons vanilla extract. Add 1 cup powdered sugar; beat until creamy. Add 3 cups powdered sugar alternately with 3 to 4 tablespoons milk, beating to spreading consistency. Makes about 2⅓ cups frosting.

Lemon Semolina Syrup Cake

2 cups semolina or farina flour
1 cup sugar
1½ teaspoons baking powder
¼ teaspoon salt
2 cups plain low-fat yogurt
2 tablespoons FILIPPO BERIO® Extra
Light Tasting Olive Oil
Finely grated peel of 1 lemon
12 to 15 walnut halves
1 cup light corn syrup
2 tablespoons lemon juice
Fresh strawberries (optional)

Preheat oven to 350°F. Grease 9-inch springform pan with olive oil.

In large bowl, combine semolina, sugar, baking powder and salt. With wooden spoon or spatula, mix in yogurt, olive oil and lemon peel until well blended. *Do not use electric mixer.* Pour batter into prepared pan. Score top of batter with tip of sharp knife, making 12 to 15 squares or diamond shapes, about ½ inch deep. (Marks will not remain completely visible before baking, but will show slightly when baked.) Place walnut half in center of each square or diamond shape.

Bake 45 minutes or until golden brown and toothpick inserted in center comes out clean. Meanwhile, in small saucepan, combine corn syrup and lemon juice. Heat over medium heat, stirring frequently, until mixture is hot.

When cake tests done, remove from oven. Make ½-inch-deep cuts through scored portions, cleaning knife after each cut. Immediately pour hot syrup over cake in pan. Let stand 1 to 2 hours or until syrup is absorbed and cake is cool. Remove side of pan; serve garnished with strawberries, if desired. Cover; refrigerate any remaining cake.

Makes 10 to 12 servings

Patriotic Cocoa Cupcakes

Pumpkin Carrot Cake

2 cups all-purpose flour
2 teaspoons baking soda
2 teaspoons ground cinnamon
½ teaspoon salt
¾ cup milk
1½ teaspoons lemon juice
3 large eggs
1¼ cups LIBBY'S® 100% Pure Pumpkin
1½ cups granulated sugar
½ cup packed brown sugar
½ cup vegetable oil
1 can (8 ounces) crushed pineapple, drained
1 cup (about 3 medium) grated carrots
1 cup flaked coconut
1¼ cups chopped nuts, divided
  Cream Cheese Frosting (recipe follows)

PREHEAT oven to 350°F. Grease two 9-inch-round baking pans.

COMBINE flour, baking soda, cinnamon and salt in small bowl. Combine milk and lemon juice in liquid measuring cup (mixture will appear curdled).

BEAT eggs, pumpkin, granulated sugar, brown sugar, oil, pineapple, carrots and milk mixture in large mixer bowl; mix well. Gradually add flour mixture; beat until combined. Stir in coconut and *1 cup* nuts. Pour into prepared baking pans.

BAKE for 30 to 35 minutes or until wooden pick inserted in center comes out clean. Cool in pans for 15 minutes. Remove to wire racks to cool completely.

FROST between layers, on side and top of cake with Cream Cheese Frosting. Garnish with *remaining* nuts. Store in refrigerator.

Makes 12 servings

Cream Cheese Frosting: COMBINE

11 ounces softened cream cheese, ⅓ cup softened butter and 3½ cups sifted powdered sugar in large mixer bowl until fluffy. Add 1 teaspoon vanilla extract, 2 teaspoons orange juice and 1 teaspoon grated orange peel; beat until combined.

Fudgey Chocolate Cupcakes

¾ cup water
½ cup (1 stick) 60% vegetable oil spread, melted
2 egg whites, slightly beaten
1 teaspoon vanilla extract
2¼ cups HERSHEY'S Basic Cocoa Baking Mix (recipe follows)
2 teaspoons powdered sugar
2 teaspoons HERSHEY'S Cocoa (optional)

1. Heat oven to 350°F. Line 16 muffin cups (2½ inches in diameter) with foil or paper baking cups.

2. Stir together water, melted spread, egg whites and vanilla in large bowl. Add Basic Cocoa Baking Mix; beat on low speed of mixer until blended. Fill muffin cups ⅔ full with batter.

3. Bake 20 to 25 minutes or until wooden pick inserted into centers comes out clean. Remove from pans to wire racks. Cool completely. Sift powdered sugar over tops of cupcakes. If desired, partially cover part of each cupcake with paper cutout. Sift cocoa over exposed powdered sugar. Carefully lift off cutout. Store, covered, at room temperature.

Makes 16 cupcakes

Hershey's Basic Cocoa Baking Mix:

Stir together 4½ cups all-purpose flour, 2¾ cups sugar, 1¼ cups HERSHEY'S Cocoa, 1 tablespoon plus ½ teaspoon baking powder, 1¾ teaspoons salt and 1¼ teaspoons baking soda. Store in airtight container in cool, dry place for up to 1 month. Stir before using. Makes 8 cups mix.

Pumpkin Carrot Cake

Cookies & Pies

Heartwarming cookies and wholesome pies have always been popular desserts and tea time snacks. Now your favorite recipes are all in one place.

Chocolate Chip Shells

2 cups all-purpose flour
1⅓ cups (about 8 ounces) NESTLÉ® TOLL HOUSE® Semi-Sweet Chocolate Morsels, divided
4 large eggs
1 cup granulated sugar
1 tablespoon orange liqueur (such as Cointreau) or 1 teaspoon orange extract
1 teaspoon vanilla extract
2 tablespoons (about 1 orange) grated orange peel
1 cup (2 sticks) unsalted butter, melted
Sifted powdered sugar

PREHEAT oven to 350°F. Generously grease and flour madeleine baking pan(s).

COMBINE flour and *1 cup* morsels in medium bowl. Beat eggs, granulated sugar, orange liqueur, vanilla extract and orange peel in large mixer bowl until light in color. Fold flour mixture and butter alternately into egg mixture, beginning and ending with flour mixture. Spoon heaping tablespoon of batter into each prepared mold.

BAKE for 10 to 12 minutes or until wooden pick inserted in center comes out clean. Cool in pan(s) for 1 minute. With tip of knife, release onto wire racks to cool completely. Wash, grease and flour pan(s). Repeat with *remaining* batter.

SPRINKLE madeleines very lightly with powdered sugar. Microwave *remaining* morsels in *heavy-duty* resealable plastic food storage bag on HIGH (100%) power for 30 seconds; knead bag to mix. Microwave at additional 10-second intervals, kneading until smooth. Cut a small hole in corner of bag; squeeze to drizzle over madeleines. Allow chocolate to cool and set before serving.

Makes about 2½ dozen madeleines

Chocolate Chip Shells

Easy Peanut Butter Chip Pie

1 package (3 ounces) cream cheese, softened
1 teaspoon lemon juice
1⅔ cups (10-ounce package) REESE'S® Peanut Butter Chips, divided
⅔ cup sweetened condensed milk (not evaporated milk)
1 cup (½ pint) cold whipping cream, divided
1 packaged chocolate or graham cracker crumb crust (6 ounces)
1 tablespoon powdered sugar
1 teaspoon vanilla extract

1. Beat cream cheese and lemon juice in medium bowl until fluffy, about 2 minutes; set aside.

2. Place 1 cup peanut butter chips and sweetened condensed milk in medium microwave-safe bowl. Microwave at HIGH (100%) 45 seconds; stir. If necessary, microwave an additional 15 seconds at a time, stirring after each heating, until chips are melted and mixture is smooth when stirred.

3. Add warm peanut butter mixture to cream cheese mixture. Beat on medium speed until blended, about 1 minute. Beat ½ cup whipping cream in small bowl until stiff; fold into peanut butter mixture. Pour into crust. Cover; refrigerate several hours or overnight until firm.

4. Just before serving, combine remaining ½ cup whipping cream, powdered sugar and vanilla in small bowl. Beat until stiff; spread over filling. Garnish with remaining peanut butter chips. Cover; refrigerate leftover pie.

Makes 6 to 8 servings

Sweet Potato Pecan Pie

1 pound sweet potatoes or yams, cooked and peeled
¼ cup (½ stick) butter or margarine, softened
1 (14-ounce) can EAGLE BRAND® Sweetened Condensed Milk (NOT evaporated milk)
1 egg
1 teaspoon grated orange peel
1 teaspoon ground cinnamon
1 teaspoon vanilla extract
½ teaspoon ground nutmeg
¼ teaspoon salt
1 (6-ounce) graham cracker crumb pie crust
Pecan Topping (recipe follows)

1. Preheat oven to 425°F. In large mixing bowl, beat hot sweet potatoes and butter until smooth. Add Eagle Brand and remaining ingredients except crust and Pecan Topping; mix well. Pour into crust.

2. Bake 20 minutes. Meanwhile, prepare Pecan Topping.

3. Remove pie from oven; *reduce oven temperature to 350°F.* Spoon Pecan Topping over pie.

4. Bake 25 minutes longer or until set. Cool. Serve warm or at room temperature. Garnish with orange zest twist, if desired. Refrigerate leftovers. *Makes 1 pie*

Pecan Topping: In small mixing bowl, beat 1 egg, 2 tablespoons firmly packed light brown sugar, 2 tablespoons dark corn syrup, 1 tablespoon melted butter and ½ teaspoon maple flavoring. Stir in 1 cup chopped pecans.

Prep Time: 30 minutes
Bake Time: 45 minutes

Caramel-Pecan Pie

3 eggs
⅔ cup sugar
1 cup (12-ounce jar) SMUCKER'S®
    Caramel Topping
¼ cup butter or margarine, melted
1½ cups pecan halves
1 (9-inch) unbaked pie shell

In mixing bowl, beat eggs slightly with fork. Add sugar, stirring until dissolved. Stir in topping and butter; mix well. Stir in pecan halves. Pour filling into pie shell.

Bake at 350°F for 45 minutes or until knife inserted near center comes out clean. Cool thoroughly on rack before serving. Cover and store in refrigerator.   *Makes 6 to 8 servings*

Holiday Cheese Tarts

1 (8-ounce) package cream cheese,
    softened
1 (14-ounce) can EAGLE BRAND®
    Sweetened Condensed Milk (NOT
    evaporated milk)
⅓ cup lemon juice from concentrate
1 teaspoon vanilla extract
2 (4-ounce) packages single-serve
    graham cracker crumb pie crusts
    Assorted fruit (strawberries,
    blueberries, bananas, raspberries,
    orange segments, cherries, kiwi
    fruit, grapes, pineapple, etc.)
¼ cup apple jelly, melted, if desired

1. In medium mixing bowl, beat cream cheese until fluffy. Gradually beat in Eagle Brand until smooth. Stir in lemon juice and vanilla.

2. Spoon into crusts. Chill 2 hours or until set. Just before serving, top with fruit; brush with jelly, if desired. Refrigerate leftovers.
     Makes 12 tarts

Prep Time: 10 minutes
Chill Time: 2 hours

Malted Dream Drops

½ Butter Flavor CRISCO® Stick or ½ cup
    Butter Flavor CRISCO® all-vegetable
    shortening
1 cup firmly packed brown sugar
1 egg
1 teaspoon vanilla
½ cup evaporated milk
1¼ cups all-purpose flour
1 cup chocolate malted milk granules
1 teaspoon baking powder
¼ teaspoon salt
1 cup semisweet chocolate chips
1 cup coarsely chopped walnuts

1. Combine ½ cup shortening and sugar in large bowl. Beat at medium speed of electric mixer until well blended. Beat in egg and vanilla. Add milk. Beat until smooth.

2. Combine flour, malted milk granules, baking powder and salt. Mix into creamed mixture at low speed until just blended. Stir in chocolate chips and nuts. Cover and refrigerate at least 1 hour.

3. Heat oven to 350°F. Grease baking sheet with shortening. Place sheets of foil on countertop for cooling cookies.

4. Drop rounded teaspoonfuls of dough 2 inches apart onto prepared sheet.

5. Bake at 350°F 10 to 12 minutes, or until set. *Do not overbake.* Cool 2 minutes on baking sheet. Remove cookies to foil to cool completely.   *Makes about 4 dozen cookies*

Chocolate Truffle Tart

Crust
- ⅔ cup all-purpose flour
- ½ cup powdered sugar
- ½ cup ground walnuts
- 6 tablespoons butter or margarine, softened
- ⅓ cup NESTLÉ® TOLL HOUSE® Baking Cocoa

Filling
- 1¼ cups heavy whipping cream
- ¼ cup granulated sugar
- 2 cups (12-ounce package) NESTLÉ® TOLL HOUSE® Semi-Sweet Chocolate Morsels
- 2 tablespoons seedless raspberry jam
- Sweetened whipped cream (optional)
- Fresh raspberries (optional)

For Crust

PREHEAT oven to 350°F.

BEAT flour, powdered sugar, nuts, butter and cocoa in large mixer bowl until soft dough forms. Press dough onto bottom and up side of ungreased 9- or 9½-inch fluted tart pan with removable bottom or 9-inch pie plate.

BAKE for 12 to 14 minutes or until puffed. Cool completely in pan on wire rack.

For Filling

BRING cream and granulated sugar in medium saucepan *just to a boil*, stirring occasionally. Remove from heat. Stir in morsels and jam; let stand for 5 minutes. Whisk until smooth. Transfer to small mixer bowl. Cover; refrigerate for 45 to 60 minutes or until mixture is cooled and slightly thickened.

BEAT for 20 to 30 seconds or just until color lightens slightly. Spoon into crust. Refrigerate until firm. Remove side of pan; garnish with whipped cream and raspberries.

Makes 8 servings

Ali's Oatmeal Cookies

- 1 Butter Flavor CRISCO® Stick or 1 cup Butter Flavor CRISCO® all-vegetable shortening
- 1 cup granulated sugar
- 1 cup firmly packed light brown sugar
- 2 eggs
- 1 teaspoon vanilla
- 1½ cups plus 1 tablespoon all-purpose flour, divided
- 1 teaspoon baking soda
- ¾ teaspoon salt
- 2½ cups oats (quick or old-fashioned, uncooked)
- 1 cup finely chopped hazelnuts
- 1 cup finely diced dried apricots
- 1 cup chopped white chocolate chips

1. Heat oven to 350°F. Place sheets of foil on countertop for cooling cookies.

2. Combine 1 cup shortening, granulated sugar, brown sugar, eggs and vanilla in large bowl. Beat at medium speed of electric mixer until well blended.

3. Combine 1½ cups flour, baking soda and salt. Add gradually to creamed mixture at low speed. Beat until well blended. Stir in oats and nuts with spoon.

4. Toss apricots with remaining 1 tablespoon flour. Stir into dough. Stir in white chocolate chips. Shape into 1½-inch balls. Flatten slightly. Place 2 inches apart on ungreased baking sheet.

5. Bake at 350°F for 11 to 13 minutes or until just beginning to brown around edges and slightly moist in center. *Do not overbake.* Cool 2 minutes on baking sheet. Remove cookies to foil to cool completely.

Makes about 3 dozen cookies

Chocolate Truffle Tart

Apple Crisp Cookies

Cookies

 1 Butter Flavor CRISCO® Stick or 1 cup Butter Flavor CRISCO® all-vegetable shortening plus additional for greasing
 1 cup firmly packed light brown sugar
 1 teaspoon vanilla
 2½ cups oats (quick or old-fashioned, uncooked)
 2¼ cups all-purpose flour
 ½ teaspoon baking soda
 ½ teaspoon salt
 6 to 8 tablespoons water

Topping

 1 can (21 ounces) apple pie filling, finely chopped
 1 cup reserved crumb mixture
 ½ cup finely chopped pecans or walnuts

1. Heat oven to 375°F. Grease baking sheet with shortening. Place sheets of foil on countertop for cooling cookies.

2. For cookies, combine shortening, brown sugar and vanilla in large bowl. Beat at medium speed of electric mixer until well blended.

3. Combine oats, flour, baking soda and salt. Add alternately with water to creamed mixture stirring with spoon. Mix well after each addition. (Mixture will be crumbly, but will hold together when shaped into small ball.) Add additional water if necessary. Reserve 1 cup for topping. Shape remaining dough into 1-inch balls. Place 2 inches apart on greased baking sheet. Flatten to ⅛-inch thickness with floured bottom of glass. Smooth edges.

4. Bake at 375°F for 5 to 7 minutes or until light brown around edges and firm. *Do not overbake.* Remove from oven. Cool on baking sheet about 5 minutes.

5. For topping, place 1 measuring teaspoonful of pie filling in center of each cookie. Spread carefully to cover.

6. Combine 1 cup reserved crumbs and nuts in small bowl. Toss until mixed. Sprinkle over apple filling.

7. Return to oven. Bake 5 minutes or until topping is light brown. *Do not overbake.* Cool 2 minutes on baking sheet. Remove cookies to foil to cool completely.

Makes about 3 dozen cookies

Holiday Double Chocolate Cookies

 1½ cups all-purpose flour
 ½ cup HERSHEY'S Cocoa
 ½ teaspoon baking soda
 ¼ teaspoon salt
 ½ cup (1 stick) butter or margarine, softened
 ¾ cup packed light brown sugar
 ½ cup granulated sugar
 1 teaspoon vanilla extract
 2 eggs
 1⅓ cups (10-ounce package) HERSHEY'S Holiday Bits, divided

1. Heat oven to 350°F. Lightly grease cookie sheet.

2. Stir together flour, cocoa, baking soda and salt. In large bowl, beat butter, brown sugar, granulated sugar and vanilla until well blended. Add eggs; beat well. Gradually add flour mixture, blending well. Stir in 1 cup Holiday Bits. Drop by rounded teaspoons onto prepared cookie sheet. Press 8 to 9 of remain bits on dough before baking.

3. Bake 7 to 9 minutes or until cookie is set. Do not overbake. Cool slightly; remove from cookie sheet to wire rack. Cool completely.

Makes about 3½ dozen cookies

Apple Crisp Cookies

Honey Almond Biscotti

½ cup butter or margarine
¾ cup honey
2 eggs
1 teaspoon vanilla
3½ cups all-purpose flour
2 teaspoons ground cinnamon
2 teaspoons anise seeds
½ teaspoon salt
½ teaspoon baking powder
¼ teaspoon baking soda
1 cup dried cranberries or candied cherries
¾ cup slivered almonds

Cream butter in large bowl with electric mixer; beat in honey, eggs and vanilla. Combine flour, cinnamon, anise seeds, salt, baking powder and baking soda in small bowl; mix well. Stir into butter mixture. Stir in cranberries and nuts. Shape dough into two 10×3×1-inch logs on greased baking sheet. Bake in preheated 350°F oven about 20 minutes or until lightly browned. Remove from oven; cool 5 minutes. Remove to cutting board. *Reduce oven temperature to 300°F.* Cut each log into ½-inch strips; place on baking sheet. Bake about 20 minutes more or until crisp throughout. Cool completely on wire racks.

Makes 3 dozen cookies

Favorite recipe from **National Honey Board**

Lemon Pecan Cookies

1 Butter Flavor CRISCO® Stick or 1 cup Butter Flavor CRISCO® all-vegetable shortening
1½ cups granulated sugar
2 large eggs
3 tablespoons fresh lemon juice
3 cups all-purpose flour
2 teaspoons baking powder
¼ teaspoon salt
1 cup chopped pecans

1. Heat oven to 350°F. Place wire rack on countertop for cooling cookies.

2. Combine 1 cup shortening and sugar in large bowl. Beat at medium speed of electric mixer until well blended. Beat in eggs and lemon juice until well blended.

3. Combine flour, baking powder and salt in medium bowl. Add to creamed mixture; mix well. Stir in pecans. Spray cookie sheets lightly with CRISCO® No-Stick Cooking Spray. Drop dough by teaspoonfuls about 2 inches apart onto prepared cookie sheets. Bake at 350°F for 10 for 12 minutes or until lightly browned. Cool on cookie sheets 4 minutes; transfer to cooling rack to cool completely.

Makes about 6 dozen cookies

Strawberry Cheesecake Pudding Pie

1½ cups strawberry, cherry or raspberry pie filling, divided
1 (6-ounce) READY CRUST® Graham Cracker Pie Crust
1½ cups cold milk
2 (4-serving-size each) packages JELL-O® Cheesecake Flavor Instant Pudding & Pie Filling
1 (8-ounce) tub COOL WHIP® Whipped Topping, thawed

1. Spoon ½ cup fruit pie filling into crust.

2. Pour milk into large bowl. Add pudding mixes. Beat with wire whisk 2 minutes or until smooth. (Mixture will be thick.) Immediately stir in whipped topping. Spoon over pie filling in crust.

3. Refrigerate 3 hours or until set. Top with remaining pie filling. Garnish as desired. Refrigerate leftovers. *Makes 8 servings*

Prep Time: 10 minutes
Chilling Time: 3 hours

European Kolacky

1 cup butter or margarine, softened
1 package (8 ounces) cream cheese, softened
1 tablespoon milk
1 tablespoon sugar
1 egg yolk - well beaten
1½ cups all-purpose flour
½ teaspoon baking powder
1 can SOLO® or 1 jar BAKER® Filling (any flavor)
Powdered sugar

Cream butter, cream cheese, milk and sugar in medium bowl with electric mixer until thoroughly blended. Beat in egg yolk. Sift together flour and baking powder; stir into butter mixture to make stiff dough. Cover and refrigerate several hours or overnight.

Preheat oven to 400°F. Roll out dough on lightly floured surface to ¼-inch thickness. Cut dough with floured 2-inch cookie cutter. Place cookies on ungreased cookie sheets about 1 inch apart. Make depression in centers of cookies with thumb or back of spoon. Spoon 1 teaspoon filling into centers of cookies.

Bake 10 to 12 minutes or until lightly browned. Remove from baking sheets and cool completely on wire racks. Sprinkle with powdered sugar just before serving.

Makes about 3 dozen cookies

Brownie Turtle Cookies

2 squares (1 ounce each) unsweetened baking chocolate
⅓ cup solid vegetable shortening
1 cup granulated sugar
½ teaspoon vanilla extract
2 large eggs
1¼ cups all-purpose flour
½ teaspoon baking powder
½ teaspoon salt
1 cup "M&M's"® Milk Chocolate Mini Baking Bits, divided
1 cup pecan halves
⅓ cup caramel ice cream topping
⅓ cup shredded coconut
⅓ cup finely chopped pecans

Preheat oven to 350°F. Lightly grease cookie sheets; set aside. Heat chocolate and shortening in 2-quart saucepan over low heat, stirring constantly until melted; remove from heat. Mix in sugar, vanilla and eggs. Blend in flour, baking powder and salt. Stir in ⅔ cup "M&M's"® Milk Chocolate Mini Baking Bits. For each cookie, arrange 3 pecan halves, with ends almost touching at center, on prepared cookie sheets. Drop dough by rounded teaspoonfuls onto center of each group of pecans; mound the dough slightly. Bake 8 to 10 minutes just until set. *Do not overbake.* Cool completely on wire racks. In small bowl combine ice cream topping, coconut and chopped nuts; top each cookie with about 1½ teaspoons mixture. Press remaining ⅓ cup "M&M's"® Milk Chocolate Mini Baking Bits into topping.

Makes about 2½ dozen cookies

Fluffy Lemon Berry Pie

4 ounces cream cheese, softened
1½ cups cold milk
2 (4-serving size) packages JELL-O®
    Lemon Flavor Instant Pudding &
    Pie Filling
1 (8-ounce) tub COOL WHIP® Whipped
    Topping, thawed
1 (6-ounce) READY CRUST® Shortbread
    or Graham Cracker Pie Crust
1 cup blueberries, raspberries or sliced
    strawberries

1. Beat cream cheese in large bowl with wire whisk until smooth. Gradually beat in milk until well blended. Add pudding mixes. Beat 2 minutes or until smooth. Immediately stir in half of whipped topping.

2. Spoon into crust. Top with remaining whipped topping.

3. Refrigerate 3 hours or until set. Garnish with berries. Refrigerate leftovers.

Makes 8 servings

Prep Time: 10 minutes
Chilling Time: 3 hours

Cinnamon Roll Cookies

Cinnamon Mixture
4 tablespoons granulated sugar
1 tablespoon ground cinnamon

Cookie Dough
1 Butter Flavor CRISCO® Stick or 1 cup
    Butter Flavor CRISCO® all-vegetable
    shortening
1 cup firmly packed light brown sugar
2 large eggs
1 teaspoon vanilla
3 cups all-purpose flour
2 teaspoons baking powder
½ teaspoon salt
1 teaspoon ground cinnamon

1. For cinnamon mixture, combine granulated sugar and 1 tablespoon cinnamon in small bowl; mix well. Set aside.

2. For cookie dough, combine shortening and brown sugar in large bowl. Beat at medium speed with electric mixer until well blended. Beat in eggs and vanilla until well blended.

3. Combine flour, baking powder, salt and 1 teaspoon cinnamon in small bowl. Add to creamed mixture; mix well.

4. Turn dough onto sheet of waxed paper. Spread dough into 9×6-inch rectangle using rubber spatula. Sprinkle with 4 tablespoons cinnamon mixture to within 1 inch from edge. Roll up jelly-roll style into log. Dust log with remaining cinnamon mixture. Wrap tightly in plastic wrap; refrigerate 4 hours or overnight.

5. Heat oven to 375°F. Spray cookie sheets with CRISCO® No-Stick Cooking Spray.

6. Slice dough ¼ inch thick. Place on prepared cookie sheets. Bake at 350°F for 8 minutes or until lightly browned on top. Cool on cookie sheets 4 minutes; transfer to cooling racks.

Makes about 5 dozen cookies

Kitchen Hint: Be careful when working with this dough. It is a stiff dough and can crack easily when rolling. Roll the dough slowly and smooth any cracks with your finger as you go.

Fluffy Lemon Berry Pie

Sensational Cinnamon Chip Biscotti

½ cup (1 stick) butter, softened
1 cup sugar
2 eggs
1 teaspoon vanilla extract
2½ cups all-purpose flour
1½ teaspoons baking powder
¼ teaspoon salt
1⅔ cups (10-ounce package) HERSHEY'S Cinnamon Chips (divided)
1 cup very finely chopped walnuts
2 teaspoons shortening (do not use butter, margarine, spread or oil)
White Chip Drizzle (recipe follows)

1. Heat oven 325°F. Lightly grease cookie sheet.

2. Beat butter and sugar in large bowl until blended. Add eggs and vanilla; beat well. Stir together flour, baking powder and salt; gradually add to butter mixture, beating until smooth. (Dough will be stiff.) Using spoon or with hands, work 1 cup cinnamon chips and walnuts into dough.

3. Divide dough into four equal parts. Shape each part into a log about 8 inches long. Place on prepared cookie sheet, at least 2 inches apart; flatten slightly.

4. Bake 25 to 30 minutes or until logs are set and wooden pick inserted in center comes out clean. Remove from oven; let cool on cookie sheet 30 minutes. Transfer to cutting board. Using serrated knife and sawing motion, cut logs diagonally into ½-inch-wide slices. Place slices close together, cut side down, on ungreased cookie sheet. Return to oven; bake 5 to 6 minutes. Turn each slice; bake an additional 5 to 8 minutes. Remove from oven; cool slightly. Remove from cookie sheet to wire rack. Cool completely. Melt remaining cinnamon chips with shortening; drizzle over each cookie. Drizzle White Chip Drizzle over top.

Makes about 5 dozen cookies

White Chip Drizzle: Place ¼ cup HERSHEY'S Premier White Chips and 1 teaspoon shortening (do not use butter, margarine, spread or oil) in small microwave-safe bowl. Microwave at HIGH (100%) 30 to 45 seconds or until smooth when stirred.

Wisconsin Ricotta Tart with Kiwi and Raspberry Sauce

⅓ cup all-purpose flour
⅓ cup packed brown sugar
3 tablespoons butter
1 cup flaked coconut
½ cup chopped pecans or macadamia nuts
2 cups (16 ounces) Wisconsin Ricotta cheese
½ cup powdered sugar
1 teaspoon grated lime peel
1 teaspoon vanilla
1 package (10 ounces) frozen raspberries, thawed
1 kiwifruit

Preheat oven to 350°F. Combine flour and brown sugar; cut in butter until mixture resembles coarse crumbs. Stir in coconut and nuts. Press into 10-inch tart pan or pie plate. Bake crust 15 minutes. Remove from oven and cool.

Combine cheese, powdered sugar, lime peel and vanilla in food processor or blender; process until smooth. Spoon mixture into prepared crust. Refrigerate 1 hour. Before serving, place raspberries in food processor or blender; process until sauce forms. Cut kiwi into slices and arrange in circle on top of tart.* Drizzle tart with ½ of the raspberry sauce. Serve with remaining sauce. *Makes 8 to 10 servings*

Recipe can be prepared to this point and refrigerated until ready to serve.

Favorite recipe from **Wisconsin Milk Marketing Board**

Sensational Cinnamon Chip Biscotti

Peanut Butter Cup Cookie Ice Cream Pie

½ cup creamy peanut butter
¼ cup honey
1 quart (2 pints) vanilla ice cream, softened
1 cup KEEBLER® Chips Deluxe™ With Peanut Butter Cups Cookies, chopped
1 (6-ounce) READY CRUST® Chocolate Pie Crust
½ cup chocolate syrup
    Whipped cream

1. Place large bowl in freezer. Mix peanut butter and honey in medium bowl. Place ice cream in bowl from freezer; add peanut butter mixture and cookies. Mix on low speed with electric mixer until blended.

2. Spoon half of ice cream mixture into crust. Spread chocolate syrup over ice cream mixture in crust. Spoon remaining ice cream mixture over chocolate syrup.

3. Garnish with whipped cream and additional chocolate syrup. Freeze leftovers.

Makes 8 servings

Prep Time: 15 minutes

Deep-Dish Peach Custard Pie

1 *unbaked* 9-inch (4-cup volume) deep-dish pie shell
3½ cups (about 7 medium) peeled, pitted and sliced peaches
1 can (14 ounces) NESTLÉ® CARNATION® Sweetened Condensed Milk
2 large eggs
¼ cup butter or margarine, melted
1 to 3 teaspoons lemon juice
½ teaspoon ground cinnamon
    Dash ground nutmeg
    Streusel Topping (recipe follows)

PREHEAT oven to 425°F.

ARRANGE peaches in pie shell. Combine sweetened condensed milk, eggs, butter, lemon juice, cinnamon and nutmeg in large mixer bowl; beat until smooth. Pour over peaches.

BAKE for 10 minutes. Sprinkle with Streusel Topping. Reduce temperature to 350°F; bake for additional 55 to 60 minutes or until knife inserted near center comes out clean. Cool on wire rack.
Makes 8 servings

Streusel Topping: COMBINE ⅓ cup packed brown sugar, ⅓ cup all-purpose flour and ⅓ cup chopped walnuts in medium bowl. Cut in 2 tablespoons butter or margarine with pastry blender or two knives until mixture resembles coarse crumbs.

Mice Creams

1 pint vanilla ice cream
1 (4-ounce) package READY CRUST® Mini-Graham Cracker Pie Crusts
Ears—12 KEEBLER® Grasshopper® cookies
Tails—3 chocolate twigs, broken in half *or* 6 (3-inch) pieces black shoestring licorice
Eyes and noses—18 brown candy-coated chocolate candies
Whiskers—2 teaspoons chocolate sprinkles

Place 1 scoop vanilla ice cream into each crust. Press cookie ears and tails into ice cream. Press eyes, noses, and whiskers in place. Serve immediately. Do not refreeze.

Makes 6 servings

Prep Time: 15 minutes

Peanut Butter Cup Cookie Ice Cream Pie

Festive Holiday Rugelach

1½ cups (3 sticks) butter or margarine, softened
12 ounces cream cheese, softened
3½ cups all-purpose flour, divided
½ cup powdered sugar
¾ cup granulated sugar
1½ teaspoons ground cinnamon
1¾ cups "M&M's"® Chocolate Mini Baking Bits, divided
Powdered sugar

Preheat oven to 350°F. Lightly grease cookie sheets; set aside. In large bowl cream butter and cream cheese. Slowly work in 3 cups flour. Divide dough into 6 equal pieces and shape into squares. Lightly flour dough, wrap in waxed paper and refrigerate at least 1 hour. Combine remaining ½ cup flour and ½ cup powdered sugar. Remove one piece of dough at a time from refrigerator; roll out on surface dusted with flour-sugar mixture to 18×5×⅛-inch-thick strip. Combine granulated sugar and cinnamon. Sprinkle dough strip with 2 tablespoons cinnamon-sugar mixture. Sprinkle about ¼ cup "M&M's"® Chocolate Mini Baking Bits on wide end of each strip. Roll dough starting at wide end to completely enclose baking bits. Cut strip into 1½-inch lengths; place seam side down about 2 inches apart on prepared cookie sheets. Repeat with remaining ingredients. Bake 16 to 18 minutes or until golden. Cool completely on wire racks. Sprinkle with powdered sugar. Store in tightly covered container. *Makes about 6 dozen cookies*

Variation: For crescent shapes, roll each piece of dough into 12-inch circle. Sprinkle with cinnamon-sugar mixture. Cut into 12 wedges. Place about ½ teaspoon "M&M's"® Chocolate Mini Baking Bits at wide end of each wedge and roll up to enclose baking bits. Place seam side down on prepared cookie sheets and proceed as directed.

Cinnamon Chip Gems

1 cup (2 sticks) butter or margarine, softened
2 (3-ounce) packages cream cheese, softened
2 cups all-purpose flour
½ cup sugar
⅓ cup ground toasted almonds
2 eggs
1 (14-ounce) can EAGLE BRAND® Sweetened Condensed Milk (NOT evaporated milk)
1 teaspoon vanilla extract
1⅓ cups cinnamon baking chips, divided

1. In large mixing bowl, beat butter and cream cheese until well blended. Stir in flour, sugar and almonds. Cover; refrigerate about 1 hour. Divide dough into 4 equal parts. Shape each part into 12 smooth balls. Place each ball in small muffin cup (1¾ inches in diameter); press evenly on bottom and up side of each cup.

2. Preheat oven to 375°F. In small mixing bowl, beat eggs. Add Eagle Brand and vanilla; mix well. Place 7 cinnamon baking chips in bottom of each muffin cup; generously fill three-fourths full with Eagle Brand mixture.

3. Bake 18 to 20 minutes or until tops are puffed and just beginning to turn golden brown. Cool 3 minutes. Sprinkle about 15 chips on top of filling. Cool completely in pan on wire rack. Remove from pan using small metal spatula or sharp knife. Cool completely. Store tightly covered at room temperature. *Makes 4 dozen cookies*

Tip: For a pretty presentation, line the muffin pan with colorful paper baking cups before pressing the dough into the muffin cups.

Ma'moul (Date Pastries)

Filling
- 1 pound chopped pitted dates
- ½ cup water
- ¼ cup granulated sugar
- 1 teaspoon almond extract
- 2 tablespoons fresh grated orange peel
- ½ teaspoon ground cinnamon

Pastry
- 1 Butter Flavor CRISCO® Stick or 1 cup Butter Flavor CRISCO® all-vegetable shortening
- ¼ cup granulated sugar
- 3 tablespoons milk
- 1 tablespoon rosewater* or water
- 2 cups all-purpose flour
- Confectioners' sugar

Rosewater is available at Middle Eastern markets.

1. For filling, combine dates, water, ¼ cup sugar and almond extract in small saucepan. Bring to boil over medium-high heat. Reduce heat to low; simmer 4 to 5 minutes, stirring often, until mixture becomes thick paste. Stir in orange peel and cinnamon. Remove from heat; cool.

2. Heat oven to 300°F.

3. For pastry, combine shortening and ¼ cup sugar in large bowl. Beat at medium speed with electric mixer until well blended. Beat in milk and rosewater. Beat in flour, ¼ cup at a time, until well blended. Knead dough in bowl until dough holds together and is easy to shape.

4. Pinch off walnut-size piece of dough. Roll into ball. Pinch sides up to form pot shape. Fill center with level tablespoonful of date filling. Pinch dough closed; press to seal. Slightly flatten and smooth top. Place on ungreased baking sheets about 1 inch apart.

5. Bake at 300°F for 16 to 20 minutes or until firm and set. *Do not allow pastries to brown.* Cool on baking sheets 3 minutes; transfer to cooling racks. Sprinkle with confectioners' sugar while still warm. Cool.

Makes about 2½ dozen pastries

Almond Rice Madeleines

- 1 cup whole blanched almonds, lightly toasted
- ¾ cup flaked coconut
- 1½ cups sugar
- 3 cups cooked rice, chilled
- 3 egg whites
- Fresh raspberries
- Frozen nondairy whipped topping (optional)

Preheat oven to 350°F. Spray madeleine pans* with nonstick cooking spray.

Place almonds in food processor fitted with metal blade; process until finely ground. Add coconut and sugar to processor; process until coconut is finely minced. Add rice; pulse to blend. Add egg whites; pulse to blend. Spoon mixture evenly into prepared madeleine pans, filling to tops.

Bake 25 to 30 minutes or until lightly browned. Cool completely in pans on wire racks. Cover and refrigerate 2 hours or until ready to serve. Run sharp knife around each shell; gently remove from pan. Invert onto serving plates. Serve with raspberries and whipped topping, if desired.

Makes about 3 dozen cookies

Substitute miniature muffin tins for madeleine pans, if desired.

Favorite recipe from **USA Rice Federation**

Very Cherry Pie

4 cups frozen unsweetened tart cherries
1 cup dried tart cherries
1 cup sugar
2 tablespoons quick-cooking tapioca
½ teaspoon almond extract
    Pastry for double-crust 9-inch pie
¼ teaspoon ground nutmeg
1 tablespoon butter

Combine frozen cherries, dried cherries, sugar, tapioca and almond extract in large mixing bowl; mix well. (It is not necessary to thaw cherries before using.) Let cherry mixture stand 15 minutes.

Line 9-inch pie plate with pastry; fill with cherry mixture. Sprinkle with nutmeg. Dot with butter. Cover with top crust, cutting slits for steam to escape. Or, cut top crust into strips for lattice top and cherry leaf cutouts.

Bake in preheated 375°F oven about 1 hour or until crust is golden brown and filling is bubbly. If necessary, cover edge of crust with foil to prevent overbrowning.

Makes 8 servings

Note: Two (16-ounce) cans unsweetened tart cherries, well drained, can be substituted for frozen tart cherries. Dried cherries are available at gourmet and specialty food stores and at selected supermarkets.

Favorite recipe from **Cherry Marketing Institute**

Almond Chinese Chews

1 cup granulated sugar
3 eggs, lightly beaten
1 can SOLO® or 1 jar BAKER® Almond
    Filling
¾ cup all-purpose flour
1 teaspoon baking powder
¼ teaspoon salt
    Powdered sugar

Preheat oven to 300°F. Grease 13×9-inch baking pan; set aside.

Beat granulated sugar and eggs in medium-size bowl with electric mixer until thoroughly blended. Add almond filling; beat until blended. Sift together flour, baking powder and salt; fold into almond mixture. Spread batter evenly in prepared pan.

Bake 40 to 45 minutes or until wooden toothpick inserted in center comes out clean. Cool completely in pan on wire rack. Cut into 2×1½-inch bars; dust with powdered sugar.

Makes about 3 dozen bars

Fudgy Pecan Pie

¼ cup (½ stick) butter or margarine
2 (1-ounce) squares unsweetened
    chocolate
1 (14-ounce) can EAGLE BRAND®
    Sweetened Condensed Milk (NOT
    evaporated milk)
½ cup hot water
2 eggs, well beaten
1¼ cups pecan halves or pieces
1 teaspoon vanilla extract
⅛ teaspoon salt
1 (9-inch) unbaked pastry shell

1. Preheat oven to 350°F. In medium saucepan over low heat, melt butter and chocolate. Stir in Eagle Brand, hot water and eggs; mix well.

2. Remove from heat; stir in pecans, vanilla and salt. Pour into pastry shell. Bake 40 to 45 minutes or until center is set. Cool slightly. Serve warm or chilled. Garnish as desired. Store covered in refrigerator.

Makes one 9-inch pie

Prep Time: 15 minutes
Bake Time: 40 to 45 minutes

Very Cherry Pie

Original Nestlé® Toll House® Chocolate Chip Cookies

2¼ cups all-purpose flour
1 teaspoon baking soda
1 teaspoon salt
1 cup (2 sticks) butter or margarine, softened
¾ cup granulated sugar
¾ cup packed brown sugar
1 teaspoon vanilla extract
2 large eggs
2 cups (12-ounce package) NESTLÉ® TOLL HOUSE® Semi-Sweet Chocolate Morsels
1 cup chopped nuts

PREHEAT oven to 375°F.

COMBINE flour, baking soda and salt in small bowl. Beat butter, granulated sugar, brown sugar and vanilla extract in large mixer bowl until creamy. Add eggs, one at a time, beating well after each addition. Gradually beat in flour mixture. Stir in morsels and nuts. Drop by rounded tablespoon onto ungreased baking sheets.

BAKE for 9 to 11 minutes or until golden brown. Cool on baking sheets for 2 minutes; remove to wire racks to cool completely.

Makes about 5 dozen cookies

Pan Cookie Variation: GREASE

15×10-inch jelly-roll pan. Prepare dough as above. Spread into prepared pan. Bake for 20 to 25 minutes or until golden brown. Cool in pan on wire rack. Makes 4 dozen bars.

Slice and Bake Cookie Variation:

PREPARE dough as above. Divide in half; wrap in wax paper. Refrigerate for 1 hour or until firm. Shape each half into 15-inch log; wrap in wax paper. Refrigerate for 30 minutes.* Preheat oven to 375°F. Cut into ½-inch-thick slices; place on ungreased baking sheets. Bake for 8 to 10 minutes or until golden brown. Cool on baking sheets for

2 minutes; remove to wire racks to cool completely. Makes about 5 dozen cookies.

Dough may be stored in refrigerator for up to 1 week or in freezer for up to 8 weeks.

Key Lime Pie

3 eggs, separated
1 (14-ounce) can EAGLE BRAND® Sweetened Condensed Milk (NOT evaporated milk)
½ cup lime juice from concentrate
2 to 3 drops green food coloring (optional)
1 (9-inch) unbaked pastry shell
½ teaspoon cream of tartar
⅓ cup sugar

1. Preheat oven to 325°F. In medium mixing bowl, beat egg yolks; gradually beat in Eagle Brand and lime juice. Stir in food coloring, if desired. Pour into pastry shell.

2. Bake 30 minutes. Remove from oven. *Increase oven temperature to 350°F.*

3. Meanwhile, for meringue, with clean mixer, beat egg whites and cream of tartar to soft peaks. Gradually beat in sugar, 1 tablespoon at a time. Beat 4 minutes or until stiff, glossy peaks form and sugar is dissolved.

4. Immediately spread meringue over hot pie, carefully sealing to edge of crust to prevent meringue from shrinking. Bake 15 minutes. Cool 1 hour. Chill at least 3 hours. Store covered in refrigerator.   *Makes 8 servings*

Prep Time: 25 minutes
Bake Time: 45 minutes
Cool Time: 1 hour
Chill Time: 3 hours

Original Nestlé® Toll House® Chocolate Chip Cookies

Coconut Cream Cheese Cookies

1 Butter Flavor CRISCO® Stick or 1 cup Butter Flavor CRISCO® all-vegetable shortening
6 ounces cream cheese, softened
1 cup granulated sugar
1 teaspoon almond extract
1 teaspoon vanilla
¼ teaspoon salt
1 large egg
2 tablespoons milk
2 cups all-purpose flour
½ cup toasted flaked coconut

1. Heat oven to 325°F.

2. Combine shortening, cream cheese, sugar, almond extract, vanilla and salt in large bowl. Beat at medium speed with electric mixer until well blended. Beat in egg and milk until well blended. Add flour and coconut; mix well.

3. Drop rounded teaspoonfuls of dough about 2 inches apart onto ungreased cookie sheets.

4. Bake at 325°F for 15 to 20 minutes or until lightly browned. Cool on cookie sheets 4 minutes; transfer to cooling racks.

Makes about 5 dozen cookies

Honey Oat Biscotti

½ cup butter or margarine
¾ cup honey
2 eggs
1 teaspoon vanilla
2 cups all-purpose flour
3 teaspoons ground cinnamon
1 teaspoon baking powder
½ teaspoon baking soda
½ teaspoon salt
2 cups quick-cooking rolled oats
½ cup chopped nuts

Cream butter in large bowl with electric mixer; beat in honey, eggs and vanilla. Combine flour, cinnamon, baking powder, baking soda and salt in small bowl; mix well. Stir into butter mixture. Stir in oats and nuts. Shape dough into two 10×3×1-inch logs on greased baking sheet.

Bake in preheated 375°F oven 12 to 15 minutes or until lightly browned. Remove from oven; cool 5 minutes. Remove to cutting board. *Reduce oven temperature to 300°F.* Cut each log into ½-inch strips; place on cookie sheet. Bake 25 to 30 minutes or until crisp throughout strip. Cool completely on wire racks. *Makes 3 dozen cookies*

Favorite recipe from **National Honey Board**

Blueberry Crumble Pie

1 (6-ounce) READY CRUST® Graham Cracker Pie Crust
1 egg yolk, beaten
1 (21-ounce) can blueberry pie filling
⅓ cup all-purpose flour
⅓ cup quick-cooking oats
¼ cup sugar
3 tablespoons margarine, melted

1. Preheat oven to 375°F. Brush bottom and sides of crust with egg yolk; bake on baking sheet 5 minutes or until light brown.

2. Pour blueberry pie filling into crust. Combine flour, oats and sugar in small bowl; mix in margarine. Spoon over pie filling.

3. Bake on baking sheet about 35 minutes or until filling is bubbly and topping is browned. Cool on wire rack. *Makes 8 servings*

Preparation Time: 15 minutes
Baking Time: 40 minutes

Island Cookies

1⅔ cups all-purpose flour
¾ teaspoon baking powder
½ teaspoon baking soda
½ teaspoon salt
¾ cup (1½ sticks) butter, softened
¾ cup packed brown sugar
⅓ cup granulated sugar
1 teaspoon vanilla extract
1 large egg
1¾ cups (11.5-ounce package) NESTLÉ®
   TOLL HOUSE® Milk Chocolate
   Morsels
1 cup flaked coconut, toasted, if desired
1 cup chopped walnuts

PREHEAT oven to 375°F.

COMBINE flour, baking powder, baking soda and salt in small bowl. Beat butter, brown sugar, granulated sugar and vanilla extract in large mixer bowl until creamy. Beat in egg. Gradually beat in flour mixture. Stir in morsels, coconut and nuts. Drop by slightly rounded tablespoon onto ungreased baking sheets.

BAKE for 8 to 11 minutes or until edges are lightly browned. Cool on baking sheets for 2 minutes; remove to wire racks to cool completely.   *Makes about 3 dozen cookies*

Note: NESTLÉ® TOLL HOUSE® Semi-Sweet Chocolate Morsels, Semi-Sweet Chocolate Mini Morsels, Premier White Morsels or Butterscotch Flavored Morsels may be substituted for the Milk Chocolate Morsels.

White Chocolate Chunk & Macadamia Nut Brownie Cookies

1½ cups firmly packed light brown sugar
⅔ CRISCO® Stick or ⅔ cup CRISCO®
   all-vegetable shortening
1 tablespoon water
1 teaspoon vanilla
2 eggs
1½ cups all-purpose flour
⅓ cup unsweetened cocoa powder
½ teaspoon salt
¼ teaspoon baking soda
1 cup white chocolate chunks or chips
1 cup coarsely chopped macadamia nuts

1. Heat oven to 375°F. Place sheets of foil on countertop for cooling cookies.

2. Place brown sugar, ⅔ cup shortening, water and vanilla in large bowl. Beat at medium speed of electric mixer until well blended. Add eggs; beat well.

3. Combine flour, cocoa, salt and baking soda. Add to shortening mixture; beat at low speed just until blended. Stir in white chocolate chunks and macadamia nuts.

4. Drop dough by rounded measuring tablespoonfuls 2 inches apart onto ungreased baking sheet.

5. Bake one baking sheet at a time at 375°F for 7 to 9 minutes or until cookies are set. *Do not overbake.* Cool 2 minutes on baking sheet. Remove cookies to foil to cool completely.
   Makes about 3 dozen cookies

"Make Your Own Sundae" Pie

1 cup hot fudge ice cream topping, warmed and divided
1 prepared (9-inch) vanilla cookie crumb pie crust
6 cups vanilla ice cream, softened
1 cup caramel ice cream topping, warmed and divided
¼ cup marshmallow cream
1 tablespoon milk
⅔ cup "M&M's"® Chocolate Mini Baking Bits
¼ cup chopped nuts
Aerosol whipped topping and maraschino cherry for garnish

Spread ½ cup hot fudge topping on bottom of crust; freeze 10 minutes. Spread 1 cup ice cream over fudge layer; freeze 10 minutes. Spread ½ cup caramel topping over ice cream layer; freeze 10 minutes. Mound scoops of ice cream over caramel layer. Cover and freeze until ready to serve. Just before serving, in small bowl combine marshmallow cream and milk. Microwave at HIGH (100%) 10 seconds; stir until well combined. Drizzle pie with remaining ½ cup hot fudge topping, remaining ½ cup caramel topping and marshmallow sauce. Sprinkle with ⅓ cup "M&M's"® Chocolate Mini Baking Bits and nuts. Garnish with whipped topping, remaining ⅓ cup "M&M's"® Chocolate Mini Baking Bits and maraschino cherry. Serve immediately.

Makes 8 servings

Low Fat Molasses Jumbles

½ cup Dried Plum Purée (recipe follows) or prepared dried plum butter
½ cup sugar
½ cup molasses
1 egg
2 cups all-purpose flour
2 teaspoons ground cinnamon
1 teaspoon ground ginger
½ teaspoon baking soda
½ teaspoon salt
Additional sugar

Preheat oven to 350°F. Coat baking sheets with vegetable cooking spray. In large bowl, mix dried plum purée, sugar and molasses until well blended. Add egg; mix well. Combine remaining ingredients except sugar; stir into dried plum purée mixture just until blended. Roll heaping tablespoonfuls of dough in additional sugar. Place on baking sheets, spacing 2 inches apart. With fork, flatten dough in crisscross fashion until ½ inch thick. Bake in center of oven about 12 to 13 minutes or until set and bottoms are lightly browned. Remove from baking sheets to wire racks to cool completely.

Makes 30 (2½-inch) cookies

Dried Plum Purée: Combine 1⅓ cups (8 ounces) pitted dried plums and 6 tablespoons hot water in container of food processor or blender. Pulse on and off until dried plums are finely chopped and smooth. Store leftovers in a covered container in the refrigerator for up to two months. Makes 1 cup.

*Favorite recipe from **California Dried Plum Board***

"Make Your Own Sundae" Pie

Amaretto Cheesecake Tart

Crust
- ¾ cup amaretti cookie crumbs
- ¾ cup zwieback crumbs
- 1 tablespoon sugar
- ¼ cup Dried Plum Purée (recipe follows) or prepared dried plum butter

Filling
- 1 carton (16 ounces) nonfat cottage cheese
- 4 ounces fat-free cream cheese, softened
- 2 eggs
- 2 tablespoons almond-flavored liqueur

Topping & Glaze
- 2 oranges, peeled and sliced into rounds
- 1 kiwifruit, peeled and sliced into rounds
- 2 tablespoons apple jelly, melted
  Fresh raspberries, orange peel and mint leaves for garnish

Preheat oven to 325°F. To prepare crust, in medium bowl, combine crumbs and sugar. Cut in Dried Plum Purée with pastry blender until mixture resembles coarse crumbs. Press onto bottom and up side of 9-inch tart pan with removable bottom. To prepare filling, process cottage cheese and cream cheese in food processor 3 to 5 minutes or until smooth. Add eggs and liqueur; process until blended. Pour into prepared crust. Bake in center of oven 30 minutes or until filling is set. Cool on wire rack; refrigerate until completely chilled. Arrange fruit on top of filling. Brush fruit with jelly. Garnish with raspberries, orange peel and mint. Cut into wedges. *Makes 10 servings*

Dried Plum Purée: Combine 1⅓ cups (8 ounces) pitted dried plums and 6 tablespoons hot water in container of food processor or blender. Pulse on and off until dried plums are finely chopped and smooth. Store leftovers in covered container in refrigerator for up to two months. Makes 1 cup.

*Favorite recipe from **California Dried Plum Board***

Black Forest Oatmeal Fancies

- 1 Butter Flavor CRISCO® Stick or 1 cup Butter Flavor CRISCO® all-vegetable shortening
- 1 cup firmly packed light brown sugar
- 1 cup granulated sugar
- 2 eggs
- 2 teaspoons vanilla
- 1⅔ cups all-purpose flour
- 1 teaspoon baking soda
- 1 teaspoon salt
- ½ teaspoon baking powder
- 3 cups quick oats (not instant or old-fashioned), uncooked
- 1 baking bar (6 ounces) white chocolate, coarsely chopped
- 6 squares (1 ounce each) semisweet chocolate, coarsely chopped
- ½ cup coarsely chopped red candied cherries
- ½ cup sliced almonds

1. Heat oven to 375°F. Place foil on countertop for cooling cookies. Combine 1 cup shortening, brown sugar, granulated sugar, eggs and vanilla in large bowl. Beat at medium speed of electric mixer until well blended.

2. Combine flour, baking soda, salt and baking powder. Mix into shortening mixture at low speed until well blended. Stir in, one at a time, oats, white chocolate, semisweet chocolate, cherries and nuts with spoon.

3. Drop rounded tablespoonfuls of dough 2 inches apart onto ungreased baking sheets.

4. Bake at 375°F for 9 to 11 minutes or until set. *Do not overbake.* Cool 2 minutes on baking sheets. Remove cookies to foil to cool completely. *Makes about 3 dozen cookies*

Mini Chip Snowball Cookies

1½ cups (3 sticks) butter or margarine, softened
¾ cup powdered sugar
1 tablespoon vanilla extract
½ teaspoon salt
3 cups all-purpose flour
2 cups (12-ounce package) NESTLÉ® TOLL HOUSE® Semi-Sweet Chocolate Mini Morsels
½ cup finely chopped nuts
Powdered sugar

PREHEAT oven to 375°F.

BEAT butter, sugar, vanilla extract and salt in large mixer bowl until creamy. Gradually beat in flour; stir in morsels and nuts. Shape level tablespoons of dough into 1¼-inch balls. Place on ungreased baking sheets.

BAKE for 10 to 12 minutes or until cookies are set and lightly browned. Remove from oven. Sift powdered sugar over hot cookies on baking sheets. Cool on baking sheets for 10 minutes; remove to wire racks to cool completely. Sprinkle with additional powdered sugar, if desired. Store in airtight containers.

Makes about 5 dozen cookies

Decadent Brownie Pie

1 (9-inch) unbaked pastry shell
1 cup (6 ounces) semi-sweet chocolate chips
¼ cup (½ stick) butter or margarine
1 (14-ounce) can EAGLE BRAND® Sweetened Condensed Milk (NOT evaporated milk)
½ cup biscuit baking mix
2 eggs
1 teaspoon vanilla extract
1 cup chopped nuts
Vanilla ice cream

1. Preheat oven to 375°F. Bake pastry shell 10 minutes; remove from oven. Reduce oven temperature to 325°F.

2. In small saucepan over low heat, melt chips with butter.

3. In large mixing bowl, beat chocolate mixture with Eagle Brand, biscuit mix, eggs and vanilla until smooth. Add nuts. Pour into baked pastry shell.

4. Bake 35 to 40 minutes or until center is set. Serve warm or at room temperature with ice cream. Refrigerate leftovers.

Makes 1 (9-inch) pie

Prep Time: 25 minutes
Bake Time: 45 to 50 minutes

Grasshopper Mint Pie

1 (8-ounce) package cream cheese, softened
⅓ cup sugar
1 (8-ounce) tub frozen whipped topping, thawed
1 cup chopped KEEBLER® Fudge Shoppe® Grasshopper Cookies
3 drops green food coloring
1 (6-ounce) READY CRUST® Chocolate Pie Crust
Additional KEEBLER® Fudge Shoppe® Grasshopper Cookies, halved, for garnish

1. Mix cream cheese and sugar with electric mixer until well blended. Fold in whipped topping, chopped cookies and green food coloring. Spoon into crust.

2. Refrigerate 3 hours or overnight.

3. Garnish with cookie halves. Refrigerate leftovers.

Makes 8 servings

Preparation Time: 15 minutes
Chilling Time: 3 hours

Chocolate Almond Cookies

1 cup (2 sticks) butter or margarine,
    softened
1 cup sugar
1 egg
½ teaspoon almond extract
½ teaspoon vanilla extract
2 cups all-purpose flour
½ cup HERSHEY'S Cocoa
¼ teaspoon baking powder
¼ teaspoon baking soda
⅛ teaspoon salt
1 cup HERSHEY'S MINI CHIPS™
    Semi-Sweet Chocolate Chips
    Additional sugar
    Slivered blanched almonds

1. Beat butter and 1 cup sugar in large bowl until fluffy. Add egg, almond and vanilla extracts; beat well. Combine flour, cocoa, baking powder, baking soda and salt; gradually add to butter mixture, beating to form smooth dough. Stir in small chocolate chips. If necessary, refrigerate dough about 1 hour or until firm enough to handle.

2. Heat oven to 350°F. Shape dough into 1⅛-inch balls; roll in sugar. Place about 2 inches apart on ungreased cookie sheet. Place three slivered almonds on top of each ball; press slightly.

3. Bake 9 to 10 minutes or until set. Cool slightly. Remove from cookie sheet to wire rack. Cool completely.

Makes about 3½ dozen cookies

Oatmeal Gorp Cookies

1¼ Butter Flavor CRISCO® Sticks or
    1¼ cups Butter Flavor CRISCO®
    all-vegetable shortening
¾ cup firmly packed light brown sugar
½ cup granulated sugar
1 large, very ripe banana
1 egg
1 teaspoon vanilla
3 cups oats (quick or old-fashioned,
    uncooked)
1½ cups all-purpose flour
1 teaspoon baking soda
1 teaspoon ground cinnamon
¼ teaspoon ground nutmeg
1 cup semisweet chocolate chips
1 cup raisins
1 cup chopped walnuts
½ cup sliced almonds
½ cup flake coconut

1. Heat oven to 375°F. Place sheets of foil on countertop for cooling cookies.

2. Combine 1¼ cups shortening, brown sugar, granulated sugar, banana, egg and vanilla in large bowl. Beat at medium speed of electric mixer until well blended.

3. Combine oats, flour, baking soda, cinnamon and nutmeg. Add gradually to creamed mixture. Beat until well blended.

4. Stir in chocolate chips, raisins, nuts and coconut with spoon. Shape heaping tablespoonfuls into 1½- to 2-inch balls with dampened hands. Place 3 inches apart on ungreased baking sheet. Flatten dough slightly.

5. Bake at 375°F for 12 minutes or until light brown. *Do not overbake.* Cool 2 minutes on baking sheet. Remove cookies to foil to cool completely.   *Makes about 3 dozen cookies*

Chocolate Almond Cookies

Strawberry Cheesecake Pie

1 *prepared* 9-inch (6 ounces) graham cracker crumb crust
⅔ cup (5 fluid-ounce can) NESTLÉ® CARNATION® Evaporated Fat Free Milk
1 package (8 ounces) fat-free cream cheese, softened
1 large egg
½ cup granulated sugar
2 tablespoons all-purpose flour
1 teaspoon grated lemon peel
1½ to 2 cups halved fresh strawberries
3 tablespoons strawberry jelly, warmed

PREHEAT oven to 325°F.

PLACE evaporated milk, cream cheese, egg, sugar, flour and lemon peel in blender; cover. Blend until smooth. Pour into crust.

BAKE for 35 to 40 minutes or until center is set. Cool completely in pan on wire rack. Arrange strawberries on top of pie; drizzle with jelly. Refrigerate well before serving.

Makes 8 servings

Basic Icebox Cookie Dough

1 cup butter or margarine, softened
1 cup sugar
1 egg
1 teaspoon vanilla
2½ cups all-purpose flour
1 teaspoon baking powder
½ teaspoon salt

Beat butter and sugar with an electric mixer. Add egg and vanilla; mix well. Combine flour, baking powder and salt. Gradually add to butter mixture; mix well.

Makes 4½ cups dough

Maraschino Cherry Cookies: Add ½ cup chopped well-drained maraschino cherries to basic dough; divide dough in half. Form dough into 2 logs, 1½ inches in diameter. Wrap in waxed paper and refrigerate at least 6 hours. Cut into ¼-inch slices. Place 1 to 1½ inches apart on *ungreased* baking sheet. Bake in preheated 375°F oven 8 to 10 minutes. Remove to cooling rack. Repeat with remaining dough. Makes 6 to 7 dozen cookies.

Maraschino Date Pinwheels: Combine 8 ounces chopped pitted dates and ¼ cup water in small saucepan; bring to a boil. Reduce heat; simmer until thickened. Add ¾ cup chopped drained maraschino cherries; mix well and cool. Divide dough in half. Roll out each half to 12×10-inch rectangle on lightly floured surface. Spread half of cooled filling on each rectangle. Roll up beginning at long ends. Pinch ends of rolls to seal. Wrap in waxed paper and refrigerate at least 6 hours. Cut rolls into ¼-inch slices. Place 1 to 1½ inches apart on *ungreased* baking sheet. Bake in preheated 375°F oven about 10 to 14 minutes or until lightly browned. Remove to cooling rack. Makes 6 to 7 dozen cookies.

Maraschino Thumbprint Cookies: Shape dough into balls, using 2 teaspoons dough for each cookie. Press thumb in center of each ball. Place whole well-drained maraschino cherry in center of each depression. Brush with beaten egg white. For a nutty variation, roll each dough ball in beaten egg white, then in finely chopped pecans before pressing with thumb and filling with cherry. Place 1 to 1½ inches apart on *ungreased* baking sheet. Bake in preheated 375°F 12 to 15 minutes. Remove to cooling rack. Makes 5 dozen cookies.

Favorite recipe from **Cherry Marketing Institute**

Strawberry Cheesecake Pie

Pumpkin Spiced and Iced Cookies

2¼ cups all-purpose flour
1½ teaspoons pumpkin pie spice
1 teaspoon baking powder
½ teaspoon baking soda
½ teaspoon salt
1 cup (2 sticks) butter or margarine, softened
1 cup granulated sugar
1 can (15 ounces) LIBBY'S® 100% Pure Pumpkin
2 large eggs
1 teaspoon vanilla extract
2 cups (12-ounce package) NESTLÉ® TOLL HOUSE® Semi-Sweet Chocolate Morsels
1 cup chopped walnuts (optional)
Vanilla Glaze (recipe follows)

PREHEAT oven to 375°F. Grease baking sheets.

COMBINE flour, pumpkin pie spice, baking powder, baking soda and salt in medium bowl. Beat butter and granulated sugar in large mixer bowl until creamy. Beat in pumpkin, eggs and vanilla extract. Gradually beat in flour mixture. Stir in morsels and nuts. Drop by rounded tablespoon onto prepared baking sheets.

BAKE for 15 to 20 minutes or until edges are lightly browned. Cool on baking sheets for 2 minutes; remove to wire rack to cool completely. Spread or drizzle with Vanilla Glaze.   *Makes about 5½ dozen cookies*

Vanilla Glaze: **COMBINE** 1 cup powdered sugar, 1 to 1½ tablespoons milk and ½ teaspoon vanilla extract in small bowl; mix well.

Peach Yogurt Pie with Raspberry Sauce

Crust
    1 cup graham cracker crumbs
    ¼ cup sugar
    3 tablespoons CRISCO® Oil*
    1¼ teaspoons water

Filling
    1 quart peach flavor frozen yogurt, softened

Sauce
    1 package (12 ounces) frozen unsweetened raspberries, thawed
    ⅓ cup sugar
    1 teaspoon cornstarch
    ⅛ teaspoon salt
    ¼ teaspoon almond extract

*Use your favorite Crisco Oil product.

1. Heat oven to 350°F. Place cooling rack on countertop.

2. For crust, combine graham cracker crumbs, sugar, oil and water in 9-inch pie plate. Mix with fork. Press firmly against bottom and up side of pie plate.

3. Bake at 350°F for 8 minutes. *Do not overbake.* Remove pie plate to cooling rack. Cool completely.

4. For filling, spread softened yogurt into cooled crust. Freeze 2½ to 3 hours or until firm.

5. For sauce, combine raspberries, sugar, cornstarch and salt in small saucepan. Cook and stir over medium heat until mixture comes to a boil and is thickened. Press through sieve to remove seeds. Stir in almond extract. Cool to room temperature. Refrigerate. Drizzle over pie just before serving. Garnish, if desired.   *Makes 1 (9-inch) pie (8 servings)*

Pumpkin Spiced and Iced Cookies

Jumbo 3-Chip Cookies

4 cups all-purpose flour
1 teaspoon baking powder
1 teaspoon baking soda
1½ cups (3 sticks) butter, softened
1¼ cups granulated sugar
1¼ cups packed brown sugar
2 large eggs
1 tablespoon vanilla extract
1 cup (6 ounces) NESTLÉ® TOLL HOUSE® Milk Chocolate Morsels
1 cup (6 ounces) NESTLÉ® TOLL HOUSE® Semi-Sweet Chocolate Morsels
½ cup NESTLÉ® TOLL HOUSE® Premier White Morsels
1 cup chopped nuts

PREHEAT oven to 375°F.

COMBINE flour, baking powder and baking soda in medium bowl. Beat butter, granulated sugar and brown sugar in large mixer bowl until creamy. Beat in eggs and vanilla extract. Gradually beat in flour mixture. Stir in morsels and nuts. Drop dough by level ¼-cup measure 2 inches apart onto ungreased baking sheets.

BAKE for 12 to 14 minutes or until light golden brown. Cool on baking sheets for 2 minutes; remove to wire racks to cool completely.   *Makes about 2 dozen cookies*

Heavenly Chocolate Mousse Pie

4 (1-ounce) squares unsweetened chocolate, melted
1 (14-ounce) can EAGLE BRAND® Sweetened Condensed Milk (NOT evaporated milk)
1½ teaspoons vanilla extract
1 cup (½ pint) whipping cream, whipped
1 (6-ounce) chocolate crumb pie crust

1. In medium mixing bowl, beat melted chocolate with Eagle Brand and vanilla until well blended.

2. Chill 15 minutes or until cooled; stir until smooth. Fold in whipped cream.

3. Pour into crust. Chill thoroughly. Garnish as desired. Refrigerate leftovers.

Makes 1 pie

Prep Time: 20 minutes
Chill Time: 15 minutes

Fruit Tart

⅓ cup FLEISCHMANN'S® Original Margarine
1¼ cups all-purpose flour
4 to 5 tablespoons ice water
1 cup EGG BEATERS® Healthy Real Egg Product
⅓ cup sugar
1 teaspoon vanilla extract
1¼ cups skim milk, scalded
1 cup sliced fresh fruit

In medium bowl, cut margarine into flour until mixture resembles coarse crumbs. Add water, 1 tablespoon at a time, tossing until moistened. Shape into a ball. On floured surface, roll dough into 11-inch circle, about ⅛ inch thick. Place in 9-inch pie plate, making ½-inch-high fluted edge; set aside.

In medium bowl, combine Egg Beaters®, sugar and vanilla; gradually stir in milk. Pour into prepared crust. Bake at 350°F for 45 to 50 minutes or until set. Cool completely on wire rack. Cover; chill until firm, about 2 hours. To serve, top with fruit.

Makes 10 servings

Prep Time: 30 minutes
Bake Time: 45 minutes

Lone Star Peanut Butter Cutouts

¼ cup smooth peanut butter
¼ cup granulated sugar
3 tablespoons butter or margarine, softened
1¼ cups buttermilk baking mix
2 tablespoons water
½ teaspoon ground cinnamon
⅔ cup dry-roasted peanut halves
½ cup semi-sweet chocolate chips

In large bowl, stir together peanut butter, sugar and butter or margarine until smooth. Stir in baking mix, water and cinnamon until well blended. Shape dough into a ball. Wrap dough with plastic wrap and chill about 1 hour or until firm. Cut dough in half. Roll each piece ⅛-inch thick on a lightly floured board. Cut dough into shapes with a cookie cutter. Transfer cutouts to ungreased cookie sheets. Press a few roasted peanut halves into the top of each cookie. Bake in 375°F oven for 8 to 10 minutes, or until golden brown around the edges. With spatula, transfer cookies to cooling rack.

Melt chocolate chips in microwave on high power for 2 minutes. Stir until smooth. Drizzle chocolate glaze over each cookie. Refrigerate until frosting is set. Store cookies in an airtight container.   *Makes about 2 dozen cookies*

Favorite recipe from **Texas Peanut Producers Board**

Hazelnut Plum Tart

1 cup hazelnuts
¼ cup firmly packed light brown sugar
1 cup all-purpose flour
⅓ cup FILIPPO BERIO® Olive Oil
1 egg, separated
   Pinch salt
3 tablespoons granulated sugar
2 teaspoons cornstarch
½ teaspoon grated lime peel
   Pinch ground nutmeg
   Pinch ground cloves
1¼ pounds plums (about 5 large), cut into halves and pitted
3 tablespoons currant jelly
   Sweetened whipped cream (optional)

Preheat oven to 375°F. Grease 9-inch tart pan with removable bottom with olive oil.

Place hazelnuts in food processor; process until coarsely chopped. Remove ¼ cup for garnish; set aside. Add brown sugar; process until nuts are finely ground. Add flour, olive oil, egg yolk and salt; process until combined. (Mixture will be crumbly.)

Spoon mixture into prepared pan. Press firmly in even layer on bottom and up side. Brush inside of crust with egg white. Place in freezer 10 minutes.

In large bowl, combine granulated sugar, cornstarch, lime peel, nutmeg and cloves. Cut each plum half into 4 wedges. Add to sugar mixture; toss until combined. Arrange plums in overlapping circles in crust; spoon any remaining sugar mixture over plums. Place tart on baking sheet.

Bake 45 to 50 minutes or until fruit is tender and juices are thickened. Cool 30 minutes on wire rack. Place currant jelly in small saucepan; heat over low heat, stirring frequently, until melted. Brush over plums; sprinkle with reserved hazelnuts. Serve tart warm or at room temperature with whipped cream, if desired.   *Makes 6 servings*

Candy Bar Pie

4 ounces cream cheese, softened
1¾ cups plus 1 tablespoon cold milk,
    divided
1 (12-ounce) tub COOL WHIP®
    Whipped Topping, thawed, divided
2 packages (2.07 ounces each)
    chocolate-covered caramel peanut
    nougat bars, chopped
1 (4-serving size) package JELL-O®
    Chocolate Flavor Instant Pudding &
    Pie Filling
1 (6-ounce) READY CRUST® Chocolate
    Pie Crust

1. Mix cream cheese and 1 tablespoon milk in medium bowl with wire whisk until smooth. Gently stir in 2 cups whipped topping and chopped candy bars; set aside.

2. Pour remaining 1¾ cups milk into another medium bowl. Add pudding mix. Beat with wire whisk 1 minute. Gently stir in ½ cup whipped topping. Spread half of pudding mixture on bottom of crust. Spread cream cheese mixture over pudding mixture. Top with remaining pudding mixture.

3. Refrigerate 4 hours or until set. Garnish with remaining whipped topping. Refrigerate leftovers.   *Makes 8 servings*

Prep Time: 15 minutes
Chilling Time: 4 hours

Macaroon Kisses

1 (14-ounce) can EAGLE BRAND®
    Sweetened Condensed Milk (NOT
    evaporated milk)
2 teaspoons vanilla extract
1 to 1½ teaspoons almond extract
5⅓ cups (14 ounces) flaked coconut
48 solid milk chocolate candy kisses,
    stars or drops, unwrapped

1. Preheat oven to 325°F. Line baking sheets with foil; grease and flour foil. Set aside.

2. In large mixing bowl, combine Eagle Brand, vanilla and almond extract. Stir in coconut. Drop by rounded teaspoonfuls onto prepared baking sheets; with spoon slightly flatten each mound.

3. Bake 15 to 17 minutes or until golden brown. Remove from oven. Immediately press candy kiss, star or drop in center of each macaroon. Remove from baking sheets; cool on wire racks. Store loosely covered at room temperature.   *Makes 4 dozen cookies*

Banana Caramel Spice Pie

1 large ripe banana, sliced
1 (6-ounce) READY CRUST® Shortbread
    Pie Crust
2 cups cold milk
2 (4-serving size) packages white
    chocolate or vanilla flavor instant
    pudding & pie filling
½ teaspoon ground cinnamon
1 (8-ounce) tub whipped topping,
    thawed
Caramel ice cream topping

1. Place banana slices in bottom of crust.

2. Pour milk into large bowl. Add pudding mixes and cinnamon. Beat with wire whisk 1 minute. Gently stir in whipped topping. Spoon into crust.

3. Refrigerate 4 hours or until set. Serve with caramel topping.   *Makes 8 servings*

Preparation Time: 10 minutes
Chilling Time: 4 hours

Candy Bar Pie

Acknowledgments

The publisher would like to thank the companies and organizations listed below for the use of their recipes and photographs in this publication.

American Lamb Council
Barilla America, Inc.
Bays English Muffin Corporation
BC-USA, Inc.
BelGioioso® Cheese, Inc.
Birds Eye®
Blue Diamond Growers®
Bob Evans®
Butterball® Turkey
California Dried Plum Board
California Poultry Federation
California Tree Fruit Agreement
California Wild Rice Advisory Board
Cherry Marketing Institute
Chilean Fresh Fruit Association
Colorado Potato Administrative Committee
ConAgra Foods®
Cucina Classica Italiana, Inc.
Delmarva Poultry Industry, Inc.
Del Monte Corporation
Dole Food Company, Inc.
Domino® Foods, Inc.
Dreyer's / Edy's Grand Ice Cream
Dromedary Pimientos®
Duncan Hines® and Moist Deluxe® are registered
    trademarks of Aurora Foods Inc.
Eagle Brand®
Egg Beaters®
Filippo Berio® Olive Oil
Fleischmann's® Yeast
Florida Department of Agriculture and Consumer
    Services, Bureau of Seafood and Aquaculture
Florida Tomato Committee
The Golden Grain Company®
Grandma's® is a registered trademark of
    Mott's, Inc.
Guiltless Gourmet®
Hebrew National®
Heinz North America
Hershey Foods Corporation
The Hidden Valley® Food Products Company
Hillshire Farm®
Holland House® is a registered trademark of Mott's,
    Inc.
Hormel Foods, LLC
Idaho Potato Commission
Keebler® Company
Lawry's® Foods

Lee Kum Kee (USA) Inc.
© Mars, Incorporated 2003
McCormick®
McIlhenny Company (TABASCO®
    brand Pepper Sauce)
Michigan Apple Committee
Minnesota Cultivated Wild Rice Council
Mott's® is a registered trademark of Mott's, Inc.
National Chicken Council / US Poultry & Egg
    Association
National Fisheries Institute
National Honey Board
National Onion Association
National Pork Board
National Turkey Federation
Nestlé USA
New York Apple Association, Inc.
Newman's Own, Inc.®
Norseland, Inc. / Lucini Italia Co.
North Dakota Beef Commission
North Dakota Wheat Commission
Northwest Cherry Growers
Pear Bureau Northwest
Perdue Farms Incorporated
The Quaker® Oatmeal Kitchens
Reckitt Benckiser Inc.
RED STAR® Yeast, a product of Lasaffre Yeast
    Corporation
Reynolds Consumer Products, A Business of
    Alcoa Inc.
Riviana Foods Inc.
Roman Meal® Company
Sargento® Foods Inc.
The J.M. Smucker Company
Sokol and Company
Sonoma® Dried Tomatoes
StarKist® Seafood Company
The Sugar Association, Inc.
Property of © 2003 Sunkist Growers, Inc.
    All rights reserved.
Texas Peanut Producers Board
Uncle Ben's Inc.
Unilever Bestfoods North America
USA Rice Federation
Veg•All®
Walnut Marketing Board
Washington Apple Commission
Wisconsin Milk Marketing Board

A

Acorn Squash Filled with Savory Spinach, 204
Albacore Salad Puttanesca with Garlic Vinaigrette, 158
Albóndigas Soup, 51
Ali's Oatmeal Cookies, 342
Almond Amaretto Loaf, 298
Almond Chinese Chews, 356
Almond Rice Madeleines, 355
Amaretto Cheesecake Tart, 364
Amaretto Glaze, 298
Angel Hair Al Fresco, 176
Angel Hair with Roasted Red Pepper Sauce, 182
Apple Cinnamon Rolls, 256

Apples
Apple and Raisin Fruit Braid, 287
Apple Brunch Strata, 8
Apple-Cinnamon Granola Bread, 306
Apple Crisp Cookies, 344
Apple Crumb Coffeecake, 288
Apple Filling, 256
Apple-Potato Pancakes, 30
Apples and Cheese Rolls, 248
Apple Sauce Cinnamon Rolls, 28
Apple Sauce Coffee Ring, 279
Apple Yogurt Muffins, 20
Arlington Apple Gingerbread Cake, 324
Breakfast Kabobs, 34
Buttery Apple Spread, 257
Easy Apple Bread, 253
Golden Cheddar Batter Bread, 257
Harvest Honey Spice Cake, 312
Maple Apple Oatmeal, 29
Roasted Turkey Breast with Cherry & Apple Rice Stuffing, 214
Scrumptious Apple Cake, 314
Turkey Kielbasa with Cabbage, Sweet Potatoes and Apples, 126

Apricot Cream Cake, 313
Arizona Pork Chili, 79
Arlington Apple Gingerbread Cake, 324

Artichokes
Frittata with Artichokes, 36
Greek Lamb Braised with Vegetables, 152
Zesty Artichoke Pesto Sauce, 168

Asparagus
Farmers' Market Salad, 200
Ham & Asparagus Brunch Bake, 44
Mostaccioli per la Pasqua, 144
Paris Pasta, 198
Pasta Primavera, 171
Stewed Mushrooms on Asparagus with Vegetarian Oyster Sauce, 208

B

Bacon
Fettuccine Carbonara, 150
Hearty Corn & Cheese Chowder, 86
Minestrone, 89
Spanish Rice and Meatballs, 119

Baja Fish Tacos, 146
Baked Banana Doughnuts, 32
Baked Eggplant with Cheese, 200
Baked Ham & Cheese Monte Cristo, 42

Bananas
Baked Banana Doughnuts, 32
Banana Caramel Spice Pie, 374
Banana Pecan Braid, 246

Bananas *(continued)*
Banana-Chocolate Chip Bread, 294
Upside-Down Hot Fudge Sundae Pie, 344

Barbecued French Bread, 298
Basic Icebox Cookie Dough, 368
Bayou Yam Muffins, 12

Beef
Albóndigas Soup, 51
Burgundy Beef Stew, 92
California Tamale Pie, 148
Corned Beef and Cabbage with Parsley Dumplings, 162
Crunchy Layered Beef & Bean Salad, 160
East Meets West Cocktail Franks, 220
Easy Slow-Cooked Chili, 90
Family Swiss Steak and Potatoes, 196
Fiesta Beef Pot Pie, 113
Greek Beef & Rice, 164
Heartland Shepherd's Pie, 138
Hearty Beef Stew with Noodles, 56
Hungarian Goulash Stew, 157
Italian Beef Burrito, 124
Italian Tomato Soup, 73
Johnnie Marzetti, 131
Layered Mexican Casserole, 157
Mexican Beef Stir-Fry, 170
Mexican Lasagna, 118
Old-Fashioned Beef Stew, 64
1-2-3 Steak Soup, 54
Original Ortega® Taco Recipe, 150
Quick Beef Bourguignonne, 134
Quick Beef Soup, 62
Red Cloud Beef and Onions, 110
Skillet Franks and Potatoes, 126
Spanish Rice and Meatballs, 119
Stick-to-Your-Ribs Hearty Beef Stew, 84
String Pie, 140
Sunflower Wheat-Beef Pot Pie, 130
Texas Beef Stew, 88
Texas-Style Deep-Dish Chili Pie, 103
Thai-Style Beef & Rice, 192
Three Bean and Franks Bake, 104
Veg•All® Beef & Cheddar Bake, 124
Zesty Mexican Stir-Fry Fajitas, 149

Berries
Berry Striped Pops, 228
Blueberry Crumble Pie, 360
Blueberry Filling, 26
Breakfast Kabobs, 34
Chilean Puff Pastry Fruit Band, 17
Fluffy Lemon Berry Pie, 348
Fruit Soup, 60
Peach Yogurt Pie with Raspberry Sauce, 370
Raspberry Shortcakes, 312
Spring Break Blueberry Coffeecake, 25
Strawberry Cheesecake Pie, 368
Strawberry Cheesecake Pudding Pie, 346
Stuffed French Toast with Fresh Berry Topping, 8
Wisconsin Ricotta Tart with Kiwi and Raspberry Sauce, 350

Berry Striped Pops, 228
Biscuits 'n Gravy, 17
Black Bean Bisque with Crab, 48
Black Bean Sausage Skillet, 158
Black Forest Chocolate Fudge Cake, 324
Black Forest Oatmeal Fancies, 364
Black Pepper-Onion Bread, 300

Blueberry Breakfast Braid, 26
Blueberry Crumble Pie, 360
Blueberry Filling, 26
Bouillabaisse, 74
Braided Sandwich Ring, 296
Bread Bowls, 250

Breads (see also pages 246-307)
Baked Ham & Cheese Monte Cristo, 42
Brunch Sandwiches, 38
Butterscotch Sticky Buns, 40
California Turkey Chili, 76
Chile Rellenos Monte Cristos, 43
Cinnamon Coffee-Crumb Muffins, 42
Cocoa Nut Bundles, 6
Country Chicken and Biscuits, 112
Easy Three Cheese Tuna Soufflé, 142
French Onion Soup, 76
Grilled Panini Sandwiches, 174
Heartland Crown Roast of Pork, 238
Holiday Bread Pudding, 224
Holiday Chicken Pinwheels, 218
Jam French Toast Triangles, 44
Johnnie Marzetti, 131
Mexicali Cornbread Casserole, 172
Pork Roast with Corn Bread & Oyster Stuffing, 224
Quick Cinnamon Sticky Buns, 14
Smoked Cheese and Muffin Strata, 38
Stuffed French Toast with Fresh Berry Topping, 8
Tomato-Bread Casserole, 212
Tomato French Onion Soup, 70
Turkey Breast with Southwestern Corn Bread Dressing, 226
Wisconsin Swiss Linguine Tart, 104

Breakfast in a Cup, 38
Breakfast Kabobs, 34

Broccoli
Baked Ham & Cheese Monte Cristo, 42
Broccoli & Cheddar Noodle Casserole, 96
Broccoli, Chicken and Rice Casserole, 114
Broccoli Lasagna, 141
Broccoli Lasagna Bianca, 123
Cheddar Broccoli Soup, 56
Cheddar Broccoli Tart, 34
Cheesy Broccoli Bake, 100
Chicken Primavera, 194
Fish Broccoli Casserole, 94
Ham and Rice Pie, 11
Lasagna Primavera, 132
Moroccan Supper, 210
No-Fuss Tuna Quiche, 97
Pasta with Shrimp, Broccoli and Red Pepper, 177
Sausage and Broccoli Noodle Casserole, 140
Tomato, Basil & Broccoli Chicken, 119
Vegetable & Cheese Platter, 212
Vegetable Cobbler, 118

Brownie Peanut Butter Cupcakes, 220
Brownie Sundae Cake, 326
Brownie Turtle Cookies, 347
Brunch Sandwiches, 38
Burgundy Beef Stew, 92
Butch's Black Bean Soup, 70
Buttermilk Doughnuts, 10
Buttermilk Pan Rolls, 284
Butterscotch Sticky Buns, 40
Buttery Apple Spread, 257

Index

C

Cabbage
Chicken and Sweet Potato Ragoût, 116
Corned Beef and Cabbage with Parsley Dumplings, 162
Hearty and Heart-Healthy Idaho Potato Soup/Stew, 80
Meatless Italian Minestrone, 50
Patrick's Irish Lamb Soup, 68
Turkey Kielbasa with Cabbage, Sweet Potatoes and Apples, 126
Vegetable Stir-Fry in Spicy Black Bean Sauce, 202
Cajun Bubble Bread, 252
Cajun Chicken Bayou, 98
Cajun Chili, 60
Cajun Garlic Bread, 287

Cake Mixes
Cherry Cupcakes, 328
Chocolate Cappuccino Cupcakes, 322
Cool and Minty Party Cake, 325
Easy Egg Nog Pound Cake, 310
Frizzy the Clown Cupcakes, 237
Merry Santa Cupcakes, 242
Pumpkin Cheesecake Bars, 240
Raspberry Crumb Coffee Cake, 16
Rich Caramel Cake, 320
Valentine's Cupcakes, 310
California Tamale Pie, 148
California Turkey Chili, 76
Calzone Italiano, 156
Candy Bar Pie, 374
Caramel-Pecan Pie, 341
Carnival Pork Stew, 90
Carolina Baked Beans & Pork Chops, 108
Catch of the Day Stew, 73
Cellentani, Italian Sausage and Mushrooms in Tomato-Gorgonzola Sauce, 172
Challah, 286
Cheddar Broccoli Soup, 56
Cheddar Broccoli Tart, 34
Cheese Pull-Apart Bread, 279
Cheesy Broccoli Bake, 100
Cheesy Chicken Pot Pie, 136
Cheesy Potato Pancakes, 4
Cheesy Vegetable Soup, 82

Cherries
Black Forest Oatmeal Fancies, 364
Cherry Cupcakes, 328
Cherry Danish, 11
Chocolate Sundae Cupcakes, 222
Dried Cherry-Almond Bread, 258
Jamaican Cherry Bread, 254
Maraschino Cherry Cookies, 368
Maraschino Date Pinwheels, 368
Maraschino Thumbprint Cookies, 368
Pineapple-Coconut Party Cake, 331
Roasted Turkey Breast with Cherry & Apple Rice Stuffing, 214
Sunday Morning Upside-Down Rolls, 24
Very Cherry Pie, 356
Cherry Swirl Coffee Cake, 294

Chicken
Broccoli, Chicken and Rice Casserole, 114
Cajun Chicken Bayou, 98
Cajun Chili, 60
Cheesy Chicken Pot Pie, 136
Chicken and Black Bean Enchiladas, 182
Chicken and Sweet Potato Ragoût, 116
Chicken and Vegetable Ragoût, 177

Chicken (continued)
Chicken Biscuit Bake, 97
Chicken Casserole Olé, 126
Chicken Florentine, 185
Chicken Jambalaya, 94
Chicken Paprikash, 180
Chicken Penne with Gorgonzola and Peas, 103
Chicken Primavera, 194
Chicken Ragoût with Chilies, Tortillas and Goat Cheese, 64
Chicken Satay, 154
Chicken Tortilla Soup, 89
Chicken Tuscany, 128
Chicken Vegetable Soup, 66
Citrus Chicken and Bell Pepper Fajitas, 189
Classic Matzoh Ball Soup, 63
Classic Veg•All® Chicken Pot Pie, 120
Coq au Vin & Pasta, 108
Cornish Hens with Citrus Chutney Glaze, 240
Country Chicken and Biscuits, 112
Country Cream of Chicken Chowder, 78
Cranberry Orange Game Hens with Vegetable Stuffing, 228
Creamy Shell Soup, 74
Garden Ranch Linguine with Chicken, 146
Holiday Chicken Pinwheels, 218
Holiday Hens with Sherry Gravy, 234
Hot Mediterranean Chicken Salad, 190
Italian Vegetable Farfalle, 194
Lemon-Garlic Chicken & Rice, 140
Mediterranean Cornish Hens, 146
Mexican Chicken Stew, 54
Paella, 122
Picadillo Chicken, 156
Saffron Chicken Risotto, 106
Salsa Chicken & Rice Skillet, 158
Savory Chicken and Biscuits, 132
Scalloped Chicken & Pasta, 142
Scandinavian Chicken, 166
Scrambled Eggs with Chicken and Sun-Dried Tomatoes, 43
Sicilian Skillet Chicken, 178
Skillet Chicken Alfredo, 189
Sonoma® Pot Pie, 100
Southwest Skillet, 108
Spicy Thai Chicken, 170
Stuffed Cornish Hens for Christmas, 236
Thai Stir Fry, 172
Thin-Sliced Panzanella, 164
Tomato, Basil & Broccoli Chicken, 119
Wine and Herb Roaster with Ham and Oyster Stuffing, 219
Yucatan Chicken Stir-Fry, 154
Chickpea and Shrimp Soup, 58
Chile Rellenos Monte Cristos, 43
Chilean Puff Pastry Fruit Band, 17
Chili Corn Soup, 83

Chocolate
Banana-Chocolate Chip Bread, 294
Black Forest Oatmeal Fancies, 364
Brownie Peanut Butter Cupcakes, 220
Brownie Sundae Cake, 326
Brownie Turtle Cookies, 347
Cherry Cupcakes, 328
Chocolate Filling, 244
Chocolate Glazed Pears, 234

Chocolate (continued)
Chocolate Intensity, 321
Heavenly Chocolate Mousse Pie, 372
Macaroon Kisses, 374
Peanut Butter & Chocolate Pull-Apart Rolls, 248
Peanut Butter Cup Cookie Ice Cream Pie, 352
Petit Pain au Chocolate, 266
Rich Chocolate Cake with Creamy Peanut Butter Milk Chocolate Frosting, 332
White Chocolate Chunk & Macadamia Nut Brownie Cookies, 361
Chocolate Almond Cookies, 366
Chocolate Cappuccino Cupcakes, 322

Chocolate Chips
Ali's Oatmeal Cookies, 342
Chocolate Almond Cookies, 366
Chocolate Cappuccino Cupcakes, 322
Chocolate Chip Coffeecake, 260
Chocolate Chip Shells, 338
Chocolate Nut Topping, 260
Chocolate Truffle Tart, 342
Decadent Brownie Pie, 365
Donna's Heavenly Orange Chip Scones, 254
Glazed Cranberry Mini-Cakes, 330
Island Cookies, 361
Jingle Bells Chocolate Pretzels, 232
Jumbo 3-Chip Cookies, 372
Lone Star Peanut Butter Cutouts, 373
Malted Dream Drops, 341
Mini Chip Snowball Cookies, 365
Mocha Dream Cake, 318
Oatmeal Gorp Cookies, 366
Original Nestlé® Toll House® Chocolate Chip Cookies, 358
Petit Pain au Chocolate, 266
Pumpkin Spiced and Iced Cookies, 370
Rich Chocolate Cake with Creamy Peanut Butter Milk Chocolate Frosting, 332
Toll House® Mini Morsel Pancakes, 32
White Chip Drizzle, 350
White Chocolate, Raspberry and Pecan Filling, 276
White Dipped Pretzels, 232
White Glaze, 330
Zesty Lemon Pound Cake, 322
Chocolate Chocolate Crescents, 304
Chocolate Drizzle, 325
Chocolate Filling, 244, 304
Chocolate Filling & Frosting, 316
Chocolate Nut Topping, 260
Chocolate Raspberry Torte, 316
Chocolate Squares with Nutty Caramel Sauce, 308
Chocolate Sundae Cupcakes, 222
Chocolate Truffle Tart, 342
Chunky Vegetarian Chili, 48

Cinnamon Chips
Cinnamon Chip Filled Crescents, 298
Cinnamon Chip Gems, 354
Cinnamon Chips Drizzle, 298
Quick Cinnamon Sticky Buns, 14
Sensational Cinnamon Chip Biscotti, 350
Cinnamon Coffee-Crumb Muffins, 42
Cinnamon Roll Cookies, 348
Cioppino, 50

Citrus Chicken and Bell Pepper Fajitas, 189
Classic Matzoh Ball Soup, 63
Classic Veg•All® Chicken Pot Pie, 120
Cocoa
 Black Forest Chocolate Fudge Cake, 324
 Chocolate Almond Cookies, 366
 Chocolate Filling, 304
 Chocolate Filling & Frosting, 316
 Chocolate Squares with Nutty Caramel
  Sauce, 308
 Creamy Cocoa Log Frosting, 216
 Easter Baskets and Bunnies Cupcakes,
  328
 Hershey's Basic Cocoa Baking Mix, 336
 Mocha Dream Cake, 318
 Patriotic Cocoa Cupcakes, 334
 Rich Chocolate Cake with Creamy
  Peanut Butter Milk Chocolate
  Frosting, 332
 Touchdown Brownie Cups, 316
Cocoa Nut Bundles, 6
Coconut
 Almond Rice Madeleines, 355
 Coconut Cream Cheese Cookies, 360
 Easter Baskets and Bunnies Cupcakes,
  328
 Island Cookies, 361
 Jamaican Cherry Bread, 254
 Macaroon Kisses, 374
 Oatmeal Gorp Cookies, 366
 Pineapple-Coconut Party Cake, 331
 Pumpkin Carrot Cake, 336
 Spicy Thai Chicken, 170
 Spring Break Blueberry Coffeecake, 25
 Wisconsin Ricotta Tart with Kiwi and
  Raspberry Sauce, 350
Color-Bright Ice Cream Sandwiches, 230
Cool and Minty Party Cake, 325
Coq au Vin & Pasta, 108
Corn
 Butch's Black Bean Soup, 70
 California Tamale Pie, 148
 Chicken Tortilla Soup, 89
 Chili Corn Soup, 83
 Chunky Vegetarian Chili, 48
 Country Cream of Chicken Chowder, 78
 Country Stew, 86
 Fiesta Beef Pot Pie, 113
 Fisherman's Soup, 52 Hearty Corn &
  Cheese Chowder, 86
 Hungarian Goulash Stew, 157
 Layered Mexican Casserole, 157
 Layered Mexican Tortilla Cheese
  Casserole, 141
 Mexican Chicken Stew, 54
 Mexican-Style Stuffed Peppers, 168
 Nacho Cheese Soup, 52
 Pork and Wild Rice Chili, 82
 Roasted Red Pepper, Corn & Garbanzo
  Bean Salad, 180
 Salsa Chicken & Rice Skillet, 158
 Santa Fe Tomato Chowder, 66
 Southwestern Soup, 62
 Stewed Mushrooms on Asparagus with
  Vegetarian Oyster Sauce, 208
 Texas Beef Stew, 88
 Tortilla Soup, 83
 Turkey, Corn and Sweet Potato Soup, 79
Corned Beef and Cabbage with Parsley
 Dumplings, 162

Cornish Hens with Citrus Chutney Glaze,
 240
Country Chicken and Biscuits, 112
Country Cream of Chicken Chowder, 78
Country Fare Breakfast with Wisconsin
 Fontina, 26
Country Sausage Macaroni and Cheese, 123
Country Skillet Hash, 37
Country Stew, 86
Cracked Wheat Bread, 288
Cranberries
 Cranberry Orange Game Hens with
  Vegetable Stuffing, 228
 Cranberry Peach Tart with Almonds,
  237
 Cranberry-Pecan Filling, 302
 Cranberry Sausage Quiche, 22
 Glazed Cranberry Mini-Cakes, 330
 Harvest Honey Spice Cake, 312
 Holiday Bread Pudding, 224
 Honey Almond Biscotti, 346
Cranberry Pecan Wreath, 302
Cream Cheese Frosting, 336
Creamy Cinnamon Rolls, 282
Creamy Cocoa Log Frosting, 216
Creamy Fruit Blintzes, 36
Creamy Holiday Tarts, 240
Creamy Shell Soup, 74
Creamy Shells with Spinach and
 Mushrooms, 208
Creamy Vanilla Frosting, 328
Crème de Brie® Heart Tarts, 220
Creole Beans and Rice, 210
Crêpes, 4
Crispy Onion Crescent Rolls, 284
Crumb Topping, 42, 288
Crunchy Layered Beef & Bean Salad, 160
Crunchy Ranch-Style Eggs, 30
Cucumbers
 Gazpacho, 92
 Idaho Potato Gazpacho, 62

D
Dates
 Banana Pecan Braid, 246
 Ma'moul (Date Pastries), 355
 Maraschino Date Pinwheels, 368
Decadent Brownie Pie, 365
Deep-Dish Peach Custard Pie, 352
Delectable Chocolate Wreath, 276
Donna's Heavenly Orange Chip Scones,
 254
Down-Home Sausage Gravy, 28
Dried Cherry-Almond Bread, 258
Dried Plum Purée, 238, 244, 325, 362,
 364
Dutch Potage, 48

E
East Meets West Cocktail Franks, 220
Easter Basket Cupcakes, 321
Easter Baskets and Bunnies Cupcakes, 328
Eastertime Leg of Lamb, 222
Easy Apple Bread, 253
Easy Egg Nog Pound Cake, 310
Easy Ham & Veg•All® Chowder, 80
Easy Peanut Butter Chip Pie, 340
Easy Slow-Cooked Chili, 90
Easy Three Cheese Tuna Soufflé, 142
Easy Turkey and Rice, 112

Eggplant
 Baked Eggplant with Cheese, 200
 Eggplant, Tomato & Cheese Casserole,
  206
 Grilled Vegetable Rigatoni, 170
 Ratatouille, 207
 Sicilian Caponata, 194
Eggs Santa Fe, 20
El Dorado Rice Casserole, 195
European Kolacky, 347
European Wheat Bread, 263

F
Family Swiss Steak and Potatoes, 196
Fancy Florida Seafood Gumbo, 51
Fanfare Dinner Rolls, 264
Farmers' Market Salad, 200
Festive Focaccia Pizza Bread, 292
Festive Holiday Rugelach, 354
Fettuccine Carbonara, 150
Fiesta Beef Pot Pie, 113
Fire & Ice Brunch Skillet, 202
Fish
 Albacore Salad Puttanesca with Garlic
  Vinaigrette, 158
 Angel Hair Al Fresco, 176
 Baja Fish Tacos, 146
 Bouillabaisse, 74
 Catch of the Day Stew, 73
 Cioppino, 50
 Easy Three Cheese Tuna Soufflé, 142
 Fish Broccoli Casserole, 94
 Fish Cakes with Thai Salsa, 162
 Fisherman's Soup, 52
 No-Fuss Tuna Quiche, 97
 Poached Seafood Italiano, 176
 Quick Mediterranean Fish, 174
 Salmon Vera Cruz, 166
 Seafood Gumbo, 80
 Tomato and Salmon Quiche, 14
 Tuna Cream Cheese Omelets, 30
 Tuna Minestrone with Parmesan Cheese,
  58
 West Coast Bouillabaisse, 88
 Yucatan Snapper, 152
Florentine Strata, 188
Fluffy Lemon Berry Pie, 348
Focaccia with Dried Tomatoes and
 Fontina, 250
Freezer Rolls, 292
French Onion Bread Stix, 302
French Onion Soup, 76
French Yule Log, 216
Frittata with Artichokes, 36
Frizzy the Clown Cupcakes, 237
Frostings & Glazes
 Amaretto Glaze, 298
 Chocolate Drizzle, 325
 Chocolate Filling & Frosting, 316
 Chocolate Sundae Cupcakes, 222
 Cinnamon Chips Drizzle, 298
 Cream Cheese Frosting, 336
 Creamy Vanilla Frosting, 328
 Easter Basket Cupcakes, 321
 Frizzy the Clown Cupcakes, 237
 Frosting, 276
 Mocha Dream Cake, 318
 Mocha Glaze, 325
 Molasses Glaze, 252
 Orange Glaze, 302

Frostings & Glazes *(continued)*
    Red's Rockin' Rainbow Cupcakes, 310
    Valentine's Cupcakes, 310
    Vanilla Frosting, 334
    Vanilla Glaze, 370
    White Chip Drizzle, 350
    White Glaze, 330
Fruit-Filled Petal Rolls, 256
Fruit Soup, 60
Fruit Tart, 372
Fudgey Chocolate Cupcakes, 336
Fudgy Pecan Pie, 356

G
Garden Ranch Linguine with Chicken, 146
Garlic Vinaigrette Dressing, 158
Gazpacho, 92
Gemelli with Baby Shrimp and Sweet Peas, 196
Giardiniera Sauce, 167
Ginger Bread, 305
Gingerbread, 238
Glazed Cranberry Mini-Cakes, 330
Golden Cheddar Batter Bread, 257
Golden Gate Wild Rice Cioppino, 46
Golden Tomato Soup, 59
Grasshopper Mint Pie, 365
Grecian Lamb Kabobs, 178
Greek Beef & Rice, 164
Greek Lamb Braised with Vegetables, 152
Greens and Gemelli, 186
Grilled Panini Sandwiches, 174
Grilled Vegetable Fettuccine, 207
Grilled Vegetable Rigatoni, 170

H
Ham
    Baked Ham & Cheese Monte Cristo, 42
    Brunch Sandwiches, 38
    Carnival Pork Stew, 90
    Cheesy Broccoli Bake, 100
    Chicken Jambalaya, 94
    Easy Ham & Veg•All® Chowder, 80
    Ham & Asparagus Brunch Bake, 44
    Ham and Beer Cheese Soup, 76
    Ham and Potato au Gratin, 142
    Hash Brown Casserole, 18
    Hearty Potato-Ham Chowder, 68
    Holiday Appetizer Quiche, 227
    Holiday Baked Ham, 227
    Mexicali Cornbread Casserole, 172
    Mostaccioli per la Pasqua, 144
    Potato-Ham Scallop, 18
    Potato Straw Cake with Ham & Gruyère, 16
    Sausage Ham Jambalaya, 103
    Tagliatelle with Creamy Sauce, 167
    Wine and Herb Roaster with Ham and Oyster Stuffing, 219
Ham and Rice Pie, 11
Harvest Honey Spice Cake, 312
Harvest Stuffing Bread, 300
Hash Brown Casserole, 18
Hazelnut Plum Tart, 373
Heartland Crown Roast of Pork, 238
Heartland Shepherd's Pie, 138
Hearty and Heart-Healthy Idaho Potato Soup/Stew, 80
Hearty Beef Stew with Noodles, 56
Hearty Corn & Cheese Chowder, 86

Hearty Minestrone Soup, 52
Hearty Potato-Ham Chowder, 68
Hearty Sausage Stew, 51
Hearty Tortilla Chip Soup, 60
Heavenly Chocolate Mousse Pie, 372
Hershey's Basic Cocoa Baking Mix, 336
Hidden Herb Grilled Turkey Breast, 232
Holiday Appetizer Quiche, 227
Holiday Baked Ham, 227
Holiday Bread Pudding, 224
Holiday Cheese Tarts, 341
Holiday Chicken Pinwheels, 218
Holiday Hens with Sherry Gravy, 234
Holiday Rye Bread, 252
Honey Almond Biscotti, 346
Honey Cloverleafs, 304
Honey Grapefruit Delight, 12
Honey Oat Biscotti, 360
Hoppin' John Skillet, 218
Hot Mediterranean Chicken Salad, 190
Huevos Con Arroz, 6
Huevos Rancheros in Tortilla Cups, 40
Huevos Rancheros Tostados, 164
Huevos y Frijoles Frittata, 29
Hungarian Goulash Stew, 157

I
Idaho Potato Focaccia, 253
Idaho Potato Gazpacho, 62
Island Cookies, 361
Italian Beef Burrito, 124
Italian Bow Tie Vegetable Soup, 92
Italian-Glazed Pork Chops, 98
Italian Herbed Oatmeal Focaccia, 273
Italian Rustico Soup, 84
Italian Sausage and Rice Frittata, 150
Italian Stir-Fried Lamb, 190
Italian Tomato Soup, 73
Italian Vegetable Farfalle, 194

J
Jalapeño Cheese Bread, 291
Jam French Toast Triangles, 44
Jamaican Cherry Bread, 254
Jambalaya, 112
Jingle Bells Chocolate Pretzels, 232
Johnnie Marzetti, 131
Jumbo 3-Chip Cookies, 372

K
Kaleidoscope Chowder, 79
Key Lime Pie, 358

L
Lamb
    Eastertime Leg of Lamb, 222
    Grecian Lamb Kabobs, 178
    Greek Lamb Braised with Vegetables, 152
    Italian Stir-Fried Lamb, 190
    Patrick's Irish Lamb Soup, 68
    Pizza-Style Stuffed Potatoes, 110
    Shepherd's Pie, 192
Lasagna Florentine, 96
Lasagna Primavera, 132
Last Minute Tomato Swirl Bread, 273
Lawry's® Garlic Bread, 286
Layered Mexican Casserole, 157
Layered Mexican Tortilla Cheese Casserole, 141
Lemon-Garlic Chicken & Rice, 140

Lemon Pecan Cookies, 346
Lemon Semolina Syrup Cake, 334
Linguine with Mixed Sweet Peppers, Dried Tomatoes, Feta, Walnuts and Basil, 98
Lone Star Peanut Butter Cutouts, 373
Low Fat Molasses Jumbles, 362

M
Macaroon Kisses, 374
Madeira Gravy, 219
"Make Your Own Sundae" Pie, 362
Malted Dream Drops, 341
Ma'moul (Date Pastries), 355
Manicotti Marinara, 106
Maple Apple Oatmeal, 29
Maple Cider Basted Turkey, 222
Maraschino Cherry Cookies, 368
Maraschino Date Pinwheels, 368
Maraschino Thumbprint Cookies, 368
Marbled Pumpkin Cheesecake Squares, 244
Meatless Italian Minestrone, 50
Mediterranean Cornish Hens, 146
Mediterranean Shrimp & Vegetable Linguine, 171
Merry Santa Cupcakes, 242
Mexicali Cornbread Casserole, 172
Mexican Beef Stir-Fry, 170
Mexican Chicken Stew, 54
Mexican Lasagna, 118
Mexican Monkey Bread, 258
Mexican-Style Stuffed Peppers, 168
Mice Creams, 352
Minestrone, 89
Miniature Biscuits, 305
Mini Chip Snowball Cookies, 365
Mini-Sticky Pecan Buns, 290
Mini Vegetable Quiches, 12
Minted Orzo, 144, 178
Mixed Vegetables
    Cheesy Chicken Pot Pie, 136
    Cheesy Vegetable Soup, 82
    Chicken Biscuit Bake, 97
    Classic Veg•All® Chicken Pot Pie, 120
    Easy Ham & Veg•All® Chowder, 80
    Garden Ranch Linguine with Chicken, 146
    Heartland Shepherd's Pie, 138
    Hearty and Heart-Healthy Idaho Potato Soup/Stew, 80
    Hearty Minestrone Soup, 52
    Mexicali Cornbread Casserole, 172
    Minestrone, 89
    Mini Vegetable Quiches, 12
    1-2-3 Steak Soup, 54
    Quick Beef Soup, 62
    Scalloped Chicken & Pasta, 142
    Smothered Mexican Pork Chops, 171
    Sonoma® Pot Pie, 100
    Texas Beef Stew, 88
    Tuna Minestrone with Parmesan Cheese, 58
    Veg•All® Beef & Cheddar Bake, 124
    Vegetable Chili, 88
    Vegetable Soup with Delicious Dumplings, 59
    Vegetable-Stuffed Baked Potatoes, 212
    Yucatan Chicken Stir-Fry, 154
Mocha Dream Cake, 318
Mocha Glaze, 325

Molasses Glaze, 252
Moroccan Supper, 210
Mostaccioli per la Pasqua, 144
Mushrooms
 Baked Eggplant with Cheese, 200
 Broccoli Lasagna, 141
 Catch of the Day Stew, 73
 Cellentani, Italian Sausage and
  Mushrooms in Tomato-Gorgonzola
  Sauce, 72
 Chicken Primavera, 194
 Chicken Tuscany, 128
 Coq au Vin & Pasta, 108
 Country Sausage Macaroni and Cheese,
  123
 Easy Three Cheese Tuna Soufflé, 142
 Easy Turkey and Rice, 112
 Fiesta Beef Pot Pie, 113
 Giardiniera Sauce, 167
 Ham and Rice Pie, 11
 Hearty Beef Stew with Noodles, 56
 Hearty Sausage Stew, 51
 Italian Stir-Fried Lamb, 190
 Lasagna Florentine, 96
 Native American Wild Rice Soup, 72
 Omelet Italiano, 10
 1-2-3 Steak Soup, 54
 Pasta Primavera, 171
 Quick Beef Bourguignonne, 134
 Saffron Chicken Risotto, 106
 Sausage & Zucchini Soup, 58
 Savory Chicken and Biscuits, 132
 Seafood Gumbo, 80
 Sicilian Skillet Chicken, 178
 Sonoma® Pot Pie, 100
 Stewed Mushrooms on Asparagus with
  Vegetarian Oyster Sauce, 208
 Stuffed Shells Florentine, 128
 Tomato and Salmon Quiche, 14
 Vegetable & Cheese Platter, 212
 Vegetable-Stuffed Turkey Breast, 230
 Zucchini Mushroom Frittata, 24

N
Nacho Cheese Soup, 52
Nacho Salad, 196
Native American Wild Rice Soup, 72
No-Fuss Tuna Quiche, 97
Norwegian Almond Muffins (for bread
 machines), 29
Nuts
 Ali's Oatmeal Cookies, 342
 Almond Rice Madeleines, 355
 Apple Crisp Cookies, 344
 Apricot Cream Cake, 313
 Banana Pecan Braid, 246
 Black Forest Chocolate Fudge Cake, 324
 Black Forest Oatmeal Fancies, 364
 Brownie Sundae Cake, 326
 Brownie Turtle Cookies, 347
 Butterscotch Sticky Buns, 40
 Caramel-Pecan Pie, 341
 Cherry Danish, 11
 Chicken Ragoût with Chilies, Tortillas
  and Goat Cheese, 64
 Chocolate Filling, 304
 Chocolate Nut Topping, 260
 Chocolate Raspberry Torte, 316
 Chocolate Squares with Nutty Caramel
  Sauce, 308

Nuts (continued)
 Cranberry Peach Tart with Almonds, 237
 Cranberry-Pecan Filling, 302
 Creamy Cinnamon Rolls, 282
 Decadent Brownie Pie, 365
 Easy Apple Bread, 253
 Easy Turkey and Rice, 112
 European Wheat Bread, 263
 French Yule Log, 216
 Fudgy Pecan Pie, 356
 Glazed Cranberry Mini-Cakes, 330
 Harvest Honey Spice Cake, 312
 Hazelnut Plum Tart, 373
 Honey Almond Biscotti, 346
 Honey Cloverleafs, 304
 Honey Oat Biscotti, 360
 Island Cookies, 361
 Jumbo 3-Chip Cookies, 372
 Lemon Pecan Cookies, 346
 Linguine with Mixed Sweet Peppers,
  Dried Tomatoes, Feta, Walnuts and
  Basil, 98
 Lone Star Peanut Butter Cutouts, 373
 Malted Dream Drops, 341
 Mini Chip Snowball Cookies, 365
 Mini-Sticky Pecan Buns, 290
 Oatmeal Gorp Cookies, 366
 Orange Carrot Cake, 330
 Original Nestlé® Toll House® Chocolate
  Chip Cookies, 358
 Peanut Dip, 154
 Pecan Topping, 340
 Picadillo Chicken, 156
 Pineapple-Coconut Party Cake, 331
 Pumpkin Carrot Cake, 336
 Pumpkin Cheesecake Bars, 240
 Pumpkin Spiced and Iced Cookies, 370
 Pumpkin-Nut Bread, 280
 Rich Caramel Cake, 320
 Roasted Turkey Breast with Cherry &
  Apple Rice Stuffing, 214
 Salmon Vera Cruz, 166
 Sensational Cinnamon Chip Biscotti, 350
 Southern Caramel Pecan Rolls, 268
 Spinach Tortellini with Roasted Red
  Peppers, 185
 Stuffed Pork Loin Genoa Style, 186
 Touchdown Brownie Cups, 316
 Turkey Breast with Southwestern Corn
  Bread Dressing, 226
 Walnut Christmas Balls, 244
 White Chocolate Chunk & Macadamia
  Nut Brownie Cookies, 361
 White Chocolate, Raspberry and Pecan
  Filling, 276
 Wild Rice Three Grain Bread, 282
 Wisconsin Ricotta Tart with Kiwi and
  Raspberry Sauce, 350

O
Oatmeal Bread, 260
Oatmeal Gorp Cookies, 366
Old-Fashioned Beef Stew, 64
Old Naples Style Penne, 160
Omelet Italiano, 10
1-2-3 Steak Soup, 54
Onion Buckwheat Bread, 290
Onion-Herb Baked Bread, 264
Onion Soup with Bel Paese®, 66
Orange Glaze, 302

Oranges
 Amaretto Cheesecake Tart, 364
 Blueberry Breakfast Braid, 26
 Cornish Hens with Citrus Chutney
  Glaze, 240
 Orange Carrot Cake, 330
 Peanut Dip, 154
 Yucatan Snapper, 152
Original Nestlé® Toll House® Chocolate
 Chip Cookies, 358
Original Ortega® Taco Recipe, 150

P
Paella, 122
Painted Bread Knots, 306
Pan de Pueblo, 274
Paris Pasta, 198
Parker House Rolls, 257
Pasta Alfredo, 120
Pasta e Fagioli, 78
Pasta Fagioli, 180
Pasta Primavera, 171
Pasta with Shrimp, Broccoli and Red
 Pepper, 177
Patrick's Irish Lamb Soup, 68
Patriotic Cocoa Cupcakes, 334
Peaches
 Berry Striped Pops, 228
 Cranberry Peach Tart with Almonds, 237
 Deep-Dish Peach Custard Pie, 352
 Peach Orchard Muffins, 44
 Peach Yogurt Pie with Raspberry Sauce,
  370
 Side by Side Southern Stuffing and
  Turkey, 242
Peanut Butter
 Color-Bright Ice Cream Sandwiches,
  230 Easy Peanut Butter Chip Pie, 40
 Peanut Butter Cup Cookie Ice Cream
  Pie, 352
 Rich Chocolate Cake with Creamy
  Peanut Butter Milk Chocolate
  Frosting, 332
 Texas Peanut Butter Pound Cake, 326
Peanut Butter & Chocolate Pull-Apart
 Rolls, 248
Peanut Dip, 154
Pears
 Chocolate Glazed Pears, 234
 Vegetable Cobbler, 118
Peas
 Cellentani, Italian Sausage and
  Mushrooms in Tomato-Gorgonzola
  Sauce, 72
 Chicken Penne with Gorgonzola and
  Peas, 103
 Fettuccine Carbonara, 150
 Gemelli with Baby Shrimp and Sweet
  Peas, 196
 Hoppin' John Skillet, 218
 Mexican-Style Stuffed Peppers, 168
 Paella, 122
 Savory Chicken and Biscuits, 132
 Shepherd's Pie, 192
 Tagliatelle with Creamy Sauce, 167
 Thai-Style Beef & Rice, 192
 Turkey-Olive Ragoût en Crust, 102
 Vegetable & Cheese Platter, 212
Pecan Topping, 340
Penne with Arrabiatta Sauce, 206

Penne with Creamy Tomato Sauce, 198
Penne with Fresh Herb Tomato Sauce, 186
Penne with Red Pepper Alfredo Sauce, 149
Penne with Sausage and Kalamata Olives, 167
Penne with Shrimp and Vegetables, 184
Pepperonata, 195
Petit Pain au Chocolate, 266
Picadillo Chicken, 156
Pimiento-Cheese Soup, 73
Pineapples
  Holiday Baked Ham, 227
  Pineapple-Coconut Party Cake, 331
  Pumpkin Carrot Cake, 336
  Spring Break Blueberry Coffeecake, 25
Pizza Soup, 72
Pizza-Style Stuffed Potatoes, 110
Poached Seafood Italiano, 176
Polish Reuben Casserole, 174
Poppy Seed Breadsticks, 274
Pork
  Arizona Pork Chili, 79
  Carnival Pork Stew, 90
  Carolina Baked Beans & Pork Chops, 108
  Country Skillet Hash, 37
  Heartland Crown Roast of Pork, 238
  Italian-Glazed Pork Chops, 98
  Pork & Rice Provençal, 116
  Pork and Wild Rice Chili, 82
  Pork Roast with Corn Bread & Oyster Stuffing, 224
  Pork Tenderloin Mole, 166
  Smothered Mexican Pork Chops, 171
  Stuffed Pork Loin Genoa Style, 186
Portofino Primavera, 188
Potato Breakfast Custard, 6
Potato-Ham Scallop, 18
Potato Rosemary Rolls, 266
Potato Straw Cake with Ham & Gruyère, 16
Pumpernickel Raisin Bread, 262
Pumpkin
  Marbled Pumpkin Cheesecake Squares, 244
  Pumpkin Cake Roll with Cream Cheese Filling, 320
  Pumpkin Carrot Cake, 336
  Pumpkin Cheesecake Bars, 240
  Pumpkin Gingerbread Surprise, 236
  Pumpkin-Nut Bread, 280
  Pumpkin Spiced and Iced Cookies, 370
  Vermont Spice Cake, 314

Q
Quick Beef Bourguignonne, 134
Quick Beef Soup, 62
Quick Cinnamon Sticky Buns, 14
Quick Mediterranean Fish, 174

R
Raspberry Crumb Coffee Cake, 16
Raspberry Shortcakes, 312
Ratatouille, 207
Red Cloud Beef and Onions, 110
Red's Rockin' Rainbow Cupcakes, 310
Rice Bran Buttermilk Pancakes, 18
Rice, Cheese & Bean Enchiladas, 149
Rich Caramel Cake, 320
Rich Chocolate Cake with Creamy Peanut Butter Milk Chocolate Frosting, 332
Rigatoni with Four Cheeses, 138

Rise and Shine Sausage Oatmeal Cups, 37
Roasted Pepper-Olive Loaf, 268
Roasted Red Pepper, Corn & Garbanzo Bean Salad, 180
Roasted Turkey Breast with Cherry & Apple Rice Stuffing, 214
Roman Meal® Cream of Rye Bread, 284
Roman Meal® Homemade Bread, 262
Roman Meal® Waffles, 43
Rosarita Refried Soup, 68

S
Saffron Chicken Risotto, 106
Salad Dressings
  Dutch Potage, 48
  Garden Ranch Linguine with Chicken, 146
  Garlic Vinaigrette Dressing, 158
  Pasta Alfredo, 120
  Spinach Tortellini with Roasted Red Peppers, 185
Salmon Vera Cruz, 166
Salsa
  Butch's Black Bean Soup, 70
  Chicken and Black Bean Enchiladas, 182
  Chicken Casserole Olé, 126
  Citrus Chicken and Bell Pepper Fajitas, 189
  Fire & Ice Brunch Skillet, 202
  Hearty Tortilla Chip Soup, 60
  Mexican-Style Stuffed Peppers, 168
  Nacho Cheese Soup, 52
  Nacho Salad, 196
  Roasted Red Pepper, Corn & Garbanzo Bean Salad, 180
  Salsa Chicken & Rice Skillet, 158
  Salsa Macaroni & Cheese, 192
  Southwest Skillet, 108
  Spam™ Fajitas, 136
  Stacked Burrito Pie, 124
  Tacos de Huevos, 34
  Tortilla Soup, 83
  Turkey Chili, 70
Santa Fe Tomato Chowder, 66
Sausage
  Apple Brunch Strata, 8
  Biscuits 'n Gravy, 17
  Black Bean Sausage Skillet, 158
  Breakfast Kabobs, 34
  Cajun Chili, 60
  Calzone Italiano, 156
  Country Sausage Macaroni and Cheese, 123
  Cranberry Sausage Quiche, 22
  Down-Home Sausage Gravy, 28
  Greens and Gemelli, 186
  Hearty Sausage Stew, 51
  Italian Sausage and Rice Frittata, 150
  Jambalaya, 112
  Paella, 122
  Polish Reuben Casserole, 174
  Potato Breakfast Custard, 6
  Rise and Shine Sausage Oatmeal Cups, 37
  Sausage & Zucchini Soup, 58
  Sausage and Broccoli Noodle Casserole, 140
  Sausage Ham Jambalaya, 103
  Skillet Spaghetti Pizza, 136
  Smoked Cheese and Muffin Strata, 38
  Stuffed Pork Loin Genoa Style, 186

Sausage (continued)
  Taco Soup, 63
  Turkey Breast with Southwestern Corn Bread Dressing, 226
  Turkey Kielbasa with Cabbage, Sweet Potatoes and Apples, 126
  Turkey Sausage Potato Pancakes, 25
  Wisconsin Sausage Soup, 86
Savory Chicken and Biscuits, 132
Savory French Bread, 280
Scalloped Chicken & Pasta, 142
Scandinavian Chicken, 166
Scrambled Eggs with Chicken and Sun-Dried Tomatoes, 43
Scrumptious Apple Cake, 314
Seafood Gumbo, 80
Seafood Marinara with Linguine, 148
Sensational Cinnamon Chip Biscotti, 350
Shellfish
  Black Bean Bisque with Crab, 48
  Bouillabaisse, 74
  Chickpea and Shrimp Soup, 58
  Cioppino, 50
  Fancy Florida Seafood Gumbo, 51
  Gemelli with Baby Shrimp and Sweet Peas, 196
  Golden Gate Wild Rice Cioppino, 46
  Jambalaya, 112
  Kaleidoscope Chowder, 79
  Mediterranean Shrimp & Vegetable Linguine, 171
  Old Naples Style Penne, 160
  Paella, 122
  Pasta with Shrimp, Broccoli and Red Pepper, 177
  Penne with Shrimp and Vegetables, 184
  Pork Roast with Corn Bread & Oyster Stuffing, 224
  Seafood Gumbo, 80
  Seafood Marinara with Linguine, 148
  Shrimp Bisque, 83
  Surimi Seafood-Zucchini Frittata with Fresh Tomato Sauce, 100
  Tangy Shrimp with Angel Hair Pasta, 134
  West Coast Bouillabaisse, 88
  Wine and Herb Roaster with Ham and Oyster Stuffing, 219
  Zesty Seafood Lasagna, 131
Shepherd's Pie, 192
Shortcut "Sourdough" Corn Bread, 297
Shrimp Bisque, 83
Sicilian Caponata, 194
Sicilian Skillet Chicken, 178
Side by Side Southern Stuffing and Turkey, 242
Simply Delicious Pasta Primavera, 176
Skillet Chicken Alfredo, 189
Skillet Franks and Potatoes, 126
Skillet Spaghetti Pizza, 136
Smoked Cheese and Muffin Strata, 38
Smothered Mexican Pork Chops, 171
Soft Pretzels, 278
Sonoma® Pot Pie, 100
Soup Mixes
  Catch of the Day Stew, 73
  Cheddar Broccoli Tart, 34
  Chicken Jambalaya, 94 Frittata with Artichokes, 36
  Onion-Herb Baked Bread, 264
Southern Caramel Pecan Rolls, 268

Index

Southwest Skillet, 108
Southwestern Soup, 62
Spaghetti Puttanesca, 184
Spam™ Fajitas, 136
Spanish Rice and Meatballs, 119
Spicy Buns, 291
Spicy Thai Chicken, 170
Spinach
 Acorn Squash Filled with Savory
  Spinach, 204
 Chicken Florentine, 185
 Creamy Shells with Spinach and
  Mushrooms, 208
 Florentine Strata, 188
 Greens and Gemelli, 186
 Ham and Potato au Gratin, 142
 Kaleidoscope Chowder, 79
 Lasagna Florentine, 96
 Lasagna Primavera, 132
 Mediterranean Cornish Hens, 146
 Pasta Fagioli, 180
 Salmon Vera Cruz, 166
 Spinach and Mushroom Soup, 56
 Spinach Tortellini with Roasted Red
  Peppers, 185
 Stuffed Shells Florentine, 128
 Zesty Seafood Lasagna, 131
Spring Break Blueberry Coffeecake, 25
Squash
 Acorn Squash Filled with Savory
  Spinach, 204
 Grilled Vegetable Fettuccine, 207
 Italian Vegetable Farfalle, 194
 Lasagna Primavera, 132
 Vegetable Cobbler, 118
Stacked Burrito Pie, 124
Stewed Mushrooms on Asparagus with
 Vegetarian Oyster Sauce, 208
Stick-to-Your-Ribs Hearty Beef Stew, 84
Strawberry Cheesecake Pie, 368
Strawberry Cheesecake Pudding Pie, 346
Streusel Topping, 352
String Pie, 140
Stuffed Cornish Hens for Christmas, 236
Stuffed French Toast with Fresh Berry
 Topping, 8
Stuffed Pork Loin Genoa Style, 186
Stuffed Shells Florentine, 128
Summer Minestrone with Pesto, 72
Sunday Morning Upside-Down Rolls, 24
Sunflower Wheat-Beef Pot Pie, 130
Super Cinnamon Bun, 272
Surimi Seafood-Zucchini Frittata with
 Fresh Tomato Sauce, 100
Sweet Potato Pecan Pie, 340
Sweet Potato Turkey Pie, 122
Swiss/Olive Rye Bread, 270

T
Taco Soup, 63
Tacos de Huevos, 34
Tagliatelle with Creamy Sauce, 167
Tangy Shrimp with Angel Hair Pasta, 134
Tex-Mex Ground Turkey Potato Boats, 120
Texas Beef Stew, 88
Texas Peanut Butter Pound Cake, 326
Texas-Style Deep-Dish Chili Pie, 103
Thai Stir Fry, 172
Thai-Style Beef & Rice, 192
Thin-Sliced Panzanella, 164

Three Bean and Franks Bake, 104
Three Cheese Baked Ziti, 114
Toll House® Mini Morsel Pancakes, 32
Tomato and Salmon Quiche, 14
Tomato, Basil & Broccoli Chicken, 119
Tomato-Bread Casserole, 212
Tomato French Onion Soup, 70
Tortilla Soup, 83
Touchdown Brownie Cups, 316
Tuna Cream Cheese Omelets, 30
Tuna Minestrone with Parmesan Cheese,
 58
Turkey
 California Turkey Chili, 76
 Country Fare Breakfast with Wisconsin
  Fontina, 26
 Country Stew, 86
 Easy Turkey and Rice, 112
 Ham and Rice Pie, 11
 Hearty and Heart-Healthy Idaho Potato
  Soup/Stew, 80
 Hidden Herb Grilled Turkey Breast, 232
 Maple Cider Basted Turkey, 222
 Roasted Turkey Breast with Cherry &
  Apple Rice Stuffing, 214
 Side by Side Southern Stuffing and
  Turkey, 242
 Sonoma® Pot Pie, 100
 Sweet Potato Turkey Pie, 122
 Tex-Mex Ground Turkey Potato Boats,
  120
 Turkey Breast with Southwestern Corn
  Bread Dressing, 226
 Turkey Chili, 70
 Turkey, Corn and Sweet Potato Soup, 79
 Turkey Enchilada Pie, 114
 Turkey-Olive Ragoût en Crust, 102
 Vegetable-Stuffed Turkey Breast, 230
 Turkey Kielbasa with Cabbage, Sweet
  Potatoes and Apples, 126
 Turkey Sausage Potato Pancakes, 25
 Tuscan Pasta & Beans, 184

U
Upside-Down Hot Fudge Sundae Pie, 344

V
Valentine's Cupcakes, 310
Vanilla Frosting, 334
Vanilla Glaze, 370
Veg•All® Beef & Cheddar Bake, 124
Vegetable & Cheese Platter, 212
Vegetable Chili, 88
Vegetable Cobbler, 118
Vegetable Soup with Delicious Dumplings,
 59
Vegetable Stir-Fry in Spicy Black Bean
 Sauce, 202
Vegetable-Stuffed Baked Potatoes, 212
Vegetable-Stuffed Turkey Breast, 230
Vegetarian Tacos, 204
Vermont Spice Cake, 314
Very Cherry Pie, 356

W
Walnut Christmas Balls, 244
West Coast Bouillabaisse, 88
Western Omelet, 22
Whipped Cream Filling, 216
White Bread, 278

White Chip Drizzle, 350
White Chocolate Chunk & Macadamia
 Nut Brownie Cookies, 361
White Chocolate, Raspberry and Pecan
 Filling, 276
White Dipped Pretzels, 232
White Glaze, 330
Wild Rice Three Grain Bread, 282
Wild Rice-Spinach-Feta Bread, 276
Wine and Herb Baste, 219
Wine and Herb Roaster with Ham and
 Oyster Stuffing, 219
Wisconsin-Cheddar Jalapeño Bread, 297
Wisconsin Cheese Pasta Casserole, 102
Wisconsin Ricotta Tart with Kiwi and
 Raspberry Sauce, 350
Wisconsin Sausage Soup, 86
Wisconsin Swiss Linguine Tart, 104

Y
Yucatan Chicken Stir-Fry, 154
Yucatan Snapper, 152

Z
Zesty Artichoke Pesto Sauce, 168
Zesty Lemon Pound Cake, 322
Zesty Mexican Stir-Fry Fajitas, 149
Zesty Seafood Lasagna, 131
Zucchini
 Catch of the Day Stew, 73
 Chicken and Vegetable Ragoût, 177
 Greek Beef & Rice, 164
 Grilled Vegetable Fettuccine, 207
 Grilled Vegetable Rigatoni, 170
 Huevos y Frijoles Frittata, 29
 Italian Bow Tie Vegetable Soup, 92
 Italian-Glazed Pork Chops, 98
 Italian Vegetable Farfalle, 194
 Lasagna Primavera, 132
 Minestrone, 89
 Pasta Primavera, 171
 Penne with Shrimp and Vegetables, 184
 Portofino Primavera, 188
 Ratatouille, 207
 Rice, Cheese & Bean Enchiladas, 149
 Sausage & Zucchini Soup, 58
 Summer Minestrone with Pesto, 72
 Surimi Seafood-Zucchini Frittata with
  Fresh Tomato Sauce, 100
 Vegetarian Tacos, 204
 Zucchini Mushroom Frittata, 24
 Zucchini-Tomato-Noodle Soup, 82

METRIC CONVERSION CHART

VOLUME MEASUREMENTS (dry)

1/8 teaspoon = 0.5 mL
1/4 teaspoon = 1 mL
1/2 teaspoon = 2 mL
3/4 teaspoon = 4 mL
1 teaspoon = 5 mL
1 tablespoon = 15 mL
2 tablespoons = 30 mL
1/4 cup = 60 mL
1/3 cup = 75 mL
1/2 cup = 125 mL
2/3 cup = 150 mL
3/4 cup = 175 mL
1 cup = 250 mL
2 cups = 1 pint = 500 mL
3 cups = 750 mL
4 cups = 1 quart = 1 L

VOLUME MEASUREMENTS (fluid)

1 fluid ounce (2 tablespoons) = 30 mL
4 fluid ounces (1/2 cup) = 125 mL
8 fluid ounces (1 cup) = 250 mL
12 fluid ounces (1 1/2 cups) = 375 mL
16 fluid ounces (2 cups) = 500 mL

WEIGHTS (mass)

1/2 ounce = 15 g
1 ounce = 30 g
3 ounces = 90 g
4 ounces = 120 g
8 ounces = 225 g
10 ounces = 285 g
12 ounces = 360 g
16 ounces = 1 pound = 450 g

DIMENSIONS

1/16 inch = 2 mm
1/8 inch = 3 mm
1/4 inch = 6 mm
1/2 inch = 1.5 cm
3/4 inch = 2 cm
1 inch = 2.5 cm

OVEN TEMPERATURES

250°F = 120°C
275°F = 140°C
300°F = 150°C
325°F = 160°C
350°F = 180°C
375°F = 190°C
400°F = 200°C
425°F = 220°C
450°F = 230°C

BAKING PAN SIZES

Utensil	Size in Inches/Quarts	Metric Volume	Size in Centimeters
Baking or Cake Pan (square or rectangular)	8×8×2	2 L	20×20×5
	9×9×2	2.5 L	23×23×5
	12×8×2	3 L	30×20×5
	13×9×2	3.5 L	33×23×5
Loaf Pan	8×4×3	1.5 L	20×10×7
	9×5×3	2 L	23×13×7
Round Layer Cake Pan	8×1½	1.2 L	20×4
	9×1½	1.5 L	23×4
Pie Plate	8×1¼	750 mL	20×3
	9×1¼	1 L	23×3
Baking Dish or Casserole	1 quart	1 L	—
	1½ quart	1.5 L	—
	2 quart	2 L	—